Microsoft® Virtualization with Hyper-V

JASON A. **KAPPEL**
ANTHONY T. **VELTE**
TOBY J. **VELTE**

New York Chicago San Francisco
Lisbon London Madrid Mexico City Milan
New Delhi San Juan Seoul Singapore Sydney Toronto

The McGraw·Hill Companies

Cataloging-in-Publication Data is on file with the Library of Congress

Microsoft® Virtualization with Hyper-V

1234567890   DOC DOC   019

ISBN   978-0-07-161403-0
MHID   0-07-161403-6

Sponsoring Editor
Jane K. Brownlow

Editorial Supervisor
Patty Mon

Project Manager
Harleen Chopra,
International Typesetting
and Composition

Acquisitions Coordinator
Joya Anthony

Technical Editor
Rodney Buike

Copy Editor
Margaret Berson

Proofreader
Christine Andreasen

Indexer
Robert Swanson

Production Supervisor
Jean Bodeaux

Composition
International Typesetting
and Composition

Illustration
International Typesetting
and Composition

Art Director, Cover
Jeff Weeks

*For Genevieve, Nils, and Amelia—without your infinite patience
and support this book would never have been written.*

—JAK

*For my parents Bill and Joyce—so many of the successes
I have experienced in life have their roots
in the quality of my life as a child.*

—TJV

*Joey, Jack, and Luke—the three of you bring much joy
to your mother and me, and all those around you.
It is truly my honor to be your father.*

—ATV

ABOUT THE AUTHORS

Jason Kappel has over 15 years of experience working in the information systems industry. He is a Solutions Architect and capability lead for one of the world's largest Microsoft-only system integrators.

Mr. Kappel holds many different infrastructure certifications and is a speaker at seminars and user groups on the topic of optimizing investments enterprises have made in their infrastructure. Mr. Kappel can be reached at jasonkappel@yahoo.com.

Toby J. Velte, Ph.D., is an international best-selling author of business technology articles and books. He is co-founder of Velte Publishing, Inc. and the co-author of more than a dozen books published by McGraw-Hill and Cisco Press. He is co-author of *Green IT: Reduce Your Information System's Environmental Impact While Adding to the Bottom Line* and the upcoming *Cloud Computing: A Practical Approach*.

Dr. Velte is currently part of Microsoft's North Central practice focused on helping thriving companies with their technology-based initiatives. He works with large organizations to create IT roadmaps that are business focused and implemented in a practical way. He can be reached at tjv@velte.com.

Anthony T. Velte, CISSP, CISA, is an award-winning author and co-founder of Velte Publishing, Inc. Recently he co-authored *Green IT: Reduce Your Information System's Environmental Impact While Adding to the Bottom Line* and the upcoming book, *Cloud Computing: A Practical Approach*. Over the last decade, Mr. Velte has authored more than a dozen books including McGraw-Hill's popular *Cisco: A Beginner's Guide*, now in its fourth edition.

Mr. Velte works for an industry-leading security software company. He speaks at seminars and helps companies identify risks and solutions that help protect their information systems infrastructure. He holds a variety of business and technical certifications. He can be reached at atv@velte.com.

About the Technical Editor

Rodney Buike is a Technology Advisor with Microsoft Canada specializing in Windows, messaging, security, and virtualization. Rodney is also the founder and publisher of http://www.thelazyadmin.com, a web site dedicated to sharing tips and tricks for managing your Microsoft infrastructure. Rodney also holds many industry certifications including MCSE and MCITP: Enterprise Administrator.

CONTENTS

ACKNOWLEDGMENTS

Robert Elsenpeter, author and guerilla ameliorator extraordinaire. Mr. Elsenpeter was a key contributor in the preparation of this book and provided his substantial expertise unfalteringly.

Tim Cerling, Microsoft Technology Specialist for Windows Server. Our conversations about the features and uses of Hyper-V provided a differing point of view, which was much needed.

Robert Fish, Security Architect at Microsoft. Bob enlightened us on his thoughts on securing the virtual network and different methods with which to achieve that.

Rodney Buike, IT Pro Advisor with Microsoft, and our Technical Editor. Rodney carefully reviewed each and every chapter in this book. Aside from being a pleasure to work with, his expertise and input were always "spot on." We appreciate his efforts and are certain that this book is better because of it.

We also acknowledge the patience and hard work of the people at McGraw-Hill, notably those involved in the process of bringing this book to fruition. Thanks to Jane Brownlow, Executive Editor and our Sponsoring Editor; Joya Anthony, our Acquisitions Coordinator; Patty Mon, Senior Editorial Supervisor; and Jean Bodeaux, Senior Production Supervisor. You can also flip back a few pages to see the rest of the people involved in the creation of this book. We acknowledge all of them and appreciate their efforts.

INTRODUCTION

WHO SHOULD READ THIS BOOK

No matter how you look at it, virtualization has become part of our day to day IT lives. Virtualization really exploded when VMware introduced their server product, and now all sorts of companies are introducing their own projects. Microsoft has entered the virtualization arena with its Windows Server 2008 Hyper-V. This tool is a good way to integrate virtualization into your Microsoft environment.

This book is geared toward IT department managers, Systems Engineers, and Operations Engineers who want to implement their own Hyper-V solution, and anyone who needs to maintain an already installed solution.

It is also useful for the professional who wants to learn more about virtualization solutions, specifically how Microsoft approaches the issue.

WHAT THIS BOOK COVERS

Virtualization, simply put, is running an operating system and applications on a virtual server and then presenting the information to the clients. It is something that has only become really feasible in the past few years and it is gaining momentum.

In May 2007, Gartner predicted that the total number of deployed virtual machines would reach 3 million by 2009, and that virtualization would be part of nearly every aspect of IT by 2015. The analysis firm says that virtualization adoption is accelerating more than expected and it is adjusting its forecasts accordingly. Gartner now expects 611 million virtualized PCs by 2011 and the IT infrastructure and operations to be deeply impacted by virtualization by 2012.

"Virtualization is hardly a new concept; storage has already been virtualized—albeit primarily within the scope of individual vendor architectures—and networking is also virtualized," said Philip Dawson, vice president and distinguished analyst at Gartner. "However, as both server and PC virtualization become more pervasive, traditional IT infrastructure orthodoxy is being challenged and is changing the way business works with IT."

Research by technology company CDW Corporation found that 63 percent of the 772 technology professionals surveyed will upgrade to Windows Server 2008, with 18 percent already installing it or planning to do so.

Why should you care about virtualization? Virtualization allows you to do more with less. By leveraging the power of existing hardware, you can run multiple server instances on one server, lowering your overall cost of ownership for each of your solutions. Virtualization also lowers your support costs; each of your virtual systems will be using the same virtual drivers so you don't have to worry about driver incompatibilities like you do with multiple versions of hardware.

Also, if you decide you need another server, you do not have to shop around and spend thousands of dollars—you simply spin up a new one on the hardware you already have and you are ready to go in a few minutes, compared to weeks.

Because you can put several virtualized servers on one physical server, you are getting optimal utilization out of that device. That is, rather than using on average less than 10 percent of its resources (but having paid for 100 percent of them), by adding more virtual machines, you can squeeze as much productivity out of it as you can.

Let us also look at virtualization from a cost perspective. Not having to buy as much physical hardware leads to a reduction in datacenter size, and you do not spend as much on hardware. And the electricity to power and cool those machines goes down in proportion to the reduction in on-site hardware.

Last but not least, you reduce your toll on the environment. Less power consumed means less greenhouse gases being produced. Fewer physical servers means less toxic chemicals introduced into the environment, both when the machines are manufactured and when they are disposed of.

This book covers these topics, as well as the nuts and bolts of Microsoft Windows Server 2008 Hyper-V. There are numerous entrants into the virtualization field including VMware, Xen, and Microsoft. The focus in this book, obviously, is Hyper-V.

Says IDC, "Microsoft is working diligently on the version 2 product and will likely address the most critical shortcomings, and with the next release (targeted for 2010) should get the product to the classic Microsoft design point: that being good enough for the vast majority of the market needs. In the interim, we can still expect that the number of footprints that Hyper-V makes (despite the product's current maturity level) will be staggering and will turn the volume metrics of the market upside down. These footprints are likely to penetrate all size class customers. Within the largest customers, many of which have already committed a substantial amount of their infrastructure to VMware solutions, expect use of Hyper-V to be within test, development, and noncritical and lower priority workloads at first."

The chapters in this book include the following:

▼   **Chapter 1: Virtualization Overview**   This chapter sets the stage to explain what is going on in the world of virtualization. Rather than just jump into a discussion of Hyper-V, we take a look at some competing products and how those products are best used. We will also look at Microsoft's initial forays into the world of virtualization and then talk about Hyper-V.

■   **Chapter 2: Planning and Installation**   You can't head down to the store, pick up a DVD of Hyper-V and install it (WalMart is not likely to have Hyper-V in one of those glass cases, anyway). As with any large-scale project, you need to sit down and spend some quality time figuring out your Hyper-V solution. How will it be used? What will your clients be doing with it? What is your network infrastructure like? We will walk you through the planning and installation process in this chapter.

■   **Chapter 3: Configuring Hyper-V Components**   Once you have got everything planned and have moved on with the install, you need to configure Hyper-V. While it is largely intuitive and easy to follow, there are still little tips, tricks, and best practices for getting it set up properly. In this chapter we will look at the best way to configure Hyper-V properly and suggest ways so you can get the most out of it.

■   **Chapter 4: Planning and Designing Systems Center Virtual Machine Manager 2008**   To manage your virtual environment, Microsoft offers its Systems Center Virtual Machine Manager 2008 (SCVMM). It is based on Microsoft's Dynamic Systems Initiative (DSI). DSI helps administrators achieve higher business value through automation, flexible resource utilization, and knowledge-driven processes. In this chapter we will talk about how to prepare for SCVMM and how you can get the most out of the tool.

■   **Chapter 5: Installing and Configuring Systems Center Virtual Machine Manager 2008**   The previous chapter covered the preparations you should do to get ready for SCVMM, and now this chapter covers installing it. SCVMM installation is reasonably straightforward, but we still walk you through the steps, especially given some of the more intricate issues as it tries to manage a complex environment.

■   **Chapter 6: Configuring Systems Center Virtual Machine Manager 2008**   Once SCVMM is installed, the work is not over—you still need to configure it. Given the reasonably complex nature of your virtualized—and non-virtualized—environment, there are a lot of boxes to check (or uncheck) and plenty to do to optimally configure SCVMM so you can get the most out of it.

■   **Chapter 7: Creating and Managing Virtual Machines**   All the installing and configuring is done, so now it is time to finally do what you want—create a virtual machine. While it is as easy as clicking on a template to create a new machine, setting up your first few VMs requires some foresight and planning. In this chapter we will look at the issues surrounding the creation of your virtual machine and warn of some pitfalls to be avoided.

- **Chapter 8: Managing Your Virtual Machines**   Since your users access their applications and data on your virtual server now, it is especially important to keep your server optimally tuned, and this means using strong management techniques. In this chapter we will talk about creating new machines, deleting old ones, and exporting the ones you like, among other management techniques.

- **Chapter 9: Backing Up, Restoring, and Disaster Recovery for Your Virtual Machines**   No one ever wants to lose data, and the issue is even more pronounced in a virtualized environment. After all, if someone's local hard drive dies and the information has not been backed up, then that data is lost. However, if everyone's data is on a virtual machine and that drive goes down, then there is real trouble. And what happens if there is a catastrophe, like the office burns down? If you do not have an off-site backup, everything is lost. In this chapter we will talk about what you can do to protect the data on a virtual machine.

- **Chapter 10: Monitoring Your Virtual Solution**   Just as you would monitor a conventional network; you also need to monitor your virtual machine. Ideally, if you do not make changes, nothing will change and you will be running at peak performance—ideally. The truth of the matter is that stuff happens and if you are not vigilantly monitoring your system, you face reduction in system operations. In this chapter we will talk about how you can monitor your Hyper-V virtual machines and what to do if you see performance issues.

- **Chapter 11: Hyper-V Security**   Security is an issue in any computer network, but a virtualized one brings its own set of issues. In this chapter we will talk about security issues specific to a virtualized environment and what you can do to keep your network safe and sound.

- **Chapter 12: Virtual Desktop Infrastructure**   Having a virtual machine is good, but ultimately your end users need to access the server. In this chapter we will talk about tools that help your clients use the virtual machine. We will also talk about issues surrounding virtual desktops, like security, centralization, and reliability.

- **Appendix A: Third-Party Virtualization Tools for Hyper-V**   Third-party vendors offer their own tools for use with Hyper-V. In this appendix we will list some of the more popular tools that you might find useful for your environment.

- **Appendix B: Windows Server 2008 Hyper-V Command-Line Reference**   Some people like to click their way through menus, and others like to just type at the command line. In this appendix we will list the command-line instructions so that you can control Hyper-V textually, rather than by pointing and clicking.

CHAPTER 1

Virtualization Overview

Virtualization has become a very popular way for IT departments to reduce the amount of equipment they use, while still providing services to their users. Dozens of different companies have dozens of different ways to virtualize, and it should come as a shock to no one that the world's biggest software maker wants a piece of the virtualization pie.

In this chapter we'll take a closer look at the issue of virtualization, itself, before we really drill into the features of Hyper-V.

Deploying Windows Server 2008 Hyper-V into a corporate environment is an involved and sometimes daunting project that will require a team to look deep into every corporate system and make a decision on whether that system should be virtualized. When we first started out with virtualization, there wasn't much information to go on; we didn't know how to put a virtual solution together or how to be successful at doing physical-to-virtual migrations or a host deployment. As time has gone by, we've learned significant lessons from trial and error while being up late nights. While many great books on virtualization technologies are available, there are few that impart the advice and wisdom needed to making a successful deployment. Our goal with this book is to make sure that you are successful in deploying your Microsoft virtual solution into your corporate environment, and that you have a reference manual moving forward to operations for Windows Server 2008 Hyper-V and System Center Virtual Machine Manager.

This book not only covers the theories behind virtualization, but also is full of screenshots and tips to getting Windows Server 2008 Hyper-V installed, configured, and running. Once we have Hyper-V running, we'll cover building a larger fault-tolerant solution using System Center Virtual Machine Manager 2008; how to migrate physical systems to your new virtual environment; and how to manage your new environment with System Center Operations Manager.

HISTORY OF VIRTUALIZATION

While computer technology continues to march forward with smaller, sleeker, more powerful machines, in many ways how we use computers has come full circle. Obviously the computers of today are way more powerful than the computers of the 1950s, but it turns out the way we are using them is harkening back to the early days of computing.

Let's take a look at the history of virtualization to see how it all began and look at some of the ways that the world of virtualization has evolved.

Mainframes

Anyone who has been around computers for a while will quickly recognize that the concept of running a client's session on a server and then displaying the results on the client machine describes the way mainframes work.

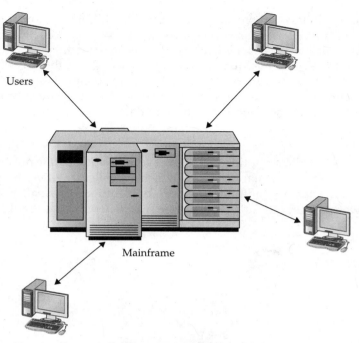

The virtualization of today is similar to how mainframes work.

While modern mainframes are certainly speedy things, they are more notable for their redundant internal engineering, ensuring a high level of redundancy, security, and backward compatibility with legacy applications. It's not uncommon for a mainframe to run constantly for years without incident, even while upgrades and repairs are performed.

Software upgrades are nondisruptive because one system can take over another's application while it is being improved.

The Evolution of the Mainframe

Between the late 1950s and 1970s, several manufacturers built the first mainframes. The group of manufacturers was known at one point as "IBM and the Seven Dwarfs." Those companies were: IBM, Burroughs, UNIVAC, NCR, Control Data, Honeywell, General Electric, and RCA.

IBM was the dominant leader in the field with its 700/7000 series, and later its 360, which continued to evolve into the current zSeries/z9 mainframes.

In the 1960s, mainframes tended not to have an interactive interface. They accepted punch cards, paper tape, and magnetic tape, operating solely in batch mode to support office functions, like customer billing.

By the 1970s, mainframes had acquired interactive user interfaces and were used as timesharing computers, able to support thousands of users simultaneously. This was done mostly via a terminal interface. These days, most mainframes have phased out terminal access and end users are able to access the mainframe using a web user interface.

In the early 1980s, less demand and competition led to a lot of companies pulling out of the mainframe arena. Also, companies realized the benefits of client-server solutions, and as a result, mainframe sales fell while server sales boomed.

By the early 1990s, it seemed that the mainframe was going the way of the dinosaur, but in the late 1990s, organizations found new uses for their existing mainframes. The growth of e-business increased the number of back-end transactions processed by the mainframe, as well as the size and throughput of databases.

Operation

Mainframes are able to host multiple operating systems, and operate not as a single computer, but as a number of virtual machines, which are called *partitions* in the mainframe world. In this capacity, a mainframe can replace hundreds of smaller servers. While mainframes were the first to function this way, we're now seeing regular servers used in this way.

Like a virtualized server, mainframes can house multiple operating systems.

Mainframes are designed to handle very high-volume input and output. Since the mid-1960s, mainframe designs have incorporated subsidiary computers called *channels* or *peripheral processors*. These computers manage the IO devices, leaving the CPU open to manage high-speed memory.

When compared to a PC, mainframes have thousands of times as much storage.

NOTE   It is not uncommon for mainframes to house enormously large databases. Gigabyte- and terabyte-sized files are common.

As bulletproof as they sound, mainframes do have disadvantages. Their primary issue is that they are centralized. This isn't a problem when everything is housed under one roof, but as the organization becomes more geographically dispersed, it's harder to justify the cost of a mainframe at several locations.

VMware

The reigning king in the world of virtualization is VMware. Their line of products (including ESX Server and VI3, which we'll discuss in a moment) has led the recent movement toward virtualized IT systems.

While VMware is a competing product to Hyper-V, it's worth talking about what VMware has to offer and why it might or might not be something you want to include in your datacenter.

ESX Server

ESX Server is a component of VMware's VMware Infrastructure, which adds management and reliability services to its core server product.

The basic server requires some sort of storage, like an array of disk drives, for storing the virtualized kernel and support files. VMware offers a variant of this product called ESX Server ESXi Embedded. This moves all the server's kernels into a dedicated hardware device.

In the VMware world, they refer to the hypervisor used as a *vmkernel*.

NOTE   We'll talk more about hypervisors and their role in virtualization later in this chapter.

VMware notes that ESX Server runs on "bare metal." That is, unlike other VMware products, it does not run on top of another operating system, but rather sets up its own kernel.

ESX Server sets up a Linux kernel first, and that kernel is used to load specialized virtualization components, including vmkernel. That first installed Linux kernel becomes the first running virtual machine and is called the *service console*.

The vmkernel has three interfaces with the user:

▼ **Hardware**   Access to other hardware is accomplished using this interface.

■ **Guest systems**   This interface simulates hardware and occurs in such a way that a guest system itself can run unmodified on top of the hypervisor.

▲ **Service console**   A general-purpose operating system used as the bootstrap for the VMware kernel and used as a management interface.

As Figure 1-1 shows, each virtualized server perceives the system resources as unique to it, and not shared with others.

ESX Server has some limitations that might restrict its deployment and use: The maximum amount of RAM for a guest system is 64GB; and there can only be 32 hosts in both High Availability (HA) clusters and Distributed Resource Scheduler (DRS) clusters.

VMware Infrastructure 3

VMware Infrastructure 3 (VI3) is a solution aimed at enterprises that are looking to consolidate full-scale production systems. It is the most scalable of the VMware platforms with new management, load-balancing, and high-availability features.

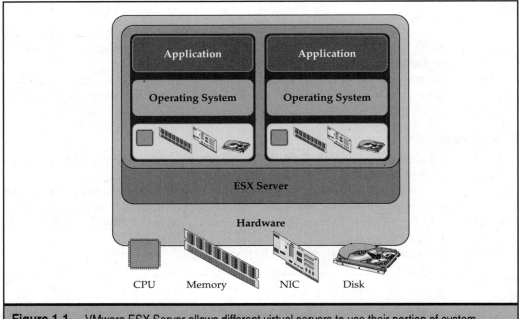

Figure 1-1.   VMware ESX Server allows different virtual servers to use their portion of system resources as if they were their own.

As VI3 is based on ESX Server, it is not dependent on a host operating system, and it can be used to host virtual machines running Windows, Linux, or other common operating systems.

Since VI3 is so scalable, it can run up to 128 concurrent virtual machines on multiple ESX servers, all managed from a central console. Those servers can all be configured to share a common file system—the VMware Virtual Machine Fine System (VMFS)—hosted on local disks, Network Attached Storage (NAS), or Storage Area Network (SAN) storage.

VMFS makes provisioning and management of virtual machines much simpler. It makes it possible to dynamically allocate resources and profess loads across both virtual machines and physical servers. In fact, you can move an entire virtual machine from one server to another, even while users and applications are actively using it. Additionally, once the virtual machines are installed, they can be managed remotely.

VI3 employs the VMware Distributed Resource Scheduler (DRS), which automatically tunes processor, memory, and other resources.

VMware High Availability (HA) adds automatic failover if there is a hardware or software problem, and VMotion makes it possible to migrate live virtual machines from one server to another. This aids in maintenance and load balancing.

Connectix

Connectix Corp. was a company that made virtualization software for Windows and Macintosh-based computers. In 2003 Microsoft acquired their virtualization technology and now uses it in their own virtualization products.

Connectix's technology allowed customers to migrate to next-generation technology from Microsoft, while still being able to use legacy applications.

Virtual PC for Mac provided integration of Windows on the Macintosh platform, enabling Mac OS customers to run Windows-based applications, access PC networks, use Windows-only Internet applications, and share files with PC-based colleagues. Virtual PC for Mac joined the Macintosh Business Unit's mix of Mac products, such as Office v.X, Entourage X, and Internet Explorer for Mac.

Virtual PC for Windows provided Windows desktop customers with an additional tool for migrating to Windows XP or Windows 2000 Professional, supported legacy applications, and enabled a range of other uses for application development, call centers, technical support, education, and training.

Virtual Server addressed customer demand for an application migration solution based on virtualization and supported by Microsoft. In addition, it provided cost efficiencies by consolidating multiple Windows NT 4.0 servers and their applications into a single Windows Server system.

Though Connectix is now defunct, Microsoft continues to develop virtual machine solutions based on the Connectix technologies.

Microsoft

Microsoft has dipped its toes into most different types of technology. Sometimes they get it right and sometimes they don't. Though this book focuses on Microsoft's Hyper-V solution, it isn't the first time they have developed virtualization solutions. In fact, in addition to Hyper-V, there are two other virtualization products from Microsoft out there. While not as grand in scope as Hyper-V, they are still a means to add virtualization to your organization. Let's talk a little more about Virtual PC, Virtual Server, and Hyper-V in an examination of what Microsoft brings to the virtualization party.

Virtual PC

Microsoft Virtual PC 2007 is a desktop virtual machine solution to help you migrate legacy applications to Windows Vista. Virtual PC offers customers a cost-effective safety net to ease their migration to Microsoft Windows Vista and a tool to help accelerate the development, testing, deployment, and support of PC applications. The configuration screen is shown in Figure 1-2.

For example, Microsoft Virtual PC allows enterprise customers to run multiple operating systems on one PC, so employees can run critical legacy applications on an interim basis while IT professionals proceed with the migration to the end user's workstation to the latest version of the Windows operating system.

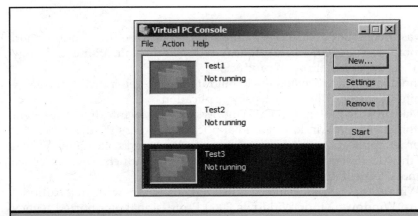

Figure 1-2. Configuring a new instance of Microsoft's Virtual PC is done through a standard window.

Benefits Virtual PC 2004 marked Microsoft's entry into the Windows-based virtual machine arena in 2003. The product was built on virtualization technology that Microsoft acquired in February 2003 from Connectix Corp.

Virtual PC offers the benefit of rapid reconfiguration. For instance, the software can enhance the productivity of technical support, help desk, or call center employees by enabling them to easily switch among operating systems without logging in and out between calls.

Virtual PC is also designed to accelerate software testing by allowing developers to test and debug their software for multiple platforms in a timely and cost-effective manner, all on one PC, improving both software quality and time to market.

Features Features of Microsoft Virtual PC include support for as many as four network adapters per virtual machine, all through the graphical user interface; Extensible Markup Language (XML) file-based configuration of virtual machines to ease the copying of a virtual machine to another computer; and support for up to 3.6GB of memory. More memory makes it possible to run more operating systems simultaneously and improves the performance of operating systems with larger memory requirements.

Key features carried over from the former Connectix product include:

▼ The virtual machine additions, that provide a high level of integration between host and guest operating systems, including integrated mouse, time synchronization, cut-and-paste, drag-and-drop, and folder sharing

■ Undo Disks, which allows users to delete any changes they make to the virtual hard disk during a session

▲ Differencing Disks, which lets multiple users and multiple virtual machines use the same parent virtual hard disk at the same time.

Virtual PC also runs most x86 operating systems in the virtual machine environment with no need for custom drivers. This compatibility positions customers to migrate legacy applications and consolidate desktops for dramatic cost savings.

NOTE   In August 2006 Microsoft announced the Macintosh-hosted version would not be ported to Intel-based Macintoshes, effectively discontinuing the product, as PowerPC-based Macintoshes are no longer manufactured.

Virtual PC supports these host operating systems:

▼   Windows Vista (32-bit and 64-bit versions of Windows Vista Ultimate, Enterprise, Business editions, and European Business N only; but not Windows Vista Starter, Windows Vista Home Basic or Home Premium, or European Vista Home N editions)

■   Windows XP Professional and Tablet PC Edition (32-bit) and Windows XP Professional x64 Edition (not Windows XP Home Edition or Windows XP Media Center Edition)

▲   Windows Server 2003

NOTE   Virtual PC 2004 was the last version to support Windows 2000 as the host OS.

Virtual PC supports these guest operating systems:

▼   Windows Vista (all 32-bit editions)

■   Windows XP (all 32-bit only)

■   Windows Server 2008 (Virtual PC 2007 Service Pack1 onward)

■   Windows 2000 Professional and Server

■   Windows 98 Second Edition

■   Windows Server 2003 Standard Edition

▲   Certain editions of IBM OS/2

NOTE   Support for Windows 95, Windows 98 original release, Windows Me, Windows NT 4.0 Workstation, and MS-DOS 6.22 as guests was formally discontinued in Virtual PC 2007, but they can still largely be run.

Virtual Server

Microsoft Virtual Server is a virtualization solution that allows virtual machines to be created on Windows XP, Vista, and Server operating systems. Like Virtual PC, it is based on technology developed by Connectix. Its configuration screen is shown in Figure 1-3.

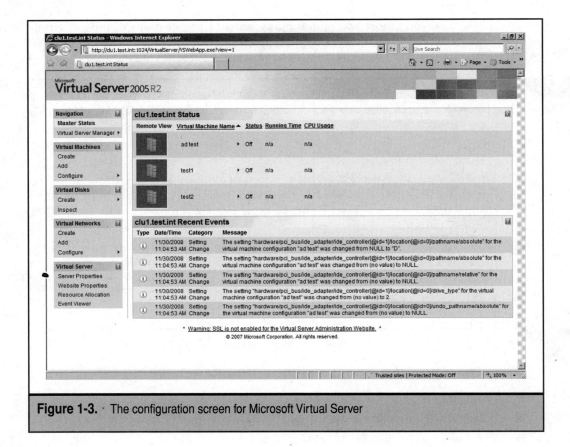

Figure 1-3. · The configuration screen for Microsoft Virtual Server

Virtual machines are created and managed through an Internet Information Services (IIS) web-based interface or through a Windows client application called VMRCplus.

The current version is Microsoft Virtual Server 2005 R2, Service Pack 1. New features in the 2005 release include:

▼ Linux support for:

- Red Hat Enterprise version 2.1–5.0

- Red Hat Linux 9.0

- SUSE Linux

- SUSE Linux Enterprise Servers 9 and 10

■ Virtual Disk Precompactor

■ Symmetric Multiprocessing (SMP)

■ x64 host OS support

■ The ability to mount virtual hard drives on the host OS

▲ Additional operating systems, including Vista and Windows Server 2008

Virtual Server also provides a Volume Shadow Copy writer, allowing live backups of the host OS on Windows Server 2003 and 2008 hosts.

Hyper-V

Following the launch of Windows Server 2008, Microsoft released Windows Server 2008 Hyper-V, the hypervisor-based virtualization technology that is a role built into 64-bit versions of Windows Server 2008.

Hyper-V offers a reliable, scalable, and high-performance virtualization platform that plugs into existing IT infrastructures, enabling users to consolidate some of the most demanding workloads. In addition, the Microsoft System Center product family gives customers a single set of integrated tools to manage physical and virtual resources, helping customers create a more agile and dynamic datacenter. Figure 1-4 shows the Hyper-V Manager interface.

Case Study: Land O' Lakes   Minnesota-based Land O'Lakes suffered from a common IT challenge resulting from tremendous growth through mergers and acquisitions. The agricultural cooperative's datacenter was packed with a compilation of aging servers running at an average utilization rate of just 3 percent, putting a considerable strain on IT resources.

Figure 1-4.   User interacts with Hyper-V via the Hyper-V Manager.

IT pros call the condition "server sprawl," and Land O'Lakes had a bad case of it.

"We faced a combination of underutilized and aging hardware, applications running on outdated operating systems, and rising datacenter power and cooling costs," said Jason Nord, the company's server administrator.

To counter the problem, Land O'Lakes did what an increasing number of similarly challenged companies are doing: It turned to a virtualization solution. Specifically, it became an early adopter of Microsoft virtualization technologies, including Windows Server 2008 Hyper-V.

The company's IT team initially rolled out a Microsoft Virtual Server 2005 R2 in its test and development environment, in which four physical servers each hosted 10 to 13 virtual machines, with each virtual machine running one application. The team plans to migrate this environment to Hyper-V and to move an additional 10 to 15 new applications directly into virtual machines in the production environment, thus saving the cost of hardware servers.

"Our Microsoft virtualization solution is a key part of a business strategy we have at Land O'Lakes called Best Cost Initiative," said Tony Taylor, the company's director of IT services. "It's not just about cutting costs, but about looking where our money is being spent and finding ways to leverage our investments across the company. Virtualization holds a lot of promise in helping us maximize the value of our IT investments."

Features   Hyper-V's scalability derives from its support for multiple processors and cores at the host level and improved memory limits at the host and guest level within virtual machines. This enables users to scale their virtualization environment to support a large number of virtual machines within a given host and to take advantage of quick migration for high availability across multiple hosts.

A major differentiator for Hyper-V is the familiarity of the Windows platform.

To help both customers and partners assess whether their existing servers are good candidates for virtualization using Hyper-V, Microsoft has released the Microsoft Assessment and Planning (MAP) Toolkit 3.2 to help accelerate virtualization planning and deployment. It is available free at www.microsoft.com/map.

In addition, more than 130 independent software vendors have certified a total of 150 applications on Windows Server 2008. Symantec, Diskeeper, and IBM are the first three vendors to have achieved the new Certified for Windows Server 2008 Hyper-V designation. This designation identifies applications that have been independently tested to exploit Hyper-V capabilities and meet mission-critical expectations in a virtualized environment.

WHAT IS VIRTUALIZATION?

Virtualization—in its simplest form—is the abstraction of hardware from the software. This can take many different forms. It can be in the form of operating system virtualization such as Hyper-V; presentation virtualization with terminal services; or application virtualization with App-V; and companies like Cisco and Hewlett Packard have network and storage virtualization.

Operating system virtualization is the most popular virtualization today. It is not only used on servers but is installed on workstations for doing development and conducting demonstrations.

Virtualization can help companies maximize the value of IT investments, decreasing the server hardware footprint, energy consumption, and cost and complexity of managing IT systems while increasing the flexibility of the overall environment. Virtualization also helps IT professionals and developers build systems with the flexibility and intelligence to automatically adjust to changing business conditions by aligning computing resources with strategic objectives.

Why Virtualize?

Companies are always looking to save more money, reduce costs, and do more with less. At one point in 1965 Intel cofounder Gordon Moore observed that the density of transistors would double about every two years. Since 1965 this has held relatively true and has become known as Moore's Law. While Moore was observing the number of transistors, another interesting phenomenon has occurred, and it seems that other components of computer architecture such as hard drives and memory seem to double in capacity at about the same rate as predicted by Moore's Law.

With the doubling of performance and capacity of the hardware components every couple of years, many business applications haven't kept up with new hardware features or just don't need the power that is available. In the 1990s and early 2000s there was a boom of building scale-out solutions, and many application components were hosted on a separate server, or because of application compatibility a small system would require its own server. The practice of scaling out and the inability to run multiple applications on one server has led to bloated datacenters. At that time the economy was extremely good and x86 virtualization technologies were still in their infancy. This ultimately led to a standard practice for many businesses.

Recent events like the cost of electricity, cooling, and the cost of running a datacenter have led to skyrocketing operational costs. Luckily, with the release of updated operating systems that can manage the running of multiple applications on the same server, and the aging of virtualization technology, we have a series of solutions to help battle server sprawl and help us reclaim the datacenter.

Usage Scenarios

Server virtualization can be used to achieve several benefits within an organization:

▼ Server consolidation

■ Business continuity and disaster recovery

■ Development and test systems

▲ Dynamic Data Center

Server Consolidation Server consolidation is the act of reducing the number of physical servers and minimizing datacenter floor space in an enterprise. Through server consolidation an IT organization can not only reduce the number of physical servers in an environment, but they can also significantly decrease the amount of money that is spent on operational costs. By reducing the physical server count, consolidation will decrease the amount of power required to run servers, which will directly impact the amount of cooling that is required to keep servers running at an optimal temperature and reduce the amount of expensive datacenter floor space required to run business systems.

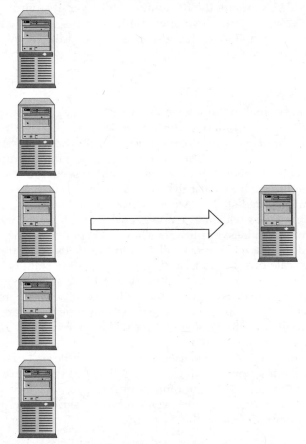

Consolidating many physical servers as virtual servers on
one machine saves datacenter space, increases CPU utilization,
and reduces the amount of electricity used.

Consolidation can also happen at a remote location. For example, a remote site may have four physical servers that are underutilized, but have to be on a separate server due to application compatibility issues; those physical servers could be migrated to a single server running the Hyper-V role as isolated virtual machines, thus saving money in power, cooling, licensing, and maintenance. This would also allow for the provisioning of an additional virtual server if the need arises at the remote location versus having to purchase and ship a new server.

Business Continuity and Disaster Recovery   The need to be able to recover from a catastrophic event as fast as possible to get back to being at a functional business state can be a costly and extremely tough situation for a company to address. Using Windows Server 2008 Hyper-V, you can pre-stage systems at a warm site, use Windows Server

Failover Clustering; or if your environment is already virtualized, and you're using the right third-party solutions, that entire environment can be replicated to another datacenter or backed up and restored at a different location. Using virtualization for business continuity and disaster recovery can significantly reduce the cost of a project as well as speed up your disaster recovery testing.

Development and Test Systems Development and test systems are a great place to start your virtualization journey. With the speed at which business moves today, IT organizations need to quickly provision development and test systems to meet business demand to develop systems faster. By creating templates and having a virtual infrastructure in place, you can provision a development or test system in a matter of minutes versus the weeks it takes to order new hardware and install that hardware in your datacenter. With the snapshot functionality that is available in Hyper-V, a developer can create a baseline configuration, take a snapshot of that configuration, and implement the new code. If there is a problem with the code, the developer or tester can revert to the snapshot and be ready to try again.

The traditional model of restoring from backup or rebuilding a machine is time in-tensive for the administrators, as well as for the developers and testers who have to re-configure each machine. If a project needs another development or test system, a person with appropriate rights can use the self-service portal of System Center Virtual Machine Manager 2008 to provision a new system without having to use a systems administrator to build that machine.

Dynamic Data Center For years you've been hearing about the Dynamic Data Center. With the release of Windows Server 2008 Hyper-V, we're one step closer to that reality. A Dynamic Data Center is a theory that systems will seamlessly be able to be provisioned, deprovisioned, and adjust to work load demands automatically. With Hyper-V and System Center Virtual Machine Manager 2008, you can configure intelligent placement to place your virtual machine on the host that is most optimized for your guests workload.

The Green Story

Another great reason to virtualize is the environmental impact that your datacenter makes. When you have hundreds or thousands of servers, you're consuming a lot of electricity, both to power the equipment and to cool the datacenter. By virtualizing serv-ers, you cut hundreds of servers out of operation. This results in less power consumed and less carbon dioxide pumped into the atmosphere.

Save Money While there's an altruistic benefit to green IT, there's also a monetary benefit. First, from an equipment standpoint, you need not replace so much gear. You can reduce the number of servers, depending on what applications you use. Assuming a 12:1 ratio after virtualization, you offload the duties of 12 machines onto one. So you've saved the cost of 11 physical servers, plus you don't have to spend as much money to power them.

NOTE You also have a leaner IT department, because you won't need as much personnel to manage the equipment.

Here's a good exercise: Chances are that you never see the electrical bill for your datacenter, but your facilities manager does. Head down to his office and take a look at the electrical bill—realizing that most of it is attributed to the datacenter.

Save the Planet   There are strong environmental reasons why you should virtualize. We talked about the ability to reduce greenhouse gas emissions by reducing the amount of hardware you have, but there are also reductions in pollution.

By reducing the number of servers you use, when it comes time to dispose of them, rather than the pollutants of 12 servers being introduced to the world, now there is just one. And if disposed of properly, those pollutants won't hurt anyone.

In addition to the end life of the server, think about what happens before you even take ownership of the server. It has to be manufactured (creating pollutants) and it has to be shipped to you. By virtualizing, you take 11 more servers worth of production and shipping out of the environmental equation.

Save Your Company   You may not care at all about saving the planet. We're not here to be your conscience, but there are solid business reasons to virtualize. First, we've already established that you can save money.

How much will you save? This number varies from business to business and state to state, but, in general, let's assume you have 100 computers and right now 35 percent of them have power-saving features enabled. The power bill runs around $2,883 per year. If you enable power saving on all your machines, it drops to $990.

The prospect of saving money should seal the deal for you, but if you need more encouragement, think about the public relations goodwill that your company will engender by striving to be more environmentally friendly.

NOTE   For more information of ecological responsibility as it relates to IT, check out the book *Green IT: Reduce Your Information System's Environmental Impact While Adding to the Bottom Line* by Toby Velte, Anthony Velte, and Robert Elsenpeter (McGraw-Hill, 2008).

What Should I Virtualize?

Virtualize everything! Well, maybe not everything; determining which servers to virtualize is probably one of the most time-consuming tasks you will do while planning your virtualization implementation. There are factors that range from performance and supported operating system to the hardest part of all, politics. We're going to leave the politics to the politicians and focus only on the technical components of virtualization.

There are five major system components that will drive your choice to virtualize a server or workstation.

- ▼   Disk IO
- ■   Memory Utilization
- ■   Processor Utilization
- ■   Network Utilization
- ▲   Operating System

Disk IO

Disk IO is the input and output (IO) of data to a hard disk. Disk IO is measured by the number of IO operations per second (IOPS) that can be performed. When planning a Windows Server 2008 Hyper-V environment, it will be critical to provide enough IO performance from your disk subsystem to the host server or servers to support the IO requirements for the host and each virtual machine you implement. When you are implementing a new virtual machine or converting a physical machine to a virtual machine, the virtual machine itself will use the same amount of IO as it did or would have if it were a physical server. Also, the total amount of IO isn't just the sum of the virtual machines; it must also include the IO of the host. While doing this, keep in mind that you will someday add more virtual servers to that host.

Memory Utilization

Memory utilization is how much Random Access Memory (RAM) a system uses for the base operating system as well as for the applications that run on that system. The amount of memory a system uses can go up and down depending on the workload a server is experiencing at any given time. Knowing how much memory your guests use at load and on average will help you determine not only how much memory you will need to purchase for your host systems, but also how many virtual machines you will be able to place on that host.

Processor Utilization

Processor utilization is how much throughput your CPU is doing at any given time. Each task or process that runs on a multitasking CPU must share CPU cycles. This is important because if a task is already heavy on the CPU, there is less time for the CPU to work with other processes. With the creation of multicore processors there are more CPU cores available to do the tasks at hand. When you do the analysis of your current machines, pay close attention to the utilization and the type of processors that are in your systems. This will help determine the number of virtual machines that can fit on a host machine.

Network Utilization

Network utilization is the amount of network usage of a system. This usage is generally expressed as the amount of bandwidth being recorded over a period of time in megabits per second.

The network utilization rate is the ratio of current traffic to the maximum traffic that the port can handle. If network utilization rates are high, then the network is busy. If they are low, then the network is idle. If the rate is too high, the result is low transmission speeds.

However, when we talk about network utilization as it relates to virtualization, we're talking about multiple virtual machines sharing a single network interface card (NIC). The result is a much more efficient strategy, and one that reduces the amount of network traffic.

Guest Operating Systems

Windows Server 2008 Hyper-V has a limited number of operating systems that are supported to run on the guest virtual machines. Table 1-1 shows the operating systems that Microsoft will support as a guest OS in a guest virtual machine on Hyper-V.

Operating System	Version	SMP
Windows Server 2008 x64 with or without Hyper-V	Standard Enterprise Datacenter Web Server	Guest configured with one, two, or four virtual processors SMP
Windows Server 2008 x86	Standard Enterprise Datacenter Web Server	Guest configured with one, two, or four virtual processors SMP
Windows Server 2003 x64	Standard with Service Pack 2 Enterprise with Service Pack 2 Datacenter with Service Pack 2 Web Server with Service Pack 2	Guest configured with one or two virtual processors
Windows Server 2003 x86	Standard with Service Pack 2 Enterprise with Service Pack 2 Datacenter with Service Pack 2 Web Server with Service Pack 2	Guest configured with one or two virtual processors SMP
Windows Server 2000	Server with Service Pack 4 Advanced Server with Service Pack 4	Guest configured with one virtual processor
Windows HPC (High Performance Computing) Server	2008	Guest configured with one, two, or four virtual processors
Windows Vista x64	Business with Service Pack 1 Enterprise with Service Pack 1 Ultimate with Service Pack 1	Guest configured with one or two virtual processors SMP
Windows Vista X86	Business with Service Pack 1 Enterprise with Service Pack 1 Ultimate with Service Pack 1	Guest configured with 1 or 2 virtual processors SMP
Windows XP x64	With Service Pack 2	Guest configured with one or two virtual processors
Windows XP x86	With Service Pack 3	Guest configured with one or two virtual processors
Windows XP x86	With Service Pack 2	Guest configured with one virtual processor

Table 1-1. Operating Systems Officially Supported by Hyper-V

Operating System	Version	SMP
Linux x64	SUSE Linux Enterprise Server 10 with Service Pack 2 SUSE Linux Enterprise Server 10 with Service Pack 1	Guest configured with one virtual processor
Linux x86	SUSE Linux Enterprise Server 10 with Service Pack 2 SUSE Linux Enterprise Server 10 with Service Pack 1	Guest configured with one virtual processor

Table 1-1.   Operating Systems Officially Supported by Hyper-V (*continued*)

Other operating systems might work with Hyper-V, but Microsoft is only supporting this list at this time. Check the Microsoft web site, www.microsoft.com/en/us/default.aspx, regularly to see if Microsoft has added any additional supported operating systems since the publication of this book.

A more in-depth view of how to calculate your server utilization and tools that you can use to collect the performance data required to help make the "to virtualize or not to virtualize" decision will be provided in the next chapter.

WINDOWS SERVER 2008 HYPER-V HIGH-LEVEL ARCHITECTURE

Windows Server 2008 is Microsoft's latest server product, and the one that introduces us to Hyper-V. Let's take a look at all the flavors of Windows Server 2008 so you can see what each one offers. The versions of Windows Server have remained mostly consistent over the years, but with each new release, more and better functionality is introduced.

Versions of Windows Server 2008

Microsoft has released several different editions of Windows Server 2008. For the purpose of this book we are only going to focus on the editions of Windows Server 2008 that include Hyper-V. Each Server 2008 edition has slightly different features and licensing models, so determining what is right for you will be critical during the planning phase of your virtualization project. The following Server 2008 editions include the Hyper-V role:

▼ Windows Server 2008 Standard x64

■ Windows Server 2008 Enterprise x64

■ Windows Server 2008 Datacenter x64

▲ Microsoft Hyper-V Server 2008

The release of Windows Server 2008 R2 will mark the first Windows Operating System to only be released only for 64-bit processors. Some companies aren't going to feel especially comfortable with that, but since you really can't buy a 32-bit processor in a server anymore it makes sense for Microsoft to do this. Also, when running as a Hyper-V host, you will be able to have up to 32 logical processors in a single host. This is an increase of 8 logical processors over the R1 release.

Standard

Windows Server 2008 standard is very similar to Windows Server 2008 Enterprise and Windows Server 2008 Datacenter except for a few components.

- ▼ Windows Server 2008 Standard supports up to four x86 sockets of processors with a maximum of 32 processor cores, or up to four x64 sockets of processors with a maximum of 64 processor cores.

- ▲ Windows Server 2008 Standard will support up to 4 gigabytes (GB) of RAM on the x86 implementation and up to 32GB of RAM on the x64 implementation.

Windows Server 2008 Standard is licensed in a per-server model. When a license of Windows Server 2008 standard is purchased, this entitles the server to the physical operating system instance plus an additional one virtual machine to run Windows Server 2008 standard on that host system.

Enterprise

Each edition of Windows Server 2008 is really the number of processors and roles/features that are available to that version.

- ▼ Windows Server 2008 Enterprise supports up to eight x86 sockets of processors with a maximum of 32 processor cores, or eight x64 sockets of processors with a maximum of 64 processor cores.

- ■ Windows Server 2008 Enterprise will support up to 64GB of RAM on the x86 implementation and up to 2 terabytes (TB) of RAM on the x64 implementation. With the Hyper-V role enabled, Enterprise will support up to 1TB of RAM on the host system, allowing each guest system to address up to 64GB.

- ▲ Windows Server 2008 Enterprise also supports up to 16 nodes in a Windows failover cluster.

Windows Server 2008 Enterprise is licensed in a per-server model. When a license of Server 2008 Enterprise is purchased, this entitles the server to the physical operating system instance plus an additional four virtual machines. That means you can run the core operating system on the hardware and you can run a mix of:

- ▼ Windows Server 2008 Enterprise or Standard 32- and/or 64-bit
- ▲ Windows Server 2003/R2 Enterprise or Standard 32- and/or 64-bit

Datacenter

When you're building a larger virtualization cluster with Windows Server 2008, the Datacenter edition makes a lot of sense as the core OS. Since the Datacenter edition supports an unlimited number of virtual machines when built in a cluster scenario, it significantly reduces licensing complexities that can occur when using Quick Motion to migrate a virtual machine from one host to another.

▼   Windows Server 2008 Datacenter supports up to 32 x86 sockets of processors with a maximum of 32 processor cores or 64 x64 sockets of processors with a maximum of 64 processor cores.

■   Windows Server 2008 Datacenter will support up to 64GB of RAM on the x86 implementation and up to 2TB of RAM on the x64 implementation. With the Hyper-V role enabled, Datacenter will support up to 1TB of RAM on the host system, allowing each guest system to address up to 64GB.

▲   Server 2008 Datacenter also supports up to 16 nodes in a Windows failover cluster.

Windows Server 2008 Datacenter licensing is purchased on a per-processor basis up to eight sockets. When the number of processor licenses has been purchased for the number of processors in the host computer, that host computer has the right to run an unlimited number of Windows Server 2008 virtual machines for no additional cost.

Hyper-V Server 2008

Hyper-V Server 2008 is a dedicated stand-alone server release that only contains the Windows Hypervisor, Windows Server driver model, and the virtualization components. This release supports the basic Hyper-V virtualization functionality, with support for up to four processors or 24 processor cores and up to 32GB of RAM. Hyper-V Server 2008 does not allow for additional server roles and does not have a graphical user interface, nor does it include the ability to create clusters for high availability. Each Windows guest virtual machine will require a respective license for the operating system installed.

For all versions of Windows Server 2008 with Hyper-V installed, Microsoft will only support up to 24 logical processors per host. For instance, if you have two dual-core processors and you have hyperthreading enabled, you would effectively have 8 logical processors. If it were possible to turn off hyperthreading in the system BIOS, you would have 4 logical processors on a system.

The Hyper-V Server 2008 R2 will continue to be a free download from Microsoft, but has a significant amount of new features. Hyper-V 2008 Server R2 now includes the features to create a highly available cluster of up to 16 nodes, 32 logical processors, and the live migration feature. Even though this is a free download, you still need to purchase licenses for each of the operating systems that you run as virtual machines on a Hyper-V Server 2008 R1 or R2 release.

What Is Windows Server 2008 Hyper-V?

Windows Server 2008 with Hyper-V is the Microsoft version of a hypervisor. A *hypervisor* is a very thin operating system that runs directly on hardware, ultimately as an operating system control program, and separates a parent partition from a child partition.

While Hyper-V is advanced in terms of what it does and its construction, it really comes down to four major pieces. Let's take a look under the hood of Hyper-V to see what is going on and what makes it tick.

The four different major components (shown in Figure 1-5) that make up Windows Server 2008 Hyper-V are:

▼   Hardware

■   Hyper-V hypervisor

■   VMBUS

▲   Partitions

    ■   Parent partition

    ■   Child partition

Hardware

When Microsoft created Hyper-V, they took into consideration the benefits that hardware manufacturers are building into today's servers for virtualization. Hyper-V leverages features such as data execution prevention and hardware-assisted virtualization from Intel and AMD.

Data execution prevention (DEP) is a mix of hardware and software that is used to help prevent code from being executed from the default heap and the stack. When it really comes down to it, DEP helps prevent malicious code from taking advantage of exception-handling mechanisms in Windows. Specifically, when you implement a new

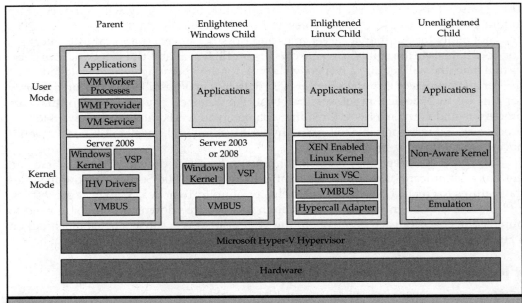

Figure 1-5.   The Hyper-V architecture has four main components.

server that is going to run the Hyper-V role, you must enable the Intel XD bit (execute disable bit) or the AMD NX bit (no execute bit).

Hardware-assisted virtualization is a set of technologies that helps to manage tasks that would generally be done by the hypervisor. This includes memory and hardware sharing. Intel and AMD have both released hardware-assisted virtualization technologies: Intel's technology is Intel VT, and AMD's technology is called AMD-V. By leveraging the advancements that Intel and AMD have made in hardware-assisted virtualization, Microsoft has developed Hyper-V to be able to put virtual machines and applications as close to the hardware as possible.

When choosing a hardware platform for your Hyper-V implementation, it's very important that the hardware model is on the approved hardware list. Microsoft has put the hardware on the approved hardware list through an extremely rigorous testing program. This testing was important for Hyper-V since the hypervisor interfaces directly with the hardware and the parent/child partitions.

When you look at the Windows Server 2008 Editions, you will see that there are x86 versions with Hyper-V available. The x86 versions of Server 2008 only host the management components for Hyper-V and do not contain the Hyper-V hypervisor. This can be very confusing when you are looking at your MSDN subscription or your select downloads, but the Hyper-V hypervisor is only available to run on x64 editions of Windows Server 2008. This actually works out to be a benefit for the enterprise to be able to leverage the memory and processing expansions that the 64-bit environment provides.

Hyper-V Hypervisor

There are two major types of hypervisors: a monolithic hypervisor and a microkernelized hypervisor. The *monolithic* hypervisor is installed directly to hardware and holds all third-party tools and drivers required for the Admin VM and guest VMs to function. A *microkernelized* hypervisor, like the monolithic hypervisor, is installed directly to the hardware but offloads driver management and the virtualization stack to the parent partition (see Figure 1-6).

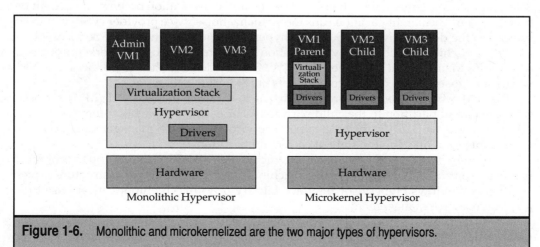

Figure 1-6.   Monolithic and microkernelized are the two major types of hypervisors.

Hyper-V is a microkernelized hypervisor architecture. What that means is that Hyper-V gives supported guest operating systems such as Windows Server 2008 and SUSE Linux the ability to work as close as possible to the hardware. Hyper-V itself doesn't contain the core system drivers that a standard monolithic hypervisor would hold. Instead, not allowing any third-party code or drivers to exist in the hypervisor has led to a very clean implementation, which also makes a very small attack surface for any malicious person or code.

The Hyper-V hypervisor handles access to physical resources such as the physical processer. The hypervisor provides a virtual view of the physical components to the partitions. Depending on the configuration, this may be a full virtual view, or the virtual view may be just a slice of the physical resources. The hypervisor uses what is called the *hypercall* as the interface of communications between the partitions and the hardware. The hypervisor will also run the advanced programmable interrupt controller (APIC), which assigns priority levels to processor interrupts. The hypervisor also manages memory address management, partitions, and memory service routines.

VMBUS

The virtual machine bus (VMBUS) is used for communication between the parent and child partition via the virtual service provider and the virtual service client. The VMBUS provides a virtualized environment if your system is running a virtualization-optimized processor.

Partitions

Hyper-V creates logical units of isolation in which a guest operating system will be installed. Each of those logical units is called a partition. There are two types of partitions that are created in Hyper-V, the parent partition and the child partition.

Parent Partition   The *parent partition*, or root partition, runs the virtualization stack and is the partition that has direct access to the hardware devices. When you install Windows Server 2008 and then implement the Hyper-V role, your initial installation becomes the parent or root partition. The parent partition runs the virtualization service provider (VSP) that talks directly to the device drivers through the hypervisor and offers hardware services when requested by child partitions. The virtualization stack consists of the VM worker processes, a Windows Management Instrumentation (WMI) provider, and the VM Services. The VM worker processes are user-mode components of the virtualization stack.

The VM worker processes provide virtual machine management (VMM) services from the parent partition to the child partitions. For each child partition there is a separate set of VM worker processes created. The virtual machine management service is responsible for managing the state of each child partition.

The parent partition also contains a specific set of WMI APIs to allow you to programmatically control and manage a virtual machine. The virtualization infrastructure driver (VID) and Windows Hypervisor Interface Library or WinHV components are used for physical resource management.

The VID provides management services for partitions, virtual processor management, and memory management. The WinHV component allows a partitioned operating system to talk to the hypervisor directly with standard Windows calling conventions. The parent partition is also used to create child partitions that will run an isolated guest operating system with applications.

Child Partition   The *child partition* runs a guest operating system that can have applications installed and running many different functions of a business. If a supported hypervisor-aware operating system is installed on the guest virtual machine or child partition, it will run the virtualization service client or VSC. The VSC consumes the services that the VSP makes available for use.

Each device type for Hyper-V—such as storage, networking, video, and input devices—has a VSP/VSC pair that Microsoft has provided. If you are using a supported device from a third-party independent hardware vendor (IHV), that vendor will supply a VSP/VSC pair for you that has undergone strict testing by Microsoft.

Hyper-V categorizes operating systems into two different categories: a hypervisor-aware operating system and a non-hypervisor-aware operating system. A hypervisor-aware operating system is extremely similar to a paravirtualized operating system. Paravirtualization is a method that lets a guest operating system know that it's being virtualized and allows for the host system and the guest system to cooperate to help reduce the performance cost on key functions of a guest operating system. Hypervisor-aware operating systems work directly with Hyper-V to realize performance and management gains by taking advantage of Enlightened I/O. Windows Server 2008 is a fully enlightened operating system right out of the box. SUSE Enterprise Linux is also a fully enlightened operating system in which older versions of Windows Server and other x86 operating systems have different levels of enlightenment.

Two different types of devices are present in a child partition: synthetic and emulated. A *synthetic* device is designed to have the lowest overhead and utilizes the VMBUS to send packaged instructions to a driver on the parent partition. An *emulated* device is a device that emulates a physical device such as a network interface card.

After you install a supported operating system onto a child partition, you will want to install the integration components on that operating system. Integration components are a set of services and drivers that help the virtual machine perform and behave in a more consistent manner. There are integration components for both Windows and Linux operating systems.

The Windows Integration Components installs the virtualization service client as well as time synchronization, heartbeat, shutdown, key/value pair exchange, and the Volume Shadow Copy Service (VSS).

The time synchronization component plays an important role in keeping child partitions in sync. This can be achieved using a network protocol as well, but the time synchronization component comes in handy when a network resource isn't available, or where a network protocol may be too slow. Having the ability to synchronize time quickly becomes very important when restoring a virtual machine from a saved state, or when bringing a virtual machine back online that has been in a dormant state for an extended period of time.

The parent partition will use the heartbeat component to send a regular request to the child partition to verify if that partition is available. If the parent partition doesn't receive a response in a timely manner, it will continue to request a status and will log events for the missing replies.

There are times when you will need to shut down one or multiple virtual machines that you may not have time to log in to or you may not have rights to log on to. The shutdown components allow for virtual machines to be cleanly shut down without having to log on to a virtual machine.

The key/value pair exchange components are used to set, delete, and gather specific information about a child partition and the operating system running on that partition. Once the integration component is installed, the parent partition will set the host name of the DNS server used by the parent partition, as well as the parent partition's fully qualified domain name (FQDN) and the local non-fully qualified system name. The child partition will provide the parent partitions with information by exposing the data that is contained in the HKLM\Software\Microsoft\Virtual Machine\Auto registry location. This information includes:

▼ **OSMajorVersion**   Specifies major version number of the OS

■ **OSMinorVersion**   Specifies minor version number of the OS

■ **OSBuildNumber**   Specifies operating system build number of the guest OS

■ **OSVersion**   Specifies operating system version of the guest OS

■ **OSPlatformID**   Specifies system platform of the guest OS (WIN9x, NT4, or later)

■ **CSDVersion**   Latest service pack that is installed on the guest OS

■ **ServicePackMajor**   Latest major service pack version installed on the guest OS

■ **ServicePackMinor**   Latest minor service pack version installed on the guest OS

■ **SuiteMask**   Specifies available product suites on the guest OS

■ **ProductType**   Specifies product type of the OS installed on the guest (Server, XP)

■ **OSname**   Specifies the name that is set in HKLM\Software\Microsoft\WindowsNT\CurrentVersion\ProductName (for example, Windows Vista Ultimate)

■ **ProcessorArchitecture**   Specifies the processor architecture such as Intel or AMD

▲ **FullyQualifiedDomainName**   Specifies the fully qualified name of the guest OS, or if the guest is part of a failover cluster, it specifies the cluster virtual server name

Third-party and other tools to manage and monitor the child partition and the guest operating system can use this exposed data.

On guest operating systems that support the Volume Shadow Copy Service (VSS), if the integration components have been installed, the parent partition can request the synchronization and quiescence of a guest operating system. This means that the parent partition can request that the guest operating system on the child partition put its data into an inhibited state so that a snapshot of that data can take place, and the data can be synchronized from one snapshot to another. If all guest operating systems installed on guest partitions support VSS, and are running the integration components, the entire host server can be backed up using a VSS snapshot.

Linux operating systems that have a XEN-Enabled Linux kernel such as SUSE Enterprise, Linux 10 will be able to take advantage of the Hyper-V integration components to help increase guest performance. When the Linux Integration components are installed, the virtualization service client is installed as well, which is named the hypercall adapter. The hypercall adapter on the child partition translates XEN virtualization calls into Hyper-V virtualization calls.

Table 1-2 illustrates which integration components are available for a specific guest operating system. Not all functions are available for each operating system.

Virtualization is a huge and important topic. In this chapter we threw a lot at you about what virtualization is, and how it has evolved. We also took an in-depth look at Hyper-V and how it works. In the next chapter we'll talk about planning for a Hyper-V installation and walk through the steps of putting it on your server.

Operating System	Time Sync	Heartbeat	Shutdown	K/V Pair Exchange	VSS
Windows Server 2008 x64	Yes	Yes	Yes	Yes	Yes
Windows Server 2008 x86	Yes	Yes	Yes	Yes	Yes
Windows Server 2003 x64 with SP2	Yes	Yes	Yes	Yes	Yes
Windows Server 2003 x86 with SP2	Yes	Yes	Yes	Yes	Yes
Windows 2000 Server with SP4	Yes	Yes	Yes	Yes	No
Windows 2000 Advanced Server with SP4	Yes	Yes	Yes	Yes	No
Windows Vista x64 with SP1	Yes	Yes	Yes	Yes	Yes
Windows Vista x86 with SP1	Yes	Yes	Yes	Yes	Yes
Windows XP x64 with SP2	Yes	Yes	Yes	Yes	No
Windows XP x86 with SP2 or SP3	Yes	Yes	Yes	Yes	No
SUSE Linux Enterprise Server 10 x64	No	No	No	No	No
SUSE Linux Enterprise Server 10 x86	No	No	No	No	No

Table 1-2. Integration Components for Guest Operating Systems

CHAPTER 2

Planning and Installation

While it would be nice to be able to simply jump into your Windows Server 2008 installation, that's not the best thing to do. In this chapter we'll cover how to plan and prepare for an installation, and then we'll walk you through the steps you need in order to perform a successful Windows Server 2008 Hyper-V installation.

Every project that you do requires planning. We know that's a bold statement, and there are some people who will disagree with us, but based on our collective project experience we have found this to be true. A project can be broken down into four distinct phases:

▼ Planning

■ Design

■ Build

▲ Installation

Project management methodology is meant to provide a standard method and guidelines to make sure that information technology projects are done in a disciplined, well-managed procedure that ensures the delivery of quality products that are completed on time and within budget.

As Figure 2-1 shows, project management in an iterative process. It isn't a step-by-step process. Indeed, some phases overlap—such as concept definition and planning—where it can be hard to do one without the other.

Other activities—like oversight and quality control—are continual and will have an impact on each cycle of the project.

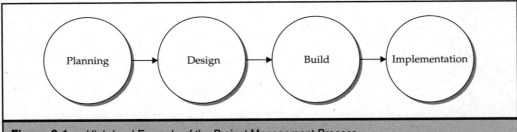

Figure 2-1.   High-level Example of the Project Management Process

THE PLANNING PHASE

Now that you have an understanding of the Windows Server 2008 Hyper-V features and the different options you have for the 2008 operating systems, let's take a look at planning your project. As we've already mentioned, the planning phase is probably the most important phase of your project.

In the planning phase, you're going to spend a majority of your time figuring out what your requirements are going to be, your communications plan, and your overall project plan for design, build, and implementation. You may also be using the data you collect about your systems to build a business case to procure funding for the remaining phases of your project.

Requirements

When we talk about IT projects and requirements, one's thought instantly goes to the side of a box of software where it tells you that you need a Windows Vista computer running 2.7 GHz, 2GB memory, and 25GB of available hard drive space. That's coming up, but we're talking about a different set of requirements at this phase.

A requirement is basically what you need a particular service or system to do or be. Requirements can come in the form of how available the service should be, how a system processes a transaction, or what the color of the user interface should be. (We're fans of cornflower blue, if you were wondering.)

A majority of requirements are going to be driven by business resources that ultimately have control of the systems that you plan to convert or build as virtual systems. You'll also want to spend time with the support organizations for each application to get a feel for how the application is acting in production.

This phase establishes the project's structure, develops pilot plans and testing strategies, and addresses deployment implications, operations management and supportability, and operational acceptance criteria.

What Do I Need to Know?

When it comes to a virtualization project, you need to know a fair amount of detail about the systems that are candidates for virtualization. Not only do you need to know what the technical details of the servers are, but you will also need to know what the systems do for your business. Knowing whether the server is a front-end access point to a product management system that is used 24 hours a day by resources globally; a shop floor scheduling system; or a single server that is used at month end by the accounting department can have an impact on how—or if—you convert or build virtual machines for those systems. You may find that adding virtual machines to an existing web farm and decommissioning the old servers is more advantageous to conducting a physical-to-virtual migration.

Talk to People

The first part of what you are going to need to do is to hold interviews with owners of the systems that you have deemed candidates for virtualization, to build what we call a candidate profile. The *candidate profile* is a collection of information that tells you what a system is, what it does, how it performs, and what the business expects of it. You can use a spreadsheet, or if you are more adventurous you can build a database with this information. During your interviews you should be gathering the following information:

▼   What does the system do?

■   Where is the system located?

■   What software is installed on that system?

■   When is it most utilized?

■   Who uses the system?

■   Are there scheduled jobs that occur, and if so, when?

■   What service level agreements does this business have with customers?

■   What are the recovery point and recovery time objectives?

■   How much data does the system have?

■   How is the system backed up?

▲   What kind of availability is required for the system?

Generally, when you're doing these types of interviews and building your candidate profile, you'll be able to gather all the above information, but also have a chance to start talking with the business units about what virtualization is and help them determine the benefits. This is also a time when you'll discover any virtualization blockers, such as a legal contract, or that the business cannot assume the risk of converting that system at this time. Once you have this information you should have a good view of what the systems do for the business, when the business needs them available, and you will start to have an idea of whether they are good virtualization candidates.

The other half of determining whether a system is a good virtualization candidate is to know the technical specifications of the system. The information that you should be gathering about your server is:

▼   Hardware make and model

■   Processor information (type, number, speed)

■   Processor utilization

■   Amount of memory

■   Memory utilization

■   Disk configuration

■   Disk IO utilization

■   Network configuration

■   Network IO utilization

■   Additional hardware cards (ISA or PCI cards)

■   Hardware dongles (USB, serial, or parallel)

■   Hardware accessories (scanners or other equipment)

- ■ Installed OS version
- ■ Patch level
- ▲ Installed software

Obtaining this information can be done in several different ways. You can configure Performance Monitor to collect the information, or you can use a tool set such as the Microsoft Assessment and Planning Toolkit or PlateSpin PowerRecon.

Performance Monitor

Using the built-in performance monitor tools in the Windows OS, you can collect the data that you will need to make decisions about whether a host is a good virtualization candidate or not. There are four areas of information that need to be collected:

- ▼ Processor
- ■ Disk
- ■ Memory
- ▲ Network

Once you collect the information, place it in the candidate spreadsheet or database that you will use later for determining host size and placement.

Windows Performance Monitor has been around since Windows NT in 1993 and the Windows Server 2008 Performance Monitor provides you with a visual tool for measuring the performance of your Windows server. You can also monitor other computers on the network.

Each item (such as the processor) that can be analyzed with the Performance Monitor is referred to as an *object*. A performance data item that can be measured for a particular object is called a *counter*. For example, the processor has a number of counters that you can view, including the % Processor Time and the Interrupts/Sec counters.

By using the counters to analyze various performance attributes of your hardware component, you can determine whether a piece of hardware on a server (such as the processor or hard drive) has become a bottleneck in terms of server performance.

The Performance Monitor can display the data as a graph, a histogram (a horizontal or vertical bar graph format), or a report. You set the performance counters that are viewed in the Performance Monitor Details pane, select a particular object, and then add the counters related to the object you want to monitor.

Processor

By collecting the processor utilization information over a period of time, you can start building an understanding of what that system does and when. Knowing this information is critical so that you don't overcommit processor resources on your host systems and possibly starve out other virtual machines. The longer you collect performance data, the closer your trend analysis of the systems will be, which will help you predict how many virtual machines you can run on each host. Use the Performance Monitor object shown in Table 2-1 to collect this data.

Object	Counter	Instance
Processor	% Processor Time	_Total

Table 2-1. Information You Can Gather about Your Processor with Performance Monitor

Also collect the number of processors in the system, including number of cores per processor, speed, cache, and front-side bus speed, and document this information in your candidate profile.

Disk

Every system, physical or virtual, requires disk space. Those systems utilize that disk space to store the operating system files, paging file, application install files and data, user data, and databases. Figuring out what a system is going to need for disk space and disk performance is pretty much the same for physical as it is for virtual, and collecting this data will help you determine your host disk requirements.

To determine the amount of disk space you are going to need, take the total amount of disk space used and add some factor for future growth. You'll need to work with the business owners and support team of the application to figure out what the growth factor will be. Once that is done, add current size and growth estimate to your candidate profile.

Determining disk performance is a little bit trickier. Disk performance is measured by the total number of physical inputs and outputs that occur over a period of time and is generally calculated as Input Outputs per second (IOPS). To calculate the total number of IOPS, your system is using Performance Monitor to track the performance objects shown in Table 2-2 over a period of time. The longer you track this information, the better the data will be to help you make a decision on whether to virtualize the system and how to scale your host system.

Object	Counter	Instance
Physical Disk	Disk Read/sec	_Total
Physical Disk	Disk Writes/sec	_Total
Physical Disk	Disk Queue Length	_Total

Table 2-2. Disk Drive Measurements in Performance Monitor

The Disk Queue Length counter will help you determine if your system has a disk subsystem bottleneck. On a well-performing system, the Disk Queue Length should be zero. Once you have collected this data, add it to your candidate profile.

Memory

Memory allocation has almost become an art rather than a science. Not allocating enough memory to a system will cause excessive paging and increase disk impact, which can give misleading information on disk IO and could create a subsystem bottleneck. Allocating too much memory can lead to the host being underutilized and thus impacting the utilization of that system, which goes directly to the cost of ownership of that system. As with all of the performance data that you are collecting, the length of time you collect will give you better data for making a decision on the candidate. This counter is shown in Table 2-3.

Pay special attention when collecting data to try to incorporate times when you know the systems are going to be at peak load. Use the preceding Performance Monitor object to track your memory usage. Once you've calculated the amount of memory you need from this counter, add an additional 32 megabytes to your estimate to account for host overhead.

Network

When documenting your candidate profile for network information, make sure that you document the number of network adapters that are in the system, what network those adapters are connected to, and the purpose of that network. The system may have an adapter for a front-end/back-end configuration, backup networks, or for iSCSI or NAS traffic. Any or all of these scenarios have an impact on your host and virtual machine design. To collect the network information of your candidate, use the Performance Monitor counter in Table 2-4.

Object	Counter	Instance
Memory	Committed Bytes	There is no instance

Table 2-3.   Memory Counter Used in Performance Monitor

Object	Counter	Instance
Network interface	Bytes total/sec	Each network adapter

Table 2-4.   Network Counter and Instance to Measure in Performance Monitor

THE MICROSOFT ASSESSMENT AND PLANNING TOOLKIT

The Microsoft Assessment and Planning Toolkit, or MAP, is a free solution accelerator that is available from Microsoft to help with planning and assessing Windows Vista and Windows Server 2008 hardware, Office 2007, security, SQL Server, power savings, application virtualization, performance monitoring, server consolidation, and virtualization. This toolkit helps to automate the collection of data we've mentioned and helps with determining host configuration and virtual machine placement. For the purpose of this book, we're only going to focus on the virtualization planning components from the MAP Toolkit.

Using the MAP Toolkit you'll be able to perform the following tasks to help build your candidate profile:

▼ Inventory the servers and workstations you are considering for virtualization

■ Collect performance data on the considered systems

■ Help determine the placement and number of your guest virtual machines on a virtual server

▲ Produce reports with detailed information on which systems can be virtualized

How Does the MAP Tool Assess Systems?

The Microsoft Assessment and Planning tool uses Windows Management Instrumentation (WMI), the Remote Registry Service, performance counters, Active Directory domain services, and SNMP (Simple Network Management Protocol) to collect inventory and performance metrics.

Windows Management Instrumentation (WMI)

The Assessment and Planning Toolkit uses WMI to collect hardware, device, and software information from remote computers. All assessment scenarios use WMI to conduct inventory tasks. In order to have a successful inventory and collection, some WMI configuration steps need to be in place prior to running an inventory. Table 2-5 describes the settings to modify in WMI.

Windows Active Directory Domain Services

If you have Windows Active Directory installed and your systems are joined to your domain, you can configure the MAP Toolkit to query a domain controller for a computer list versus having to create a text file for the MAP tool to read in.

Remote Registry Service

The MAP Toolkit uses the Remote Registry Service to find installed roles and run the Performance Metrics Wizard. In order for the MAP tool to be successful, make sure the following items have been performed on the systems you plan to inventory.

Consideration	Description	Setting
Local Account Password	If a system is in a workgroup configuration, the local user account used for inventory must have a password.	Set a password for any local accounts used for inventory and data collection.
Network Access Policy	If a system is in a workgroup configuration, the Network Access – Sharing and security model for local accounts is set to Guest Only.	Change the policy from Guest Only to Classic.
Firewall ports	The MAP Toolkit requires that TCP port 135, TCP port 139, TCP port 445, and UDP ports 137 and 138 be open.	Enable Remote Administrator Exception and File and Printer Sharing exception in Windows Firewall or open TCP port 135, TCP port 139, TCP port 445, and UDP ports 137 and 138 on the system firewall.

Table 2-5.   Settings in WMI

▼   Remote Registry Service is started.

■   Windows Firewall Remote Administration Exception is enabled or TCP port 135 is open.

▲   An account with Local Administrator Privileges is being used.

Using the Microsoft Assessment and Planning Toolkit

When installing MAP, the following software prerequisites need to be met prior to the installation.

▼   A supported operating system:

■   Windows XP 32-bit or 64-bit with SP2 or SP3

■   Windows Vista Ultimate, Enterprise, or Business 32-bit or 64-bit with or without SP1

- Windows Server 2003 R2 32-bit or 64-bit
- Windows Server 2008 32-bit or 64-bit
- Microsoft Works 2007 or Word 2003 with SP2
- Microsoft Word Primary Interop Assemblies
- Microsoft Excel 2007 or Excel 2003 SP2
- Microsoft Windows Installer Version 4.5
- .NET Framework Version 3.5 SP1
▲ Microsoft SQL Server 2005 or 2008 with a "MAPS" instance. If you don't have a SQL Server available for use, the MAP installer will download and install SQL Server 2008 Express Edition.

MAP also has a set of hardware requirements, as shown in Table 2-6, depending on the number of systems that will be scanned and assessed.

As with any system that will have a significant amount of data flowing through it, a gigabit network card is a good idea. One additional point you will want to take into consideration is whether you're going to be scanning and collecting data from 10,000 or more systems. If so, you will want to install SQL Server 2005 or 2008 to handle the amount of data. Also, if your company has 50,000 or more systems that you are going to be conducting an assessment on, you may want to break up your inventory into manageable divisions and possibly inventory systems per site or per network segment.

OK, now that you've configured your systems with the prerequisites, let's get MAP installed and start it collecting your system's information.

Number of Systems Being Assessed	Type of System	CPU	RAM
1–9,999	Desktop or laptop	Multicore 1.5 GHz or faster	2.5GB RAM
10,000–19,999	Workstation or server	Multicore 2.0 GHz or faster	4GB or more
20,000+	Server	Multiprocessor with Multicore 2 GHz or faster	4GB RAM or more

Table 2-6. Hardware Requirements for MAP

Installing MAP

MAP installation, like most any Microsoft product, is fairly straightforward. You just need some pieces of information to fill in as you run the installer. Let's look at the steps to install MAP.

1. To install MAP, download it from Microsoft and click on the setup file. The Microsoft Assessment and Planning Solution Accelerator Setup Wizard will open.

2. Click Next.

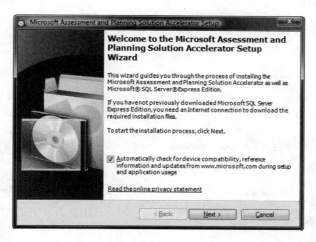

3. Read and accept the terms of the license agreement and then click Next.

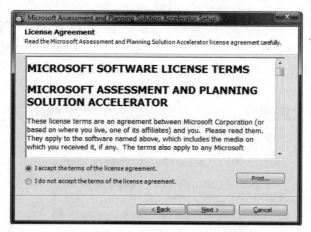

4. Choose your installation path and then click Next.

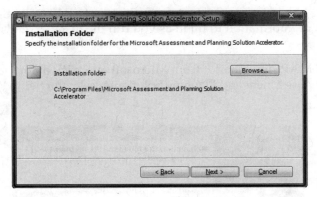

5. Choose to download and install SQL Server Express or install from previously downloaded installation files and then click Next.

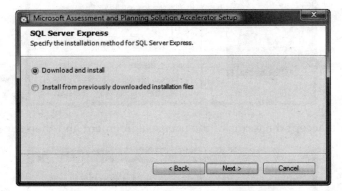

6. Read the SQL Server Express License agreement, accept the terms, and then click Next.

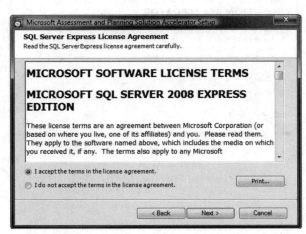

7. Click Install.

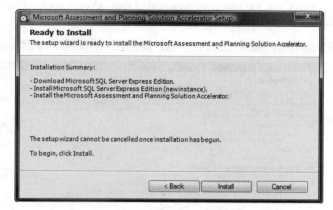

SQL Server Express will now download and install to your MAP computer. Once the SQL Server Express install is completed, the MAP installer will begin. Once Map is finished installing, choose whether or not to open MAP and click Finish.

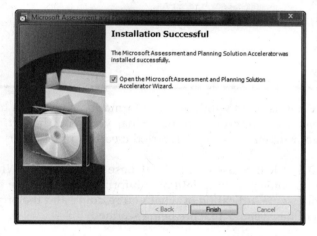

Using MAP to Collect Data

MAP is a very large tool, so large that a book could be written specifically about it. For this book we're going to accelerate directly to using it for assessing your server environment for virtualization. To learn more about MAP, we highly recommend reading the *Getting Started Guide* and the Microsoft Assessment and Planning online help information:

http://technet.microsoft.com/en-us/library/bb977556.aspx

OK, now that you have MAP installed, let's start collecting data so that you can see which of your systems are virtualization candidates. When MAP first opens, it's the familiar Office interface:

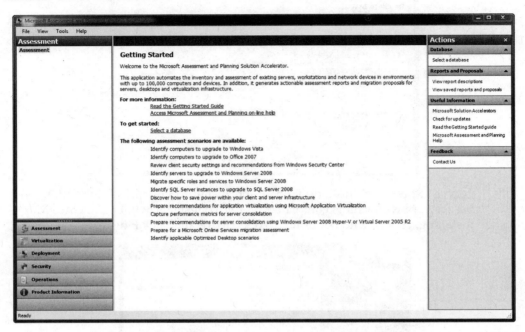

Each tab on the left is filled with links to information about each topic. In the main Getting Started pane, we highly recommend that you read the *Getting Started Guide* prior to starting your inventories. To get started creating an inventory with MAP, click Select a Database.

Specify a name that will be used for this database then click OK. When creating your name, try to include some sort of identifiable information. What we mean is that you may want to include some indication of what you're doing and the organization or network information of the systems that are being scanned.

Once the database is created, several options become available for the next steps:

Click the link Prepare Recommendations for Server Consolidation Using Windows Server 2008 Hyper-V or Virtual Server 2005 R2.

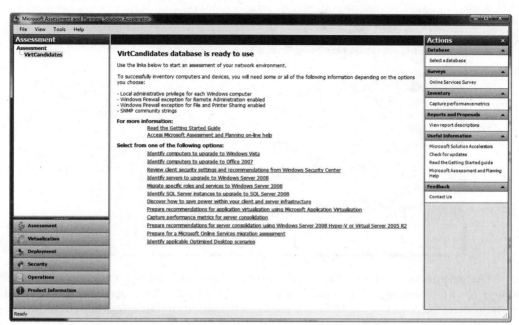

Click on the link Capture Performance Metrics for Computers in Your Environment.

In order to assess systems that are virtualization candidates, the Performance Metrics Wizard must be provided with information on what systems to collect data from, the credentials to collect data with, and how long to collect that data. There are sets of prerequisites that need to be met for the Performance Metrics Wizard to be successful in connecting via WMI. For systems that are running a firewall on the operating system, the ports listed in Table 2-7 need to be allowed.

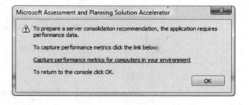

Function	Ports
File and Printer Sharing	TCP 139 and 445
	UDP 137 and 138
Remote Administration	TCP 135

Table 2-7. Ports That Need to Be Open to Allow the Performance Metrics Wizard to Function

Enter a path to the text file you created or click Browse to find the file, and then click Next.

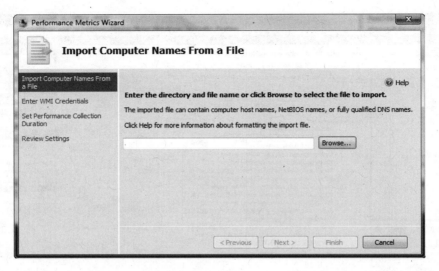

MAP requires a user that has local administrative privileges on each system from which you are going to collect data. This user can be a local system account or it can be a domain-based account. More than one user can be added if your environment requires.

Click the New Account button.

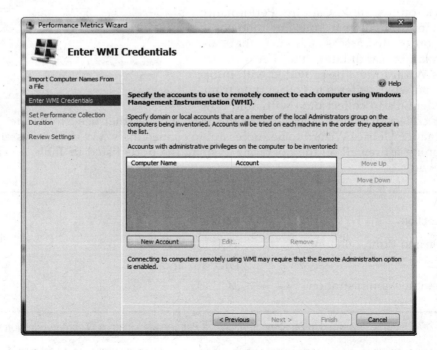

Enter the account information, leaving the domain name blank if you are specifying a local account, enter the password, and choose whether this account will be used on all computers or on a specific computer. Once that information is entered, click Save or Save and New if you need to enter more than one account.

Set the amount of time that you want the MAP tool to collect data and click Next. The longer you can collect data, the more accurate the analysis of your systems will be. Depending on the function of a system, it may have peak times in the middle of the night every night, or it may really only be utilized at the end of a month or end of the year.

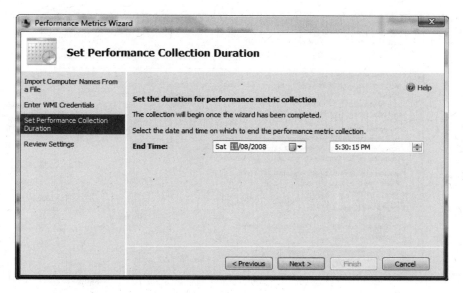

Verify that your settings are correct and click Finish.

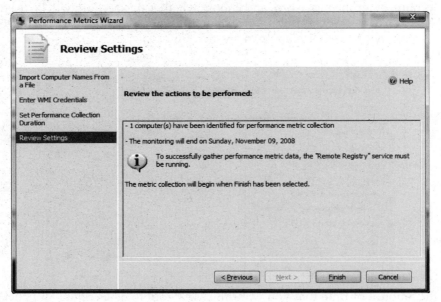

The Performance Metrics Wizard will now reach out and start collecting information on your systems. Once the assessment tool is done collecting information about your systems, you will be able to view reports about the system characteristics. These reports will help you to determine your virtualization candidates.

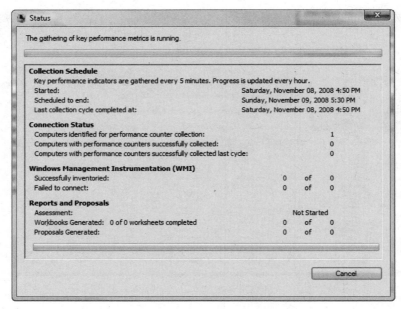

Click the Close button and we can now go view the reports. Remember that the longer you run the performance collection, the better idea you will have of how your systems are running.

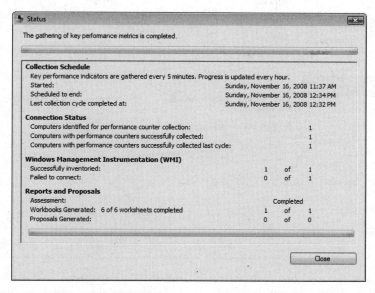

To view the reports on the systems that you just collected information about, click the link Prepare Recommendations for Server Consolidation Using Windows Server 2008 Hyper-V or Virtual Server 2005 R2.

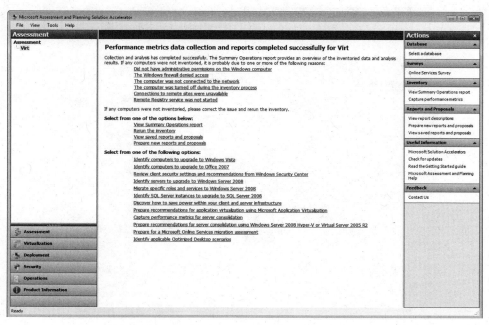

Choose the Windows Server 2008 Hyper-V option. Once you click Next, the assessment tool will walk you through a series of questions about what your future host system may look like to help build the report for your virtualization strategy.

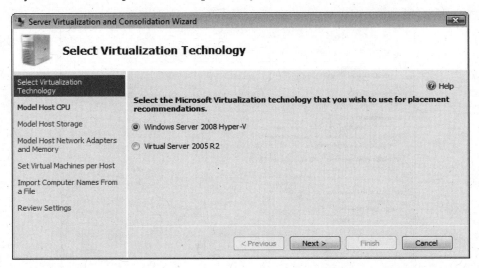

Define your future host system configuration. This includes selecting the process vendor (Intel or AMD), which model of processor you have purchased, the number of processors, speed, number of cores, cache size, and bus speed. Once you have entered that information, click Next.

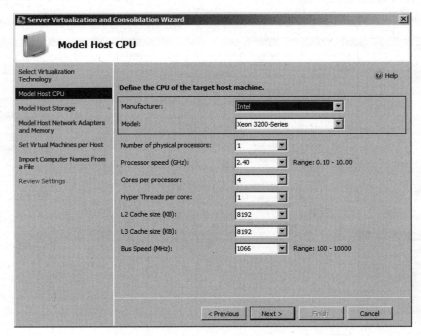

Configure the physical disk layout for your host system. Pay special attention to the type of disks that you choose; the RPM and throughput can make a significant impact on the performance of your server. Enter the number of disks that you will be using, the disk controller cache size, and which RAID configuration you are going to use for your disk. Once you have entered this data, click Next.

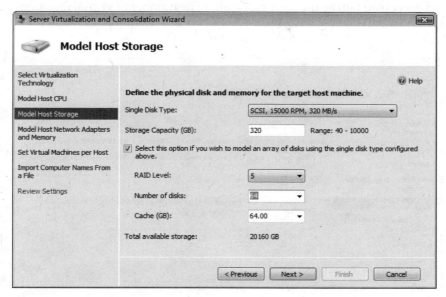

Define the number and type of network adapters as well as the amount of memory that will be in the host machine and click Next.

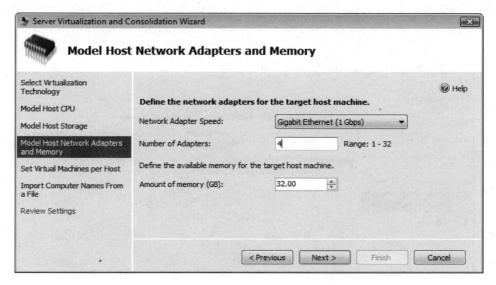

To set the maximum number of virtual machines a host can have running, click the Select This Option check box and enter the maximum number. For Windows Server 2008 Hyper-V the maximum number of virtual machines that can be on any host is up to 128 concurrent running virtual machines, and up to 512 configured virtual machines. While Hyper-V supports up to 128 concurrent virtual machines, your hardware, specifically RAM and processor, will be the limiting factors. The number of virtual machines that can reside on a host will change with Windows Server R2. Continue to check the Microsoft web site for Hyper-V to check on the current limits. Click Next.

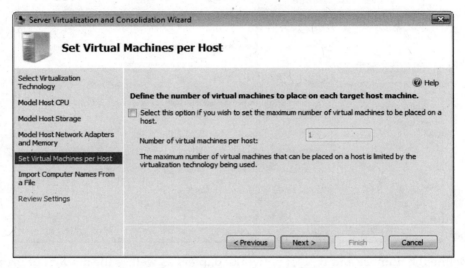

Enter the path to your text file that contains the system names of the systems you just inventoried and click Next.

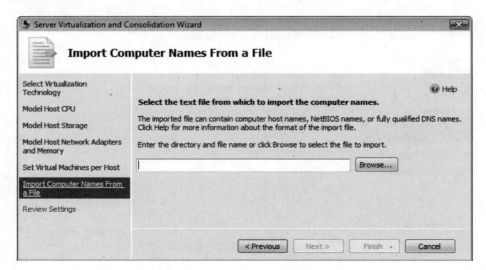

Review your settings to make sure they are correct. If you need to make adjustments click Previous, or click Finished. When you click Finish, the MAP toolkit will start creating a workbook and proposal for you to review.

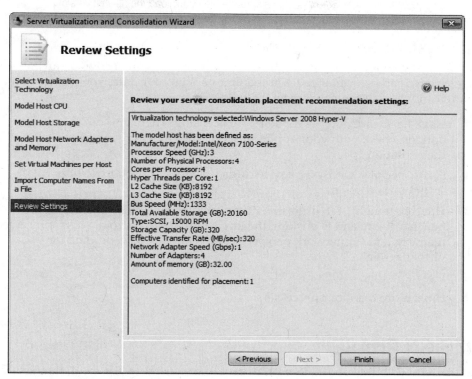

Once the MAP Toolkit is finished, click Close and click the Save Reports and Proposals link. This link will bring you to a folder with the same name as the database you created. In the folder there will be a Word document and one or more Excel spreadsheets. The Word document is the assessment proposal document, and the spreadsheets are the collected data from your inventory and the configuration that you created of a host system.

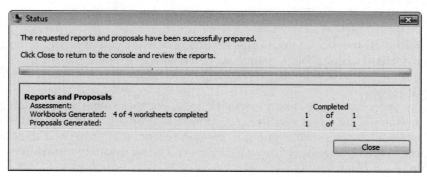

NOTE The current version of the assessment toolkit does not collect memory statistics. Use the Performance Monitor to collect that information and record that data separately. Microsoft is always making updates to the MAP toolkit, make sure that you download the newest version.

Which Systems Should I Convert?

Now that you've built candidate profiles of your systems, you need to do an analysis of which systems can be virtualized. On the first pass of your data, you can immediately drop out candidate systems that meet the following criteria:

▼ Have hardware dongles for software licensing. There are some hardware options; check with your application provider for support and availability for their solution.

■ Have specialty hardware device cards (scientific collection devices, retail scanners, and so on).

■ Have extremely high utilization. If a system is already built on relatively new hardware and is pushing the limits of that server from a disk, processor, memory, and/or network perspective, it is not a good candidate for virtualization.

■ Use more than 64GB of RAM.

▲ Have more than four processors.

THE DESIGN PHASE

Now that you've built candidate profiles and have narrowed the candidate list down, let's focus on designing your virtual infrastructure environments. From a macro point of view, there are three scenarios that you'll want to consider when designing your infrastructure:

▼ Core datacenter

■ Hub locations

▲ Branch offices

Depending on the size of your organization and what you're trying to accomplish with your virtualization project, you may be considering one or all of the scenarios. Throughout the book we will be commenting on design and build for each component as we go.

Each location has needs that are specific to it. For example, the core datacenter is going to contain your mission-critical equipment and be a location of centralized file storage, while a branch office is going to contain servers that only need to access files. And adding Hyper-V to either of those locations will be set up somewhat differently, and with its unique needs in mind.

Core Datacenter

The core datacenters are generally great places to start your virtualization project; there is generally lots of "low-hanging fruit" and you can see some of the biggest impact in this area since cost is generally higher for full datacenter items such as space, power, and cooling.

The core datacenter is where your mission-critical servers are located, and also the place where redundancy is going to be especially important. It is also the location where changes affect the entire company. It is likely that servers in hub and branch locations will access data stored in the datacenter.

Benefits to virtualization in the datacenter include:

▼ Standardization is achieved across the organization.

▲ The return on investment (ROI) is maximized.

Problems with datacenter virtualization include:

▼ All the costs of the virtualization project are incurred before the project is completed, so no benefits are realized until project completion.

▲ There is a high level of risk, given the fact that key systems are tinkered with.

Hub Locations

In this scenario, virtualization technologies are deployed in hub locations. A *hub* is a physical location with key workers, computers, and network technologies. Additionally, remote locations may need to access the resources at the hub site.

Benefits to this virtualization scenario include:

▼ The opportunity to pilot a virtualization deployment and prove the process and benefits of your project before deploying it on a larger scale.

■ Standardization can be delivered to an entire region.

▲ The ROI can be increased as compared to a decentralized approach.

The downsides of virtualization in this scenario include:

▼ The upfront costs of virtualization can be high.

■ There is some risk because a large number of systems are virtualized at one time. However, the risks do not extend back to the main datacenter.

▲ It is disruptive, because many systems will be affected at the same time.

Branch Offices

Deploying a virtualization project at a branch office brings its own pluses and minuses. A branch office is much smaller than the main organization or a hub location. These locations have more limited network connectivity to the rest of the organization because there is less bandwidth available.

Benefits of a branch office virtualization deployment include:

▼   Smaller upfront costs because the project is smaller than in the datacenter or hub.

■   Less risk, because there are fewer systems virtualized at one time.

▲   A pilot environment is provided and gives you an opportunity to prove the benefits of virtualization, but without affecting key systems.

Problems with virtualizing on this scale include:

▼   There's a chance that nonstandard configuration is developed in remote locations.

■   Since there's less IT staff at a branch office, it is more complex to implement the solution. It's also more difficult to provide support and troubleshooting.

▲   When compared to a larger project, there's less ROI in a smaller environment.

Choices

Taking the scenarios and the client profile into consideration, you should be able to determine how you want to build your Hyper-V infrastructure. The major components that you need to figure out are:

▼   How many guest virtual machines will I have?

■   Where are my guest virtual machines located?

■   Do I need high availability for my guest virtual machines?

■   Do I need high availability for the services running in my guest virtual machines?

■   Do I need to back up the host systems, guest systems, or just the data in the guest systems?

■   How many IOPS (Input Output per second) can my host system handle?

■   How many IOPS are my guest systems using as a physical server?

▲   How much bandwidth can my host system handle?

Taking this information into consideration, you can make the choices on how to scale your host servers with number of processors, amount of memory, and network cards. You will also be able to determine whether your virtual hosts should be in a cluster configuration, which will help you to determine what kind of disk you should use (SAN, iSCSI, internal) and in what configuration.

THE BUILD PHASE

The build phase is pretty much what it sounds like; it's building the core infrastructure components of your virtual environment. During this phase you will also be conducting testing to verify that your processes work and the infrastructure does what you want it to do, as well as testing migrations of your physical machines or virtual machines to this environment.

Scaling Your Host Server

In order to figure out just what hardware you need in your host server, it's a good idea to sit down with a sheet of paper and figure out all the little details. This allows you to know exactly how much machine you need, without going overboard and buying more than you need.

CPU Calculations

▼   Calculate current processor requirements of machines to be virtualized (data comes from MAP reports):

Number of CPUs × CPU speed × CPU utilization
Two processors × 2000 MHz × 10 percent utilization= ~400 MHz

■   Calculate target CPU capacity of the Hyper-V host:

Number of processors × CPU speed
Two processors × 3600 MHz = 7200 total MHz

▲   Reserve 25 percent for the host:

.25 × 7200 = 1800 MHz
7200 − 1800 = 5400 MHz available

If I have 12 servers that have current processor requirements of 400MHz, that totals 4800 MHz, which is less than the 5400 MHz CPU capacity of the Hyper-V host.

Network Capacity Planning

▼   Determine current bandwidth requirements (number comes from MAP tool):

Number of VMs × NIC speed × NIC utilization
12 VMs × 100 Mb/s × 40 percent utilization = 480 Mb/s
4 VMs × 1000 Mb/s × 25 percent utilization = 1000 Mb/s
Total needed = 1480 Mb/s

■   Calculate target NIC capacity:

Number of NICs × NIC speed
2 NICs × 1000 Mb/s = 2000 Total Mb/s bandwidth

▲   Assume 75 percent GB Ethernet efficiency

.75 × 2000 = 1500 Mb/s available

Again the total bandwidth requirements of all NICs on the machines to be virtualized needs to be less than the total available on the Hyper-V host.

Memory Capacity Planning

Add up the total amount of physical memory in the servers to be virtualized and add that to the recommended memory for a Windows Server 2008 Hyper-V server (1–2GB).

Disk Capacity Planning

Calculate IOPS for each machine to be virtualized and add up. Ensure that the disk subsystem in the Hyper-V host can support that level of IOPS. A virtual machine has the same IOPS requirements as its physical counterpart.

INSTALLING HYPER-V

Installation of the Hyper-V role on Server 2008 is the same on all editions of the operating systems. As discussed in Chapter 1, the major differences are number of processors, amount of memory, and the licensing model.

Roles

Before building Server 2008, Microsoft spent time trying to figure out how users use their server products, and they learned that organizations use them to do specific things—that is, they don't buy a server just for the sake of having a server. To that end, Microsoft grouped those organizational uses into broad terms called *workloads*. For example, there is a database workload and an application server workload. Within this broad grouping of workloads are subgroups called *roles*.

A *role* is a single, specific thing that the server is expected to do. For example, on your network you likely have a file server, a print server, a web server, and so forth. Windows Server 2008 takes the same approach, and has three main categories of roles:

▼   **Identity and Access Management**   These sorts of roles are part of Active Directory.

■   **Infrastructure**   These include file servers, print servers, DNS, and so forth.

▲   **Application**   These roles include servers like the Web Server role and Terminal Service role.

All total there are 17 server roles, including

▼   Active Directory Certificate Services

■   Network Policy and Access Services

▲   Windows Server Virtualization

Microsoft plans to add additional roles that can be downloaded, including the Streaming Media Services role.

Some things simply won't exist as roles, like BitLocker Drive Encryption or Network Load Balancing, because they are not something a system is specifically installed to provide. Remember, the organization buys a system to perform a specific role.

Rather than configure Server 2008 with all these roles installed, you are given the option of which role the server will have in your organization. By leaving it as an option until install time, you improve stability and security and you need not worry about resources being consumed for a role you don't need. And you also don't have to worry about troubleshooting or support for roles that you don't need.

System Requirements

With each successive release of a Windows Server product, system requirements demand more and more resources. Windows Server 2008 is no exception. You're going to need beefy equipment to install the product. Luckily, these computers aren't hard to come by; it's just the nature of the beast. Table 2-8 lists the system requirements for Windows Server 2008.

GUI or Core

With the release of Windows Server 2008, Microsoft has released a new mode of the operating system, Core. The Windows Server 2008 Core installation option is a command-driven interface that allows for a minimal operation systems installation.

Component	Requirement
Processor	Minimum: 1 GHz (x86 processor) or 1.4 GHz (x64 processor)
	Recommended: 2 GHz or faster
	Note: An Intel Itanium 2 processor is required for Windows Server 2008 for Itanium-based systems.
Memory	Minimum: 512MB RAM
	Recommended: 2GB RAM (or greater)
	Maximum: x86: 4GB (Standard) or 64GB (Enterprise or Datacenter)
	Maximum: x64: 32GB (Standard) or 2TB (Enterprise or Datacenter)
Available Disk Space	Minimum: 10GB
	Recommended: 40GB or greater
Drive	DVD-ROM
Display and peripherals	Super VGA (800×600) or higher-resolution monitor.
	Keyboard
	Mouse

Table 2-8.   System Requirements for Windows Server 2008

Installing Hyper-V on the Full Version of Windows Server 2008

Once you've performed a clean installation of Windows Server 2008, installed all drivers, and verified the system to be in good health, installing Hyper-V is a very straightforward install. First open Server Manager and click the Roles option in the left navigation bar.

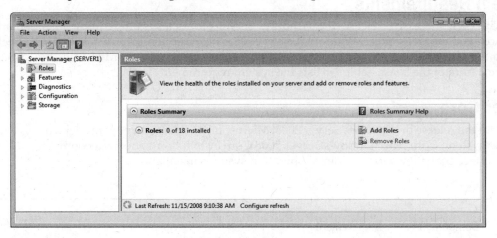

Click the Add Roles link. The installation wizard will appear. Read the information and click Next.

Choose the Hyper-V role and click Next.

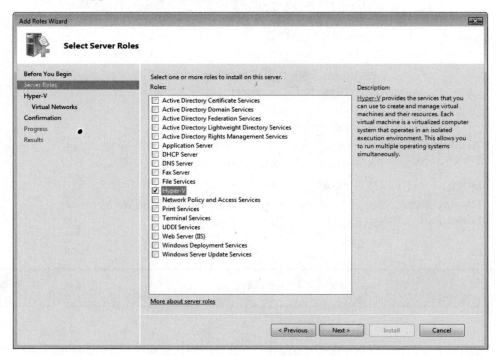

NOTE It's a best practice when you are building a host server that you only run the Hyper-V role. The reason for this is that every additional role that you run in the parent partition will take away resources that you could use for a child partition. If you need to run things like DHCP or a web server, we recommend that you create a child partition and install the operating system that you want to run those services on.

Windows Server 2008 offers you a vast number of roles, but you have the flexibility to choose only the roles that apply to your organization. Examples of roles include:

▼ Active Directory (AD) Certificate Services

■ AD Domain Services

■ Application Server

■ DHCP Server

■ DNS Server

■ Web Server

▲ Terminal Server

As described in the sections that cover the prerequisites, verify that your server is a 64-bit installation, Hardware Data Execution Prevention (DEP) has been enabled, and the hardware-assisted virtualization features have been enabled in your server's BIOS. Click Next.

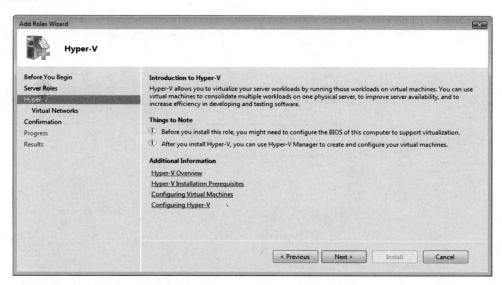

Choose the network adapters that will be used for virtual networks on your host systems and click Next. You will want to have at least two network cards in each of your host systems. This allows you to separate the traffic that your virtual machines and your parent partition have.

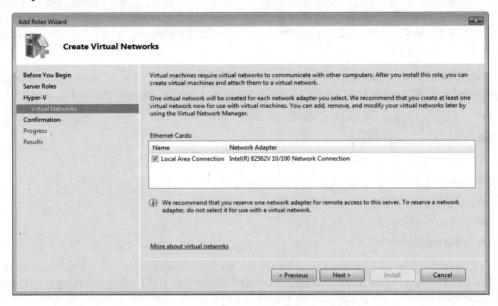

Verify that the information is correct on the system and click Install to start the installation of Hyper-V.

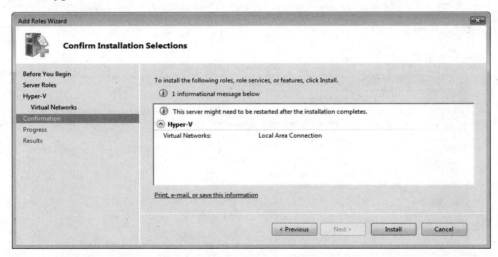

Once the installation is complete, click Close and reboot the server. When the system reboots, the operating installation becomes the parent partition and the Hyper-V hypervisor is injected between the hardware and the parent partition. After the server reboots, log back in to the server to allow the installation to complete. Once the installation is completed, click Close, and you're ready to finish the configuration of Hyper-V.

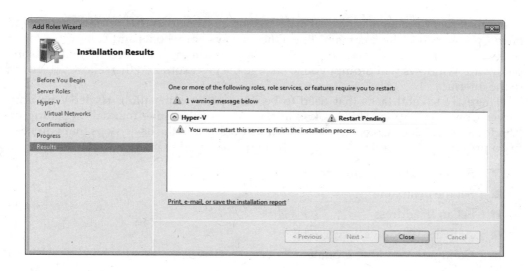

Installing Hyper-V on the Core Version of Windows Server 2008

Server Core is an installation option while installing Server 2008. To install Server Core chose the corresponding version of Server you would like to install and choose the Core installation option.

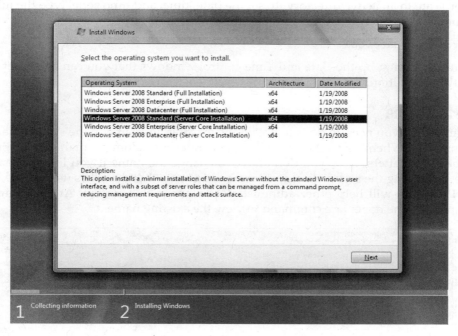

The rest of the installation steps are exactly the same as installing the GUI version.

With Server Core there is no GUI interface and every step to configuring a server will have to be done via the command line. Once the system reboots and comes to a logon screen, press CTRL-ALT-DELETE to log on, choosing the Administrator account with a blank password. Windows will prompt you to change the password and then allow you access to the interface.

There are several tasks that need to be done prior to installing Hyper-V on your Server Core installation. This book is in no way an exhaustive manual on setting up Windows Server 2008 Core, but we will walk you through the basic steps that you need to do prior to implementing Hyper-V. The tasks that need to be done are:

- ▼ Set date, time, and time zone
- ■ Set the hostname
- ■ Set an IP address
- ■ Activate Windows Server 2008
- ■ Configure Windows Update
- ▲ Install the Hyper-V role

Set Date, Time, and Time Zone

Having the correct system time is extremely important to managing a system. This could help with troubleshooting when something goes wrong with the system being able to authenticate to an active directory. To set the date, time, and time zone, type the following command sequence at the command prompt:

```
Control timedate.cpl
```

This will bring up the Date and Time control windows that you can use to set your specific information.

Set Hostname

The first thing you need to do is to obtain the existing hostname of the system that you just installed. When Server 2008 installs, it generates a random hostname consisting of numbers and letters. Now you don't have to change the name if you like the random name, but giving the server an easy-to-remember name that describes its purpose, such as "HVHost1," will help other administrators manage this system. At the command prompt enter the hostname command to view the existing name.

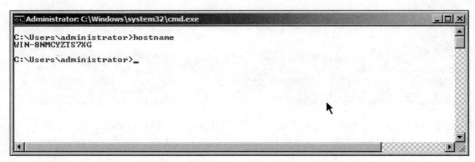

To change the name of the server, you're going to use the `netdom` command. The `netdom` command can be used to change the server name or for other tasks such as joining a server to a domain. At the command prompt, type the following command sequence:

```
Netdom renamecomputer <yoursystemscomputername> /NewName:<NewComputerName>
```

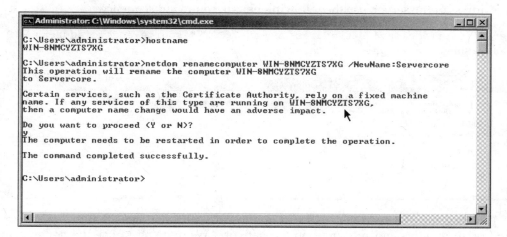

To reboot the system in core you will use the `shutdown` command. At the command prompt, type **Shutdown /r /t 0** to reboot.

Set an IP Address

Windows Server 2008 sets the IP address to automatically be assigned via DHCP by default. To change the IP address of a server in core you will use the `netsh` command. More information can be found about the `netsh` command at http://technet.microsoft .com/en-us/library/cc785383.aspx. The first thing we need to do is to find out what adapters we have available on our system. To show the available interfaces on your system, type the following command on the command line:

```
netsh interface ipv4 show interface
```

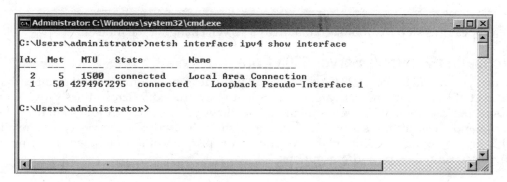

Choose which network adapter you would like to set the IP address for. In this example we only have the one adapter and the loopback interface. Your server may have multiple connections, so planning what network each connection will be on and what IP address those adapters get is important. To set the IP Address, find the adapter you want in your list and make a note of the IDX number shown on the left of the screen. This number will be used to specify which adapter you set the IP Address on. To set the IP Address of the server, use the following netsh command sequence:

```
Netsh interface ipv4 set address name ="<IDX>" source=static address=<IP>
mask=<SubnetMask> gateway=<GatewayIP>
```

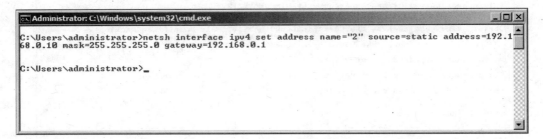

The last step we need to do is to set up the DNS information so that the system can find other systems and resources on the network. We're going to use the netsh command again with the add dnsserver option. Type the following command at the command prompt:

```
Netsh interface ipv4 add dnsserver name="<IDX>" address=<DNSIP> index=<index>
```

Repeat this step for your secondary DNS server, changing the index to 2.

Activating Windows Server 2008 Core

When you install Server 2008 Core, Microsoft provides a time-limited serial number that needs to be changed and activated. To help with this process, Microsoft has provided a Visual Basic script in the Core installation that allows you to activate the system from the command line since there is no GUI. The slmgr.vbs utility script has server options available for managing licensing on the system; for the purpose of this book we are going to focus on using the ipk and ato options.

If you've purchased a product key from Microsoft or you're using an MSDN or Tech-Net key, there are two steps to the process: installing the new product key and activating the server. These steps need to be done in that order or your activation will fail.

To install your product key, type the following command at the command line:

```
Slmgr.vbs -ipk <productkeywithdashes>
```

Once that has finished, run the following command to activate your server:

```
Slmgr.vbs -ato
```

This process may take a few minutes and is silent unless an error occurs.

Configuring Windows Update

Part of having a healthy and secure system is installing updates and patches. Microsoft provides the Windows Update service with several options that help make this process more painless. In Windows Server 2008 Core, Windows Update is installed by default, but automatic updates are not configured. To configure auto updates we are going to use the scregedit.wsf script that is located in the c:\windows\system32 directory.

At the command prompt, type the following command to enable Automatic Updates:

```
Cscript SCregEdit.wsf /AU 4
```

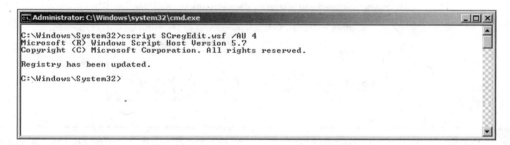

For the changes to take effect, it's best to stop and restart the Automatic Updates service. To do this you're going to use the net command. The net command is a very robust command for managing your servers. To stop the Automatic Updates service, type the following command at the command prompt:

```
net stop wuauserv
```

Once that has stopped successfully, let's restart the Automatic Updates service by typing the following command at the command prompt:

```
net start wuauserv
```

Now that the service has been restarted, type the following command at the command prompt to force an update:

```
wuauclt /detectnow
```

Add Hyper-V Role

Now that you've configured your server core installation, you can install the Hyper-V role. Type the following command at the command prompt:

```
start /w ocsetup Microsoft-Hyper-V
```

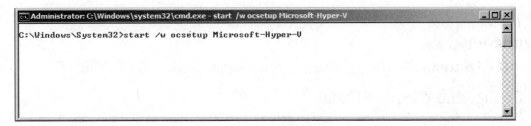

This will install the Hyper-V components and will ask for a reboot. If you use this method, two reboots will occur.

Once the components are installed, the system must be rebooted for the changes to take effect. Choose Yes to reboot your system at this time.

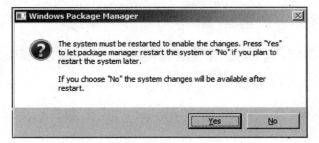

NOTE To cut down the number of reboots to one, run the following command prior to the above command:

```
bcdedit /set hypervisorlaunchtype auto
```

After the system has finished its reboots, the configuration of this system will need to be done via the Hyper-V Manager on a Server 2008 server, or the system can be configured by Systems Center Virtual Machine Manager.

Installing Hyper-V Server

Microsoft Hyper-V server is a stand-alone implementation of the Hyper-V hypervisor. It still allows for the great features of Hyper-V but doesn't give you the high-availability features that come with Windows Server 2008, and all licensing is done on a per virtual model.

Install the Hyper-V server disk in your server and boot to it.
Choose your language.

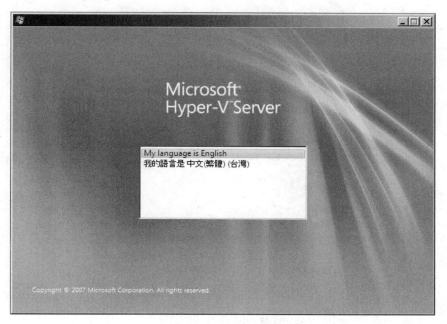

Choose your language, time and currency formation, and your keyboard or imput method and click Next.

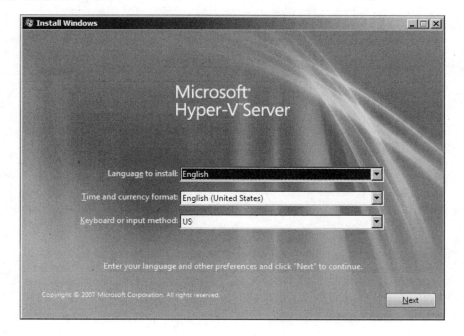

Click Install Now to install Hyper-V Server.

Read and accept the license terms and click Next.

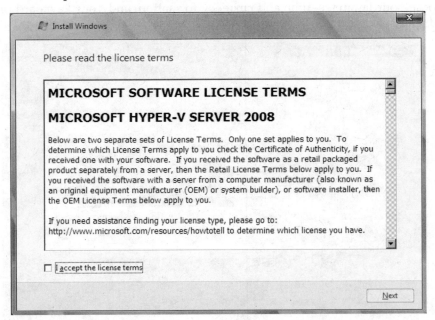

At this time there is no upgrade path to Windows Hyper-V server. Click Custom to configure your disks.

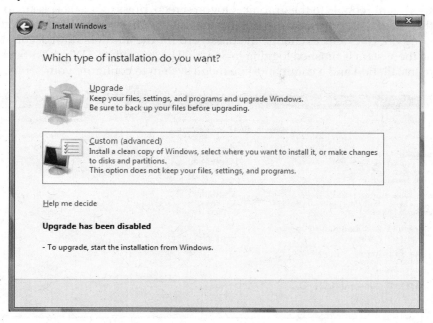

Configure the drives the way you want them to be, click Next, and the installer will start copying files to your system. We recommend that you at least run mirrored drives for the hypervisor and parent partition, and an additional set of RAID drives for child partitions. This will give the parent partition some redundancy from a disk standpoint as well as separating the parent disk usage and child disk usage.

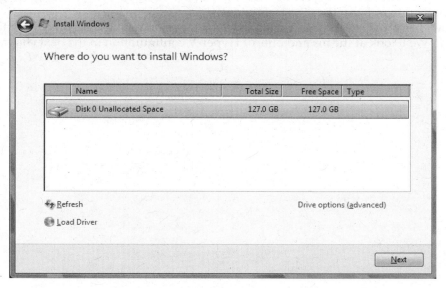

Once the installer is finished copying files to your system, the system will reboot to finish installing features. There will be one more reboot into the graphical interface. When the system reboots to the graphical logon screen, press CTRL+ALT+DELETE to log on, click Other User, enter a username of Administrator with no password, and click the arrow to log on. Click OK to change the password for the administrator account.

When the system is finished logging in, you will be greeted by a Windows Server 2008 Core-like installation and a command-line menu system to configure your server with.

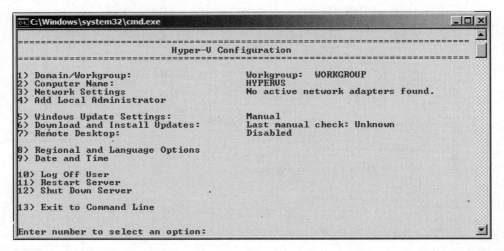

Use the command-line menu to configure your server to be ready to run virtual machines.

Sure, you can just plop the Windows Server 2008 Hyper-V DVD-ROM in the drive and install, but to do a better job—and even determine whether virtualization is an option for your system or systems—it's a good idea to do the heavy lifting of figuring out how your company uses the technology.

Now that we've got Hyper-V installed, let's move on to a discussion of how to configure it. We'll look at the ins and outs of Hyper-V configuration in the next chapter.

CHAPTER 3

Configuring Hyper-V Components

Now that you've got Windows Server 2008 with Hyper-V installed on your server, you need to go through a few steps to configure it. Depending on your requirements and what you've planned out, you're going to have to set up networking, storage, and possible clustering.

In this chapter we'll talk about your options for configuring your network for the ideal Hyper-V deployment, and the measures that Microsoft has built in to ensure that your server achieves optimum uptime.

HYPER-V MANAGER

Part of the installation of Hyper-V in the GUI install is the installation of the Hyper-V Manager.

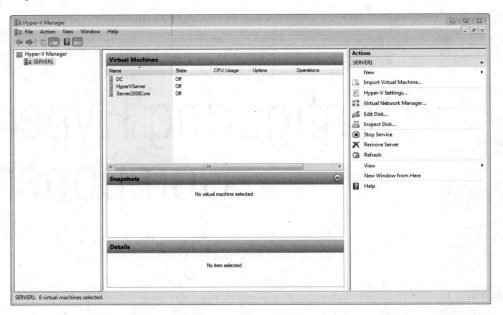

The Hyper-V Manager console is built on the Microsoft Management Console (MMC) 3.0 platform. The Hyper-V Manager is divided into three distinct panes. The pane furthest to the left is the console Explorer pane. In the console Explorer pane you can load one or many MMC snap-ins. In this pane you can choose which Hyper-V host machine you want to manage, and you can right-click on a Hyper-V server and run actions.

The middle pane of the MMC with the Hyper-V Manager snap-in is the Information pane. The Information pane will provide information about the snap-in that you have selected in the Explorer pane on the left. If you choose the Hyper-V Manager level in the Explorer pane, you will be provided with an introduction and some resources. When you select a host server, the Information pane will show which virtual machines are on that host. If you select a virtual machine, it will show you what snapshots have been created as well as an image of the virtual machine and some information about it.

To the right is the Actions pane. The Actions pane is new in MMC 3.0 and, in our opinion, a great addition. Depending on what you have selected in the Explorer pane, the Actions pane will show what actions are available for that selection. For instance, if you have selected the Hyper-V Manager level, the major action will be to connect to a Hyper-V server. If you select the server level and a virtual machine action, both the server and the virtual machine will be displayed. The same actions are accessible by right-clicking the object in the Information pane or the Explorer pane.

NETWORKING

Windows Server 2008 with Hyper-V gives your organization multiple different options for networking your virtual machines. There are several different methods that you can use for your virtual machines. You can have many virtual machines sharing one NIC; you can have dedicated a physical NIC to one virtual machine; or you can have a combination of the two. Determining what you need from a network standpoint will be driven by your customers' requirements or your virtualization candidate requirements, which you documented in your candidate profile.

Networking Options

By default Hyper-V comes with three different networking settings: External, Internal, and Private. The external network setting creates a connection to a physical NIC so that guest virtual machines can access the physical network to which that NIC is connected. The Internal setting creates a network that the host and the guest virtual machines can communicate on. The Private network setting creates a network that only virtual machines can communicate on. More than likely, if you are mixing production, development, and test workloads on your virtual environments, you will have a mix of external, internal, and private networks.

VLAN Tagging and Hyper-V

In Windows Server 2008 Hyper-V networking, there is an additional option to enable VLAN tagging. A VLAN is a virtual local area network that can be split across multiple switches, routers, and locations, allowing for network devices to be grouped together even though they may be in different parts of the world. *VLAN tagging* or frame tagging was developed by Cisco Systems to help identify packets travelling across trunked network links. A *trunked network* is a network link that has multiple VLANs associated with it.

By leveraging VLAN tagging and trunks, you can connect a single NIC to several different networks at the same time. In virtualization this becomes extremely useful as part of a consolidation effort. If you are consolidating web servers, application servers, and database servers onto the same host that resides on separate networks, you can maintain those separate networks by implementing VLAN tagging. VLAN tagging can be done at the parent or the child partition level.

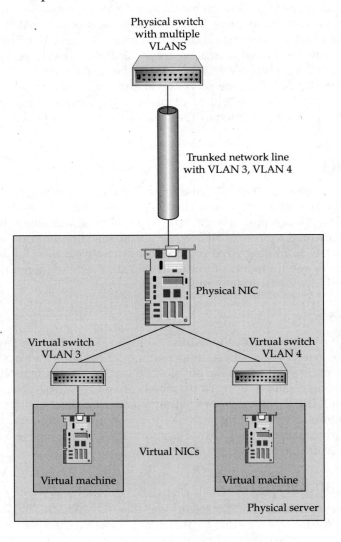

Design Considerations

As you design your host system, you will want at least two network cards available. The first network card should always be used for managing the parent partition, and the second network card should be used for virtual machine networking. The number of network cards you will need will depend on what your candidate profiles look like (amount of bandwidth used), whether you need high availability for your hosts, and whether you are using iSCSI. When you are ordering your hardware, you will be limited to the number of NICs you can have by the configuration of your server.

Let's take a look at a couple of different networking scenarios using multiple network cards.

Scenario 1

In Scenario 1 we have four network cards in the server. The first network card is used for managing the parent partition and the other three network cards will be used for virtual machines.

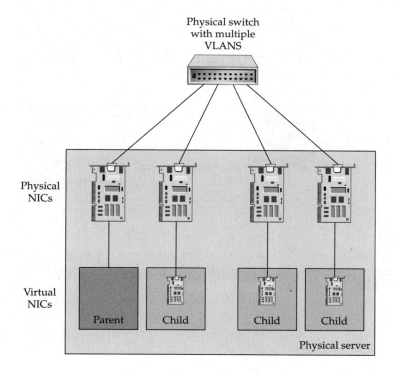

Scenario 2

In Scenario 2 we again have four network cards. The first network card is used for managing the parent partition; the second network card will be used to present the server disk via iSCSI; and the third and fourth network cards will be used as virtual machine networks.

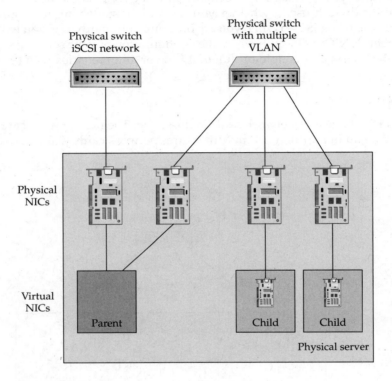

Scenario 3

For Scenario 3 we are going to use five network cards and the host server is going to be a part of a failover cluster. With Scenario 3 we are adding an additional NIC for a heartbeat NIC for the cluster.

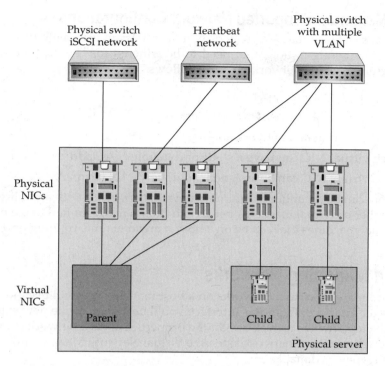

Keep in mind that each network card can be connected to different networks with multiple network switches on each network card, and each virtual network on a guest operating system can be configured to point to multiple network switches. Each switch can be configured with a VLAN tag ID, or each guest network card can be configured with a VLAN tag ID. VLANs cannot be nested, so keep in mind that if you configure a VLAN ID on the parent, you will not be able to configure a different VLAN ID in the child partition. With the flexibility this gives you, make sure that you spend time planning which networks you will be connecting to. Keep in mind that if you create a high-availability cluster, then each cluster node that you want to migrate a virtual machine to must have those networks configured and available for the virtual machine.

NOTE   When planning your network infrastructure, if you are planning to use failover clustering, then add an additional network card to each server for the cluster heartbeat communications.

Hyper-V Maximum Supported Network Configurations

While virtual machines that are created with Hyper-V are extremely flexible, there are some maximum configurations that need to be adhered to. The maximum configurations for virtual machine networking are as follows:

▼ Up to 12 virtual NICs per VM:

■ Eight synthetic network adapters

■ Four emulated network adapters

■ Each virtual NIC can have a static or dynamic MAC address.

■ Each virtual NIC can be assigned a unique VLAN channel.

▲ There can be an unlimited number of virtual switches with an unlimited number of virtual machines per switch (this is really limited to the number of virtual machines that can be on a host at any one time, running or dormant).

Creating and Managing Networks

To create and manage virtual networks on a host machine you will use the Virtual Network Manager interface. From this interface you'll be able to create new external, internal, and private networks as well as edit the properties of each network connection.

To create a new virtual network, open the Virtual Network Manager from the Actions pane in the Hyper-V Manager.

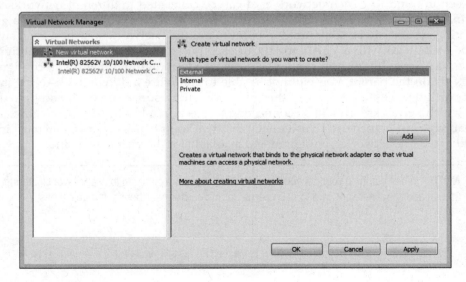

Click on the New Virtual Network option in the left pane, choose what type of network you would like to create, and click Add.

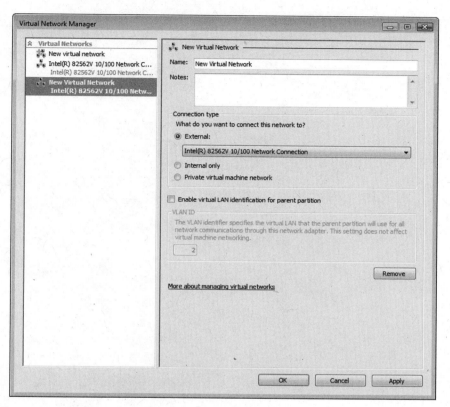

Enter a descriptive name for your network and any notes that you may want to describe what the network will be and what it should be used as. Choose what type of connection this network should be: If you are going to use this as an external network, use the drop-down box to choose the network adapter you want for this virtual network. If you choose this as an external network and you want this particular card to be on a VLAN, check the Enable Virtual LAN Identification for Parent Partition check box and enter your VLAN ID number in the box. If you choose to use a VLAN ID on the parent, you will not be able to use VLAN tagging on the child. Click Apply and OK.

To edit a network that you have already created, open the Virtual Network Manager and select the network you would like to edit in the left pane.

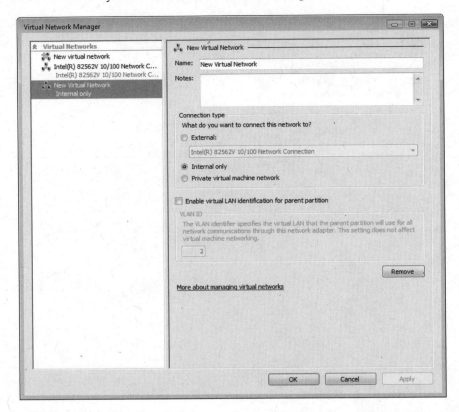

Choose which options you would like to edit and select OK or Apply. If you would like to delete the network, click the Remove button.

STORAGE

Windows Server 2008 supports several different types of storage. You can either connect to storage physically, or by using a virtual hard drive (VHD).

When Hyper-V is installed on a host, it can access the many different storage options that are available to it, including direct attached storage (DAS, such as SATA or SAS) or SAN storage (FC, or iSCSI). Once you connect the storage solution to the parent partition, you can make it available to the child partition in a number of ways.

Hyper-V Storage Options

Windows Server 2008 with Hyper-V supports the use of direct attached storage, NAS, iSCSI, and Fibre Channel storage.

VHD or Pass-through Disk

A virtual hard drive (VHD) can be created on the parent partition's volume with access granted to the child partition. The VHD operates as a set of blocks, stored as a regular file using the host OS file system (which is NTFS).

Within Hyper-V there are different types of VHDs, including fixed size, dynamically expanding, and "differencing" disks:

▼ **Dynamically expanding**   This type of virtual hard drive starts small but automatically expands to react to need. It will expand up to the maximum size indicated when the virtual hard drive is created. "Dynamic," in this context, is sort of a misnomer. Dynamic implies that the size of the virtual drive changes up and down based on need. But in actuality, the hard drive will keep expanding until it reaches the maximum limit. If you remove content from the virtual hard drive, it will not shrink to meet the new, smaller capacity.

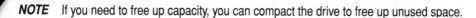

NOTE   If you need to free up capacity, you can compact the drive to free up unused space.

■ **Fixed**   This type of virtual hard drive is created at a certain size and it remains at that size. While fixed virtual hard drives are created to be a certain size, their size can be adjusted—just not automatically. To change the size of the virtual hard drive, you use the Hyper-V Manager Edit Disk action to make changes.

▲ **Differencing**   The third type of virtual hard drive is the differencing drive. In this scheme, a parent disk and a child disk are used. In this configuration, the parent disk contains a baseline hard disk image with the operating system (and maybe some applications and data). When this parent drive is configured, a differencing disk is allocated to a child. When the virtual machine to which the child virtual disk is assigned makes changes, those changes are made to the child differencing disk and the parent disk is left alone. Several child disks may be assigned to a parent disk, thus allowing multiple virtual machines to share the same parent disk. Differencing disks can also be chained together. The changes on one differencing disk can be merged to the parent disk. On the other hand, a new virtual hard disk can be created via the merger of a child and parent disk. This leaves the parent disk unaltered. When a differencing disk is created, a parent disk needs to be specified. The size of the differencing disk grows as space is needed.

NOTE   The maximum size of a VHD is 2 TB.

In Hyper-V, you can expose a host disk to the guest without putting a volume on it by using a pass-through disk. Hyper-V allows you to bypass the host's file system and access the disk directly. This disk is not limited to 2,040 GB and can be a physical hard drive on the host or a logical one on a SAN.

Hyper-V ensures that the host and guest are not trying to use the disk at the same time by setting the drive to be in the offline state for the host.

Pass-through disks have their downsides. You lose some VHD-related features, like VHD snapshots and dynamically expanding VHDs.

IDE or SCSI on the Guest

Configuring the child partition's virtual machine settings requires you to choose how the disk will be shown to the guest (either as a VHD file or pass-through disk). The child partition can see the disk as either a virtual ATA device or as a virtual SCSI disk. But you do not have to expose the drive to the child partition the same way as you exposed it to the parent partition. For example, a VHD file on a physical IDE disk on the parent partition can be shown as a virtual SCSI on the guest.

What you need to decide is what capabilities you want on the guest. You can have up to four virtual IDE drives on the guest, but they are the only type the virtualized BIOS will boot from. You can have up to 256 virtual SCSI drives on the child partition, but you cannot boot from them.

iSCSI to Guests

You can also expose drives directly to the child partition by using iSCSI. This bypasses the parent partition completely. All you have to do is load an iSCSI initiator in the child partition and configure your partition accordingly.

Hyper-V does not support booting to iSCSI, so you still need another boot drive.

Fibre Channel

A Fibre Channel Storage Area Network (SAN) is the most widely deployed storage solution in enterprises today. SANs came into popularity in the mid- to late 90s and have had huge growth numbers with the boom of data that customers are keeping and using every day. Ultimately, a SAN is really just a network that is made up of storage components, a method of transport, and an interface. A SAN is made up of a disk array, a switch, and a host bus adapter. Most hardware providers such as HP, Dell, and SUN have a SAN solution and there are companies such as EMC, Hitachi, NetApp, and Compellent that focus primarily on SAN and storage technology.

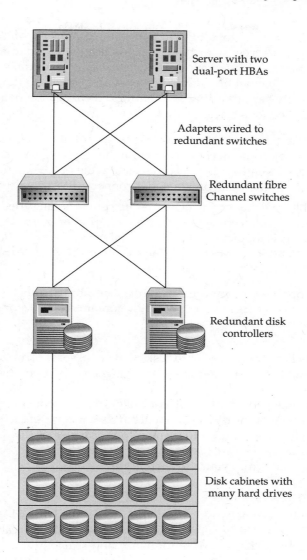

Server with two
dual-port HBAs

Adapters wired to
redundant switches

Redundant fibre
Channel switches

Redundant disk
controllers

Disk cabinets with
many hard drives

Fibre Channel Protocol

The Fibre Channel Protocol is the mechanism used to transmit data across Fibre Channel networks. There are three main fabric topologies that are used in Fibre Channel: point-to-point, arbitrated loop, and fabric.

Point-to-Point   *Point-to-point* topology is a direct connection between two ports, with at least one of the ports acting as a server. This topology needs no arbitration for the storage media because of separate links for transmission and reception. The downside is that it is limited to two nodes and is not scalable.

Arbitrated Loop   *Arbitrated loop* topology combines the advantages of the fabric topology (support for multiple devices) with the ease of operation of point-to-point topology. In the arbitrated loop topology, devices are connected to a central hub, like Ethernet LAN hubs. The Fibre Channel hub arbitrates (or shares) access to devices, but adds no additional functionality beyond acting as a centralized connection point.

Within the arbitrated loop category, there are two types of topologies:

▼   **Arbitrated loop hub**   Devices must seize control of the loop and then establish a point-to-point connection with the receiving device. When the transmission has ended, devices connected to the hub begin to arbitrate again. In this topology, there can be 126 nodes connected to a single link.

▲   **Arbitrated loop daisy-chain**   Devices are connected in series and the transmit port of one device is connected to the receive port on the next device in the daisy chain. This topology is ideal for small networks but is not very scalable, largely because all devices on the daisy chain must be on. And if one device fails, the entire network goes down.

Fabric   The fabric topology is composed of one or more Fibre Channel switches connected through one or more ports. Each switch typically contains 6, 16, 32, or 64 ports.

Disk Array

The SAN disk array is a grouping of hard disks that are in some form of RAID configuration and, just as with any RAID configuration, the more disks you have, the more I/O you will receive.

In most modern disk arrays, the disk controller (the component that controls RAID configuration and access to the disk array) will have some form of cache built into it. The cache on the disk controller is used to increase performance of the disk subsystem for both reads and writes. In the case of virtualization, the more cache available, the better performance you will see from your virtual machines.

Fibre Channel Switch

A Fibre Channel switch is a networking switch that uses the Fibre Channel protocol and is the backbone of the storage area network fabric. These switches can be implemented as one switch or many switches (for redundancy and scalability) to provide many-to-many communications between nodes on the SAN fabric. The Fibre Channel switch uses zoning to segregate traffic between storage devices and endpoint nodes. This zone can be used to allow or deny a system access to a storage device. In the past few years three companies have really cornered the market on Fibre Channel switches: Cisco Systems, QLogic, and Brocade. When purchasing a switch, pay close attention to the back plane bandwidth that it has as well as how fast the ports are. You can get a Fibre Channel switch that supports port speeds of 2, 4, or 8 gigabits per second.

Tiered Storage

Using a technique called *tiered storage*, you assign different categories of your data to different types of storage media, in order to reduce total storage cost. Categories may be based on the levels of protection needed, performance issues, frequency of access, or whatever other considerations you have.

Because assigning data to a particular form of media is an ongoing and complex activity, some vendors provide software that automatically manages the process based on your organization's policies.

For example, at tier 1, mission-critical or frequently accessed files are stored on high-capacity, fast-spinning hard drives. They might also have double-level RAIDs on them. At tier 2, less important data is stored on less expensive, slower-spinning drives in a conventional SAN. As the tiers progress, the media gets slower and less expensive. As such, tier 3 of a three-tier system might contain rarely used or archived material. The lowest level of the tiered system might be simply putting the data onto DVD-ROMs.

RAID Levels

A technology called RAID minimizes the loss of data due to drive failures. RAID was created by a group of scientists at University of California at Berkeley in 1987. When they designed the first RAID systems, RAID stood for Redundant Array of Inexpensive Disks. "Inexpensive" was later changed to "Independent," but both terms are used interchangeably.

The idea is that using two or more drives simultaneously can be faster and more fail-safe than using a single, larger drive. Using two drives in parallel (one is a copy of the other) is much safer than a single drive.

RAID technology offers both solutions at varying levels of coverage. No single RAID level is superior to any other. The RAID level you implement will depend on your needs and budget.

Level 0 – Striping

RAID level 0 is not fault tolerant because no information is duplicated on the disk system. However, performance is enhanced because the data is striped in 64k strips across all the drives in the array. For example, suppose you had three drives in your array. When the controller needs to write a block of data 256k in size, it writes the first 64k block to disk 1, the next 64k block to disk 2, the next 64k block to disk 3, and the last 64k block to disk 1. Additionally, the total available space is the same as the total physical space. Because the probability of failure is greater for this RAID level, it is not used widely.

Level 1 – Mirroring

RAID level 1 is called *mirroring* because it maintains an identical twin of the first drive. Since all data that is written to disk 1 (original disk) is also written to disk 2 (shadow disk), disk utilization is only 50 percent. There is also a slight write performance loss due to the overhead of writing to two drives. However, there is a performance gain on disk reads and there is very good fault tolerance. To eliminate the single point of failure here, you can use two controller cards, each responsible for writing to a single disk. This completely duplicates the I/O system and is called *duplexing*. You should use mirroring if you

▼ Require a high level of redundancy

■ Demand high read performance

▲ Do not want to deal with the complexity of other RAID systems

Level 2

Level 2 RAID uses striping (like RAID 0), but it is performed at the bit level. This method of writing data to the disk requires a good deal of CPU processing and is inefficient. It is thus not adopted and there are no commercially available RAID 2 solutions.

Level 3

Level 3 RAID uses byte striping similar to level 0 but includes a drive dedicated for parity. The parity can be thought of as the sum of all the bytes contained in the stripes of the other disks. The parity disk provides true fault tolerance because if any of the other drives fail, the information on it can be calculated by subtracting the bytes in the other stripes from the parity stripe.

The capacity of RAID level 3 arrays can be expressed as a percentage: n-$1/n$ where n is the total number of drives. Since all disks are involved in every read or write (to calculate the parity stripe), RAID level 3 arrays can process only one transaction at a time. They are not suited for random access of many small data blocks. These systems are best suited for large sequential requests, but it's pretty rare that you'll ever see this.

Level 4

Level 4 RAID uses striping at the block level to improve efficiency. Otherwise it dedicates a drive to the parity information like level 3 RAID, and thus has the same capacity of RAID level 3 systems.

Level 5

A popular RAID configuration is level 5 RAID. Here the parity is stored in 64k blocks and placed evenly on all drives. Since the controller can process multiple writes in parallel across the array, RAID level 5 can outperform levels 3 and 4. It doesn't perform as well as level 0 or 1, however, because of the computation used to calculate the parity information.

The capacity of RAID level 5 is the same as levels 3 and 4 and should be considered when redundancy is required but you do not have the money for a mirrored solution or if you require the overall larger capacity afforded by arrays as opposed to single, mirrored drives.

Advanced Levels

RAID level 10 is a striped array that is mirrored. This configuration provides excellent fault tolerance and a performance boost. Any single drive in each array or an entire array can fail without data loss. The capacity is reduced to 1-$n/2n$ for every n drives.

RAID level 55 requires three RAID 5 arrays that are combined into one larger RAID 5 array. Just replace each drive in RAID 5 with an array of drives each with its own controller, and you have massive capacity, excellent performance, and nearly perfect redundancy. The ratio of total usable space is the same as in RAID 5 systems (1-n/n).

HBA

The host bus adapter (HBA) is used to connect a server or workstation to a network or storage device. Host bus adapters can be used to connect multiple different devices such as Fibre Channel, iSCSI, and ESATA. With iSCSI becoming increasingly popular, an iSCSI HBA has been developed that is similar to an Ethernet NIC, but has a dedicated TCP offload engine to increase iSCSI performance. When you hear people speak or write about an HBA, they are generally referring to the Fibre Channel type of host bus adapter. Similar to an Ethernet NIC, the HBA has a unique identifier called a World Wide Name (WWN). The HBA is connected to a Fibre Channel switch, which is connected to the disk controller. From the switch, a zone is created and the WWN of the host system is granted access to disk resources on the disk controller. Like a Fibre Channel switch, HBAs support speeds of 2, 4, or 8 Gbps.

SAN Features

Today SANs come with features that can really help your enterprise manage your data and your virtual machines.

iSCSI

iSCSI is a type of SAN that uses industry technologies such as Ethernet and Ethernet NICs for transport and an interface. So far iSCSI has proven to be a great lower-cost solution to the Fibre Channel SAN solutions that are available. If, for instance, you are building your virtualization environment on servers that are worth U.S. $4,000 and you want to connect them to your Fibre Channel SAN, you will have to purchase Fibre Channel adapter cards that are compatible with your SAN. Each one of the Fibre Channel cards you implement into your server can range from $1,000 to $2,000 each. That can really start to be an additional cost if you are building out one or more 16-node clusters.

Now we're sure some of you reading this are saying, "Well yeah, but I've already implemented my Fibre Channel architecture. Now you want me to implement another infrastructure just for this?"

Well, no, that's not the case. What we're saying is that if you don't already have an infrastructure in place, iSCSI would be a great technology for you to research. One other consideration you will want to keep in mind when you are determining whether or not to implement iSCSI is whether you want to implement iSCSI on separate physical switches than your production network. You can do this, but we don't recommend it. The reason we don't recommend this is that an iSCSI network can become saturated extremely quickly and use all of the bandwidth on your back plane, creating network contention for your production services.

There are four major components that you need to implement an iSCSI infrastructure:

- ▼ Target
- ■ Disk
- ■ Network
- ▲ Initiator

Target   A *target* can be a hardware device or a server running a piece of software that is basically a storage location. Companies such as EMC, Hitachi, NetApp, and pretty much every disk vendor provide a hardware-based target that also acts as a storage controller. There is also plenty of open-source and commercial iSCSI target software that is available for you to try out and find the right option for your environment from companies such as Microsoft (Windows Storage Server Edition), Rocket Division Software, Youngzsoft, and Nimbus Data Systems.

Disk   No matter what storage solution you go with, the type and number of disks that you have as part of the solution are going to be the most important part. If you have a single terabyte drive and you plan on putting several virtual machines on that drive—even though it's on an iSCSI or Fibre Channel infrastructure—the performance is going to be terrible, and you risk losing your virtual machines in the event of a disk failure.

The idea behind having a redundant array of independent disks or RAID configuration is that it gives you a higher rate of performance from seek time to data read and write, and your RAID can be configured to allow for a disk failure. The more disks you have in your RAID configuration, the more I/O that configuration can provide for your virtual machines.

Network   You have a target with a disk and now you need a way to get to it. The concept of iSCSI is that SCSI disk commands are being encapsulated into IP packets and being transported using standard Ethernet. Now, depending on the number of virtual machines that will be "living" on your iSCSI infrastructure, the amount of I/O and bandwidth consumed can be quite large. Consideration need to be given to the host-to-guest I/O for management and the I/O of every system that is virtualized that could be running file copies, database lookups, or doing an antivirus scan. Having a dedicated network-switching infrastructure for your iSCSI solution is almost a necessity to keep your production and storage network separated so there isn't contention between the two networks.

Initiator   You've got a target, storage in the target, and a way to get to the storage on the target, and now you need some way to know what this all means. That is where the iSCSI initiator comes into play. The iSCSI initiator can, like the target, be software or hardware. Most implementations that we are seeing today are running free software iSCSI initiators that come with most operating systems. Depending on the servers that you are buying, you can also buy hardware iSCSI initiators. If you find that a software initiator isn't giving you the performance that you need, you can purchase hardware initiator cards that also have TCP/IP offload engines to help speed up the traffic.

NOTE   It is very important that you work directly with your storage vendor and Microsoft to verify that you have the correct level of drivers, firmware, and support configurations prior to implementing your SAN.

Direct Attached Storage

Direct attached storage (DAS) is a storage array that is directly connected, rather than connected via a storage network. The DAS is generally used for one or more enclosures that hold multiple disks in a RAID configuration.

DAS, as the name suggests, is directly connected to a machine, and is not directly accessible to other devices. For an individual computer user, the hard drive is the most common form of DAS. In an enterprise, providing storage that can be shared by multiple computers tends to be more efficient and easier to manage.

The main protocols used in DAS are ATA, SATA, SCSI, SAS, and Fibre Channel. A typical DAS system is made of one or more enclosures holding storage devices such as hard disk drives, and one or more controllers. The interface with the server or the workstation is made through a host bus adapter.

NAS

Network attached storage (NAS) is a hardware device that contains multiple disks in a RAID configuration that purely provides a file system for data storage and tools to manage that data and access. An NAS device is very similar to a traditional file server, but the operating system has been stripped down and optimized for file serving to a heterogeneous environment. To serve files to both UNIX/Linux and Microsoft Windows, most NAS devices support NFS and the SMB/CIFS protocols.

NAS is set up with its own network address. By removing storage access and its management from the server, both application programming and files can be served faster, because they are not competing for the same processor resources. NAS is connected to the LAN and assigned an IP address. File requests are mapped by the main server to the NAS server.

NAS can be a step toward and included as part of a more sophisticated SAN. NAS software can usually handle a number of network protocols, including Microsoft's Internetwork Packet Exchange and NetBEUI and Novell's Netware configuration.

NOTE   NAS is typically configured using a web browser.

Design Considerations

When designing the storage for your Hyper-V infrastructure, you will need to refer to the candidate profiles that you created and the requirements and vision that you defined in the planning phase to determine the I/O that you are going to need right away and to plan for additional I/O that you will need in the future.

If you already have a SAN in place, spend time with your SAN administrator to analyze your candidate profiles and the utilization of your SAN. Keep in mind that existing workloads that are already on the SAN will remain, and that you are planning to add additional workloads. The additional workloads are the guest operating systems, the data that they host, and the jobs that are running on those systems, such as batch and antivirus scans.

HIGH AVAILABILITY

There are several different scenarios that are available to achieve high availability with Hyper-V. Depending on your requirements and candidate profiles, you may implement one or a multiple of the scenarios.

It should come as no surprise that high availability is important. Certainly it's important in a conventional LAN, but it is even more important with a virtualization solution. In a traditional LAN, if the server fails or the switch falters, it is still possible for workers to get at least some of their work done. They won't be online, but if there is work they can do offline; it can still be accomplished. However, in a virtualized environment, if the server fails, then everyone on that server gets to go home early that day. That's because everyone's work environment has been offloaded onto that server.

Overview of Windows Server 2008 High Availability Options for Hyper-V

One of the greatest virtues of virtualization is the ability to consolidate multiple servers to a single server. While this will significantly drive down costs in your datacenter, it is rather frightening to have all of your servers on one physical server. That server would thus be a single point of failure, or to put it simply, you are putting all of your eggs in one basket. Microsoft has thought a lot about this and has created Windows Server 2008 Hyper-V to be a cluster-aware application that can be configured as part of a Windows Server failover cluster. A failover cluster is a group of servers with shared resources so that if one server becomes unresponsive or maintenance needs to be performed, the virtual machines running on that server can be migrated to another server, so that there is minimal impact on your end users. Failover clustering can be implemented at the Hyper-V host level and at the child level. Clustering at the host level will provide high availability for the virtual machine, but it doesn't really provide high availability for the service that is being run inside that virtual machine. To provide high availability for the services running on a virtual machine, you can create failover clusters between child partitions.

Cluster Types

With the release of Windows Server 2008 and the Windows Failover Cluster feature, there are four types of clusters that you can create for your environment.

▼   Node Majority

■   Node and Disk Majority

■   Node and File Share Majority

▲   No Majority - Disk Only

Node Majority   In a Node Majority cluster, there is no file share or disk witness associated with a cluster and all of the votes are assigned to the nodes. With a Node Majority cluster, you need to have at least 50 percent of the nodes in the cluster active to make quorum. The Node Majority cluster works best if you are creating a cluster that

▼   Is an odd number of nodes

■   Is a multisite cluster

■   Is a single-node cluster

▲   Doesn't have shared storage

The following illustration shows an example of a Node-Majority cluster with two failed nodes.

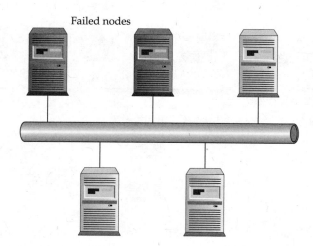

Failed nodes

Node and Disk Majority   A Node and Disk Majority cluster exists when the Node and the Disk witness both have shared votes in the quorum of the cluster. With a Node and Disk Majority cluster, you need to have at least 50 percent of the nodes in the cluster active, as well as the disk witness, to make quorum. The Node and Disk Majority cluster works best if you have an even number of nodes in your cluster. A great example of when you would use a Node and Disk Majority cluster is when you are creating a four-node cluster for Hyper-V with SAN-based storage.

The following shows an example of a Node and Disk Majority cluster with two failed nodes.

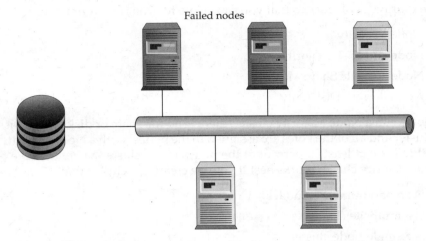

Failed nodes

The following figure shows an example of a Node and Disk Majority cluster with a failed node and a failed Witness Disk.

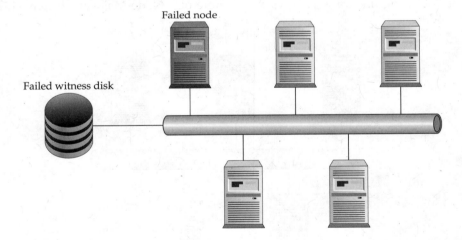

Failed node

Failed witness disk

Node and File Share Majority   A Node and File Share Majority cluster is the same as a Node and Disk Majority cluster, except instead of your cluster having shared disk from a SAN, the shared disk is a file share. Just as with the Node and Disk Majority cluster, you need to have at least 50 percent of the nodes in the cluster active, as well as the disk witness, to make quorum. The Node and File Share Majority cluster works best if you are creating a cluster that

▼   Is an even number of nodes

■   Is a multisite cluster

■   Is a two-node cluster

▲   Doesn't have shared storage

The following shows an example of a Node and File Share Majority cluster with two failed nodes.

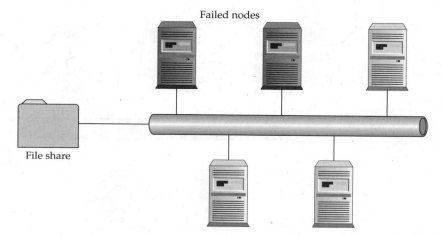

Failed nodes

File share

The following shows an example of a Node and File Share Majority cluster with a failed node and a failed Witness Disk.

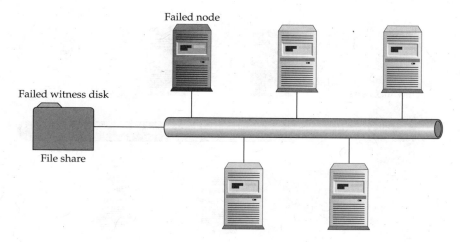

Failed node

Failed witness disk

File share

No Majority–Disk Only   In a No Majority–Disk Only cluster, the Disk Witness has all of the votes for quorum. Here's an example of how this works. Let's say that you have a four-node Hyper-V cluster and three of the four nodes fail. In a No Majority–Disk Only configuration, your cluster would still have quorum as long as the disk witness is still available. If your disk witness isn't available, it doesn't matter if you have all four nodes or one node up—your cluster will not have quorum.

The following shows an example of a No Majority–Disk Only cluster with four failed nodes; the cluster will still have quorum.

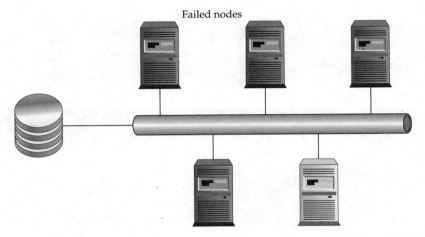

Failed nodes

The following shows an example of a No Majority–Disk Only cluster with a single failed node and a failed witness disk, which causes the cluster to not have quorum.

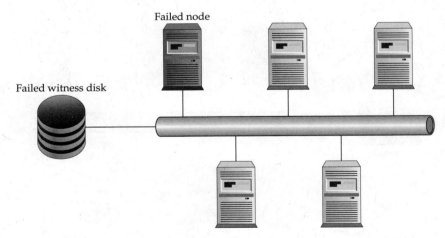

Failed node

Failed witness disk

Table 3-1 is a view of the cluster types and when you should consider using them.

| | Scenario | | | | |
Cluster Type	Single Node	Even Node	Local Two Node	Multisite	Cluster with No Shared Storage
Node Majority	Yes	No	No	Yes	Yes
Node and Disk Majority	No	Yes	Yes	No	No
Node and File Share Majority	No	Yes	Yes	Yes	Yes
No Majority–Disk Only	No	No	No	No	No

Table 3-1.   Cluster Types and When You Should Use Them

Cluster Infrastructure

A *cluster infrastructure* is made up of cluster node (servers), shared storage, and networking equipment. A *cluster node* is a server that has passed the qualifications and received the designation "Certified for Windows Server 2008." To help make sure that you're building a supported cluster configuration, Microsoft has included the Cluster Validation Wizard in the Failover Cluster Management MMC snap-in.

The Cluster Validation Wizard is not only used to validate your configuration; it also runs a series of tests that simulate cluster actions, such as:

▼ Are all nodes of the cluster running the same operating system?

■ Are all nodes at the same patch level?

■ Do all nodes have the correct components installed?

■ Can all of the nodes communicate on network interfaces?

▲ Is your storage configured correctly and in a supported configuration?

Cluster Infrastructure Design Considerations

We hate to make this work sound repetitive, but like designing your network itself, designing your failover nodes will take some work. Sure, you could just slap something out there that would be better than nothing, but spending some time to weigh your options will result in the best failover cluster for your organization.

There are several points that you will want to take into consideration when building your cluster infrastructure, including networking considerations, your disks, and which Hyper-V availability options you want.

Networking   When you're designing your cluster hardware, you'll want to consider the networking scenarios in the preceding section. As well, you will want to add an additional network card for a heartbeat network. The heartbeat network is a private network that is used by the cluster nodes to speak to each other to make sure they are available and healthy. You will also want to use dedicated network cards for parent communications and to manage iSCSI traffic.

When you build the cluster node servers, verify that you use the same configuration (duplex type, speed, and so on) on each NIC, and that the network cards are plugged into the same networks. For instance, if you have NIC 1 plugged into network 1, verify that this is the same configuration between all nodes.

Disk   When planning disk space for your virtual machines in a cluster configuration, you will want to create a dedicated LUN for each virtual machine you create if you are using Windows Server 2008 R1. By creating a LUN for each VM, you will be able to migrate each virtual machine to other hosts independently of other virtual machines. With Windows Server, 2008 R2, you will create a single large LUN, leveraging Cluster Shared Volumes that houses all virtual machines."

You may also consider having a separate set of local disks for the page file. This will increase the performance of your system since there will be less disk contention between the parent operations and the paging. You will also want to check with your hardware vendor on their recommended page file configuration for the amount of memory you should configure for your servers. Having to have a LUN per virtual machine is true if you are using Windows Server 2008 R1 with Windows Server 2008 R2. Microsoft has released Cluster Shared Volumes (CSV) which allows you to have multiple virtual machines on a single LUN and to migrate a single virtual machine between hosts using live or quick migration, while the other virtual machines on that same LUN remain unaffected.

This is possible because CSV allows all the nodes in the cluster to write to the shared disk at the same time. While each of the nodes in the cluster can write to the CSV, CSV itself is only mounted to one of the nodes called the coordinator node. The coordinator takes care of all the NTFS meta data updates and allows the cluster nodes to perform block mode reads and writes directly to the CSV. To sum it up, one node takes care of all the NTFS meta data updates while the other node just worry about the virtual machines that are running on that host. At this time, CSV is only available to Hyper-V and cannot be used for other cluster aware applications.

Hyper-V High-Availability Scenarios

There are a few different high-availability scenarios that are available when building and designing your Hyper-V implementation.

Host-Based Failover Cluster

A host-based failover cluster is a very common scenario where there are anywhere from 2 to 16 Hyper-V hosts that make up a failover cluster. This scenario provides high availability for the guest virtual machine and allows for failover in the event of hardware failure or during maintenance windows.

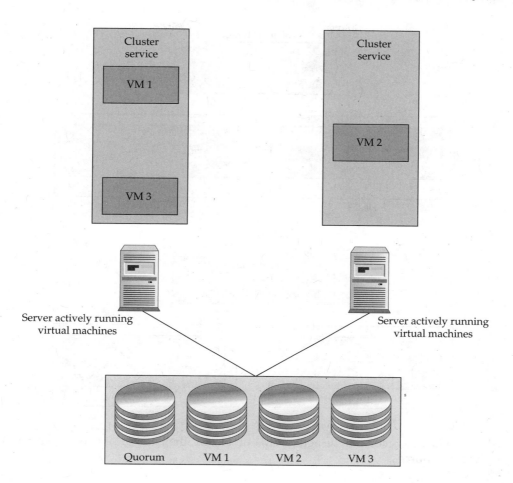

Guest Failover Clustering

Failover clustering can be implemented at the child level to provide high availability for the services that are running on your guest virtual machines. In this scenario you would create multiple child partitions on more than one of your host systems in the host-based cluster. While you can create a failover cluster on a single server for the highest level of availability, create multiple child partitions on other host systems.

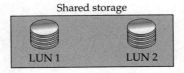

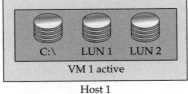

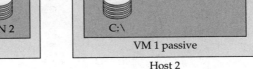

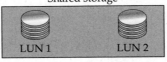

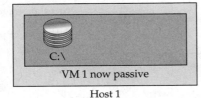

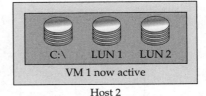

When a failure occurs on the active VM1 on Host 1, the Passive VM1 on Host 2 starts the cluster resources.

Physical-to-Virtual Clustering

Creating physical failover clusters that have low utilization can be an expensive design option if you only use one node of a failover cluster. To help lower the costs of creating high availability, a mixed cluster can be created between a physical and a virtual system.

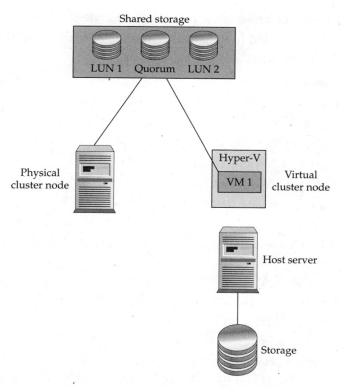

If the active physical server has a failure, the cluster service brings the services up on the virtual cluster node.

Configuring Hyper-V Host High Availability

In order to achieve a high level of availability in Hyper-V, there are some configuration steps. This ensures that you'll get the best results from your Hyper-V solution as well as achieve as little downtime as possible.

Prerequisites

There is a list of prerequisites for building a failover cluster in Windows Server 2008 that need to be met prior to building the cluster. The follow prerequisite sets should be completed prior to your cluster build-out.

1. Confirm that the entire cluster solution (servers, drivers, and so on) is compatible with Windows Server 2008. This can be done by visiting the Windows Server Catalog website, http://www.windowsservercatalog.com/.

2. Plan the names of each node and the cluster name.

3. Install all network and host bus adapters and verify that they are functional.

4. Configure all networks and storage:
   a. Plug cables in.
   b. Configure NIC and/or HBA settings to be identical between nodes.
   c. Configure IP and/or WWN.
   d. Configure DNS for name resolution.
   e. Configure VLAN and Zones.
   f. Verify connectivity between nodes.
   g. Configure disks and/or LUNS.
   h. Verify that each host can see disk(s).

5. Install the same version of Windows Server 2008 (Enterprise or Datacenter edition) on all nodes.

6. Add servers to an Active Directory domain:
   a. All servers in the cluster must be in the same Active Directory domain.

7. Patch all nodes to the identical patch level.

8. Create a cluster administrator account:
   a. When you create the cluster, you must be logged in to the domain with an account that has administrator rights on all nodes and the ability to create computer objects in the logged-in domain.

9. Install the Hyper-V feature.

10. Install the Failover Cluster feature.

11. Create a virtual network for each physical network adapter that will be used with Hyper-V.

Validating Your Cluster Configuration

After you have configured each node that you have planned for your cluster, log on to the first node of the cluster with the domain account you created in the prerequisites section and open the Cluster Manager by clicking Start | Administrative Tools, and choose Failover Cluster Management.

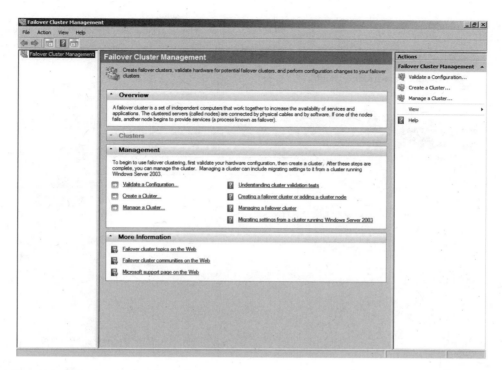

From the Management Console, choose to validate a configuration.

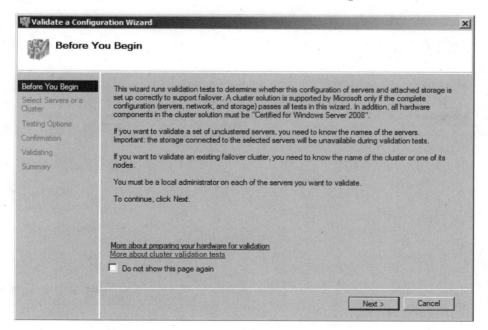

Click Next.

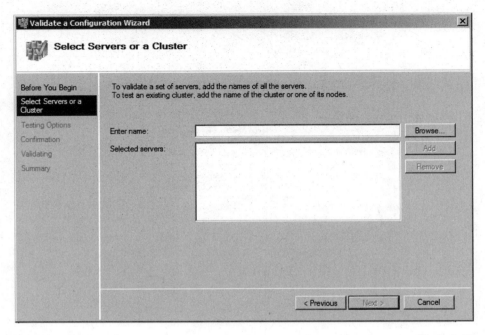

Enter the names of the servers that will become nodes in the cluster and click Next.

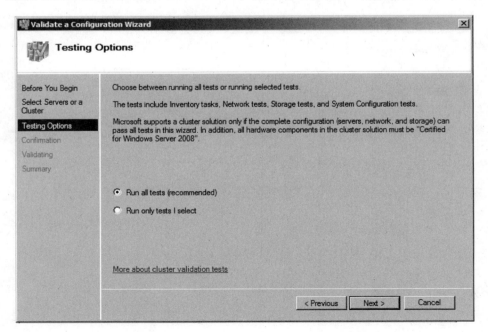

Select to run all tests and click Next.

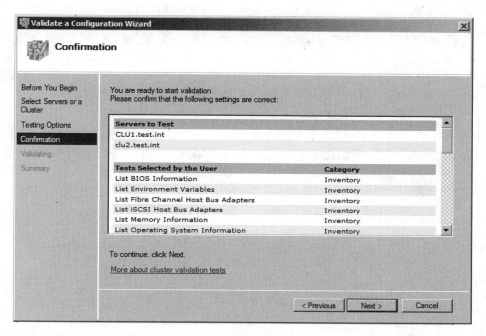

There are 36 different tests that the validation wizard will run, from checking the BIOS to finding viable disks that can be used in the cluster. Click Next.

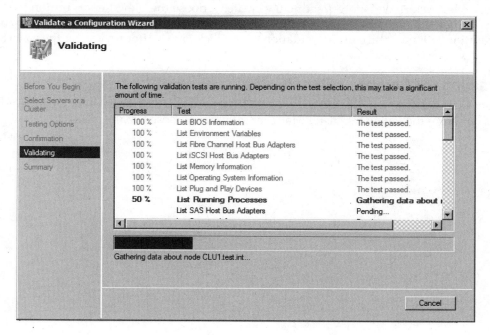

The cluster wizard will run the tests on each node of the cluster. Depending on the number of nodes that you have in your cluster, this could take a few minutes.

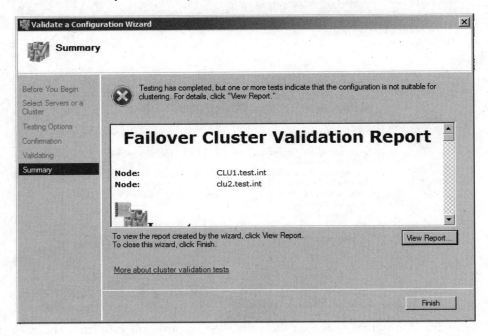

When the validation wizard has completed, you may have remediation steps that need to be performed before creating the cluster. Choose the View Report button to find any actions that need to be remediated and then rerun the test to verify that your configuration will pass the cluster validation tests. Click Finish after reviewing the report to go back to the Cluster Manager.

Creating the Cluster

Now that you have a validated cluster configuration, you can move on to creating your cluster. From the Failover Cluster Manager interface, choose Create a Cluster.

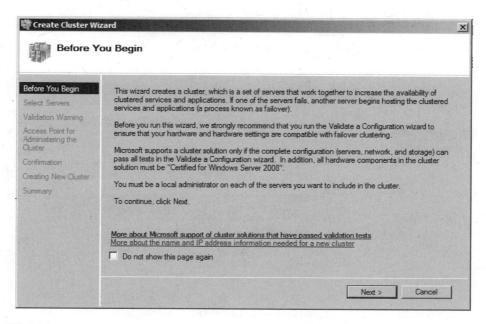

Click Next.

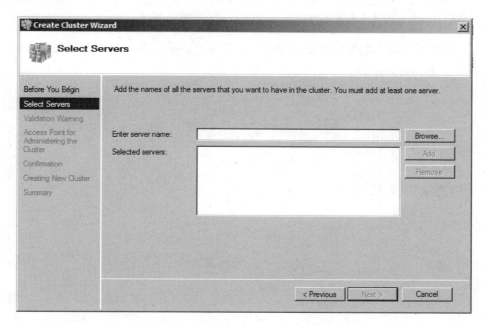

Enter the server names of the systems that will become nodes of the cluster and click Next.

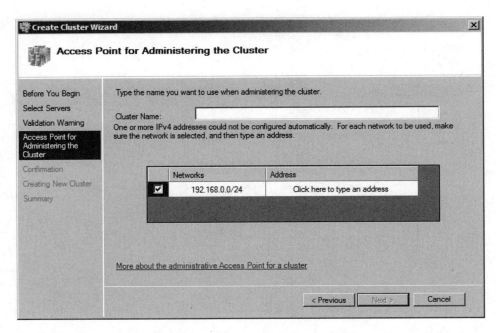

Enter the virtual name that will be used for the cluster and an IP address that virtual name will be assigned. Click Next.

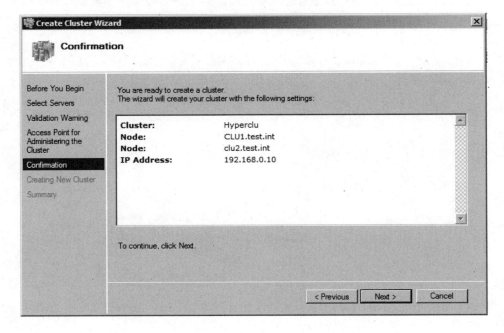

Validate your configuration and click Next. The Create Cluster Wizard will now configure each node in the cluster.

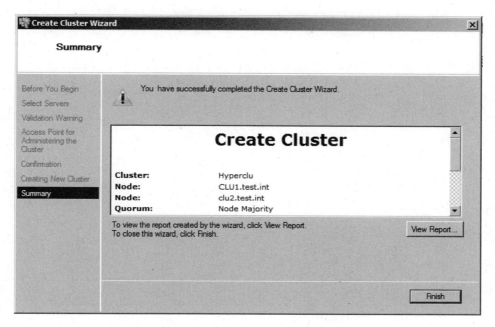

Once the cluster configuration has been completed, view the report to verify that your cluster configuration completed successfully and click Finish. You now have a working Hyper-V high-availability cluster. In the next chapter we will go over creating and managing virtual machines, including creating a highly available virtual machine.

CHAPTER 4

Planning and Designing System Center Virtual Machine Manager 2008

In Chapter 3 we configured our Hyper-V host servers, network, and storage, and created a highly available cluster environment. In Chapter 4 we are going to focus on System Center Virtual Machine Manager 2008. We'll talk about what it is, why you need it, its different components, and how to design Virtual Machine Manager for your environment.

THE DYNAMIC SYSTEMS INITIATIVE

It seems as if every time we open a magazine or check our email, there is a new business device or a new product that we need to make our business lives easier and more productive. The funny thing about that is that it's mostly true for the business user, but it almost always complicates our lives as administrators. Businesses today demand that the IT organizations can design and provision new systems faster to help drive a competitive advantage, while at the same time being able to predictably manage those systems in a cost-effective manner that doesn't take away from the bottom line.

The fact of the matter is that a successful business is a dynamic, multiheaded dragon that can turn on a dime to meet the needs of the market it lives in. It must also be able to find new markets in order to thrive. An IT organization needs to be more agile than the business it supports. By that we mean the IT organization should be able to provide value in being able to quickly provision new solutions and be able to proactively manage systems.

Microsoft has taken a close look at this issue and has developed the Dynamic Systems Initiative (DSI). DSI helps administrators achieve higher business value through automation, flexible resource utilization, and knowledge-driven processes—including the Distributed Management Task Force (DMTF) acceptance of the Web Services for Management (WS-Management) specification as a preliminary standard and the intention to build a service desk offering that will serve as a key foundational piece for the System Center family of solutions.

As a key deliverable on the company's DSI road map, Operations Manager 2007 is an end-to-end service management solution that works seamlessly across Microsoft software and its custom line-of-business applications to deliver intelligent monitoring and reporting. With Operations Manager 2007, customers can easily identify and resolve issues, accelerate problem resolution, scale management responsibility across their infrastructure and organization, and automate routine administration to improve service levels, increase efficiencies, and achieve greater control of the IT environment.

Design with DSI

There are three components of the dynamic systems technology strategy:

▼ **Design for operations**   Addressing the needs of people such as business architects and managers, application developers, IT professionals, and industry partners. This is accomplished by embedding DSI within the IT infrastructure through the use of system models.

- ■ **Knowledge-driven management** Systems are enabled to capture desired states of configuration and health in models based on business priorities and demands. This is used to provide a level of self-management to systems.

- ▲ **Virtualized infrastructure** Greater flexibility and leverage are provided to the existing infrastructure by consolidating system resources into a virtual service pool. Virtualized infrastructure makes it is easier for a system to quickly add, subtract, move, or change the resources it draws upon.

These elements are the basis for building dynamic systems. A virtualized infrastructure makes the system more robust; knowledge-driven management provides a way to put those resources to work; and design for operations ensures that systems are built with your organization's needs in mind.

Interoperability

As enterprises look to reduce costs while improving flexibility, the movement toward self-managing, dynamic systems gives administrators the tools needed to manage complexity, drive costs out of the infrastructure, and create an interoperable system. The DMTF's WS-Management specification has been approved and will be published as a preliminary standard. An essential part of the efforts to make DSI a cross-platform initiative, the specification provides a common way for systems of all types to access and exchange management information across the infrastructure.

THE SYSTEM CENTER SUITE

The System Center Suite is a major component of the DSI. The System Center Suite of products enables you to build a true end-to-end management framework in your enterprise. Microsoft has provided a significant amount of functionality, and with a little bit of elbow grease and some determination you'll be able to take advantage of those functions and build out an operationally aware environment. What we mean by that is that with time and some ingenuity, you'll be able to automatically migrate a virtual machine to a different host, providing more capacity for a workload. Or you'll be able to automatically fix issues without your end users ever knowing that something was broken. We're not sure about you, but we would much rather be out on the boat or spending time with our families than doing systems management work. By using the System Center Suite, we've been able to stop fighting fires and start doing more productive work, like creating more management intelligence and being able to provide business-critical services to our businesses in a much timelier manner.

Dynamic IT

Dynamic IT is Microsoft's strategy for providing technologies that enable IT and development organizations to become more strategic to their businesses. A dynamic infrastructure is Microsoft's vision for what an agile business looks like. It works within a business to meet the needs of a rapidly changing and adaptable environment. Dynamic IT is Microsoft's technology strategy for technologies that enhance the capabilities of an organization's people, processes, and IT infrastructure.

System Center and Dynamic IT

Microsoft System Center solutions play a central role in Microsoft's vision for helping IT organizations benefit from self-managing, dynamic systems. System Center solutions capture and aggregate knowledge about the infrastructure, policies, processes, and best practices so that IT pros can optimize IT structures to reduce costs, improve application availability, and enhance service delivery.

These integrated and automated management solutions enable IT organizations to be more productive service providers to their businesses. Aiming to enable self-managing, dynamic systems, System Center solutions close the gap between development, operations, and IT—connecting people, processes, and tools—by evaluating dependencies and optimizing business process performance from deep inside the operating system, applications, and composite services and workflows.

MICROSOFT SYSTEM CENTER PRODUCTS

Microsoft System Center has been around in one form or another for quite some time; it just wasn't called System Center. As part of the DSI, Microsoft grouped together its systems management products and rebranded them as System Center. Aside from System Center Virtual Machine Manager, the System Center suite is composed of four other products:

▼ System Center Configuration Manager—formerly System Management Server

■ System Center Operations Manager—formerly Microsoft Operations Manager (MOM)

■ System Center Data Protection Manager

▲ System Center Essentials

System Center Configuration Manager

System Center Configuration Manager (SCCM) is a configuration management solution that is used for patch management, application inventory, software deployment, operating system deployment, and remote control. The features of SCCM—along with the concepts of the DSI—make SCCM a very powerful tool to have in your enterprise.

From a virtualization perspective you will be able to patch your virtual machines from a single location, and you'll also be able to create server roles and do role-based software deployments from SCCM to your virtual machines. With the use of third party partner tools, SCCM can be used to manage your Windows and your *NIX systems.

More about SCCM can be found on the official system center web site (http://www .microsoft.com/systemcenter/configurationmanager/en/us/default.aspx), and there are many books available for SCCM. There is also a wealth of SCCM knowledge available on many other web sites. The SCCM console is shown in Figure 4-1.

SCCM delivers important capabilities that enable your IT department to assess, deploy, and update servers and mobile devices. The Software Distribution tool, which is a part of SCCM 2007, simplifies the complex task of distributing security updates and applications to the cruiser workstations.

Figure 4-1.   The SCCM console is used to manage SCCM.

Your IT team will be able to reduce the time it spends manually pushing out security and application updates. As a result, you can spend more time doing important IT work, not updating servers and mobile devices. The ability to have an in-depth view of the network has also helped enhance the security and stability of your IT environment. Further, SCCM allows you to strengthen your disaster recovery capabilities.

By implementing the Software Distribution feature within Configuration Manager, you have a simplified task of distributing applications and updates. The reduction of manual touch points also means patches, updates, and new applications are delivered to vehicles faster.

The new solution also provides your IT department with better asset intelligence and, in turn, better control over its IT infrastructure. By translating and compiling inventory data into a single report, IT managers can easily optimize their hardware and software usage and take action when necessary.

Microsoft SCCM also helps you quickly make adjustments in times of crisis. The system's failover capabilities let the organization deal with increased demand and make any necessary system changes.

System Center Operations Manager

System Center Operations Manager (SCOM) is an event-monitoring and performance-management tracking solution. By using SCOM you can create a true end-to-end monitoring environment. You can monitor all components of a solution. For instance, if you have a three-tier web, application, and database application, you can monitor the core components of the hardware, operating system, web server, application server, database platform, as well as the code that is running in those platforms. Synthetic transactions can be created and used to track end-user experience.

SCOM can also be used to *alert on* or *run actions against* events that are being tracked. For example, this means if disk space is getting low, SCOM can send an email alert to the system owner letting them know that action is required. SCOM can also run multiple actions if an event is triggered, such as alerting the system owner, running a script or managed code, or restarting a service. With the release of System Center Virtual Machine Manager (SCVMM) 2008, you can integrate SCOM with SCVMM to report on virtual system usage; determine if a physical system is a good virtualization candidate; and also be able to intelligently place and move virtual machines on host systems.

You're probably asking, "Well, that's cool that I can manage my Windows stuff, but what about my *NIX systems and my hardware?" To manage *NIX systems, Microsoft released the Operations Manager Cross Platform Extensions. You can also use SNMP, or there are also third-party partner add-on solutions that can be used to manage your *NIX systems and your physical hardware devices such as switches, routers, server hardware, and even your environmental systems.

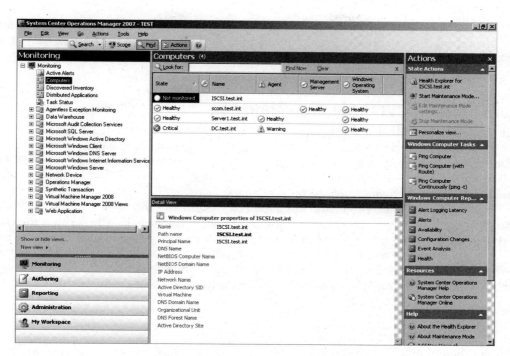

For cross-platform usability, SCOM uses an Agents and Management Pack. This is a big step toward monitoring heterogeneous environments, with the look and feel of the Windows Server platform. As such, you don't need to be an UNIX administrator to see what is going on and solve basic tasks on a UNIX or SUN computer. As with running a task for a Windows server, you can launch a service, mount a drive, or restart a service without ever getting in the Linux shell.

SCOM 2007 connects to the server over SSH with the possibility of a security-based super-user account that can be elevated to root if needed. The following cross-platform monitoring options are supported:

▼ HP-UX 11i v3 PA-RISC

■ HP-UX 11i v3 IA64

■ Solaris 10 SPARC

■ Solaris 10 x86

■ Red Hat Enterprise Linux 5 Server

▲ SUSE Linux Enterprise Server 10 SP1

SCOM 2007 is integrated with SCVMM 2008. Inside SCVMM 2008, the movement of virtual machines across Virtual Server, ESX, and Hyper-V is supported. SCVMM 2008 provides you options on where to move a virtual machine and which hosts are the best options.

System Center Data Protection Manager

In today's competitive marketplace, nightly backup is not sufficient for customers of any size. Data Protection Manager (DPM) enables you to monitor data changes in real time, enabling zero data loss recovery using a patent-pending agent technology. DPM allows a seamless integration of tape and disk, to ensure minimal downtime and reliable application recovery.

System Center Data Protection Manager is a backup and recovery solution for Windows Server and Microsoft server technologies. DPM was specifically written to take advantage of Volume Shadow Copy and other advanced technologies in Windows Server operating system to be able to provide continuous backups and protection for Windows Server functions. DPM has extended capabilities that allow for a higher level of protection above the base operating system for the following products:

- ▼ Hyper-V
- SQL Server 2008
- SharePoint 2007
- ▲ Exchange 2007

With the release of DPM 2007 Service Pack 1, you can use DPM to do online and offline backups of your operating systems. Being able to do an online backup means that for virtual machines that are running Windows Server 2008 and Windows Server 2003, you will be able to do backups while the virtual machine is running. If you are running Linux or other Microsoft Windows-based operating systems, you will be performing an offline backup. Being able to do an offline backup means that DPM 2007 SP1 will pause the running virtual machine, take a snapshot of that virtual machine, bring the virtual machine back to an online state, and then back up the snapshot of that machine.

NOTE We'll spend more time on Data Protection Manager in Chapter 9, Backup and Recovery.

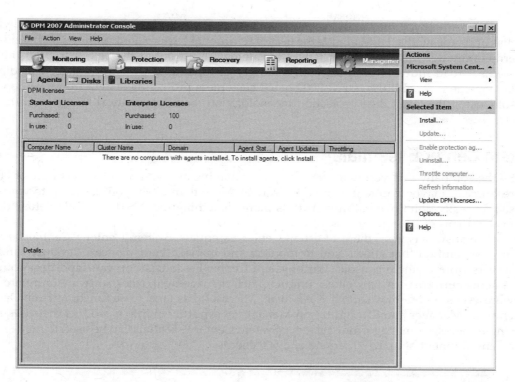

DPM 2007 extends the recovery-centric design of DPM 2006 to Microsoft Exchange Server, SQL Server, and SharePoint Portal Server, and enhances its file-server protection capability. Traditionally, the backup and recovery of an application required the identification and maintenance of various stores of user data, application binaries, and configuration data, as well as a list of procedures to recover both the data and the application. With DPM 2007, IT administrators help protect and recover all applications or application objects by using application terminology and concepts such as mailboxes for Microsoft Exchange Server or file shares for Windows file servers. Too often, current backup solutions fail because of the incorrect configuration of what data gets backed up or how. DPM 2007 unifies the application recovery process and the application backup process into one highly integrated continuous data protection solution.

DPM 2007 brings together continuous data protection with traditional tape backup/restore capabilities to provide a comprehensive disk-to-disk-to-tape data recovery solution. By combining continuous protection delivered through a real-time block-level filter, along with an advanced backup platform that uses both disk and tape, DPM 2007 brings advanced data protection technologies to enterprises of all sizes.

The block-level replication technology reduces the input/output needed to keep large data sets synchronized across all distances, offering significantly greater efficiencies. DPM 2007 provides fully integrated support for tape media that builds upon the established disk protection capabilities found in DPM 2006.

By enabling you to quickly recover applications and files from seamlessly integrated disk and tape media, DPM blends the best of traditional backup methodology with modern continuous data protection (CDP) technology. With out-of-the-box encryption for media, broad industry support with a variety of tape libraries, and advanced media management capabilities, DPM 2007 helps customers protect their data from one console, using the latest data protection technology on their most critical Microsoft infrastructure.

System Center Essentials

So the company that you work for really isn't that big and you're one of a couple of IT resources—maybe you're the only IT resource. More than likely you're saying to yourself, "I really don't need all this stuff. Is there something that is sized a little better for my company?"

The answer is yes—there's System Center Essentials. System Center Essentials is a unified solution that allows you to monitor and manage your devices, desktops, and servers from a single console. With System Center Essentials you can report on your systems performance, as well as conduct patch management, track software and hardware assets, and deploy software. All in all, Microsoft has taken core functions from Operations Manager and Configuration Manager and put them into a product that uses a single console to manage your systems. System Center Essentials can be used to manage an environment of up to 30 servers and 500 clients.

According to Microsoft, here are the top 10 reasons to use Essentials:

▼ **Unify your IT management experience**   Essentials 2007 provides a single console for core management needs. That means a single product to purchase, deploy, and learn.

■ **Keep your applications and your network up and running**   Essentials provides multiple views of the application data in your network. You can track database growth in SQL Server databases or connectivity to Exchange servers using some of the many provided charts, tables, and reports. Essentials also tracks the status of all the SNMP 1.0 and 2.0 devices in your network, allowing you to receive alerts when something important goes down.

■ **Troubleshoot problems more quickly**   Essentials provides a knowledge base out of the box to help you diagnose and fix critical alerts for key products like Exchange Server and SQL Server. These management packs are optimized so you only focus on the alerts that matter. Essentials often provides simple inline tasks to click and "fix it now." Additional management packs are available from Microsoft and third-party providers for both Windows and non-Windows environments.

■ **Simplify your patch management**   Essentials 2007 provides integrated patch management for Microsoft products in the Microsoft Update catalog. Additionally Microsoft has worked with key industry vendors to integrate their updates into Essentials, providing a single point of control for patch management. You can choose to automatically deploy critical updates or have them be subject for approval, and track compliance across your network. You can deploy a patch automatically by initiating deployment in real time.

■ **Deploy applications easily**   Using a three-step wizard, you can deploy applications to a target set of computers without worrying about having to deal with packaging or other complex processes. Additionally, Essentials uses Background Intelligent Transfer Service 2.0 (BITS) to optimize traffic over your network. Essentials even offers a means to uninstall a previously deployed application.

■ **Keep track of hardware and software assets**   Essentials 2007 gathers more than 60 hardware attributes and a complete inventory of the applications running on each machine. A summary inventory is available for quick troubleshooting or in the detailed report by machine groups.

■ **Improve your users uptime**   Agentless Exception Monitoring (AEM) allows you to collect application and OS errors that would otherwise remain anonymous. Use built-in tasks to remotely execute important tasks on users' computers, from performing a simple `ipconfig` to a remote desktop session.

■ **Get up and running fast**   Essentials 2007 uses a smart setup to check for prerequisites, ensuring that you have a successful installation. Post-installation configuration is quickly completed using three simple wizards. The built-in integration with Active Directory will allow you to manage a computer automatically as soon as it's added to your environment, without any intervention.

■ **Gain visibility into your IT environment**   You can view a Daily Health Report, providing a quick status of your IT environment and any action items required. For more detail, you can go to the Essentials console and consult the more than 180 standard reports to show how your IT environment is performing.

▲ **Get an affordable comprehensive IT management solution designed for you**   Essentials is priced for the budgets of midsize businesses, allowing you to purchase only what you need and then grow as your business requires it.

SYSTEM CENTER VIRTUAL MACHINE MANAGER 2008

System Center Virtual Machine Manager 2008, or SCVMM for short, is Microsoft's solution to centrally managing virtual hosts and guests. By leveraging the features and functions of SCVMM, you'll be able to speed up the provisioning of virtual machines, allow end users the ability to manage their own host and guests, and to monitor and increase your host systems utilization.

SCVMM 2008 offers a number of benefits for IT professionals who are tasked with managing virtual infrastructures. It provides a solution for unified management of physical and virtual machines, Performance Resource Optimization (PRO) for dynamic and responsive management of virtualized infrastructure, consolidation of physical servers, and rapid provisioning of new virtual machines.

Among the benefits of SCVMM 2008 are the following capabilities:

▼ **Maximized datacenter resources**   SCVMM 2008 delivers end-to-end support for consolidating physical servers into a virtual configuration. Virtualization can be performed quickly and reliably. Also, virtual machines can be placed intelligently on physical servers that match workload requirements. This can all be done from a centralized console.

■ **Rapid provisioning and agility**   SCVMM 2008 allows for virtual machines to be rapidly deployed. Control of the machines' "building blocks" can be performed from a centralized console, and authorized end users can allow provisioning duties. PRO can respond to failure scenarios or inadequately configured components that are identified in hardware, operating systems, or applications.

▲ **Leverage datacenter expertise**   Anyone familiar with the Windows environment will be comfortable using SCVMM 2008, which reduces the amount of personnel training, both for IT administrators, as well as help desk technicians.

In the next section, we'll take a closer look at the features of SCVMM 2008.

SCVMM Features

SCVMM 2008 has a number of useful features that can help you manage your virtualized machines. The features will help you maximize your datacenter resources, rapidly provision resources, and leverage your existing Windows knowledge.

SCVMM 2008 provides the following features:

▼ **Multivendor support**   With SCVMM you can manage both your Microsoft virtualization environments and your VMware ESX virtualization environments from a single console.

■ **Host and virtual machine management**   The host and virtual machine management functions of SCVMM can be used to quickly provision virtual machines on Windows Server 2008 with Hyper-V, Microsoft Hyper-V Server, and Virtual Server 2005 R2 SP1 hosts. This feature can also be used to enable the Hyper-V role on a Windows Server 2008 system.

■ **Intelligent placement**   The intelligent placement feature analyzes performance data of the managed host machines and guest workload requirements to determine the proper host placement when a virtual machine, or guest, is being provisioned.

■ **Library management**   The library feature in SCVMM is used to store file-based resources such as virtual machine templates, virtual hard drives, ISO files, and scripts. SCVMM also allows for SAN integration. The virtual machine templates and ISO files that you create and manage will be very large, and copying these files across a network between hosts can take a very long time. To handle this issue, Microsoft configured SCVMM to be SAN integrated. This means that instead of copying large files across the network, large files can be copied via the SAN, saving both time and networking resources.

■ **Physical-to-virtual migrations and virtual-to-virtual migrations**   The physical-to-virtual (P2V) and virtual-to-virtual (V2V) migration feature allows for physical machines to be virtualized, and also allows for the conversion of VMware virtual machines to Microsoft virtual machines.

■ **Self-service portal**   The self-service portal enables users to access, manage, and provision virtual machines.

■ **Centralized monitoring and reporting**   SCVMM includes a base set of monitoring and reporting features. To increase the flexibility of SCVMM, Microsoft has integrated SCVMM with System Center Operations Manager to provide a much deeper user experience when monitoring and reporting on performance. These reports can also be used to identify candidates to be migrated from physical machines to virtual machines.

■ **Physical Resource Optimization**   The PRO feature is used to ensure that your virtual infrastructure is running at optimal levels. PRO can also be used in a similar fashion as VMware's HA functionality, and can migrate virtual machines to different hosts in a Hyper-V cluster in the event of a hardware failure. PRO relies on PRO-enabled management packs that are installed on System Center Operations Manager.

■ **Failover cluster integration**   In Chapter 3 we covered building out a highly available host cluster. From the cluster manager you can then quickly migrate your virtual machines from one cluster node to another. SCVMM was built to be cluster-aware and adds additional functionality for easily creating highly available virtual machines, detecting Hyper-V clusters through Active Directory. It can easily move virtual machines between cluster nodes.

■ **Role-based administration**   The role-based administration feature allows you to create different user roles (administrator, group administrator, self-service group) and grant those roles appropriate rights to do the job functions they need to perform.

▲ **PowerShell automation**   SCVMM has been written from the ground up using PowerShell. SCVMM fully supports using PowerShell to automate manual administrative functions such as creating a virtual machine or other batch-type processes on multiple virtual machines.

SCVMM High-Level Architecture

There are several components that make up SCVMM. These components can all be installed on a single server, or they can be installed on multiple servers to take advantage of shared environments and to scale your implementation to the correct size of your environment. The components of SCVMM are

▼ Virtual Machine Manager Server

■ SQL Server

■ Administrators Console

■ Self-Service Web Portal

▲ SCVMM Library Server

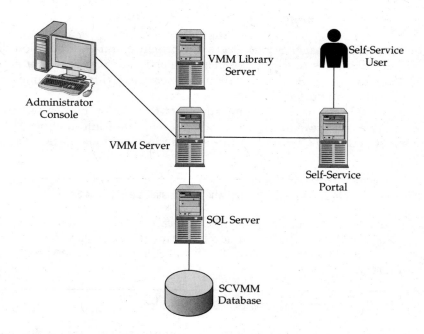

Virtual Machine Manager Server

The Virtual Machine Manager Server is the core of the SCVMM components and communicates with the virtual server hosts. To access the Virtual Machine Manager Server, you can use the administrator console, PowerShell, or the self-service provisioning web site. The SCVMM server houses the SCVMM service. The SCVMM service is the workhorse for SCVMM—it will run commands and transfer files, and is the communications traffic cop for the SCVMM components and host systems.

The SCVMM server also communicates with a SQL Server database. That database stores the SCVMM configuration. The database can be accessed to configure SCVMM by using the SCVMM Administrator Console, or by using the Windows PowerShell, which is the SCVMM command shell.

The SCVMM server is also the default library server. The SCVMM library is used to store file-based resources, like virtual hard disks, templates, ISO images, PowerShell scripts, answer files, and virtual machines.

NOTE   Additional SCVMM library servers can be set up, and it is recommended to do so if you have a number of hosts to manage.

SQL Server

The Virtual Machine Manager Server stores performance and configuration data in a SQL Server back end. This can either be in a full version of SQL Server or an Express version. SCVMM also uses SQL Server reporting services, with SCOM integration, to report on the health and performance of your systems.

Given the complexity of a virtual machine (not to mention numerous virtual machines), SCVMM makes use of the powerful SQL Server to store information. All SCVMM information is stored in a SQL Server database and is accessed via the SCVMM Administrator Console.

NOTE   The SCVMM database is specified when you install the SCVMM Server.

The SQL Server can be specified as either a local or remote instance of an existing SQL Server database. Alternately, if you don't have an existing SQL Server database you want to use, you can tell the Setup Wizard to install SQL Server 2005 Express Edition on the SCVMM server.

NOTE   The Setup Wizard also installs SQL Server 2005 tools.

If you are planning a particularly robust deployment—that is, managing more than 150 hosts or integrating Operations Manager 2007 with SCVMM to implement PRO tips and reporting—you should use SQL Server Standard or Enterprise.

Table 4-1 lists the system requirements when you have fewer than 150 hosts.

If your organization is one that will manage more than 150 hosts, see Table 4-2 for the system requirements for your SQL Server deployment.

Also, certain versions of SQL Server support the SCVMM database. Table 4-3 lists which versions of SQL Server are supported and which are not.

Component	Minimum	Recommended
Processor	Pentium 4, 2.8 GHz	Dual-core 64-bit, 2 GHz
RAM	2GB	4GB
Hard drive space (for SQL Server Express Edition)	14GB	14GB
Hard drive space	80GB	150GB

Table 4-1.   SQL Server System Requirements for Fewer Than 150 Hosts

Component	Minimum	Recommended
Processor	Dual-core 64-bit, 2 GHz	Dual-core 64-bit, 2.8 GHz
RAM	4GB	8GB
Hard drive space	150GB	200GB

Table 4-2.   SQL Server System Requirements for More Than 150 Hosts

SQL Server Versions	Supports Reporting in SCVMM?
SQL Server 2008 Express Edition	No
SQL Server 2008 (32-bit and 64-bit) Standard Edition	Yes
SQL Server 2008 (32-bit and 64-bit) Enterprise Edition	Yes
SQL Server 2005 Express Edition SP2	No
SQL Server 2005 (32-bit and 64-bit) Standard Edition SP2	Yes
SQL Server 2005 (32-bit and 64-bit) Enterprise Edition SP2	Yes

Table 4-3.   SQL Server System Versions for SCVMM

Administrator Console

The SCVMM Administrator Console is a graphical user interface, or GUI, that can be installed on the SCVMM server or on a supported operating system for an administrator or end user to utilize. The SCVMM Administrator Console is used to manage host systems, library servers, configuration, and virtual machines. The SCVMM Administrator Console is written as a PowerShell application; when the console is installed, if PowerShell is not available, the installation will install PowerShell automatically. The Administrator Console is shown in Figure 4-2.

The Administrator Console is used to interact and work with the SCVMM. It provides the administrator with a full suite of virtual machine management functions. This GUI helps administrators easily manage state transitions such as starting, stopping, and pausing their virtual machines. Microsoft designed this to be easy, and it is as simple as clicking on the virtual machine and then selecting the action to perform.

The console also allows the administrator to create virtual machine templates and then clone those machines elsewhere.

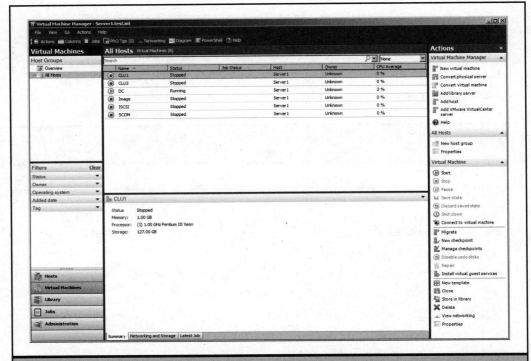

Figure 4-2. The SCVMM Administrator Console is a GUI for working with the SCVMM.

The Administrator Console works with Operations Manager 2007 to allow examination of the physical and virtual environments. For instance, the ability to map virtual and physical assets enables administrators to plan hardware maintenance. And since the SCVMM Administrator is built on the Operations Manager user interface, administrators can quickly and easily master the management of their virtual machines.

Virtual Machine Host

The virtual machine host is a physical server where virtual machines reside. SCVMM is a very flexible platform and manages several different host configurations. To manage a host, SCVMM installs an agent on the host, and if you choose, you can have SCVMM install and enable the virtualization components. Once the host has been added to your SCVMM instance and the virtualization components have been installed, you can begin to create and manage your virtual machines.

Self-Service Web Portal

The SCVMM Self-Service Portal is a web site where users can provision and manage their own virtual machines. This tool is shown in Figure 4-3.

The web portal allows authorized users to provision new virtual machines without directly involving IT staff. This capability especially targets software test and development teams, who often set up temporary virtual machines to try out new software. IT administrators retain control over access to resources.

SCVMM Library Server

The SCVMM library server is a central repository used to store virtual machine templates, ISO files, scripts, and other file-based objects that may be used by an administrator. When you install the SCVMM server, that server will become the default library server. Once the default library is created, it cannot be removed, but you can create additional library servers on the same system or on other system.

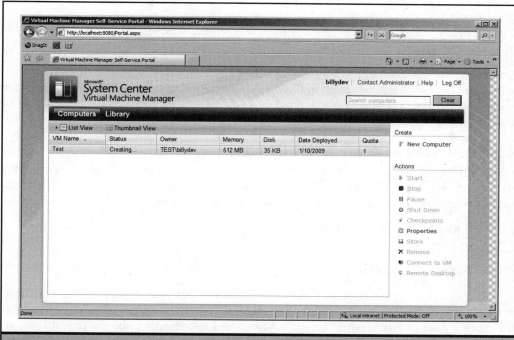

Figure 4-3.   The Self-Service Web Portal allows users to manage virtual machines.

The SCVMM library is a central repository for virtual assets, or "building blocks" used to create virtual machines quickly and consistently, including:

▼ Stored virtual machines

■ Virtual hard disks

■ CD/DVD software images, also called ISO files

■ Operating system profiles

■ Post-deployment customization scripts

■ Sysprep answer files

■ Hardware profiles

▲ Templates

In small organizations in a single location, administrators can create the library on the same machine as the SCVMM application. For larger, distributed organizations, IT administrators can implement library stores at each datacenter location, so they do not need to send files across wide area networks (WANs) and incur associated performance penalties.

Designing SCVMM

Now that you know about the features and components of SCVMM, let's talk about how to design your SCVMM topology. In this section we're going to go over figuring out how many instances of SCVMM you will need, how many servers you may need, and how to scale those servers for your environment.

What Do I Need to Know for My Design?

When designing your SCVMM implementation, there are a number of questions you need to answer that will help guide you to the correct design model for your environment. The major design considerations that you will need to explore are:

▼ Project scope and requirements

■ Locations

▲ System Center Operations Manager integration

We recommend that as you collect information about your environment, you keep this data in a SCVMM design profile spreadsheet. Once you collect all of your information about your environment, the spreadsheet will become valuable in performing an analysis on your SCVMM design.

Project Scope and Requirements

In the preceding chapters, we talked about planning prior to installing your environment, and the same concept holds true for SCVMM. You will want to work to figure out the scope and requirements for SCVMM with the business users and administrators who may be using SCVMM. Here are a couple of examples of the information that you will need to gather in your scope and requirements meetings:

▼ What would the business and administrator representatives like SCVMM to do?
- Self-service
- Department test lab

■ Organization—Some reading this book work for companies that centralize some IT functions but leave some functions at either a branch office or with a sister company.

▲ Service level agreements
- At what hours of the day does this service need to be available to your users?
- If downtime occurs, how long before the service is available again?
- Once the service is available, to what point in time should the system have been recovered?

NOTE If you're planning on implementing SCVMM and Hyper-V at the same time, you can develop your SCVMM scope and requirements at the same time as you develop your overall virtualization project scope and requirements.

System Requirements

SCVMM includes the SCVMM server, the SCVMM Administrator Console, the SCVMM Agent, and the SCVMM Self-Service Portal, an optional component.

By default, the SCVMM server is also a library server. If you do not set up a dedicated library server, you will need additional hard disk space on the SCVMM server for storing library objects. You can also install the Administrator Console on a different computer than the SCVMM server.

When you add a host or a library server in the Administrator Console, the SCVMM server automatically installs an agent locally on the host. You can also manually install an agent locally on a host, which is required if the host is on a perimeter network or in a nontrusted domain.

Before you begin installation, make sure that all prerequisite software is installed and all computers meet the minimum hardware requirements.

Software Requirements The following tables detail the software requirements needed for SCVMM components.

Table 4-4 lists the software requirements for the SCVMM server.

Table 4-5 lists the software requirements for the SCVMM Administrator Console.

Operating System	Windows Server 2008 x64 with Hyper-V
Database	If Microsoft SQL Server 2005 Express Edition SP1 is not already installed, the SCVMM installation process will install it on the local computer from the Setup Wizard. This also installs the SQL Server 2005 Express Edition Toolkit and creates a SQL Server instance named MICROSOFT$SCVMM$ on the local computer.
	Alternately, you can use an existing local or remote instance of the following versions of Microsoft SQL Server 2005 or Microsoft SQL Server 2008:
	■ Microsoft SQL Server 2005 Express Edition SP1
	■ Microsoft SQL Server 2005 Standard Edition SP1 or SP2
	■ Microsoft SQL Server 2005 Enterprise Edition SP1 or SP2
	■ Microsoft SQL Server 2008
	■ Microsoft SQL Server 2008 Standard Edition
	■ Microsoft SQL Server 2008 Enterprise Edition
Other software	■ Microsoft .NET Framework 2.0
	■ Microsoft .NET Framework 3.0
	■ Windows Remote Management (WinRM)
	■ Microsoft Core XML Services (MSXML) 6.0

Table 4-4.   Software Requirements for SCVMM Server

Operating system	Microsoft Windows Server 2008
	Microsoft Windows Server 2003
	Microsoft Windows Vista SP1
	Microsoft Windows XP SP3
Other software	Microsoft .NET Framework 2.0
	Microsoft .NET Framework 3.0
	Windows PowerShell 1.0

Table 4-5.   SCVMM Administrator Console Software Requirements

Operating system	Microsoft Windows Server 2008
	Microsoft Windows Server 2003 SP2
Other software	Microsoft .NET Framework 2.0
	Microsoft .NET Framework 3.0
	Windows PowerShell 1.0
	Windows Server Internet Information Services (IIS)

Table 4-6. SCVMM Self-Service Software Requirements

If you are planning to use the SCVMM Self-Service Portal, see Table 4-6 for the software prerequisites.

To use the SCVMM agent, each virtual machine host must have the software listed in Table 4-7.

For monitoring and reporting, you must have the software listed in Table 4-8.

Operating system	Microsoft Windows Server 2003 SP1 or above
	Microsoft Windows Server 2008
Other software	Windows Remote Management (WinRM) Microsoft Core XML Services (MSXML) 6.0

Table 4-7. SCVMM Virtual Machine Host Requirements

System Center software	System Center Operations Manager 2007
	System Center Operations Manager 2007 Reporting Server
	Virtualization Management Pack for System Center Operations Manager 2007

Table 4-8. System Center Software Requirements

Processor	2.8 GHz
RAM	2GB
Disk space if using local SQL Server 2005 Express Edition	7GB
Disk space if using remote SQL Server database	1GB
Disk space if using SCVMM Server as library server	200GB

Table 4-9.   Hardware Requirements for SCVMM Server

Hardware   What list of system requirements would be complete without a mention of the hardware minimums that apply? Table 4-9 lists the hardware requirements for the SCVMM server.

Table 4-10 enumerates the hardware requirements for your SCVMM Administrator Console and the SCVMM Self-Service Console (they are both the same).

The minimum hardware requirements for each virtual machine host will vary depending on the number and type of guest operating systems, the applications you plan to install on the virtual machines, and the anticipated workload.

The minimum hardware requirements for a library server vary widely depending on the number and size of virtual machine templates, virtual hard disks, virtual floppy disks, ISO images, scripts, hardware profiles, guest operating system profiles, and stored virtual machines. The recommended hard disk capacity for a computer with a SCVMM library is 200GB.

Network Requirements   This section details network requirements and considerations for installing Virtual Machine Manager.

▼   **Connections**   Due to the size of virtual machines, at least a 100Mbps Ethernet connection is suggested to connect all computers in a SCVMM configuration. A 1Gbps Ethernet connection will ensure adequate bandwidth and improved performance. However, if you use a 1Gbps Ethernet connection, your setup will likely see further performance enhancements if you use a more powerful processor for the SCVMM server than the recommended processor.

Processor	Pentium 500 MHz
RAM	256MB
Disk space	512MB

Table 4-10.   Hardware Requirements for the SCVMM Administrator Console and Self-Service Console

- ■ **Domains**   Before installing the SCVMM server, you must join the computer to a domain in Active Directory Domain Services (AD DS). Virtual machine hosts may be part of a domain but they do not need to be. Hosts in the DMZ are supported, as are VMware ESX hosts that are not joined using AD.

- ▲ **Firewalls**   If you want to manage a host across a machine-specific firewall, you must install the SCVMM agent locally on the host, which automatically opens port 80. The agent also uses port 443 by default. In order to manage hosts across a network firewall, you need to open the ports in that firewall manually to allow communication between the SCVMM server and the host. Once you open the ports, you can add the host to the SCVMM server.

Location

The number of locations and the systems that are contained in those locations will have a direct impact on the design of your SCVMM deployment. The information that you will want to collect about your locations includes:

- ▼ **Number of hosts that will be managed**   If you don't have any hosts yet, you will want to review your candidate profiles and design out your host infrastructure before you figure out your SCVMM.

- ■ **Number of virtual machines that will be managed by SCVMM**   Not only will you need to know how many hosts you have, but you will also need to figure out how many guest systems will reside on those hosts and whether or not those guests are development, test, or production, or if a majority of the hosts are going to be used for self-service.

- ■ **Virtualization technologies that will be used**   There are a lot of different virtualization products on the market today. While it would be amazing to have a tool that could manage all of them, it's really just not practical to develop such a tool while things are still changing at such a rapid pace as in the virtualization market. Knowing this and knowing that VMware has a big chunk of the market today, Microsoft has limited virtualization technologies they will support today. This doesn't mean that there won't be a broader scope of supported technologies in the future, but today SCVMM supports:

  - ■ Hyper-V
  - ■ Virtual Server
  - ■ VMware ESX 3.5 update 2 via Virtual Center

- ■ **Network information**   SCVMM installs a client on each host that will be managed, and the client sends data back to the SCVMM server. When you connect to a virtual machine via Remote Desktop Protocol (RDP) or the Virtual Machine Viewer, both of those operations are sensitive to bandwidth and latency on your network. Knowing the following information will help you decide on your SCVMM server placement and overall topology.

- ■ Connection and utilization between locations
- ■ Location-specific networks
  - ■ Corporate network
  - ■ DMZ networks
  - ■ Isolated networks
- ■ **Active Directory domain and forest information**   Knowing the AD forest and domain model will help you determine how you will be able to deploy the SCVMM client to your host machines. SCVMM can manage both trusted and nontrusted forests.
  - ■ Host locations by forest and domain
  - ■ Trust model
- ▲ **Images and other files that will be used by those virtual machines**   These files include:
  - ■ Templates
  - ■ ISO
  - ■ Scripts

Intelligent Placement

SCVMM uses a smart, holistic approach to placement called Intelligent Placement, which differentiates this solution from alternative products. Intelligent Placement works with both Microsoft and VMware virtualization platforms. When choosing physical hosts for virtual machines, IT administrators need to pay special attention to small details, such as the processor and memory specifications of host servers. Additionally, the performance of servers is constantly fluctuating based on usage trends, so IT administrators need some way of tracking ongoing requirements and historical performance data.

Consequently, placement is one of the most complicated aspects of virtualization. SCVMM provides administrators with a toolset to handle this task. The Intelligent Placement tool in SCVMM uses data from the Windows Server System to help administrators achieve specific goals. SCVMM selects appropriate hosts based on these factors:

- ▼ The workload's resource consumption characteristics
- ■ Minimum CPU, disk, RAM, and network capacity requirements
- ▲ Performance data from virtual machine hosts

SCVMM incorporates these considerations into algorithms that IT administrators can fine-tune to maximize resource utilization or balance workloads among hosts. Also, after a virtual machine is deployed, SCVMM continues to analyze performance data and resource requirements for both the workload and the host so that administrators can have an opportunity to further optimize their resources. IT administrators can add more virtual machines by repeating the same process.

System Center Operations Manager Integration

In our opinion, the integration with SCOM is one of the best things that Microsoft did with the 2008 release of SCVMM. Being able to monitor, make intelligent decisions on candidates or virtual machines, and report on performance will make your life as a virtual administrator so much easier and bring you closer to a self-healing dynamic environment.

SCVMM and SCOM reporting is integrated through the use of the Operations Manager Connector Framework. The Operations Manager Connector Framework is used to share data between management tools, leveraging on the strengths of multiple tools, and to provide administrators a single user interface to view systems data. The data between SCVMM and SCOM is limited to the hosts that are in a single management group in SCOM.

So, what if you have multiple management groups and hosts in each management group? Well, you have two options for handling this situation:

1. Create a new SCVMM instance for each SCOM management group that has host systems.
2. Create a SCOM management group for collecting reporting data and multihome your host systems.

Remember that if you create multiple SCVMM instances, those instances aren't integrated and you will not have a single console to manage your host and guest systems. On the flip side of things, if you create a management group purely for SCVMM and you multihome the hosts, you will have to implement the management group as well as the hardware and other infrastructure to support that. Since you know your environment best, you will have to weigh the costs of a SCVMM instance and a SCOM management group and determine your best course of action.

Number of SCVMM Systems You Need

For most organizations the most popular method for deploying SCVMM is in the single-server scenario. In the single-server scenario you will be installing all of the SCVMM components on a single server, with the exception of installing the database on an existing SQL Server. Depending on your budget this may be a good way to get yourself up and running, and if you need to, you can add additional library servers as needed. Now this doesn't necessarily mean that this will be the only instance of SCVMM in your environment. You may need to have multiple instances for isolated networks, business units, or test environments. There are a series of questions that you will need to answer to determine how many instances of SCVMM you may need to have in your environment. Keep in mind, as you're planning your environment, that if you implement multiple instances of SCVMM, they are not integrated and they don't share information. What this means is that you can't build a hierarchical structure as you can with System Center Configuration Manager or System Center Operations Manager where data can be configured to flow to a top-level server.

We're going to assume that you've already collected your location information and determined whether or not you are going to use SCVMM per SCOM management group, or you're going to multihome your hosts. There are some other tidbits that you need to take into consideration for your SCVMM design.

Maximum Number of Hosts and Virtual Machines   As with almost anything we do, there are limits and maximum configurations. SCVMM is definitely not immune. The maximum numbers of hosts and virtual machines that a single instance of SVCMM can handle are:

▼   400 hosts

▲   8,000 virtual machines

If you have built your SCVMM solution to be used primarily with the self-service function, then we recommend that your maximum numbers of hosts and virtual machines per single instance of SCVMM are:

▼   400 hosts

▲   1,000–4,000 virtual machines

Server Configuration   As we previously discussed, the SCVMM server is a major component of SCVMM—it is the product through which all other SCVMM components interact. As such, this is the first product that must be installed. The SCVMM server communicates with the SCVMM database and with managed computers—the virtual machine hosts and library servers.

Before installing the SCVMM server, you must join the computer to a domain in Active Directory Domain Services. All your virtual machine hosts must also be connected to domains in AD DS.

Normally, a single SCVMM server is enough and you'll be able to grow your system by adding more virtual machine hosts and library servers as your infrastructure expands. Having just one SCVMM server with a single database makes it possible to centrally manage your virtual environment.

However, there may be cases when having more than one SCVMM server is necessary:

▼   When you want to manage your development and test environment away from your production virtual environment

■   When your virtual environment grows beyond 400 hosts and 8,000 virtual machines

▲   When you have a large number of self-service virtual machines—between 1,000 and 4,000

There are some things to keep in mind when installing more than one SCVMM server:

▼   Each SCVMM server must be installed on a separate computer and each database must have a separate SCVMM database. Multiple SCVMM servers can use the same database server, but not the same database.

- Only one SCVMM server must manage each host or library server.

- Multiple SCVMM environments cannot be integrated and cannot share data.

▲ SCVMM does not provide a way to replicate physical files in the SCVMM library or metadata for objects that are stored in the SCVMM database. If you want to replicate data, the files need to be copies outside of SCVMM, and metadata has to be transferred by using scripts or other means.

Branch Offices   If your organization uses branch offices, there are other thoughts to keep in mind when deploying SCVMM. First, it is best to deploy an SCVMM library server and one or more hosts at the remote site. Users can build virtual machines by using resources from a local library server rather than copying multigigabyte files from a central server over the corporate WAN. This ensures that users can take advantage of those resources in the event of a WAN outage.

Also, you should consider installing a host and library on the same computer. This topology is ideal when you have 150 or fewer images. Having the host and library on the same computer also allows for rapid deployments. Since the files for building virtual machines do not need to traverse the network, this configuration is much faster for virtual machine deployments.

Naturally, there are some downsides to this topology. First, it requires more disk space. Maintaining multiple copies of the same files rather than using a central library consumes a lot of space. Also, intelligent placement is not as advantageous because you want to use the local host as, it is closest to the library server.

Virtual Machine Manager Library Servers

The SCVMM library server is a collection of resources that can be used when you create and configure your virtual machines. These files can be ISO files, hardware templates, or preconfigured virtual machines. When you create a virtual machine from a preconfigured virtual machine, the library server will copy that template to the host that you've chosen to deploy the VM to. This copy can happen via a SAN copy if your library server and host servers are on the same SAN. Then the data is copied from its storage LUN connected to the library server to its new home LUN connected to the host system via the SAN. This type of transfer is extremely quick and doesn't use networking resources.

If your SAN doesn't support SAN copy, the library server will copy the template from the library to the host via a network connection. That doesn't seem too bad, but when you take into consideration that many of your templates will be multiple gigabytes in size, that can take a long time on a 100Mbps link, and a very long time over a WAN link. It can potentially use up all of your WAN bandwidth and impact your business. With SCVMM you can implement a distributed model for your library servers, but SCVMM doesn't provide a method for replicating the files and metadata associated with those files to the distributed library servers. Keep in mind that SCVMM doesn't support Distributed File System (DFS) or Distributed File System Replication (DFSR), so you will have to write a script that will manage the replication of that data.

Designing SCVMM High Availability

Depending on the requirements that you gathered, you may or may not need to build your SCVMM implementation in a high-availability configuration. There are four components of the SCVMM implementation that you can make highly available:

▼ Virtual machines (this will be covered in Chapter 8, Managing Your Virtual Machines)

■ SCVMM Database

■ SCVMM Service

▲ SCVMM library servers

SCVMM Database

The SCVMM database can be installed on a version of SQL Server 2005 or SQL 2008 that supports failover clustering. You will want to build and configure a supported failover cluster on Windows Server 2008 or Windows Server 2003 Enterprise or Datacenter editions. Once the cluster has been built and configured, you can install SQL Server 2005 or SQL Server 2008 Enterprise Edition and create the database cluster.

After the database cluster has been installed and configured, you can install the SCVMM database to that cluster. The database cluster that you install the SCVMM database on must either be in the same Active Directory domain as the SCVMM server, or in a domain that has a two-way trust. When you install your database on the cluster, you will need to associate a Service Principal Name (SPN) with the account that SQL Server is running as. This is done because SCVMM requires mutual authentication under Kerberos.

In order to ensure successful database failovers, you may need to change SCVMM's built-in retry mechanism for the SCVMM database. By default, the retry mechanism has the following settings:

▼ Number of retries: 5

▲ Retry interval: 2 seconds

If your SQL Server database is located on a cluster, the failover duration should be shorter than the default settings. Those values can be changed in the Windows registry on the SCVMM server. The following registry keys show those default values:

NOTE   The registry is not a tool to be tinkered with if you don't know what you're doing. You can do some real damage if you don't know what you're doing.

```
HKEY_LOCAL_MACHINE\SOFTWARE\Microsoft\Microsoft System Center Virtual
Machine Manager Server\Settings\SQLValue
Name=DBRetryIntervalValueType=REG_DWORDSample value=00000002

HKEY_LOCAL_MACHINE\SOFTWARE\Microsoft\Microsoft System Center Virtual
Machine Manager Server\Settings\SQLValue
Name=DBRetryCountValueType=REG_DWORDSample value=00000005
```

SCVMM Service

At this time the SCVMM service is not supported in a high-availability failover cluster configuration. This is in part because the SCVMM service is a stateless service. What this means is that the SCVMM database holds all configuration and state information for the SCVMM service. If the server that hosts the SCVMM service becomes corrupted, that server can be rebuilt or have SCVMM reinstalled and pointed to the existing SCVMM database.

You can also install the SCVMM service into a virtual machine. In the event of a failure, that virtual machine can be re-created very quickly. You're probably asking: Well, what if the host fails? Glad you asked. The SCVMM virtual machine can be created as a highly available VM. If you build the SCVMM server as a highly available VM, we recommend that you only manage that virtual machine through the Hyper-V Manager and the cluster management tools.

You can use the Cluster Configuration Management snap-in in Windows Server 2008 to create a failover cluster. Next, manage the highly available virtual machines (HAVM) in which the SCVMM server is running in Hyper-V.

NOTE If you run the SCVMM server in a virtual machine, it is best not to use SCVMM on that machine. You run the risk of deleting the virtual machine if you do that.

If the SCVMM server does fail, recovery depends on following a solid backup plan for the database.

SCVMM Library Servers

You have two different options to provide high availability to your library servers.

1. Use clustered file servers and shares created in Windows Server 2008.
2. Use DFS.

When you're using a clustered file server, if the active server that is hosting the library share fails, the share will become active on the passive node of the cluster. When you use DFS, you will create a namespace that can have multiple replicas on different servers. You then point your library share to that DFS namespace, and if one of the servers that houses a copy of the library share fails, DFS will redirect requests to one of the replicas.

You will need to determine whether implementing a cluster or using DFS will meet your recovery time objective or you can better meet that objective by doing a restore.

To ensure high availability, file servers and shares hosted by a failover cluster should be created on Windows Server 2008 Enterprise Edition or Windows Server 2008 Datacenter Edition. SCVMM is not aware of failover clusters created in Windows Server 2003. Also, SCVMM does not support using a failover cluster that contains the SCVMM server as an available library server.

We've spent the past chapter looking under the hood of SCVMM and examining how it's put together. In the next chapter we will be looking at how to size, install, and configure your SCVMM implementation.

CHAPTER 5

Installing and Configuring Systems Center Virtual Machine Manager 2008

Systems Center Virtual Machine Manager (SCVMM) is a flexible platform that can be scaled to meet the needs of your business. In Chapter 4 we talked about designing your System Center Virtual Machine Manager topology. In this chapter we are going to focus on scaling of your hardware and the prerequisites, installation, and configuration of the SCVMM components.

SCVMM is a very useful tool that has a lot of components. Happily, installation and configuration are not overly difficult, but they do require some effort on your part. We'll talk about the steps involved in installing SCVMM on a single system, a multiple-server system, and the details of what system requirements you must have.

SCVMM ON A SINGLE SYSTEM

If your company is a smaller one that is planning on having only a few host machines, installing SCVMM on a single system is the way to go. We recommend that if you are installing SCVMM on a single machine, you install this as a physical system. The reason is that when you want to create template systems in your library, the system has to have the Hyper-V role enabled. If you implement SCVMM into a virtual machine, you will not be able to enable the role because the VM will not be able to see the hardware-assisted virtualization components.

Not withstanding your organization's size, there are some great benefits to having a single-system deployment with SCVMM, including the following:

▼ **Initial configuration**   You only need to install and configure Windows Server 2008 and the Hyper-V role one time.

■ **Licensing**   Only one Windows Server 2008 license is required.

■ **Backup and restore**   The backup procedure for a single server is simpler and demands fewer resources.

▲ **Space and cooling**   A single server uses less physical space, uses less electricity, and is less expensive to cool.

Hardware Requirements

As of the writing of this book, there is not a solid method to accurately scale your SCVMM implementation. But the information that is available from the product group pertains to a maximum configuration for managing 8,000 virtual machines and 400 hosts with the VMM component utilizing two dual-core processors with 8GB of RAM. If you are planning on installing all SCVMM components on one system, it is recommended that you only manage up to 20 hosts. If you are planning on managing more than 20 hosts, you will want to plan on scaling your SCVMM implementation to multiple servers and a full version of SQL Server.

The requirements listed in Table 5-1 are based on information from the Microsoft product groups at the time of writing.

Component	Up to 10 Hosts	Between 11 and 20 Hosts
Processor	64-bit dual-core Pentium 4, 3.2GHz or faster	64-bit dual-core Pentium 4, 3.2GHz or faster
RAM	2GB	4GB
Hard disk space	150GB	200+GB depending on the number of management hosts and the number of templates, ISOs, and other files stored in the library

Table 5-1.   Single Server System Requirements for SCVMM

Software Prerequisites

Along with hardware requirements, in order to run SCVMM on a single server there are
also software requirements.

▼ **Windows Server 2008 with Hyper-V**   This can be Standard, Enterprise, or
Datacenter edition—remember that Hyper-V only runs on the 64-bit OS.

■ **Windows Power Shell 1.0**

■ **Windows Remote Management (WinRM)** (started and set to Automatic start)

■ **Windows Automated Installation Kit (WAIK) 1.1**   If you haven't already
installed it on the planned server, this will be installed by the SCVMM installer.

▲ **Windows Server Internet Information Services (IIS) 7.0**   Use the Add Role
Wizard to add the Web Server (IIS) role with the following services:

  ■ IIS 6 Metabase Compatibility

  ■ IIS 6 WMI Compatibility

  ■ Static Content

  ■ Default Document

  ■ Directory Browsing

  ■ HTTP Errors

  ■ ASP.Net

  ■ .Net Extensibility

  ■ ISAPI Extensions

  ■ ISAPU Filters

  ■ Request Filtering

SCVMM ON MULTIPLE SERVERS

If you are planning on having more than 20 hosts, you will need to install the components onto multiple systems. Each component can be on a different server, or a mix of components can be installed on different servers. For example, you may choose to install the database and Web Portal to an existing SQL Server cluster and web farms, while the VMM component and library are on the same server. The systems that are going to be the most utilized are the VMM server and the library server. If you are planning on having over 150 hosts or a large number of self-service users that will be building and destroying virtual machines on a regular basis, you will want to consider having each component on a separate server.

Earlier we talked about the benefits of a single-server deployment. Let's continue the "glass-is-half-full" discussion, and mention why deployment on multiple servers works so well. Benefits include

▼ **Lower hardware requirements**   Servers with less memory and storage space can be used, thus allowing you to repurpose existing hardware.

■ **Redundancy**   With multiple servers, if one fails, the whole system doesn't go out. Critical services such as the domain controller and the DNS Server service can be placed on separate servers to eliminate a single point of failure.

■ **Performance**   Disk reads can be spread over multiple spindles on separate servers, which can reduce disk latency.

▲ **Backup and restore**   While single systems allow for easier backup, multiple servers provide more options and flexibility for data and system backup.

Virtual Machine Manager Server Installation Requirements

As we stated above, there isn't a good formula available to correctly size your server implementation, but the product group has given us some guidelines on how the hardware should be scaled for VMM.

Hardware Requirements

Hardware requirements will vary, based largely on how many hosts your system has. If you have 150 or fewer hosts, your system requirements will be smaller than in systems with more than 150 hosts. The differences are small, however. Chances are good that even if you have 150 hosts or fewer, your system will still meet the requirements for the larger deployment.

Table 5-2 lists the hardware requirements based on information from the Microsoft product groups at the time of writing.

The VMM component can be installed in a virtual machine or on physical hardware. Just keep in mind that if you are going to create templates in SCVMM, the library server that will house those templates will need to be on a physical server with the Hyper-V role enabled. From a maximum-configuration perspective, if you are planning on having up to 400 hosts and up to 8,000 virtual machines, Table 5-3 lists the hardware requirements.

Component	Up to 150 Hosts	More than 150 Hosts
Processor	Dual 64-bit dual-core Pentium 4, 3.2GHz or faster	Dual 64-bit dual-core Pentium 4, 3.6GHz or faster
RAM	4GB	8GB
Hard Disk Space	2GB with a remote DB 10GB with SQL Server Express loaded (SQL Server Express has a 4GB DB size limit)	2GB We recommend the full version of SQL Server 2005 for this many hosts and to offload SQL Server onto another server.

Table 5-2.   Hardware System Requirements for Multiple Server Installation

In this configuration the library, web portal, and SQL Server database components are installed on separate servers.

Software Prerequisites

The software prerequisites for the VMM component are very similar to the prerequisites for installing all the components on a single server minus the web components. To install the Virtual Machine Manager component, the following software requirements need to be met:

▼   Windows Server 2008 64-bit Standard, Enterprise, or Datacenter

■   Windows Remote Management (WinRM)

■   Microsoft .NET Framework 3.0

▲   Windows Automated Installation Kit (WAIK) 1.1

Component	Configuration
Processor	Dual 64-bit dual-core processors
RAM	8GB
Hard disk	10GB

Table 5-3.   Hardware for SCVMM Maximum Support Configuration

If you plan on running the database on the same server, a supported version of SQL Server will need to be installed. Keep in mind that SQL Server Express supports up to a 4GB database.

> **NOTE** If you have previously enabled WinRM by using the Management and Monitoring Tools components group in Add/Remove Windows Components, that version will not work with Virtual Machine Manager. You must install the version of this software from the following site, which will overwrite your existing version: http://go.microsoft.com/fwlink/?LinkId=84599.

SQL SERVER

SCVMM uses SQL Server 2005 to store system information, such as configurations and performance data. When deployed together with Operations Manager, SCVMM allows administrators to take advantage of SQL Server 2005 Reporting Services functions. SQL Server Reporting Services is a comprehensive, server-based solution that enables the creation, management, and delivery of both traditional, paper-oriented reports and interactive, web-based reports. An integrated part of the Microsoft Business Intelligence framework, Reporting Services combines the data management capabilities of SQL Server and Windows Server with familiar and powerful Microsoft Office system applications to deliver real-time information, support daily operations, and drive decisions.

The SQL Server database for SCVMM stores VMM configuration data as well as averaged performance data from the VMM component on each of the virtual machines. This data is then used by VMM to determine virtual machine placement when you are using the Intelligent Placement feature. The data that is in the database is updated by default every 9 minutes. Once the first record is written for a virtual machine, that data is updated and not created multiple times.

Hardware Requirements

As with a single-server system, the hardware requirements differ just subtly between systems with fewer than 150 hosts and systems with more than 150 hosts. Chances are good that your system will meet both sets of requirements. But these are the minimum requirements. The beefier your processor, the more RAM, and the larger disk space you have, the better.

The hardware requirements listed in Table 5-4 are based on information from the Microsoft product groups at the time of writing.

Software Prerequisites

In order to install the SCVMM database, you must be running a server with one of the following versions of SQL Server installed:

▼ **SQL Server 2008** Standard or Enterprise Edition (32-bit or 64-bit)
▲ **SQL Server 2005** Standard or Enterprise Edition (32-bit or 64-bit)

Component	Manage Up to 150 Hosts	More Than 150 Hosts
Processor	Dual 64-bit dual-core Pentium 4, 3.2GHz or faster	Dual 64-bit dual-core Pentium 4, 3.6GHz or faster
RAM	4GB	8GB
Hard Disk Space	150GB	200GB

Table 5-4.   SQL Server System Requirements

NOTE   If you are planning on using SQL Server 2008 for the SCVMM database, the SQL Server management tools must be installed onto the VMM server prior to installing the database.

Configuring SQL Server

There is a little bit of prep work that needs to be done prior to installing the SCVMM Database on an existing or a new SQL Server:

▼   Enable the SQL Server to accept remote connections. This may include configuring the Windows Firewall on the server. Work with your SQL Server DBA to ensure that your systems can accept remote connections.

▲   Create a Service Principal name for the SQL service if your SQL Server is running under a domain account or network service account.

To help secure the communications between your SCVMM database and the VMM server, we recommend that you enable Secure Sockets Layer (SSL) encryption for the communication channel.

Based on the information that you collected and the topology that you designed in the previous chapter, you may be running multiple instances of VMM to support your multiple networks or locations. There can be only one VMM database per instance of SQL Server on a server. This means that if you are running multiple instances of SQL Server on a server, you can point multiple instances of SCVMM to the same SQL Server, as long as each SCVMM database is installed in a unique SQL Server instance on that server.

LIBRARY SERVER

The Virtual Machine Manager library server stores files that can be used to create and manage your virtual machines. The library server can store ISO installation media, virtual machine hardware profiles, and virtual machine templates. By using the library, you can significantly decrease the amount of time it takes to "spin" up a new virtual machine, and it can help to drive standards in your virtual machine creation. Ultimately, the VMM library server is just a file server, and designing the hardware for a library server is very similar to a file server.

The SCVMM library is a central repository for virtual assets, or "building blocks" used to create virtual machines quickly and consistently. Those building blocks include

- ▼ Stored virtual machines
- ■ Virtual hard disks
- ■ CD/DVD software images, also called ISO files
- ■ Operating system profiles
- ■ Post-deployment customization scripts
- ■ Sysprep answer files
- ■ Hardware profiles
- ▲ Templates

In small organizations in a single location, administrators can create the library on the same machine as the SCVMM application. For larger, distributed organizations, IT administrators can implement library stores at each datacenter location so they do not need to send files across wide area networks (WANs) and incur associated performance penalties.

Software Prerequisites

The VMM library component can be installed on a stand-alone server or on a highly available failover cluster. The following operating systems are supported to run the VMM library role as a stand-alone server:

- ▼ **Windows Server 2008 with or without Hyper-V 64-bit**   Standard, Enterprise, Datacenter editions
- ■ **Windows Server 2008 without Hyper-V 32-bit**   Standard, Enterprise, Datacenter editions
- ■ **Windows Server 2008**   Core Standard, Enterprise, Datacenter editions
- ■ **Windows Server 2003 R2 SP2**   32-bit and 64-bit
- ▲ **Windows Server 2003 SP2**   32-bit and 64-bit

The following operating systems are supported to run the VMM library role in a failover cluster configuration:

- ▼ Windows Server 2008 with or without Hyper-V 64-bit—Standard, Enterprise, Datacenter editions

Hardware	Minimum	Recommended
Processor	Pentium 4, 2.8GHz	Dual-core 3.2GHz or greater 64-bit
Memory	2GB	4GB
Hard disk space	Varies based on the number of ISO files and templates you plan on storing	Varies based on the number of ISO files and templates you plan on storing. We recommend you have SAN storage on the same SAN as your host machines to take advantages of SAN copies.
Network	One Gigabit Ethernet or better network card	One or more Gigabit Ethernet or better network card(s)

Table 5-5.   Library Server System Requirements

- Windows Server 2008 without Hyper-V 32-bit—Standard, Enterprise, Datacenter editions
- ▲ Windows Server 2008—Core—Standard, Enterprise, Datacenter editions

If you are installing the library role on a supported Windows Server 2003 server, the Windows Remote Management components will need to be downloaded and installed from the Microsoft website at http://go.microsoft.com/fwlink/?LinkId=84599.

Hardware Requirements

Since the files that you are going to be storing in the library are quite large, the main components that are going to be taxed during a typical day in the life of a library server are the network connections and disk. Currently, there isn't a cut-and-dried algorithm available to determine the scale of the Web Portal, but Microsoft has provided some recommended guidelines for hardware, which are listed in Table 5-5.

SELF-SERVICE WEB PORTAL SERVER

The VMM Self-Service Web Portal is used to allow users to create and manage their own virtual machines. You're probably saying to yourself that it doesn't seem like a good idea to let your users have access to your host systems. When we first heard about this, we thought the same thing, but Microsoft also thought of this when they designed this feature.

To help, secure, and limit the functionality of created users, Microsoft has implemented role-based access to the web portal. A role-based group can be created so that an administrator can limit which host groups and what actions a user can perform on their virtual machines. To help get a handle on subscription of host resources when a user creates a virtual machine, that machine is given a quota point value, and the virtual machine is created on the most available host. Once a user or group reaches the number of points they are assigned, they can no longer create virtual machines. This functionality is very valuable with development groups.

We've found that development teams tend to rebuild their test machines regularly during the initial testing phases, and that can take up a significant amount of system admin resources. Using the Self-Service Portal, you can allow the development team to have their own host servers and be able to manage their own rebuilds.

One of the most commonly referenced virtualization scenarios is testing newly developed applications on virtual infrastructure. In test and development environments, IT professionals are constantly provisioning and tearing down virtual machines. And while virtualization does simplify this task, IT administrators typically still play a role.

Provisioning a new virtual machine using the SCVMM Self-Service Web portal is a simple process consisting of several straightforward steps. After opening the SCVMM Self-Service Web portal, users choose from a prescribed list of virtual machine templates and initiate the setup process.

The self-service provisioning process is limited because many functions are automated by SCVMM, according to the self-service policy set by the administrator for the individual user or user group.

After the new virtual machine is created, SCVMM automatically runs the Intelligent Placement process and places the new virtual machine on the appropriate physical server host.

Software Prerequisites

The following operating systems are supported to run the VMM Self-Service Web Portal server role:

- ▼ Windows Server 2008 with or without Hyper-V 64-bit—Standard, Enterprise, Datacenter editions
- ■ Windows Server 2008 without Hyper-V 32-bit—Standard, Enterprise, Datacenter editions
- ■ Windows Web Server 2008
- ■ Windows Server 2003 R2 SP2—32-bit and 64-bit
- ▲ Windows Server 2003 SP2—32-bit and 64-bit

Once you have a supported operating system installed on a server, the following software needs to be installed prior to installing the VMM Self-Service Web Portal:

▼ Server 2003

■ Windows Server IIS 6/0 components

■ PowerShell 1.0

■ .NET Framework 2.0

▲ Server 2008 with Web Server Role

■ IIS 6 Metabase Compatibility

■ IIS 6 WMI Compatibility

■ Static Content

■ Default Document

■ Directory Browsing

■ HTTP Errors

■ ASP.NET

■ .NET Extensibility

■ ISAPI Extensions

■ ISAPI Filters

■ Request Filtering

Hardware Requirements

The hardware that is required for the Web Portal server is determined by the number of concurrent users. Currently, there isn't a cut-and-dried algorithm available to determine scale of the web portal, but Microsoft has provided some recommended guidelines for hardware. Table 5-6 lists hardware requirements.

Hardware	Up to 10 Concurrent Users	More Than 10 Concurrent Users
Processor	Pentium 4, 2.8GHz	Dual-core 3.2GHz or greater 64-bit
Memory	2GB	8GB
Hard disk space	20GB	40GB

Table 5-6.   Self-Service Web Server Portal Prerequisites

ADMINISTRATOR CONSOLE

The Administrator Console can be installed on the VMM server or on another system that is used for administration. The Administrator Console provides administrators with a full suite of virtual machine management functions. This graphical user interface (GUI) helps administrators easily manage state transitions such as starting, stopping, and pausing virtual machines simply by clicking on the virtual machine and then on the action to perform.

Administrators can also save virtual machine setups as templates and then clone those machines elsewhere. In addition, the Administrator Console works seamlessly with Operations Manager 2007 to provide insight into both the physical and virtual environment. For example, with the ability to map the relationship of virtual and physical assets, IT administrators can more effectively plan hardware maintenance. And since the SCVMM Administrator Console is built on the Operations Manager user interface, administrators can quickly and easily become proficient at managing their virtual machines.

Hardware Requirements

Table 5-7 lists the hardware requirements for machines that will house the administrator console. As with other SCVMM components, the requirements vary slightly depending on whether fewer than 150 hosts are managed or more than 150 hosts are managed.

Software Requirements

The following software requirements must be in place prior to installing the VMM Administrator Console:

▼ Windows Server 2008 with or without Hyper-V 32-bit or 64-bit—Standard, Enterprise, Datacenter Full installation (core installations are not supported for the Administrator Console since there is not a GUI for the Administrator Console to run in)

■ Window Server 2003 32-bit or 64-bit with Service Pack 2—Standard, Enterprise, and Datacenter

■ Windows Vista 32-bit or 64-bit with Service Pack 1

▲ Windows XP Professional 32-bit or 64-bit with Service Pack 3

Hardware	Up to 150 Hosts	More than 150 Hosts
Processor	Pentium 4, 1GHz or better	Pentium 4, 2GHz or better
Memory	1GB	2GB
Hard disk space	2GB	4GB

Table 5-7. Administrator Console Hardware Requirements

VIRTUAL MACHINE

It would be a lovely thing to be able to just install SCVMM, point the server to some hosts, and everything would just work. Unfortunately, there isn't a product on the market that does that for us today. In order to manage your host systems, SCVMM needs to install a client on that host to be able to collect data and run actions. At this time there are a select number of supported virtualization environments that can be managed via SCVMM, and each of those platforms has a set of prerequisites that need to be installed.

Virtual Server 2005

To manage Microsoft Virtual Server 2005 with SCVMM, Virtual Server 2005 R2 with SP1 32-bit or 64-bit must be installed on one of the following operating systems:

▼   Windows Server 2003 with SP2 or later (32-bit or 64-bit)

▲   Windows Server 2003 R2 with SP2 or later (32-bit or 64-bit)

The Windows Remote Management software must also be installed for the SCVMM client to function properly.

Windows Server 2008

More than likely, most of the host systems that you are going to manage with SCVMM are going to be running Windows Server 2008. To manage a Windows Server 2008 system, the following requirements need to be met:

■   Windows Server 2008—Standard, Enterprise, or Datacenter 64-bit with the Hyper-V role enabled

Non-Windows Systems

Managing ESX Server and Hyper-V SCVMM provides a centralized management platform for enterprise virtualization of both Microsoft virtualization products as well as VMware virtualization products. Many organizations are running both virtualization platforms, but before SCVMM 2008, they needed to manage each different product using separate and distinct management tools. SCVMM 2008 provides virtualization management in a single tool.

With SCVMM, you can manage Microsoft's Virtual Server 2005 R2 and Hyper-V virtualization products as well as VMware's ESX Server via VirtualCenter Server. For example, SCVMM enables you to use features like VMware's VMotion technology to transfer VMs between different ESX Servers with no downtime, HA and DRS features, resource pools, and really all the features of vCenter. Using SCVMM 2008 to manage your VMware hosts also gives you the ability to use PRO tips, intelligent placement, and PowerShell to manage your VMware hosts.

Likewise, SCVMM allows you to take advantage of Microsoft's Quick Migration to quickly move VM between Microsoft Hyper-V hosts. VMware's VirtualCenter Server is required to manage VMware ESX servers using SCVMM.

As of the writing of this book, SCVMM only supports the management of VMware as a non-Microsoft host. The following versions of VMware are supported:

▼ VMware ESX 3.5 Update2

■ VMware ESX 3.02

▲ VMware ESX 3i

In order to manage the VMware hosts, SCVMM installs the SCVMM client on a VMware VirtualCenter server and then runs VirtualCenter. One of the following versions of VMware VirtualCenter must be implemented in order to manage ESX systems:

▼ VirtualCenter 2.5

▲ VirtualCenter 2.0.1

INSTALLING SYSTEM CENTER VIRTUAL MACHINE MANAGER 2008

Now that you have a plan for how many servers you need, what the size of those servers will be, and where you are going to place those servers, let's get into the mud and start doing the installation.

To start the installation of VMM, place the System Center Virtual Machine Manager media in the server's CD/DVD drive, or connect to the media via the network and run setup.exe.

VMM Configuration Analyzer

The VMM Configuration Analyzer is a tool that is used to verify your SCVMM configuration. This should be run on the system that you are planning for SCVMM 2008 or on a system that already has SCVMM 2008 loaded.

The VMMCA is a diagnostic tool you can use to evaluate important configuration settings for computers that either are serving or might serve VMM roles or other VMM functions. The VMMCA examines the hardware and software configurations of the computers you specify, checks them against a set of predefined rules, and then provides you with error messages and warnings for any configurations that are not optimal for the VMM role or other VMM function that you have specified for the computer.

Some notes about the VMMCA:

▼ The VMMCA must be installed and run on the computer that will be the VMM 2008 server.

■ You should use this version of the VMMCA with VMM 2008 only. To download the VMMCA for VMM 2007, go to http://go.microsoft.com/fwlink/ ?LinkID=132136.

■ Before you install the VMM, the VMMCA can be used to evaluate the configuration of computers serving the following roles:

    ■ VMM server

    ■ VMM Administrator Console

    ■ VMM Self-Service Portal

▲ Once the VMM has been installed, VMMCA can be used to evaluate the configuration of computers that you are currently using and/or considering using for the aforementioned roles. Additionally, VMMCA can be used to check machines that might perform any of the following functions:

    ■ Windows Server–based host

    ■ VMware VirtualCenter Server

    ■ P2V source computer

    ■ Operations Manager Agent

Prerequisite for VMM Configuration Analyzer

The Virtual Machine Manager Configuration Analyzer has a prerequisite that must be installed first: the Microsoft Baseline Configuration Analyzer. This is mentioned on the download page for the Analyzer package, and a link is provided for the download.

The Microsoft Baseline Configuration Analyzer can be found at http://go.microsoft .com/fwlink/?LinkID=97952.

Once the analyzer is installed, it can be used to scan computers to verify whether they are suitable to function as a VMM server, run the VMM Administrator console, function as a Self-Service Portal, or be a managed host.

Other prerequisites include:

▼ **OS**   Windows Server 2008 Datacenter or Windows Server 2008 Enterprise

▲ **Updates**   KB956589 or KB95671 and BITS update KB956774

From the setup screen, in the Prepare section, choose the VMM Configuration Analyzer. This will take you to a Microsoft website where you can download the MSCA-Setup64.MSI file.

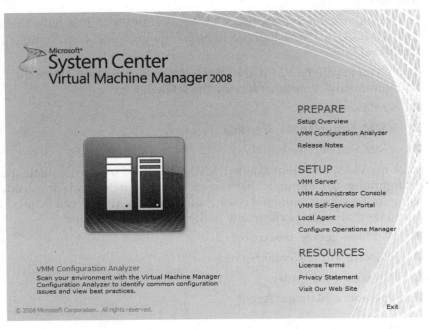

Install the Microsoft Baseline Configuration Analyzer

Run the MSCASetup64.MSI file that you just downloaded. Click Next.

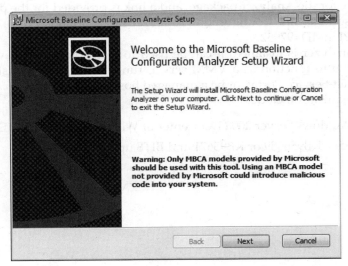

Read and then accept the license agreement and click Next.

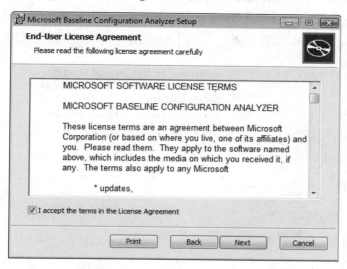

Choose the path that you want to install to and choose Next.

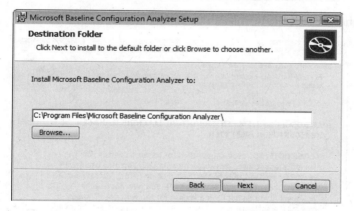

Click Install. Once all the files have finished copying, click Finish.

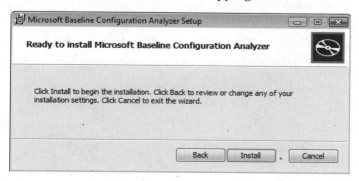

Installing VMM Configuration Analyzer

Run the VMMCA.MSI file. Click Next.

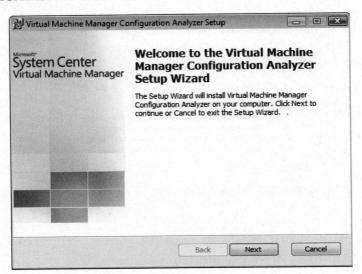

Read and then accept the license terms and click Next.

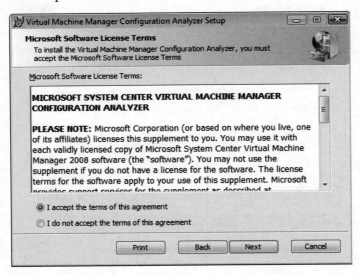

Choose your installation path and click Next.

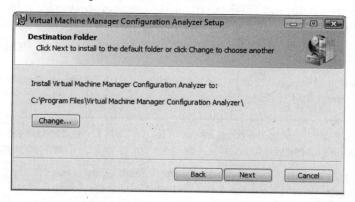

If you're ready to install, click the Install button. Once the files have been copied and installed, click Finish.

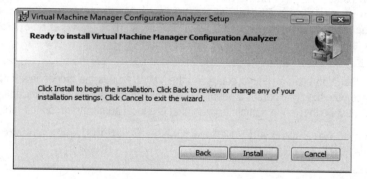

Running VMMCA

There are two ways you can elect to use VMMCA, and it depends on whether you've already installed SCVMM, or whether you are going to use VMMCA without having installed SCVMM. In this section we'll take you through the steps of running VMMCA with either option.

Using Without Installing VMM   To use VMMCA before installing VMM, follow these steps.

1. Click Start | All Programs | Virtual Machine Manager Configuration Analyzer, and then click Configuration Analyzer. On a computer that is not yet a VMM server, when you open the VMMCA, by default, the following VMM roles are selected with the name of the local computer prepopulated for all VMM roles:

   ■ VMM server

   ■ VMM Administrator Console

   ■ VMM Self-Service Portal

2. In the VMM Roles and Computer Names area, specify the VMM roles you want to evaluate, and enter the names of the computers you want to scan by doing one of the following:

    ■   To scan the local computer for all VMM roles, do not change the default settings.

    ■   To scan the local computer for only some VMM roles, clear the check box for each VMM role that you do not want to scan the local computer for.

NOTE   You cannot change the computer name for the VMM server because the VMMCA must be installed on the VMM server. You can clear its check box to exclude it from the scan.

When you scan the local computer, the VMMCA uses the credentials that you logged on with, which must be those of a local administrator. You cannot provide different credentials for scanning the local computer. To scan a remote computer for either the VMM Administrator Console or VMM Self-Service Portal role, enter the name of the remote computer and, if necessary, provide different credentials in the Credentials area. You can scan different computers for the VMM Administrator Console role and the VMM Self-Service Portal role at the same time.

NOTE   When you scan a remote computer, the VMMCA uses the credentials that you logged on with, unless you specify different credentials in the Credentials area. The credentials for a remote computer must be those of a domain account that is a local administrator on the remote computer.

3. After you have specified all VMM roles or functions, and associated computer names, click Scan.

NOTE   If you are scanning remote computers, the VMMCA must authenticate the credentials on all remote computers before it can begin scanning. This might take several minutes.

Using after Installing VMMCA   If you're installing VMMCA after installing VMM, follow these steps.

1. Click Start | All Programs | Virtual Machine Manager Configuration Analyzer, and then click Configuration Analyzer. On a computer that is already a VMM server, when you open the VMMCA, the following VMM roles are selected with the name of the local computer prepopulated for all VMM roles:

    ■   VMM server

    ■   VMM Administrator Console

    ■   VMM Self-Service Portal

    Additionally, the following VMM functions are also available:

    ■   Windows Server-based host

    ■   VMware VirtualCenter server

- P2V source computer
- Operations Manager Agent

2. In the VMM Roles and Computer Names area, specify the VMM roles and functions that you want to evaluate and enter the names of the computers you want to scan by doing one of the following:

   - To scan the local computer for all VMM roles, do not change the default settings.

   - To scan the local computer for only some VMM roles, clear the check box for each VMM role for which you do not want to scan the local computer.

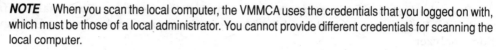

NOTE   When you scan the local computer, the VMMCA uses the credentials that you logged on with, which must be those of a local administrator. You cannot provide different credentials for scanning the local computer.

When you scan the local VMM server and the VMM database is installed on a remote SQL Server instance, the name of the remote computer is prepopulated and it is also scanned. The credentials for scanning a remote VMM database computer must be those of a member of the sysadmin server role on that computer and usually are the same account that you used to install VMM. Unless you specify different credentials, the VMMCA uses the credentials that you logged on with. To specify different credentials, click Credentials, and then in the Remote Database Administrator Credentials dialog box, enter the appropriate credentials.

You cannot change the computer name for the VMM server or the VMM database server. You can clear the VMM Server check box to exclude it and the VMM database server from the scan.

- To scan a remote computer for either the VMM Administrator Console or VMM Self-Service Portal role, enter the name of the remote computer and, if necessary, provide different credentials in the Credentials area. You can scan different computers for the VMM Administrator Console role and the VMM Self-Service Portal role at the same time.

NOTE   When you scan a remote computer, the VMMCA uses the credentials that you logged on with, unless you specify different credentials in the Credentials area. The credentials for a remote computer must be those of a domain account that is a local administrator on the remote computer.

- To scan the configuration of one or more computers that either are serving or might serve a specific VMM function, do the following:

   a. Select the Other Computers check box, and then, in the Other Computers list, click a VMM function.

   b. Type the name of a computer that you want to scan, and then click Add. Repeat this step until all the computers that you want to scan are included in the list.

NOTE You can scan computers for only one VMM function at a time, but you can scan multiple computers for the same VMM function.

Before you can scan a computer for the VMware VirtualCenter server function, you must first add a VMware VirtualCenter server to VMM.

3. After you have specified all VMM roles or functions, and associated computer names, click Scan.

NOTE If you are scanning remote computers, the VMMCA must authenticate the credentials on all remote computers before it can begin scanning. This might take several minutes.

Once the installation is complete, you can start the Configuration Analyzer from Start | All Programs | Virtual Machine Manager Configuration Analyzer | Configuration Analyzer.

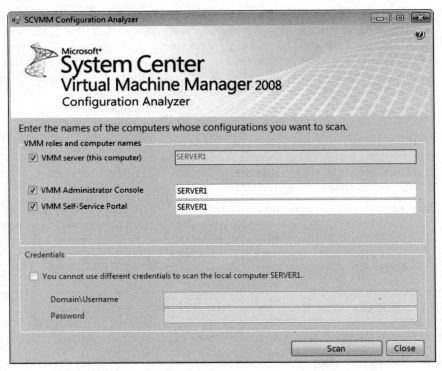

You cannot change the VMM server name because VMMCA needs to be run on the server that will be the eventual SCVMM server. You can, however, change the server names for systems that could possibly run the VMM Administrator Console and or the VMM Self-Service Portal.

INSTALLATION

Installation is a pretty straightforward affair. But before you install SCVMM, keep these issues in mind:

▼   Install the latest Microsoft Quick Fix Engineering (QFE) updates for Hyper-V and clustering through Windows Server Update Services.

■   Make sure that your shared storage solution is compliant with both Windows Server 2008 and Hyper-V clustering. Some solutions may be Windows Server 2008–compliant but not support Hyper-V clustering. You can check this by confirming with your storage vendor to find out whether updates to existing firmware and drivers are necessary.

■   Use the Node and Disk Majority option for the cluster witness model (this is also called the *quorum* in previous Windows Server versions) in most single-site cluster deployments. Check with your storage vendor for the optimal selection.

■   Use Server Core deployments as often as possible for host servers and VMs. Not only do they provide administrative benefits, but VMs using Server Core installations can also fail over much more quickly than VMs using similarly configured full installations with a GUI. Additionally, because Server Core installations require less memory and fewer hard disk resources than full installations, the same host space can support additional VMs.

■   For hard disks, provision one or more discrete logical units (LUNs) to each VM to enable individualized VM failover. Also, use highly available mount points for implementing more than 21 drive letters (LUNs) within a cluster, and use fixed virtual hard disks for optimal flexibility and best performance.

▲   For scalable solutions, add a single dedicated Gigabit Ethernet NIC port for every four VMs, depending on individual VM network I/O requirements. These guest network NIC ports are in addition to the other required ports recommended for Hyper-V parent partition accessibility, cluster heartbeats, and iSCSI connectivity (if required).

Once all prerequisites are configured for the scenario that you've chosen, insert the Systems Center Virtual Machine Manager 2008 disk into your SCVMM server.

From the initial setup screen you can verify your configuration or start setup. Since you've already run the VMM Configuration Analyzer in the last section, click on VMM Server under the Setup section to start the installation wizard.

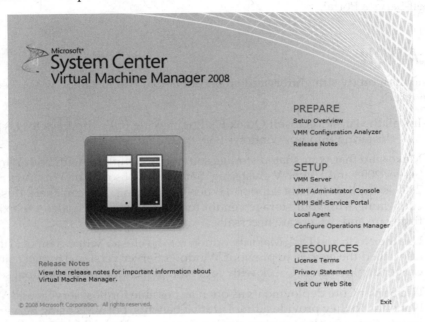

Read and then accept the license agreement and click Next.

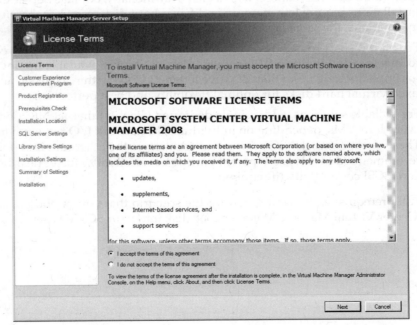

Choose whether you would like to participate in the Customer Experience Improvement program. The Customer Experience Improvement program collects non-identifiable anonymous information about your configurations and sends that information back to Microsoft for analysis. Click Next.

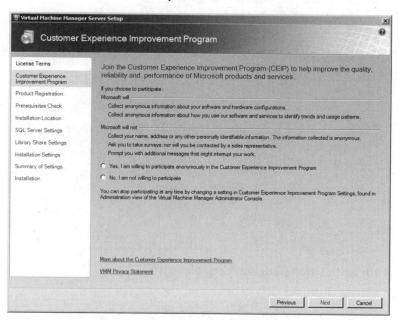

Enter your company information and click Next.

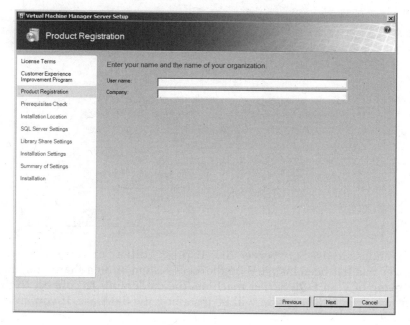

SCVMM will scan your system to verify that your prerequisites are in place. Click Next.

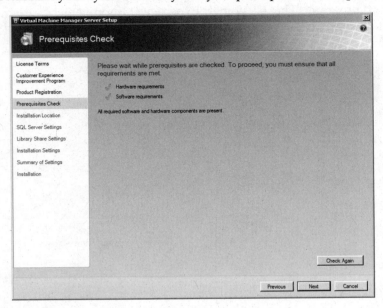

Choose your installation path and click Next.

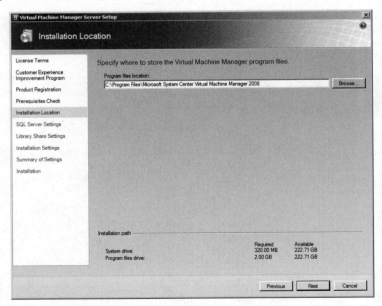

You can choose to use SQL Server 2005 Express Edition, or you can use an instance of SQL Server that has been installed on the local system or on a shared database server. Enter the name of your SQL Server machine, the credentials to connect to that server, and the instance name where you will be installing the database. If you are rebuilding the VMM component, choose the instance where the VMM database resided and click Next, or choose the server, the instance, and then choose to create a new database and Click Next.

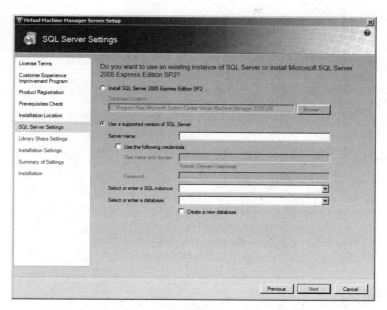

When you install the VMM components, a default library is created. Additional library shares can be created after the install, but if you are going to have only one library, make sure that you plan accordingly and have your library storage configured prior to installation, since you will not be able to change the default library share.

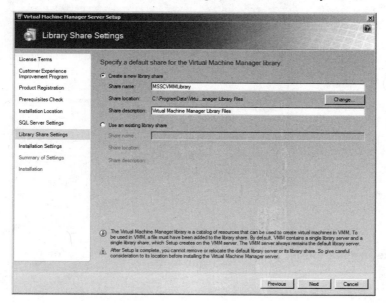

Enter the port numbers that you planned in the design section and set the VMM Service account. Click Next.

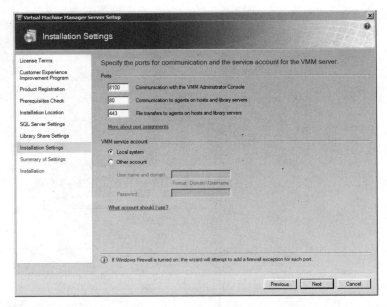

Review your settings to verify with your plan. Click Install.

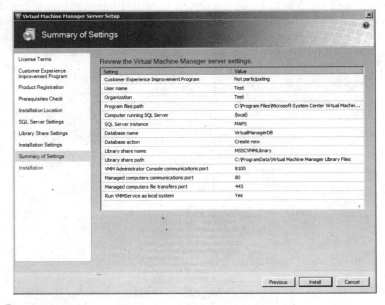

Once the installation is complete, you can choose to check for the latest update. Click Close.

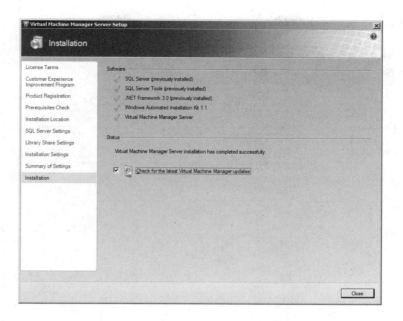

Installing the Administrator Console

By default, when you install SCVMM, the Administrator Console is not installed. To install the Administrator Console, start the setup of SCVMM and choose VMM Administrator Console.

Read and then accept the license agreement and click Next.

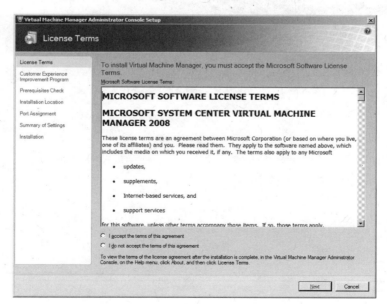

Click Next.

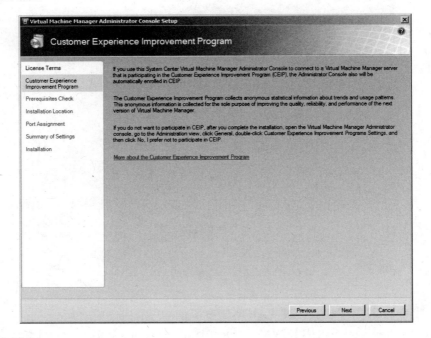

Click Next.

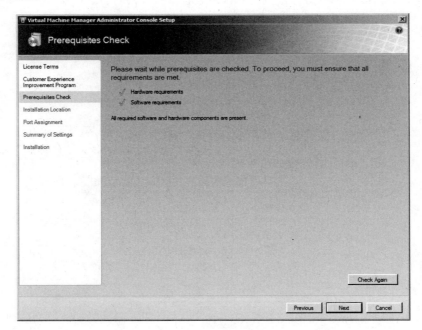

Enter the installation path for the VMM Administrator Console and click Next.

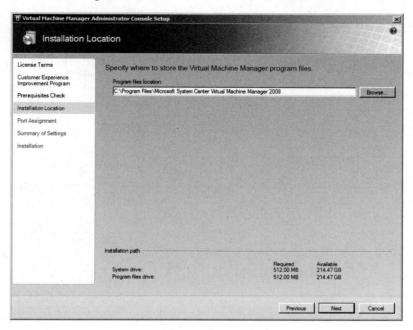

Enter the port number that you set the VMM server to conduct communications on for the VMM Administrator Console and click Next.

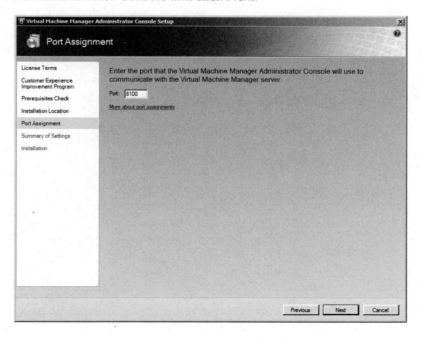

Verify your configuration and click Install.

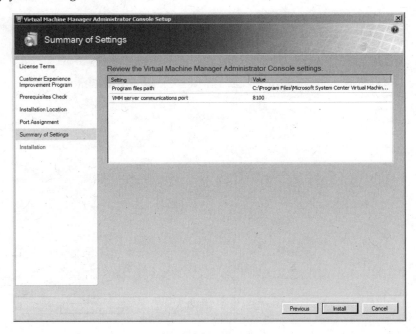

Choose whether to look for updates, create a shortcut, or open the Administrator Console, and click Close.

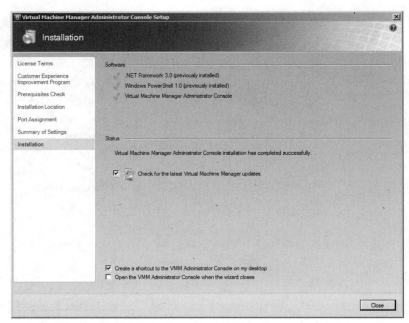

When you first open the SCVMM Administrator Console, you will be asked to enter the name of the server that you want to connect to and the port number on which to communicate. Since we've installed the Administrator on the VMM server, the VMM server name will be pre-populated.

Click Connect.

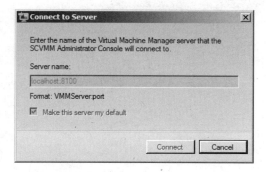

Installing the Self-Service Portal

To install the Self-Service Portal, click on the VMM Self-Service Portal link under the Setup heading on the installation pop-up.

Read and accept the license agreement and click Next.

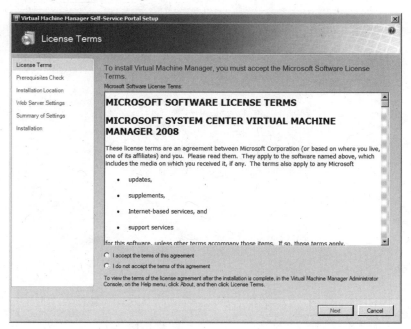

The Self-Service Portal installer will run a prerequisite check to verify your hardware and software configuration. If your server doesn't pass, you will need to remediate your configuration issues and recheck your server. Click Next.

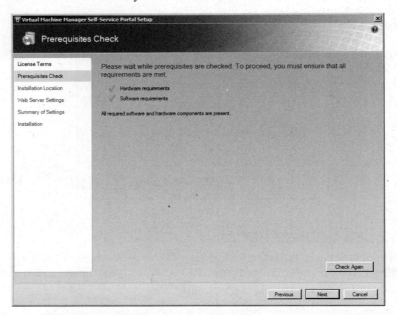

Enter your installation path and click Next.

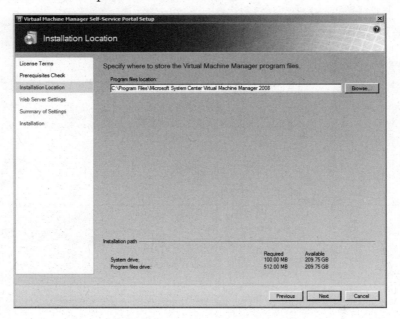

Enter the name of the server that houses the Virtual Machine Manager Service and the port that was configured for server communications. By default VMM communicates on TCP port 8100. By default the Self-Service Portal uses TCP port 80 for the web server. If port 80 is being used, you will either have to set up a host header or use a different port. Click Next.

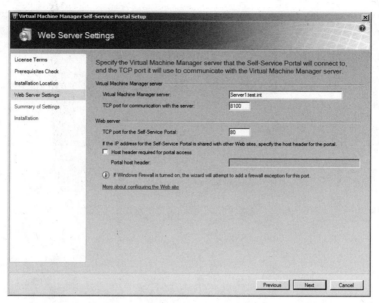

Review your settings and go back and make any changes that may be needed. Click Install to start the installation of the Self-Service Web Portal.

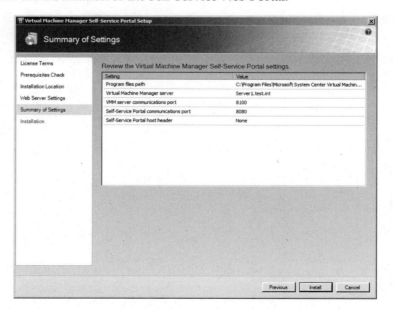

The installation of the Self-Service Portal is now complete. Choose to look for the latest VMM updates and click Close. When you install the Self-Service Web Portal, it installs in a non-secure model. We recommend that you enable SSL on the web server on which you installed the Self-Service portal to secure the communications between your clients and the server.

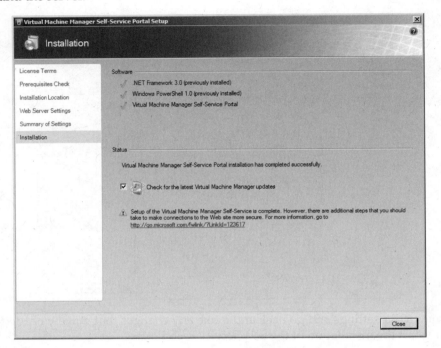

In this chapter we covered the steps necessary to install SCVMM. In the next chapter, we'll move on to its configuration.

CHAPTER 6

Configuring Systems Center Virtual Machine Manager 2008

I n the previous chapter, we talked about SCVMM and went through the steps to install it. Now it's time to configure it for the management of your virtual machines. We'll look at basic configuration steps, as well as connecting SCVMM with VMware, if you have a mixed environment. This chapter covers SCVMM 2008, as opposed to SCVMM 2007, which was limited to managing Virtual Server only. So to avoid any confusion, please note that all references to SCVMM are for SCVMM 2008.

CONFIGURING SCVMM

Now that you have SCVMM and the related components installed, let's configure your hosts, the library, and users. The first component we are going to configure is the SCOM integration for Performance and Resource Optimization (PRO) and for reporting. Having this configured first will help as you add hosts to your SCVMM environment by giving intelligent placement information as you add guests to your system.

If you don't have SCOM implemented in your environment, either because you have other tools or just haven't gotten around to it yet, we recommend that you work with your company to implement SCOM, at least for your Hyper-V, SCVMM, and guest system implementations. SCOM is by no means an absolute requirement for the installation, configuration, and operation of a Hyper-V and SCVMM environment. However, as you add more virtual machines, it will be extremely beneficial to be able to take advantage of the monitoring capabilities of SCOM to troubleshoot any issues as well as to help with capacity planning.

As IT environments grow more diverse and complex across desktops, datacenters, physical and virtual deployments, and heterogeneous infrastructures spanning Windows and non-Windows environments, Microsoft has worked closely with customers to deliver an enterprise strategy for an integrated management solution.

System Center Operations Manager 2007 R2 builds on the existing Operations Manager 2007 technology and capabilities, which are designed to help extend the value of the Microsoft System Center investments. SCOM provides end-to-end IT system–monitoring capability that incorporates industry standards and proven open source technologies, including Web Services for Management (WS-Management) and OpenPegasus, extending the capabilities across both physical and virtualized Windows and non-Windows operating systems and applications.

Microsoft delivers the core foundational cross-platform support out of the box for HP-UX, Red Hat Enterprise Linux, Sun Solaris, and SUSE Linux Enterprise Server operating systems so that partners can focus on adding their deep domain expertise in the form of management packs.

Companies such as Novell Inc., Quest Software Inc., and Xandros Inc. have delivered monitoring abilities for applications made by organizations such as The Apache Software Foundation, MySQL AB, and Oracle.

System Center Virtual Machine Manager 2008 tightly integrates with Operations Manager 2007 to deliver a new feature called Performance and Resource Optimization (PRO). Using deep knowledge of the IT environment including operating systems, applications, and hardware, Operations Manager identifies opportunities for more efficient physical and virtual resource allocation and generates "PRO tips" within the Virtual Machine Manager console. Administrators can implement these PRO tips and dynamically optimize their datacenter based upon predefined policies and the real-time, changing demands of users. When used in conjunction with the broad System Center management suite, System Center Virtual Machine Manager 2008 enables IT departments to manage both their virtualized and physical servers and applications across their desktops and datacenters with a single set of consistent, compatible tools.

The SCVMM 2008 Console

The SCVMM Console is built on the familiar MMC 3.0 graphical user interface (GUI). The Administrator Console provides administrators with a full suite of virtual machine management functions. This graphical user interface helps administrators easily manage state transitions such as starting, stopping, and pausing virtual machines simply by clicking on the virtual machine and then on the action to perform.

Administrators can also save virtual machine setups as templates and then clone those machines elsewhere. In addition, the Administrator Console works seamlessly with Operations Manager 2007 to provide insight into both the physical and virtual environment. For example, with the ability to map the relationship of virtual and physical assets, IT administrators can more effectively plan hardware maintenance. And since the SCVMM Administrator Console is built on the Operations Manager user interface, administrators can quickly and easily become proficient at managing their virtual machines. The SCVMM Administrator Console is shown in Figure 6-1.

As you can see in Figure 6-1, the SCOM console shares a lot of the same features with Microsoft Office Outlook, including the Navigation pane and navigation buttons. In the upper left of the console, you can select which host or virtual machine you want to manage. Figure 6-1 shows the console set up to manage hosts, but if Virtual Machine were selected, it would show such machines as virtual servers and different cluster types (like VMware or Hyper-V).

Selecting a host or a virtual machine in that pane calls up a more detailed description of the machine or host. This is shown in the large pane in the center of the manager. This pane shows details of your machine or host, including hardware information about the host, the type of virtualization software installed, and so forth. If a virtual machine was chosen, it would show information about that virtual machine and also a live thumbnail, showing what is happening in the machine's virtual world.

Also, as seen in Figure 6-1, the center pane on the left side contains a list of filters that you can use to help sort your hosts and virtual machines. This is especially helpful if you have many hosts or machines and you are looking for a specific device.

The bottom-left pane contains the management selection chooser. This allows you to switch between hosts, virtual machines, library, jobs, and administrative tasks.

The rightmost pane is the Actions pane. This contains several icons that allow you to click to perform such tasks as convert a physical server, add a host, remove a host, and so forth. The tasks will vary depending on whether you are managing a host, virtual machine, library, job, or administrative task.

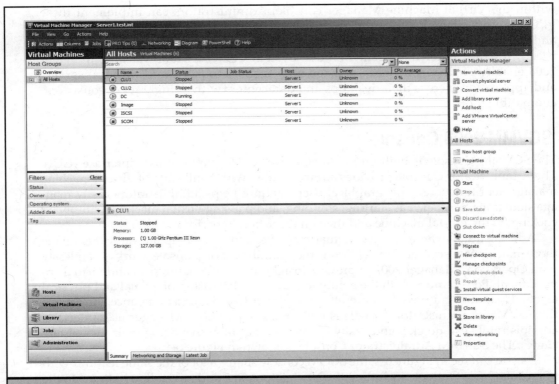

Figure 6-1.   The SCVMM Administrator Console is used to manage your virtualized environment.

Configuring SCOM Integration

In our opinion some of the best features of implementing SCVMM 2008 are enabled when you integrate with Operations Manager 2007. Once you integrate SCVMM with SCOM, the following features will become available:

- ▼ Performance and Resource Optimization (PRO)
- ■ VMM reports
- ■ Diagram view
- ▲ Health monitoring of hosts, guests, and other SCVMM components via SCOM

Additionally, the integration with SCOM provides a number of reports pertaining to virtualization:

- ▼ Virtualization candidates
- ■ Virtual machine allocation

- Virtual machine utilization
- Host utilization
- ▲ Host utilization growth

Since the SCOM integration adds a significant amount of functionality to the SCVMM implementation, we're going to configure this first. We're going to assume that you've already installed and configured SCVMM and SCOM prior to starting this configuration step.

Customers who are already using SCOM can leverage the integration between SCOM and SCVMM to drive consolidation efforts in a powerful way. The host utilization growth report is helpful in determining capacity allocation and to project future resource needs. SCVMM also leverages an SDK connection to SCOM to provide real-time updates to SCOM as VMs are created, migrated, or decommissioned.

There are three major steps that we're going to go through to configure SCOM and SCVMM integration.

- ▼ Configure the VMM Server
- Configure the SCOM Server
- ▲ Configure SCOM in VMM

Configure the VMM Server

There are two steps that need to be done to configure the VMM Server.

1. Install the SCVMM Administrator Console. If your SCOM server and VMM server are on the same physical server and OS instance, hold off on installing the SCVMM Administrator Console.

2. Install the SCOM Operations Console.

Installing the SCOM Operations Console

There are a few software prerequisites that need to be met prior to installing the SCOM Operations Console. On your VMM Server you must have

- ▼ .NET Framework 2.0
- .NET Framework 3.0
- ▲ Windows PowerShell

Log on to your VMM server and install the prerequisite software. Once these components have been installed, you can run SetupOM.exe from the SCOM installation media.

Click the Check Prerequisites link under the Prepare section to bring up the prerequisite viewer.

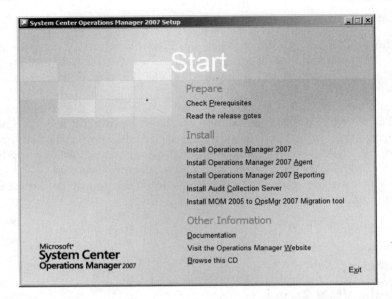

The prerequisite viewer allows you to check for required hardware and software on a server for a particular role or group of roles you would like that server to hold. Choose Console and click Check. If all tests pass, click Close. Otherwise, remediate any errors and rerun the check.

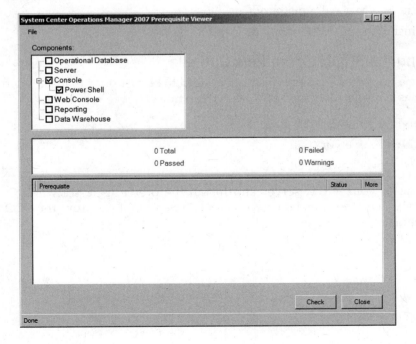

Once all checks have passed, click the Install Operations Manager 2007 link below the Install heading to start the installation of the Operations Manager Administrator Console.

Click Next.

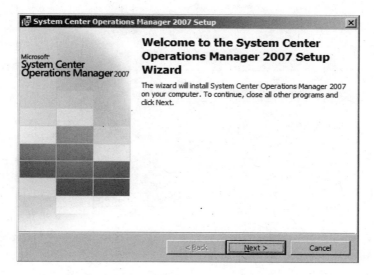

Read the license terms. Choose I Accept the Terms in the License Agreement, and click Next.

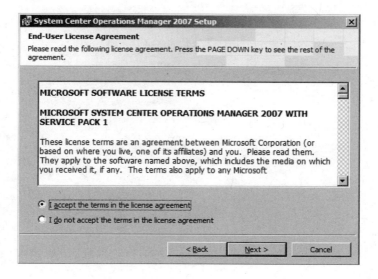

Enter your user, organization, and CD key information and click Next.

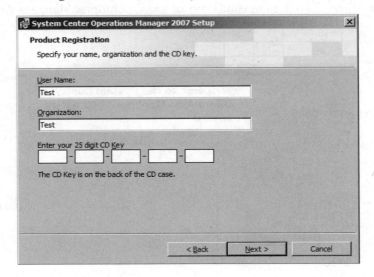

Since you are only installing the Console, you need to deselect Database, Management Server, and Web Console and click Next.

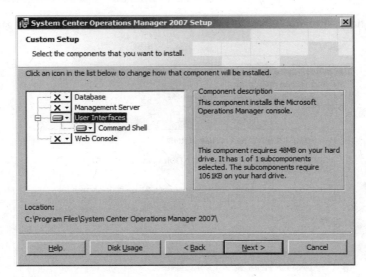

Choose to join the Customer Experience Improvement Program or not and click Next.

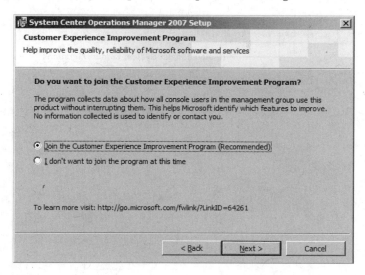

When you are ready to start the installation, click Install. Depending on the hardware configuration of your VMM server, this may take a couple of minutes.

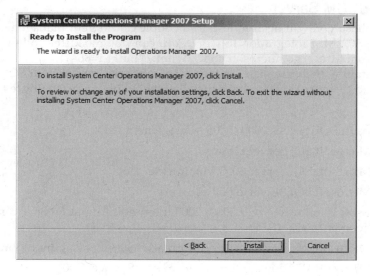

For now, let's choose to not to start the console at this time. Click Finish to end the installation.

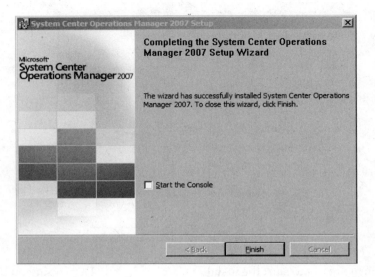

Configure SCOM Server

During this phase you will need to import a couple of different management packs for the SCOM to SCVMM integration to work. You can download the following management packs from http://go.microsoft.com/fwlink/?LinkId=86411.

Before installing the virtualization management packs, you or your SCOM administrator will need to verify that you have installed the following prerequisite management packs:

▼ Microsoft SQL Server 2000/2005 Management Pack

■ Microsoft.SQLServer.Library

■ Microsoft.SQLServer.2005.Monitoring

■ Microsoft.SQLServer.2005.Discovery

▲ Microsoft Windows Server 2000/2003 Internet Information Services Management Pack

■ Microsoft.Windows.InternetInformationServices.CommonLibrary

■ Microsoft.Windows.InternetInformationServices.2003

NOTE If you have installed any of the SCVMM 2008 management packs that were prerelease, make sure that you remove those management packs from your SCOM installation.

Log on to your root management server with a user account that is both a Local Administrator and an SCOM Administrator, and run setup.exe from the SCVMM 2008 installation source.

Click the Configure Operations Manager link under the Setup heading to start the SCOM configuration setup.

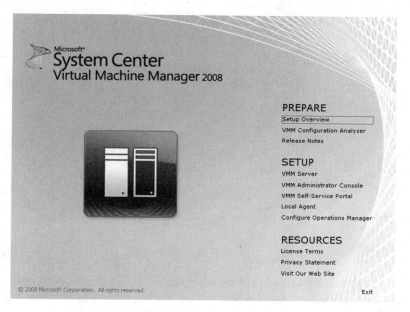

When you run SCOM configuration setup, the installation will import the virtualization and PRO management packs. It will grant the run-as account of the VMM server rights to access Operations Manager, and it will install the VMM Administrator Console to the root management server.

Read the license agreement. Choose I Accept the Terms of This Agreement, and click Next.

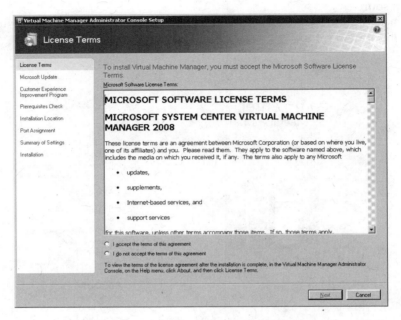

You can choose to have Microsoft Update check for SCVMM updates using automatic updates. You may want to consult with your security team on your patch management policies and then choose to use Microsoft Update or not. Click Next.

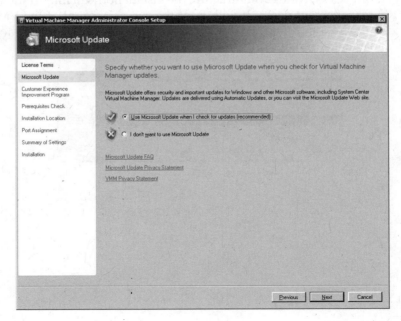

Click Next.

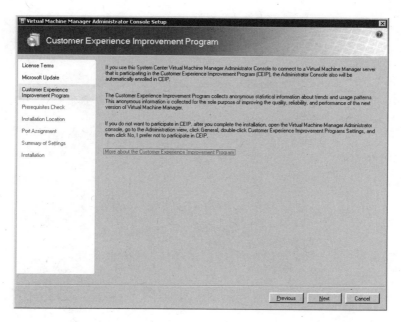

Setup will now check for system hardware and software prerequisites. If your system prerequisites do not pass, remediate those issues and check again. Once all prerequisites have been met, click Next.

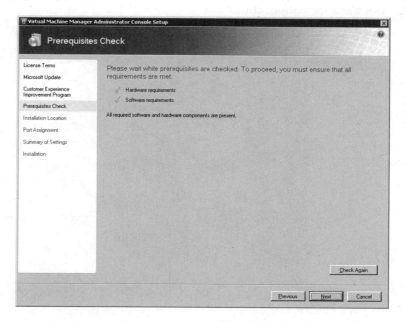

Choose your installation path for the Administrator Console and click Next.

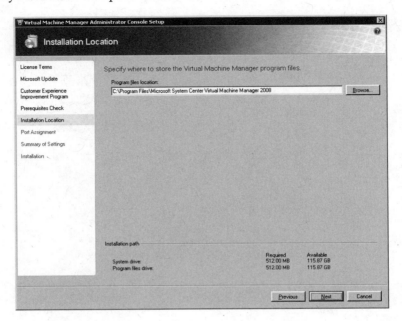

Enter your VMM server name and the port that you chose for Administrator Console communications during your SCVMM setup. The default port 8100 is prepopulated, since that is the default communications port for VMM console communications. Once you've filled out the information, click Next.

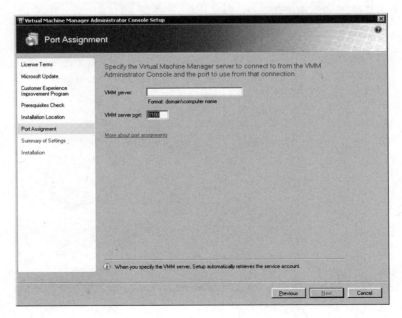

Check your chosen installation parameters. If you need to change any settings, click the Previous button or click Install to install the Administrator Console.

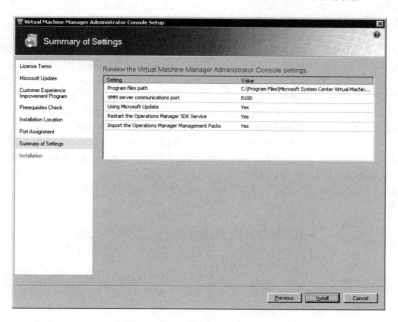

Once the installation is complete, you can choose to check for updates, create a short-cut, and open the VMM Administrator Console. Choose not to open the VMM Administrator Console at this time. Let's move on to updating the management packs.

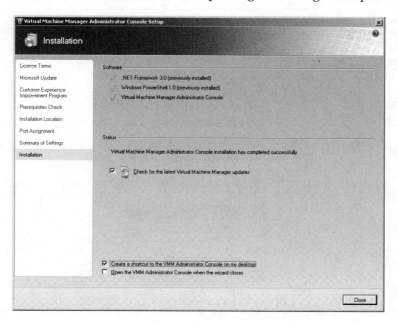

NOTE   By the time this book has been published, the SCVMM management packs for SCOM 2007 will probably have been updated. You can download the newest management packs from http://go.microsoft.com/fwlink/?LinkId=82105.

Once the VMM components have been installed, and before you import the updated management packs, you or your SCOM administrator will need to delete any management packs and dependent management packs with names beginning with "System Center Virtual Machine Manger 2008 PRO."

Once you have updated the management packs, proceed to install the VMM Administrator Console on any other management servers that you have in this management group.

Now, open the VMM console on your SCOM root management server. In order for the integration to work, we need to add the default action account for each of the SCOM management servers into the Administrator role of SCVMM.

When you first open the SCVMM Console, enter your VMM server information and click Connect.

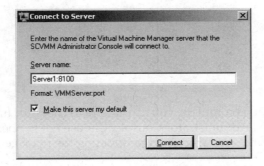

Click the Administration tab in the Navigation pane on the left of the Administrator Console.

Click User Roles in the Administration heading of the Navigation pane.

Right-click on the Administrator profile in the User Roles results pane and choose Properties.

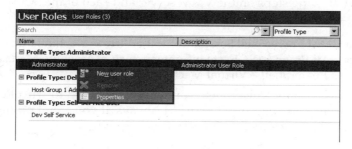

Click the Add Button to bring up the Select Users window.

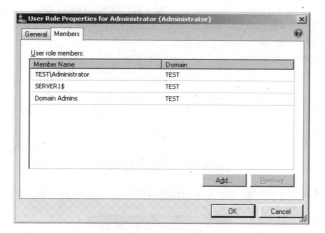

Enter the name of the Operations Manager action accounts and click OK. Then click OK on the User Role Properties window.

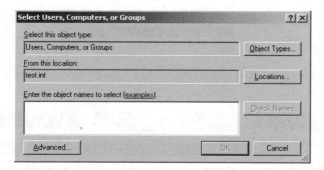

We next need to enable each of the management servers and the VMM server to allow PRO to be able to run scripts remotely on the servers.

Repeat the following steps on the VMM server and each of the SCOM Management servers:

1. Open a CMM PowerShell Session from the Virtual Machine Manager folder in Start | All Programs | System Center | Virtual Machine Manager 2008 | Windows PowerShell – Virtual Machine Manager.

2. When you open the PowerShell, you will be prompted to Trust Remote Signed Scripts from This Snap-In. Choose [A] Always. If you aren't prompted, your PowerShell policy already allows PRO to run scripts.

Configure SCOM in VMM

Now for the final step of configuring the SCOM SCVMM integration, we're going to configure the SCOM information in the VMM Administrator Console.

Open the VMM Administrator Console.

Click the Administration tab in the Navigation tab.

Click System Center under the Administration heading in the Navigation tab.

In the System Center results pane, right-click Operations Manager Server and click Modify.

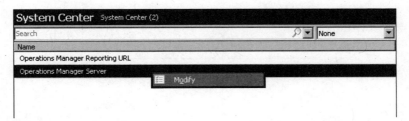

Enter the name of your SCOM Root Management server. This can be either the NET-BIOS name or the FQDN. If your server is in a disjointed name space, you will have to use the FQDN. Click OK. VMM will contact the SCOM server to do final configurations. When the process is complete, the configuration screen will disappear.

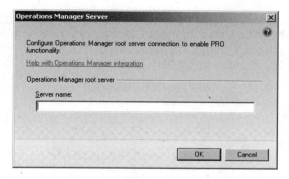

To verify that your installation is working properly, open the SCOM Operations Console.

Click the Monitoring tab on the Navigation tab.

Expand the Virtual Machine Manager 2008 views and click the Diagram View. If the diagram comes up, everything is working. If you get an error that says that the Discovery Failed, then your integration isn't working, and you'll have to go back over your steps to verify your installation and the integration steps.

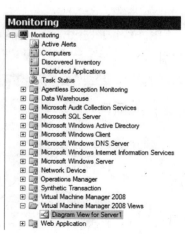

Configuring Reporting

Setting up the reporting integration between SCOM and SCVMM is a little less tricky than setting up the initial SCOM/SCVMM integration. We're going to assume that you've already done the initial SCOM integration steps and have set up SCOM reporting in general for your environment.

The first step to setting up the reporting integration is for you or your SCOM administrator is to import the Systems Center Virtual Machine Manager 2008 Reporting Management Pack. The SCVMM Reporting Management Pack can be downloaded from the SCOM Management Pack catalog at http://go.microsoft.com/fwlink/ ?LinkID=86411.

Once you've downloaded and imported the reporting management pack, you need to add each user that will be using reports to the Operations Manager Reports Operator role. To do this, open the SCOM Operations Console.

Click the Administration tab in the Navigation pane.

Click User Roles under the Administration heading of the Navigation pane.

Right-click on the Operations Manager Report Operators profile in the User Roles results pane and choose Properties.

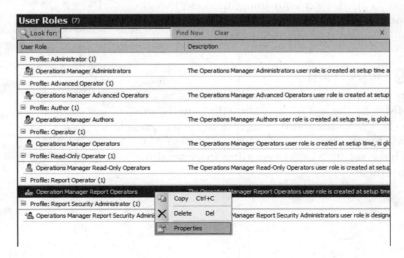

Click the Add button to bring up the Select Users and Groups window.

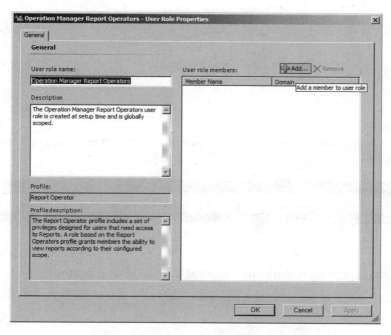

Enter the names or group name for the users that require reporting access. We recommend using groups to help make your user management easier. Click OK, and when you return to the Operations Manager Report Operations – User Role Properties, click OK.

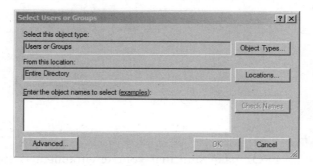

Open the System Center Virtual Machine Manager Administrator Console. Click the Administration tab of the Navigation pane.

Click System Center under the Administration heading of the Navigation pane.

In the Systems Center result pane, right-click on Operation Manager Reporting URL and click Modify.

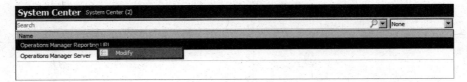

Enable the reporting feature and enter the URL to your reporting server. Click OK.

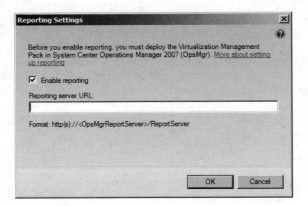

Configuring PRO

Before you configure PRO, make sure that your environment is stable and running smoothly. Also try to clear out any errors that you may have in the Event Viewer on your Hyper-V hosts and your SCVMM servers. This will help the PRO system accurately create PRO tips.

The SCVMM Physical Resource Optimization (PRO) feature provides monitoring and correction of problems for virtual machines managed by SCVMM. PRO leverages the capabilities of Operations Manager to provide management of both the physical virtual server host as well as the virtual machines that are run on that host. If Operations Manager is not installed, SCVMM still provides all its other virtual machine management features, but the extended PRO capabilities will not be available.

PRO Tips

Using PRO, the administrator can set up tips to display when a given operations threshold has been exceeded. PRO tips can consist of either text descriptions that an operator must respond to manually, or they can be scripts that either take action automatically or when the operator interacts with the PRO tip.

SCVMM's PRO tips display the predefined diagnostic message that the administrator has created as the appropriate response for the given operations condition. For instance, the remedial action in the PRO tip could state, "Add another IIS server to the Order Tracker Web farm."

The expanded definition in the Detail View pane at the bottom of the screen could explain that the web traffic has exceeded the expected level, and that adding another web server will increase the available web capacity. In this example, the PRO tip could be implemented as a script that the operator can execute at his or her discretion. The operator can click Dismiss to ignore the error, or click Implement to execute a script that will add an additional web server VM to the Order Tracker Web farm.

To configure PRO, you can choose to configure PRO globally on the top-level host group, or you can configure PRO on a per–host group basis. Depending on your Hyper-V implementation, you may choose to implement PRO at the global level to track critical alerts for all servers, and then implement PRO on certain host groups that will show warnings and critical events. You will also want to make the decision about whether or not you want PRO to be able to implement PRO tips automatically.

PRO is implemented through PRO tips that recommend an action to return a host, virtual machine, or other software or hardware in a virtualized environment, to a healthy state based on monitors in specially designed PRO-enabled management packs for System Center Operations Manager 2007.

There are three types of PRO tips:

▼ **PRO tips for hosts**   PRO tips for hosts can recommend actions, like creating a virtual machine, to return a host to a healthy state. Health is based on resource usage or other performance measures.

■ **PRO tips for virtual machines**   PRO tips for virtual machines can advise action, like a configuration update, to ensure that a virtual machine stays healthy.

▲ **PRO tips for VMM**   PRO tips can specify action for Virtual Machine Manager to resolve issues that affect multiple VMM-managed computers throughout your virtualized infrastructure. For instance, a PRO tip for VMM might recommend action for an overheated blade chassis, or a performance issue with a distributed application.

If you enable PRO for a specific host group or host cluster, enable PRO for each host and virtual machine within them. PRO tips for Virtual Machine Manager can be turned on or off through the VMM Pro settings.

PRO tips can be shown automatically or manually, and you can set the severity level of PRO tips that are shown.

> **NOTE** Not all PRO tips are designed for auto implementation.

These choices can be configured in the properties of individual host groups and host clusters and, for VMM-level PRO tips, in the VMM PRO settings.

When you see a PRO tip, you can review detailed information about the issue that generated the PRO tip—along with the recommended resolution—in the PRO Tips window of the VMM Administrator Console. The window is opened by clicking PRO Tips on the toolbar. This displays active PRO tips for the host groups that the logged-in administrator supervises. When the issue that generated the PRO tip is fixed, the PRO tip goes away.

To manage PRO tips, there are two buttons that appear along with the notification: an Implement button that automatically performs the recommended task; and a Dismiss button that closes the PRO tip and removes it from the display.

The following capabilities are provided through the PRO-enabled management pack included with VMM:

▼ **PRO tips for hosts**   The monitors in VMM recommend a virtual machine migration when CPU or memory usage exceeds the threshold set by one of two PRO monitors. The default threshold for a CPU is 75 percent of capacity on the host, and the default threshold for memory is 90 percent. PRO will migrate the virtual machine that has the highest resource usage on the host to the most suitable host in the same host group or cluster.

▲ **PRO tips for virtual machines**   The PRO monitors in VMM will recommend configuration changes if it is using 90 percent or more of the CPU memory that allocated it.

VMM currently does not include any VMM-level PRO monitors. As you add management packs, there may be VMM-level monitors included.

> **NOTE** Once you establish a performance baseline, you can fine-tune the rules in PRO-enabled management packs to customized PRO to meet the needs of your organization. For instance, once you establish how much of your processor is being used, you can adjust the PRO setting to alert you sooner than at 90 percent.

There are a number of pros and cons when you consider enabling PRO tips. On the plus side, PRO tips allow you to:

▼ Automatically fix problems when they arise.

■ Have your system automatically monitored for poor performance.

- If an alert is tripped, you just need to click one button to implement the changes that will make your system healthy again.

▲ Establish your own baselines for notification.

On the other hand, PRO is not without issues:

▼ You're relying on the VMM to tell you when there's a problem.

- Some people might not like to use the feature, relying on their own "tried and true" troubleshooting measures.

▲ The answer to a problem might be overly cryptic.

PRO Planning

When you plan your PRO implementation, consider these issues:

▼ Which host group and host clusters do you want to participate in PRO? To get the best benefit from PRO-initiated migrations, you should place your hosts and virtual machines based on the needs of your organizational units. Plan groups and clusters to support your organization's needs. Use delegated administration to filter PRO tips so your host group administrators see only the PRO tips that they need to deal with.

- Do you want to automatically let PRO fix problems, or review the tips before they are addressed? What severity level of PRO tips do you want to receive for the host group or cluster—Warning and Critical, or just Critical? Also, what level of severity do you want to be automatically implemented, Warning and Critical, or just Critical?

▲ Do you have any virtual machines that you'd rather exclude from host-level PRO actions? If you have mission-critical workloads and you cannot have any downtime, you can prevent a migration by excluding the virtual machine from host-level PRO actions. If resources are too severely tapped, another virtual machine will be migrated, even if the anchor workload has the highest resource usage on the host.

Let's start with configuring PRO at the global level.

Configure Global PRO settings

Open the SCVMM Administrator Console as an SCVMM administrator user.
   Click the Administration tab on the Navigation pane.

Click General under the Administration heading of the Navigation pane.

Right-click on PRO Settings in the General section of the results pane and choose Modify to bring up the PRO Settings window.

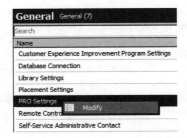

Choose to enable PRO and select the severity level on which you would like to have PRO track. You may also want to enable PRO to automatically implement PRO Tips based on Severity and click OK.

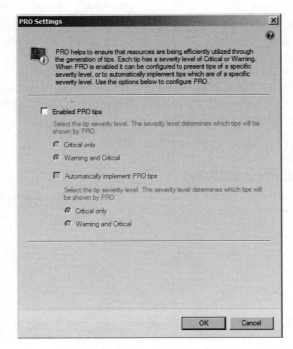

Configure PRO on a Host Group

Open the VMM Administrator Console.

Right-click on All Hosts and choose Properties to bring up the All Hosts Settings window.

Click the PRO tab and enable PRO and the level of severity you would like it to track to. Also establish whether or not you want to have PRO automatically implement PRO tips and at what severity those tips should be implemented. You will also notice that there is a grayed-out box titled Inherit PRO Settings from Parent Host Group. If you have nested host groups, by default they will not inherit the parent host group PRO settings. If you want a child host group to have the same PRO settings, enable this check box. Since this is the top-level host group, that option is not available.

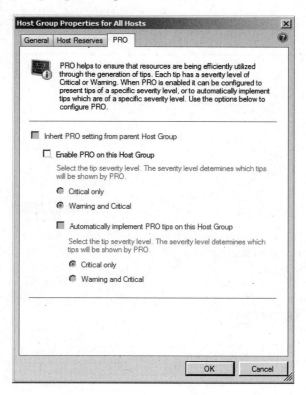

Once you've made your selections, click OK.

When your system has PRO tips available, you can view them from the PRO Tips tab on the top of the toolbar.

Adding Hosts to SCVMM

To add hosts to your SCVMM installation, open the SCVMM Administrator Console.

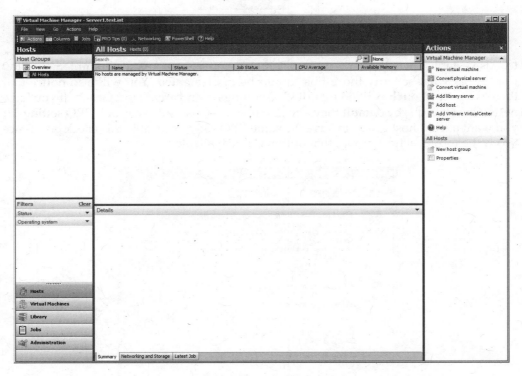

Click the Add Host action in the Actions pane.

Choose the type of host that you would like to manage and the credentials to connect to that server. If the host server you are trying to connect to isn't in a domain that has a two-way trust with the domain that the VMM server is installed in, click to clear the check box. Note that this changes the process slightly, but it's outlined a bit later in the section "Adding a Perimeter Host."

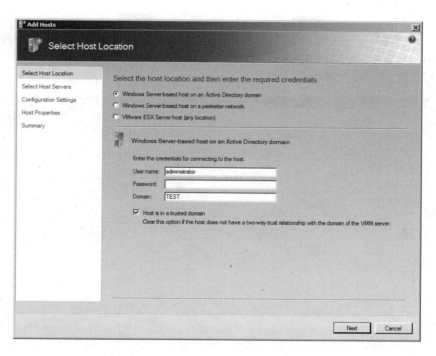

Click Next.

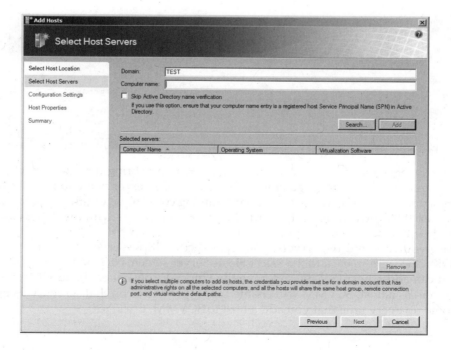

Enter the fully qualified name of the host that you want to be managed in the Computer Name field and click the Add button. If you want to add multiple servers, you can add each server to the Computer Name field and click Add or you can click the Search button to search for servers.

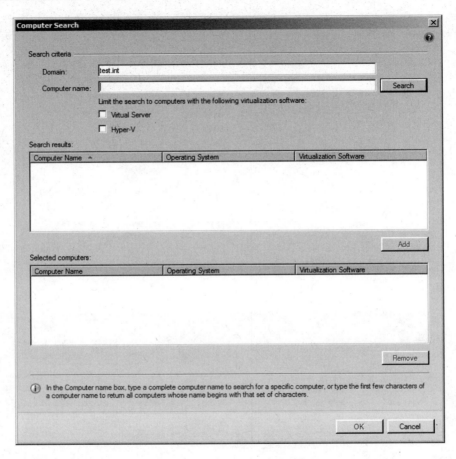

You can leave the search box blank and click Search to bring up a full list of systems in your environment, or you can enter a few letters of a server name to find a group of servers. For instance, if you have a standard naming convention of function and number like virtserv001, you can search by "virt" to find all computers with that letter combination in their name.

Once you've found the servers, you can select multiple servers and click Add and then OK. Once you're back to the Select Hosts Server screen, click Next.

You can add a host that doesn't have the Hyper-V role enabled and when you add that system as a host, SCVMM will enable the Hyper-V role on that server. This pop-up will come up every time that you add a host to SCVMM. Click Yes.

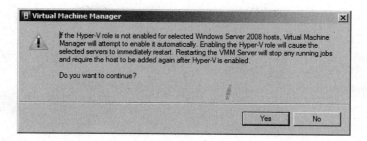

In the following section we will discuss host groups in more detail. If you have already configured host groups, choose the host group you would like your host or hosts to be associated with and click Next. If you are selecting multiple hosts, all the hosts that you select will be installed into the same host group. If you are reassociating a host that is managed by another SCVMM implementation, you can enable the check box that will reassociate that host. Click Next.

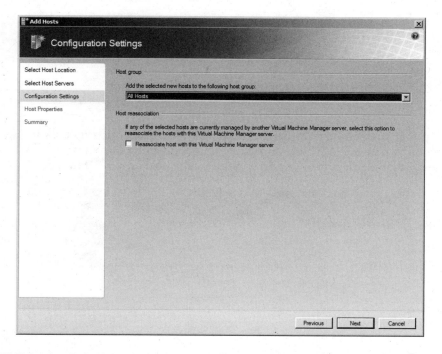

SCVMM uses default paths to store virtual machine files on the host server. When determining the default path for your virtual machines, you'll want to make sure that you don't have a default path that is on the same drive as the operating system. When you specify the default path, the SCVMM client install does not automatically create those folders. You will need to go in prior to adding the host, or after adding the host to

SCVMM, and create the folders that you choose. Enter the default paths that you want and click Next.

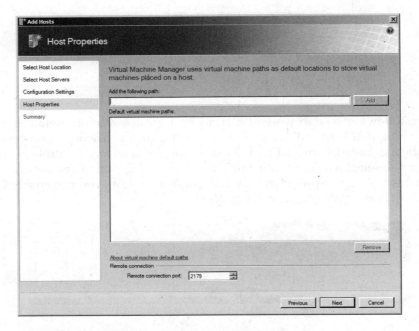

Verify that the settings are correct and click Add Hosts or Previous to alter your configurations. The SCVMM Jobs window will open, and you can track the Add Virtual Machine host job while it installs and configures the host and SCVMM client.

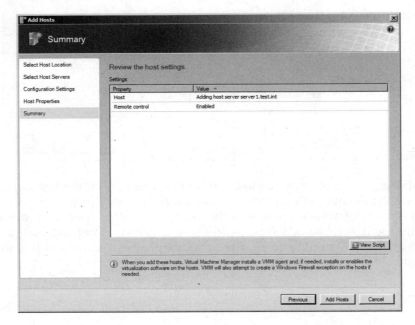

Adding a Perimeter Host

If you are installing a host that is on a perimeter, workgroup, or is an untrusted host, you will need to follow three steps to do that:

1.   Manually install the VMM Agent locally on the computer you want to be a host.
2.   Generate a security file for that host.
3.   Copy the security file to the system that you are running the VMM Administrator Console on.

To install the client on a host:

1.   Log on to the target system and connect to the SCVMM media either by putting the DVD in the server or mapping a network drive.
2.   Choose the location where you would like to install the client bits and click Next.
3.   Enter the port settings that you set for agent communications during the VMM server installation and click Next.
4.   On the Security File Folder page, click the check box This Host Is on a Perimeter Network and do one of the following:

> Enter a certificate thumbprint for a certificate you received from your certification authority.

> Enter an encryption key into the Security File Encryption Key box—making sure that you write this down or make a copy of it so that you can create a security file that will be entered into the VMM Administrator Console.

> Once you've done one of the above options, choose where you would like to store the encrypted security file and click Next.

5.   You can have the client contact the host using either a host name or an IP address. If you don't have DNS set to resolve the host name for that network, you will want to make sure to use IP Address. Click Next.
6.   Click Install to start the installation.
7.   Once the installation is complete, you need to navigate to the location that you chose to install the bits to get the security file. If you chose the default location, the path is %SystemRoot%\Program Files\Microsoft System Center Virtual Machine Manager and the file that you need is SecurityFile.Txt.
8.   Copy the SecurityFile.Txt file to the system that you are using the VMM Administrator Console to add the host with.
9.   Click the Add Hosts button in the Virtual Machine Manager tab in the Actions pane on the right of the console.
10.   Select the Windows Server-Based Host on a Perimeter Network radio button and click Next.
11.   Enter the name of the computer or the IP address of the system that you want to add.

12. Enter the encryption key you used during the agent install in the Encryption Key box and the Confirm box.

13. Click the Browse button to navigate to where you stored the SecurityFile.Txt file and select that file.

14. Click Add, then click Next.

15. Select the host group that you would like the host to be a part of, or if the system was being managed by another VMM, you can reassociate that host with this VMM implementation.

16. Select whether or not you would like to allow remote connections to the virtual machines that will be on the host or hosts you are adding, and set the port where you would like remote connections to take place. The default is port 5900. Then click Next.

17. Review the summary and verify that the settings are correct. Click Add Host to start the add host processes.

Host Groups

To help manage your hosts, you can group hosts together in what is called a *host group*. Host groups come in handy when you are delegating access to users, want to dedicate hosts to the self-service portal, or just want to be able to better organize your host machines.

Creating a Host Group

Open the SCVMM Console.

From the Virtual Machines pane, right-click All Hosts and select New Host Group.

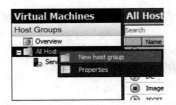

Enter a name for your host group.

CONFIGURING USER ACCESS

There are two types of users that you will configure for your SCVMM implementation: a delegated administrator and a Self-Service Portal user.

Delegated administrators are a new type of user in SCVMM. In the first version of SCVMM, there were two types of users—self-service users and administrators. With virtualization deployments growing in size, IT professionals need a way to delegate chunks of their environment to regional or departmental administrators. This capability was added in this version of SCVMM, and a single SCVMM server can manage a large enterprise environment flexibly.

SCVMM also provides a web portal where authorized users can provision new virtual machines without directly involving IT staff. This capability especially targets software test and development teams, which often set up temporary virtual machines to try out new software. IT administrators retain control over access to resources.

Creating a Delegated Administrator

Open the SCVMM Administrator Console.

Click the Administration tab.

Click User Roles.

In the Actions pane on the left side of the console, click the New User Role action in the User Role pane.

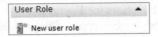

The user role that you create can be a Self-Service User that will use the SCVMM Self-Service Portal or PowerShell to create and manage virtual machines. You can also choose to create a delegated administrator that can be used to limit administrator functions to certain hosts, virtual machines, and library servers.

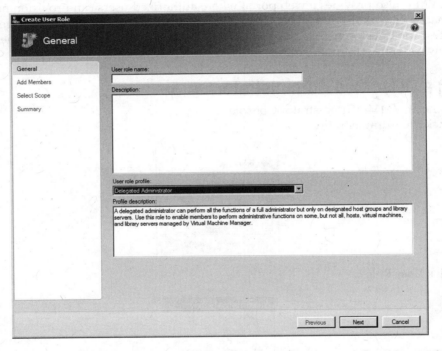

Enter the user role name, a description of what the user or role will be, and select whether the role will be for self-service or a delegated administrator. We're going to select a delegated administrator and give that administrator only access to the host group we created earlier. Enter your planned information and click Next.

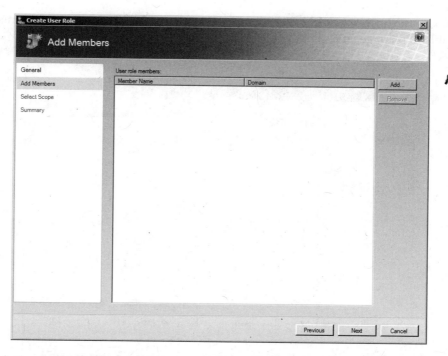

Click the Add button to add users to your delegated administrators group. When you click the button, a Select Users, Computers, or Groups window will pop up.

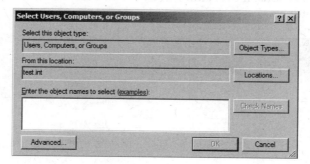

Enter the name of the user or group of users that you want as a delegated administrator. We recommend that you create Active Directory groups and manage your user membership from the group level, not necessarily from this console. Once you've entered your information, click OK. If you have any other groups or users, you can add them now or click Next.

Choose the hosts groups and/or libraries that you want this delegated administrator to be able to manage, and click Next.

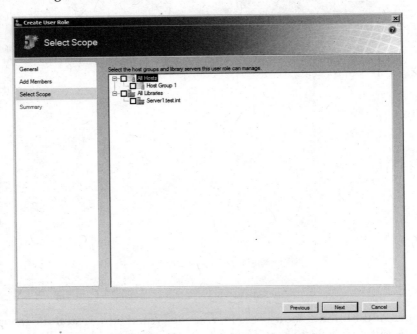

Review your selections. If everything is OK, click Create or click Previous to go back and adjust your settings.

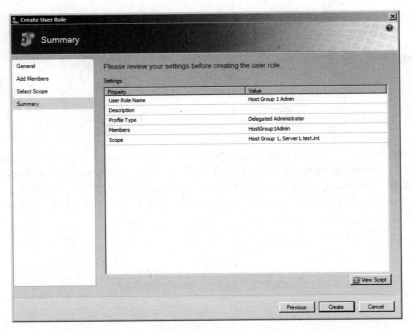

Creating a Self-Service User

Now we're going to walk you through the creation of a self-service user. You will need to create a self-service user prior to connecting to the Self-Service Portal. Click the New User Role action in the Actions pane in the VMM Administrator Console.

Enter the user role name and a description and choose the Self-Service User profile in the drop-down. Click Next.

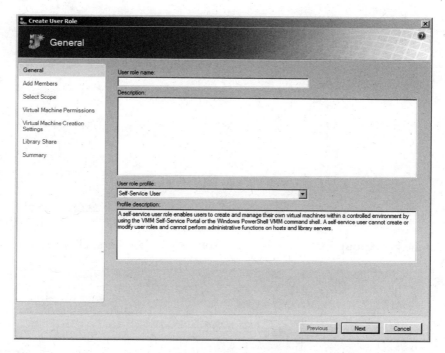

Enter the name of the user or a group of users that you want as a self-service user. We recommend that you create Active Directory groups and manage your user membership from the group level and not necessarily from this console. Once you've entered your information, click OK. If you have any other groups or users you need to add, you can add them now or click Next.

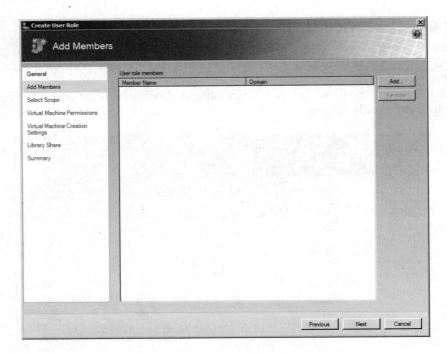

Select the host group that will have your self-service hosts and click Next.

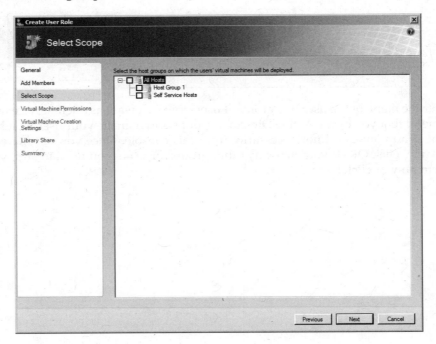

Select the permissions for actions that you want this self-service user or group to be able to perform, and click Next.

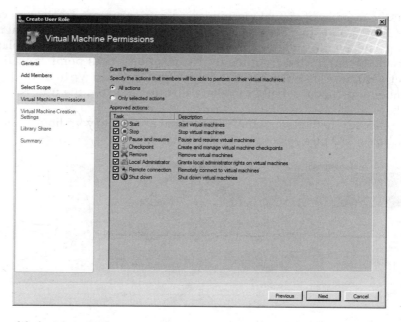

You should decide whether or not you want users to be able to create virtual machines. If you have decided to let users create virtual machines, then check the box for Allow Users to Create New Virtual Machines. Self-service users can only create virtual machines from templates.

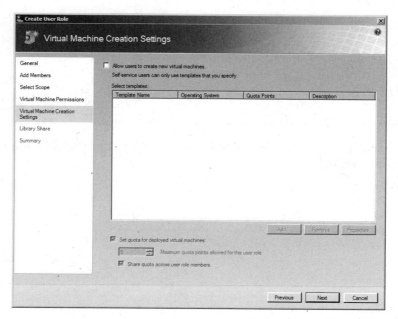

NOTE   Chapter 7 covers template and virtual machine creation.

To limit the number of virtual machines a user or group can create, you can set the number of quota points that each user or group must have to create virtual machines. When you create a template in the next chapter, you can assign that template a point value that will be subtracted from the user's or group's total point allocation. If you want to set a quota, check the box Set Quota for Deployed Virtual Machines. Set a quota number and choose whether to share that quota across the user role members. Click Next.

You can choose whether or not this user will have access to your library share to store virtual machines, ISO files, or scripts. Click Next.

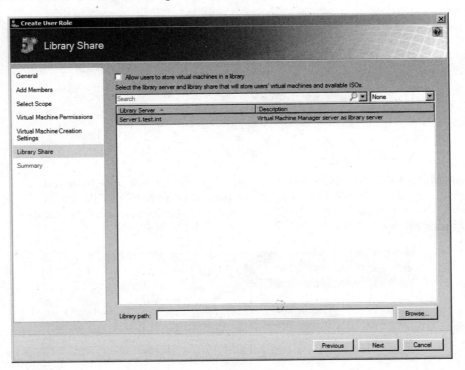

Review your selections. If everything is OK, click Create or click Previous to go back and adjust your settings.

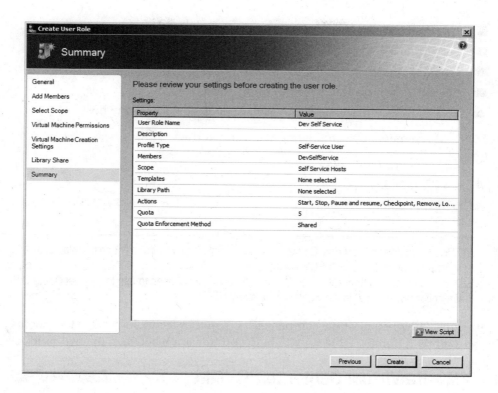

CONFIGURING VMWARE INTEGRATION

If you already have an ESX and Virtual Center or VCenter implementation, a very cool feature of SCVMM is the ability to connect and manage that environment. How this works is SCVMM will manage your ESX hosts through the Virtual Center or VCenter web service using Virtual Center APIs, effectively becoming a manager of managers. Since this integration happens via a web service, there is no need to deploy a VMM agent to the Virtual Center server or the ESX hosts. The idea behind this methodology is to allow your organization to add SCVMM in a controlled manner, and doesn't force you to have to rip out your ESX environment. Actually, if you have multiple Virtual Center or VCenter implementations, you can use SCVMM to manage all those implementations from a single console.

Once the integration is set up, you will be able to

▼   Create and edit virtual machines

■   Leverage intelligent placement

■   Use PRO tips for your guests

- Use PowerShell
- Set virtual machine state
- Use V-Motion
- Store VMware virtual machines in the VMM library
▲ Use intelligent placement for VMware guests on a VMware host

SCVMM can manage the following VMware products

▼ ESX Server 3.0 or newer
- ESX Server 3.5i
▲ Virtual Center 2.5

NOTE   If you don't have Virtual Center or VCenter implemented, you will need to install Virtual Center or VCenter prior to configuring SCVMM integration. While the APIs are similar between managing an ESX host directly and through Virtual Center, Microsoft has chosen to use the Virtual Center APIs so that functions such as VMotion would still be available.

It seems that when multiple companies have similar technologies, the terminology is always slightly different. Table 6-1 will help you transition between the two products.

Adding VMware Virtual Center to SCVMM

Open your SCVMM console with an administrator account.

From the Actions pane on the right side of the console, click Add VMware Virtual Center server to bring up the Add window.

Enter the computer name of your Virtual Center server and an administrator account for virtual center and click OK. SCVMM will contact the Virtual Center server and create the integration path adding the Virtual Center, datacenters, hosts,

VMware Terminology	SCVMM Terminology
Host and host clusters	All hosts
Datacenter	Host group
Folder	Host group
Cluster	Host cluster

Table 6-1.   Differentiation Between VMware and SCVMM Terminologies

and guests to SCVMM. Depending on the number of objects in your Virtual Center, this may take a few minutes.

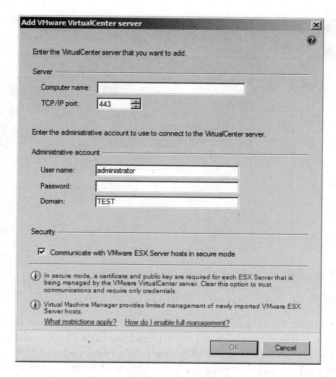

Adding a VMware ESX host to SCVMM

Once you've completed the integration of Virtual Center and SCVMM, you still may need to add a host. This can be done by opening the SCVMM Administrator Console with an account that has the rights to add hosts.

From the Actions pane on the right of the console, choose Add Host to bring up the Add Host Wizard.

Select the VMware ESX Server Host radio button and enter the root credentials of the local ESX host server.

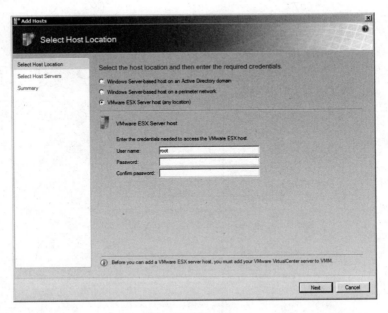

Enter the computer name or IP address of the ESX host, the virtual center that you want to use to deploy the Virtual Center client, and the host group on the SCVMM server you would like the ESX host assigned to. Once you've entered this information, click the Add Host button and repeat this process for additional hosts. Once you've added all of your hosts, click Next.

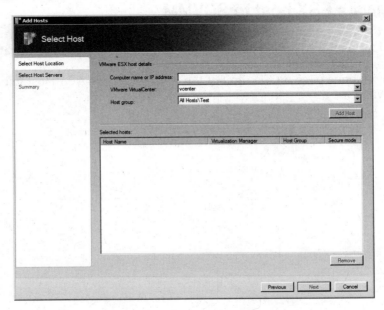

Check to make sure your information is correct and click Add Hosts to start the client install.

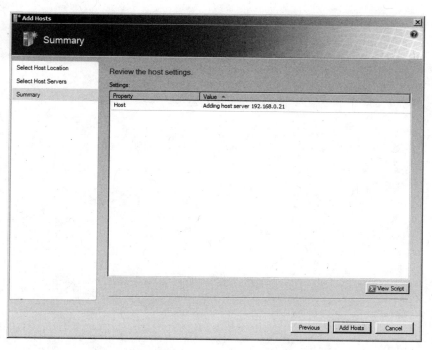

Now that you've got SCVMM installed and configured, in the next chapter we'll talk about how to create new virtual machines. You can build them from scratch, or have custom templates designed to quickly build new deployments. Chapter 7 covers the details of virtual machine creation.

CHAPTER 7

Creating and Managing Virtual Machines

What good is a virtual environment if you don't run any virtual machines on it? Virtual machines are software instances of physical machines. That is, what you used to be able to do on a single server can now be done as a software instance, multiple times on a physical server.

In this chapter we will go over what a virtual machine is; what components make up a virtual machine; how to use templates in the creation and management of your virtual machines; and how to create virtual machines in both the Hyper-V Manager and System Center Virtual Machine Manager.

WHAT IS A VIRTUAL MACHINE?

A *virtual machine* is a piece of software that can run its own operating systems and applications as if it were a physical computer. A virtual machine acts exactly like a physical computer and contains it own virtual (software-based) CPU, RAM, hard disk, and network interface card (NIC).

Operating systems can't tell the difference between a virtual machine and a physical machine; neither can applications or other computers on the network. Even the virtual machine thinks it's a "real" computer. But all that being said, the virtual machine is made completely of software and has no hardware components at all. Virtual machines have several advantages over physical machines:

▼ **Compatibility**   Virtual machines are compatible with all x86 operating systems and applications. Since virtual machines host their own guest operating systems and applications, they contain all the components in a physical computer (such as a motherboard, VGA card, network controller, and so forth). Because of this, virtual machines are compatible with all standard x86 operating systems and applications. You can use the virtual machine to run all the same software that you could on a physical x86 machine, provided your application doesn't have unique hardware requirements.

■ **Isolation**   Virtual machines, even if on the same physical machine, are isolated from each other as if they were separate physical machines. For instance, if there are four virtual machines on a single server and one of the virtual machines fails, the other three keep running, unaware of the fourth's failure. Isolation is a key reason why there is a high level of availability and security of applications running in a virtual environment, as opposed to a system running on a traditional, non-virtualized system.

■ **Encapsulation**   Virtual machines are encapsulated to provide a complete computing environment. A virtual machine bundles a complete set of virtual hardware resources, as well as an operating system and its applications, inside one package. Encapsulation makes virtual machines compact and easy to move from one location to another. They can be distributed around your datacenter, or even written to a portable USB drive.

▲   **Independence**   Virtual machines run independently of underlying hardware. For instance, you can configure a virtual machine with virtual components (such as a CPU, network adapter, or SCSI controller) that are different from the physical components that are present on the physical machine. As such, different virtual machines on the same physical machine can be configured completely differently. They can run different operating systems, different applications, different drivers, and so forth.

With all these benefits, you can move a virtual machine from one type of physical computer to another without having to change the operating system, applications, or drivers. Hardware independence allows you to run a heterogeneous mixture of operating systems and applications on a single machine.

COMPONENTS OF A VIRTUAL MACHINE

As we noted earlier, a virtual machine can be loaded out just like a physical machine. The difference, of course, is that you don't have to physically install components; you just start a software instance of it and add as needed. For example, you could set up your virtual machine to have a network adapter. You can set up an additional hard drive on your virtual machine, but without having to open a box and plug in a new one.

Virtual machine components include:

▼   Virtual disk (whether fixed, dynamic, differencing, or pass-through)
■   Networking components
■   Memory
■   Processor
■   DVD drive
■   COM ports
■   Floppy drive
▲   Integration services

Adding the components is a straightforward affair. They can be added through a GUI—which is what we'll show you in this chapter—but they can also be added via a script. The following code shows how a virtual DVD drive can be added using a Visual Basic script:

```
On Error Resume Next

Set objVS = CreateObject("VirtualServer.Application")
Set objVM = objVS.FindVirtualMachine("Windows 2000 Server")

errReturn = objVM.AddDVDROMDrive(0,1,0)
```

TEMPLATES AND PROFILES

A huge benefit of System Center Virtual Machine Manager (SCVMM 2008) is the ability to create templates and profiles. A *template* is basically a shell of a virtual machine. A template contains a hardware template, a guest operating system profile, and a virtual hard disk. The benefit of a profile is that it allows you to create a standard configuration for your virtual machine and deploy that standard in a very rapid fashion. Depending on your environment and your business requirements, you may find it best to create one template or many varied templates. We've found that in most cases you will probably create templates and profiles for some of the following scenarios:

- ▼ Different operating systems
- ■ Self-service users
- ■ Different virtual machine configurations
- ▲ Developer systems

Hardware Profile

A hardware profile is used to define a common set of hardware for a virtual machine or template. In the hardware profile you can set the number of processors, memory, network, and so on. The hardware profile is stored in the profiles section of your SCVMM 2008 library. To create a new hardware profile that will be stored in the library, open the SCVMM 2008 console.

1. Click the Library tab in the navigation pane on the left of the console.
2. From the Library actions tab in the Actions pane on the right of the console, click New Hardware Profile to start the New Hardware Profile Wizard.

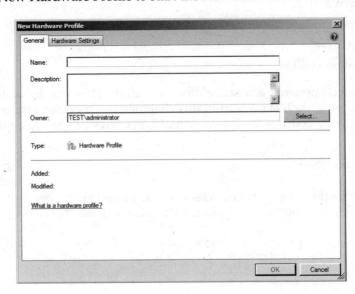

3. Enter a name and description for the new hardware profile. This might be a standard workstation or standard medium-size server. Click the Hardware Settings tab.

By default the Network Adapter is the first item that is selected, so let's start by configuring the network. In this configuration screen you can choose which network you want to connect your virtual machine to. This is accomplished by using the Network Location drop-down. You can also set the network tag using the Network Tag drop-down. Enable a VLAN ID for this network adapter, and set a dynamic or static MAC address. If you need to add an additional network card for your virtual machine, you can do this by using the New Hardware toolbar.

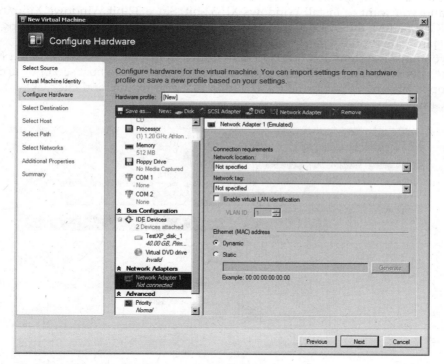

When you click the Network Adapter button, a drop-down will allow you to choose between an emulated adapter and a synthetic adapter.

Choose an emulated adapter if the operating system you are installing isn't supported by the integration components.

Let's move up to the top of the Hardware Profile list and work our way back down through the rest of the options. Click BIOS.

From this screen you can choose the device order your virtual machine will use when it boots. Do this by using the up and down arrow buttons on the right of the selection pane. You can also choose to enable the Number Lock for virtual machines; this feature is only available on Hyper-V hosts. Click Processor in the Hardware Profile pane.

From here you can choose the number of processors the virtual machine will have and what type of processor the virtual machine will be using. The processor type that you choose will be used by SCVMM 2008 to calculate host ratings on where it would be best to place the virtual machine. For example, if you are creating a virtual machine that will run Windows NT 4.0, you will want to limit the CPU functionality. Click Memory in the Hardware Profile pane.

Choose the amount of RAM you want to have in the virtual machine. You can use the drop-down box to choose MB or GB, which is nice so that you don't always have to enter 1024, 2048, and so forth for the amount of RAM. You can just choose 2GB, 4GB, and so on. Remember, when you are allocating virtual machine memory, there are operating system limits for the guest. For instance, let's say you give the virtual machine 4GB of RAM and you want to install Windows XP 32-bit. Since 32-bit Windows XP only supports 2GB of RAM, the other 2GB that you allocated will go unused. Click Floppy Drive in the Hardware Profile pane.

If you have a system that needs to boot from a floppy or access data from a floppy, you can choose to connect directly to the physical floppy in the host server or use a virtual floppy disk file. Choose the radio button that you require and click COM 1 in the Hardware Profile pane.

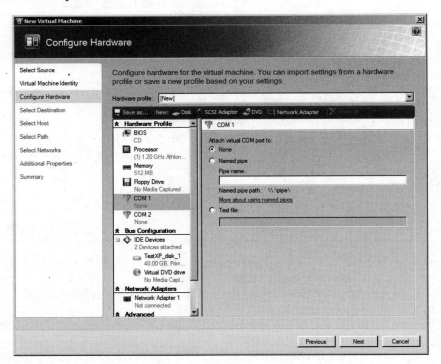

You can create up to two virtual COM ports that can be directed to use either a named pipe on the same server or a remote server or a text file. Configure COM 1 and repeat the process on COM 2 if required. Now let's configure the virtual IDE controller.

The virtual IDE controller is where you connect your hard drives and any CD/DVD drives that you need. To edit the bus configuration for the hardware profile, you can either choose to edit the DVD drive or add a SCSI adapter. Click Virtual DVD Drive in the Bus Configuration pane.

From here you can choose how you want to mount media. You can either link the virtual device to the physical drive on the server, or you can choose an ISO file that has been loaded into your library. You can choose to create additional DVD drives from the New Hardware toolbar.

Click DVD to add the new virtual DVD device. Virtual DVD drives can only be associated with IDE controllers, so by default when the DVD device is created, it is associated with the IDE controller. Since you've already configured networking, click Priority in the Advanced pane.

You can define the priority that a virtual machine will get for CPU time. The virtual machines with a higher priority will be given the CPU resources before virtual machines with a lower priority. If you are planning on having a mixed workload (production and non-production systems), you may want to consider giving your production systems a higher priority rating than your non-production systems. You might also want to give the virtual machines with mission-critical applications a higher priority than any other virtual machine on the host or cluster.

This brings us to availability. Click Availability in the Advanced pane.

Creating a highly available virtual machine with SCVMM 2008 is much easier than without SCVMM 2008. The steps of having a cluster and creating dedicated logical unit numbers (LUNs) per virtual machine still apply, but enabling the VM to be highly available takes just a click of the button. To make your virtual machine profile highly available, click the Make the VM Highly Available check box.

Guest OS Profile

A guest operating system profile is similar to an answer file that's used to provide information to the operating system during an unattended installation. In a guest OS profile you can enter information such as the computer name, the admin password, the type of OS, and networking information. To create a new guest operating system profile that will be stored in the library, open the SCVMM 2008 console.

Click the Library tab in the navigation pane on the left of the console.

From the Library Actions tab in the Actions pane on the right of the console, click New Guest OS profile to start the New Guest OS Profile Wizard.

Enter a name and description for the guest OS profile. This might be Windows Server 2008 Standard or Windows Vista. Then click the Guest OS tab.

Click the Identity Information options in the General Settings pane. In this section enter the computer name for the OS, or you can use * as a wildcard to create a randomly generated name. Enter your organization information and click the Admin Password tab.

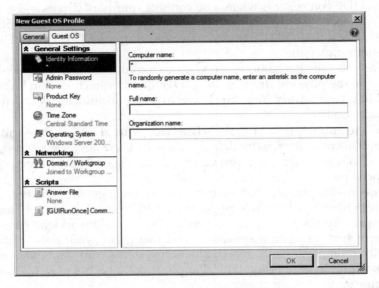

Enter the administrator password that will be used for the guest operating system. Click the Product Key tab.

Enter the product key for the Support Microsoft OS that will be associated with this OS profile. Click the Time Zone tab.

Set the time zone where the guest will be residing, and click the Operating System tab.

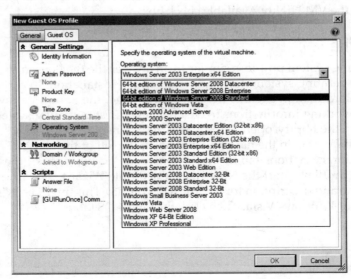

Click the drop-down box, and select the operating system that this guest OS profile represents. Click the Domain/Workgroup tab.

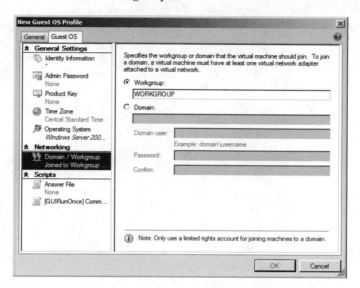

From this screen you can set the workgroup name for your virtual machines that will use this profile. You can also set the domain that you want this OS to join when it's installing. Enter your information and click the Answer File tab.

If you've already configured a sysprep.inf or unattend.xml file for the OS you've chosen, you can add that file to the library share and then specify that file in this screen. Click the GUIRunOnce tab.

From the GUIRunOnce screen, you can specify commands and actions that will be executed the first time a user logs on to the virtual machine. This comes in very handy if you have configuration scripts that you want to run in a specific order. Once you're done configuring each of the settings, click OK and the profile will be stored in the Profiles area of your library.

Templates

A *template* is a combination of a hardware and software profile. A template can be created from an existing virtual machine or it can be created with a blank virtual hard disk.

To create a new template that will be stored in the library, open the SCVMM 2008 console.

Click the Library tab in the navigation pane on the left of the console.

From the Library Actions tab in the Actions pane on the right of the console, click New Template to start the New Template Wizard.

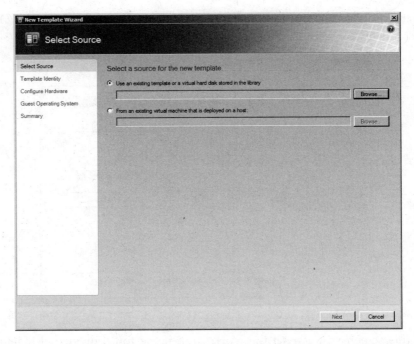

To create a template, you can use an existing template or hard disk in the library. Alternately, you can use a virtual machine that you've built and is running on a host. If you decide to use a virtual machine that is already deployed, that virtual machine will be destroyed. If you have information on it or somebody uses that machine, you will want to first create a clone of the machine, and then create a template from it. For this process click the Use an Existing Template or Virtual Hard Disk Stored in the Library radio button, and click Browse to bring up the Select Template Source window.

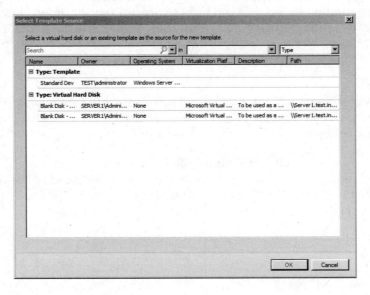

The install of SCVMM 2008 adds two blank virtual hard disks to the library.

▼   Blank Disk – Large

▲   Blank Disk – Small

Both blank disks are dynamically expanding disks; the difference is that the small disk is 16GB and the large disk is 60GB. Choose either of the blank disks and click OK. Click Next.

Give your template a name and description so that you know what it is and how it should be used. For instance, you may want to call it Windows 2008 Standard Server. Once you've entered your information, click Next to configure the hardware.

You can choose a preconfigured hardware profile, or you can edit this profile and save it as a new profile. Follow the information in the earlier section "Hardware Profile" to create a hardware profile or for more information on hardware profiles. Click Next.

You can choose a pre-created guest operating system profile, edit the information here and save as a guest operating system profile, or make edits for this particular virtual machine. Once you've completed your settings, click Next.

Review your information in the Summary page and verify that it is correct. Click Create to create your new template. The Jobs window will pop up and show you the status of your template creation. Once the template is created click the Library tab and the template will be listed.

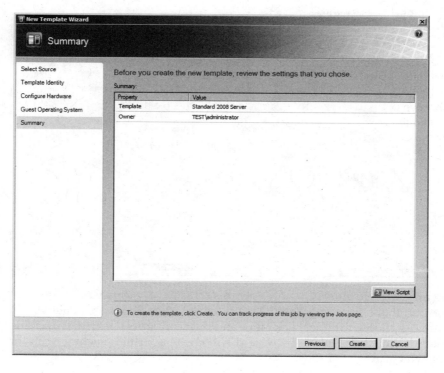

CREATING VIRTUAL MACHINES

In this section we'll talk about how to create a virtual machine in the Hyper-V Manager console, in SCVMM 2008, and in the Self-Service Portal. While these processes share similarities, each has its own unique aspects that you will need to be familiar with. You can create a virtual machine in SCVMM 2008 or Hyper-V Manager for a host machine or cluster. We recommend that you choose one or the other to create your virtual machines. If you have SCVMM 2008, we recommend that you stick with that.

Creating a Virtual Machine with Hyper-V Manager

Open the Hyper-V Manager console and choose the host server on which you would like to create the virtual machine. There are several different ways to create a new virtual machine in the Hyper-V Manager. You can right-click on a host machine and choose New | Virtual Machine, or you can choose Action from the toolbar and then choose New | Virtual Machine, or you can also activate the host server by single-clicking it in the navigation pane and choosing New | Virtual Machine from the Actions pane on the right side of the console.

Use any of the above methods to start the New Virtual Machine Wizard.

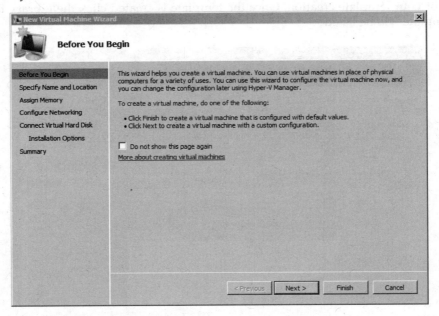

You may want to choose to not show this screen every time you create a virtual machine, and if that's the case, click the check box Do Not Show This Page Again. At this point you can choose to either click Next, and then configure the virtual machine settings you want. If you click Finish, the wizard will create a virtual machine with the default settings, which are:

▼ One processor

■ 512 MB RAM

■ A single 127GB dynamic hard drive

■ Network connection not connected to a network

▲ The virtual machine and disk stored in the location that you specified when you configured Hyper-V

Click Next.

Enter a descriptive name for your virtual machine. If you've configured a default location in Hyper-V, it will show up in the Location text box. If you want to store the virtual machine in a new location, click the check box Store the Virtual Machine in a Different Location and choose Browse to select your location. Click Next.

Assign the amount of memory for your virtual machine. When you are giving a virtual machine memory, remember there are operating system limits for the guest. For instance, let's say you give the virtual machine 4GB of RAM and you want to install Windows XP 32-bit: Since 32-bit Windows XP only supports 2GB of RAM, the other 2GB that you allocated will go unused. Once you've set your memory, click Next.

In the drop-down, choose the network you want this virtual machine assigned to and click Next.

You can choose to create a virtual hard disk now, use an existing virtual hard disk, or attach one later. Click Next.

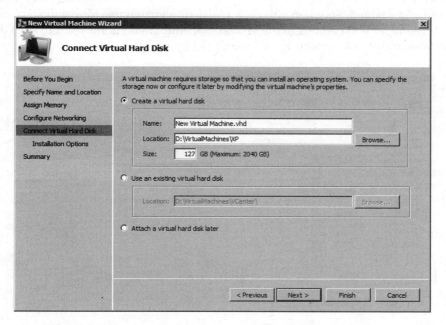

On the Installation Options screen, you can choose to install an operating system later, from a CD/DVD, ISO, or virtual floppy disk, or you can choose to boot from a network installation server. Click Next.

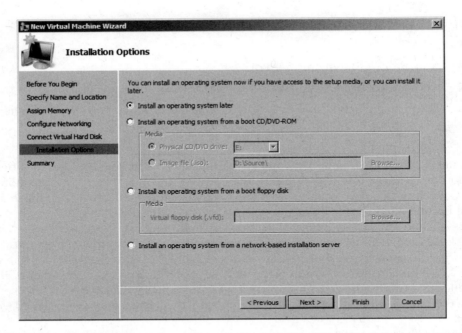

Verify that your settings are correct, and if needed, go back by clicking the Previous button to make any changes. By default the Start the Virtual Machine After It Is Created setting is enabled. So when you click Finish, the virtual machine will start, and the Hyper-V Manager will connect to the virtual machine. If you don't want to start the virtual machine right away, uncheck the box. Click Finish.

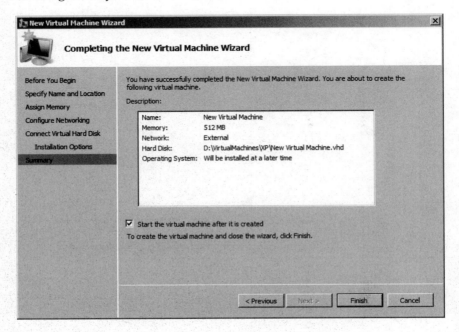

Creating a Highly Available Virtual Machine

To create a highly available virtual machine with the Hyper-V Manager, there are a series of prerequisites and steps that you need to do prior to the creation of the virtual machine. The prerequisites are:

▼ You have a healthy Hyper-V host cluster.

■ For Windows Server 2008 R1, each highly available guest will require that a dedicated LUN is created on your shared storage environment and configured as a cluster disk prior to creating the VM. If you have multiple virtual disks that you are going to attach to the virtual machine, either you can have those disks on the same LUN, or we recommend that you put each disk on its own dedicated LUN.

■ For Windows Server 2008 R2, CSV should be enabled and CSV storage added to the cluster prior to creating the VM. The virtual machines will be kept in the "SystemDrive" \ClusteredStorage directory.

▲ Format the disk or disks as NTFS.

Once you've created the disk space and configured the disk to be available on each node of your cluster, you can start the creation of your virtual machine.

Follow the process above to create a virtual machine with the Hyper-V Manager on the cluster node on which the cluster disk is active. When you reach the Specify Name and Location page, you will need to change your location to the new cluster disk that is available for that virtual machine, or the CSV location and volume you would like to store that VHD.

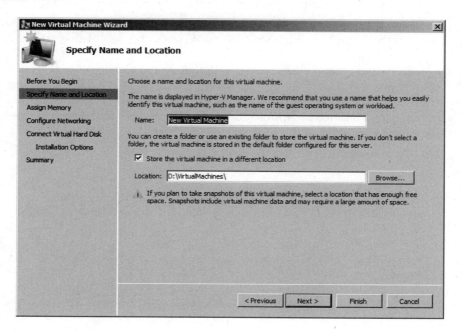

Enter a location that is the shared disk or CSV location on the cluster. Continue with the virtual machine configuration. When you reach the Connect Virtual Hard Disk page, you will need to choose a virtual hard disk that is already deployed to the cluster disk, or create a new virtual disk with a location on the cluster disk.

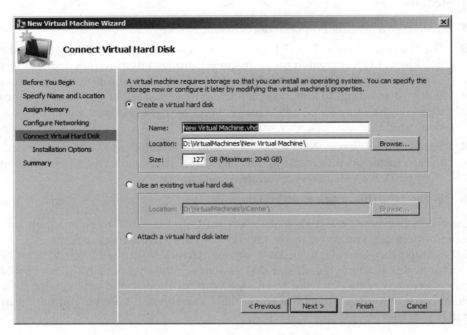

Enter a location for the new disk or an existing disk that is on a clustered disk. On the Summary page of the New Virtual Machine Wizard, choose not to start the virtual machine after it is created.

When your virtual machine has been created, open the Cluster Manager and navigate to your cluster.

Expand your cluster and click Services and Applications.

Click Configure a Service or Application under the Service and Applications tab in the Actions pane on the right of the console to start the High Availability Wizard.

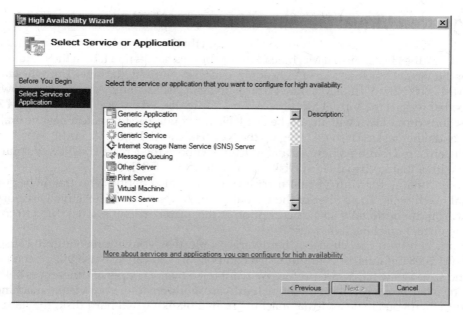

Click Next.
Click Virtual Machine and click Next.

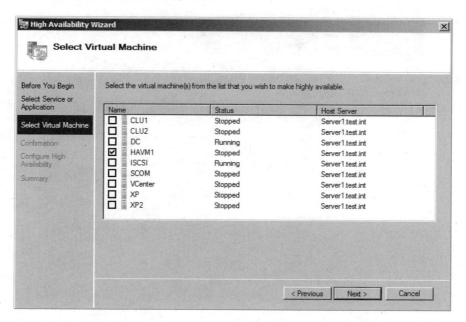

Select the virtual machine that you want to create as highly available. Keep in mind that the virtual machine must be on a shared disk or CSV that is part of the cluster. Click Next.
Confirm your selection and click Next to configure the VM as highly available.
Review the report to verify your configuration. Click Finish.

Creating a New Virtual Machine with SCVMM 2008

Open the SCVMM 2008 console with a user account that has the rights to create a virtual machine. Click the Hosts, Virtual Machines, Library, or Jobs navigation tab. In the Actions pane under the Virtual Machine Manager heading, click New Virtual Machine. This will start the SCVMM 2008 New Virtual Machine Wizard. You can also click the Actions drop-down on the toolbar to start the Virtual Machine Wizard. No matter where you are in SCVMM 2008, the Actions drop-down will always be available for you to use to create a new virtual machine and other tasks. This will bring up the New Hardware Profile Wizard.

Since we're creating a new virtual machine, choose the Create the New Virtual Machine with a Blank Virtual Hard Disk radio button and click Next.

Enter a name for your virtual machine. You can also define who the owner of the virtual machine is. The owner of the virtual machine must have an Active Directory account. You can optionally add a description of the virtual machine. Click Next to configure the virtual machine hardware.

From here you can choose a hardware profile that you've preconfigured, use the SCVMM 2008 defaults, or configure each component. You can also use this screen to create and save a new hardware profile. We want to go over a couple of differences between creating a hardware profile and editing hardware while creating your virtual machine. By default when you create a virtual machine from a blank virtual hard disk, the hard disk is created as a 40GB dynamic disk and is associated as an IDE disk. To change the virtual hard drive configuration, click on the virtual disk in the Bus Configuration pane.

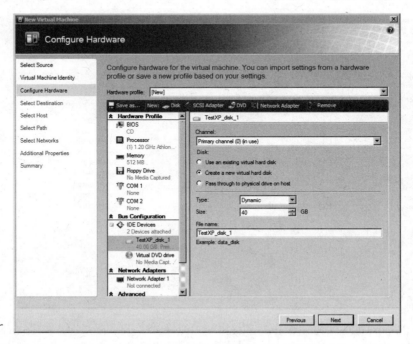

From here you can choose which channel you want the virtual hard drive associated to, and you can choose to change the disk from the IDE adapter to a SCSI adapter.

Before you can switch the disk to a SCSI adapter, you first need to create the SCSI adapter from the New Hardware toolbar.

Once you click SCSI Adapter, a new SCSI adapter will be added to the bus configuration. If you choose to define the drive as a SCSI drive, the drive will be associated to the newly created SCSI adapter. At this point you can choose to use an existing hard drive, create a new virtual drive, or create a pass-through to a physical drive on a host. Since we are creating a new virtual machine, let's choose to create a new virtual hard disk. Choose either dynamic or fixed from the Type drop-down box, and set the size and name of the virtual disk.

You can also choose to create additional disks at this time as well. To do this, click the Disk button on the New Hardware toolbar.

By default the new hard drive will be associated with the IDE bus. If you want the disk to be a SCSI disk—and you've already created a SCSI controller—you can change the channel on which the disk is configured to a SCSI channel. If you want to remove a device from your hardware profile, click on that device and then click the Remove button.

Once you have configured the hardware profile, you can choose to save the profile configuration and move forward. You can also click Next to proceed to the next configuration step. To save your hardware profile, click the Save As button on the Hardware Profile toolbar.

Enter a name and description. All of your settings will be brought forward into the wizard. If you want to make any changes to the settings, you can click the Hardware Settings tab. Click OK to save the profile and click Next to continue configuring the virtual machine.

You can choose whether to deploy the virtual machine to a host machine, or you can store the virtual machine in a library. Since we're creating a new virtual machine, let's deploy this virtual machine to a host. Click the Place the Virtual Machine on a Host radio button and click Next.

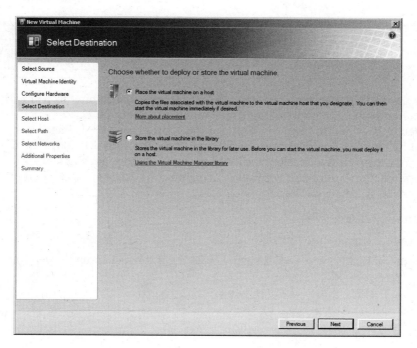

Choose the host that you would like to deploy the virtual machine to. The hosts are listed by the rating, host name, and the transfer type. SCVMM 2008 will provide a rating on which server is the best server for the virtual machine you are creating. The transfer type refers to how the virtual machine will be sent to the host machine. This can occur in two ways: network transfer and SAN-based transfer. If your host is configured for the SAN-based transfer, the transfer will utilize the SAN, which is much faster than transferring over a network. Click Next to proceed.

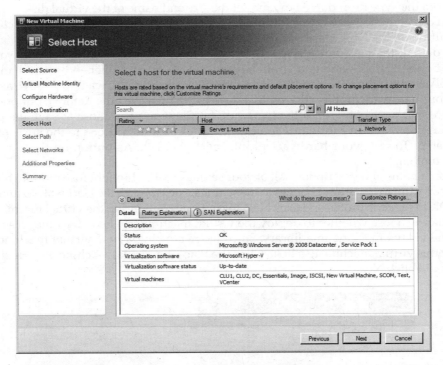

Enter the path on the host where you want the virtual machine to reside. If you are creating a highly available virtual machine, make sure that you choose a location that is a dedicated cluster-aware LUN or a CSV for that virtual machine. Click Next.

If you haven't configured a virtual network for your network adapters, use the Virtual Network drop-down to select the network for each adapter. Click Next.

Choose whether or not you want the virtual machine to be started when the physical host server starts. You can choose:

▼ Never automatically start.

■ Always turn on the virtual machine.

▲ Automatically turn on the virtual machine if it was running when the physical server stopped.

Choose the action that you would like to have happen if the physical server stops. You can choose:

▼ Save state.

■ Turn off virtual machine.

▲ Shut down guest OS.

You can also specify which operating system you are going to install on the virtual machine. From the drop-down box there are 26 different options to choose from. Choose an operating system option and click Next to view the virtual machine summary.

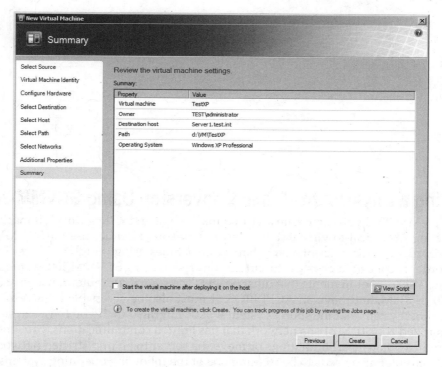

If everything looks correct, choose whether or not to start the virtual machine after it's deployed, and click Create. Once you click Create, the Jobs window will pop up and will show you the progress of the virtual machine creation job.

Creating a Virtual Machine in the Self-Service Portal

Open the Self-Service Portal and log in with a user that has been granted rights to create a virtual machine.

Click the New Computer link.

Choose a template in which you would like to create the virtual machine. Depending on the rights of the currently logged-in user, you may see one or many templates to choose from. Fill out the name of the VM, the computer name, password and product key information, and then click Create.

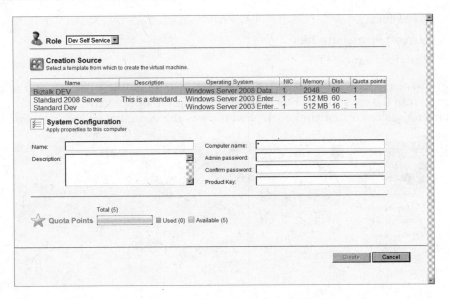

Conducting a Physical-to-Virtual Conversion Using SCVMM 2008

With SCVMM 2008 you can create a virtual machine of an existing physical machine by conducting a physical-to-virtual (P2V) conversion. You can either use the SCVMM 2008 P2V Wizard, or you can script a large batch of machines using Windows PowerShell.

In order to conduct a physical-to-virtual conversion using SCVMM 2008 as the source, there are a set of requirements that must be met. The source computer must have at least 512 MB of RAM, and have an ACPI BIOS. It must also be accessible by SCVMM 2008 and the host system that the source system will be migrated to. If you have a system in a demilitarized zone (DMZ) or a network that has limited communications, you will either need to turn off any port limitations or move the server to an unrestricted network. The source computer also needs to be running one of the following operating systems:

- ▼ Windows 2008 32-bit or 64-bit
- ■ Windows Server 2003 32-bit or 64-bit with SP1 or later
- ■ Windows 2000 Server SP4 or later
- ■ Windows 2000 Advanced Server SP4 or later
- ■ Windows XP 32-bit or 64-bit with SP2 or later
- ▲ Windows Vista 32-bit or 64-bit with SP1 or later

You can use third-party tools such as PlateSpin Migrate and Vizioncore VConverter to convert physical servers to virtual machines. For the workloads that we tend to deal with, Hyper-V and SCVMM 2008 P2V tools work for about everything.

When you conduct a P2V with the SCVMM 2008 tools, your source computers can be converted to either Windows Server 2008 with Hyper-V, or Windows Server 2008 with Virtual Server R2 SP1 or later. They can also be converted to Windows Server 2003 with Virtual Server R2 SP1 or later. The hosts that you convert to need to have at least 256MB of RAM for the host, plus the memory required for the virtual machine, as they cannot have any port restrictions through a firewall or an IPSEC policy.

The P2V process is done in one of two ways: The source computer can be converted in an online state or in an offline state. In an online P2V, the source computer continues to be available and conduct transactions. During the online P2V, SCVMM 2008 leverages Volume Shadow Copy Service (VSS) to make a local copy of the NTFS volumes and VSS-aware applications data. SCVMM 2008 continues to use VSS to keep the data between the real-time system and the backup in sync while the P2V process is being conducted.

In an offline P2V, the source computer is offline while the P2V process occurs. The source computer is rebooted into the Windows Preinstallation Environment (WinPE) and the source disks are cloned to virtual hard drives on the host system. If you are going to be converting Windows 2000 systems, FAT volumes, or domain controllers, offline conversion is the way for you to go since it is the most reliable method to ensure the consistency of the source data.

The P2V process is relatively straightforward; an image of the source machine's disk is made and the P2V process modifies the operating system so that the source operating system will run on Hyper-V or Virtual Server. The online and offline conversion processes are similar but differ in how the data is actually copied.

There are several steps in the online P2V:

1. SCVMM 2008 installs a P2V agent on the source computer to gather configuration information.

2. SCVMM 2008 signals the P2V agent to gather information about hardware, software, services, and updates.

3. The P2V agent sends that data back to the SCVMM 2008 server as XML where it is stored in the SCVMM 2008 database.

4. Once the information is received, SCVMM 2008 determines if the source machine can be virtualized by checking that the source operating system is supported, and that the physical configuration can be made into a virtual configuration.

5. If all is good with the configuration, a VSS image is captured for each volume and a separate virtual hard drive is created per physical volume. If you choose to use a dynamic disk, only the data is captured and the white space is left. We recommend that if you are converting a server, you use static disks to take advantage of the performance gains you get from a static disk.

6. Once the virtual drives have been created, the P2V client uses the Background Intelligent Transfer Service (BITS) to transfer the data from the source system to the host.

7. SCVMM 2008 then prepares the operating system and virtual hard drives in what is called the fix-up phase.

8. SCVMM 2008 creates the virtual machine.

9. SCVMM 2008 connects the virtual hard drives, NICs, DVD/CD, and memory.

The offline process differs in that the server is rebooted into WinPE and all data is copied while the system is offline. This is the most reliable way to transfer your data, and we recommend that you use it whenever you can versus doing an online P2V.

1. SCVMM 2008 installs a P2V client on the source computer.

2. The P2V agent installs a WinPE image on the source computer, edits the boot file, and reboots the source computer so it loads into WinPE.

3. Once the system has been rebooted into WinPE, then the physical volumes are copied to the host system.

4. SCVMM 2008 then prepares the operating system and virtual hard drives in what is called the fix-up phase.

5. SCVMM 2008 creates the virtual machine.

6. SCVMM 2008 connects the virtual hard drives, NICs, DVD/CD, and memory.

Conducting a P2V

Log in to the SCVMM 2008 console with an account that has rights to conduct a P2V.

From the Virtual Machine Manager heading in the Actions pane on the left side of the console, choose Convert Physical Server. This can also be achieved by clicking on the Actions drop-down on the toolbar.

Choose Virtual Machine Manager and select Convert Physical Server to start the P2V Wizard.

Enter the name or IP address of the system that you want to convert, and enter administrative credentials to connect to that machine. This can be a domain-level or local-level account. Click Next.

Enter the virtual machine name. This name is only used to identify the system to SCVMM 2008 and it doesn't have to be the same name as the actual system. If you use the same name as the system name it will still display correctly in System Center Operations Manager 2007. Enter the name of the owner of the system and any comments, and then click Next.

Click the Scan System button to have SCVMM 2008 begin collecting data about the system. Depending on the source system configuration, this could take a couple of minutes to complete. Once the scan is complete, click Next to configure your volumes.

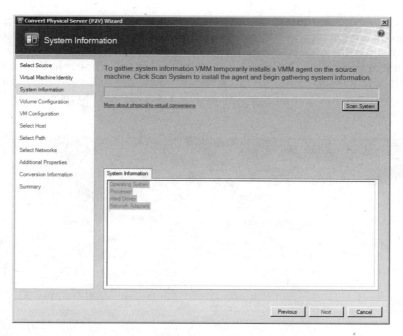

Make any necessary changes to configure your virtual drive. You can set the disk size, whether the disk is dynamic or fixed, whether the disk is IDE or SCSI, and what channel the disk will reside on. Click the Conversion Options button on the bottom left of the Volume Configuration pane.

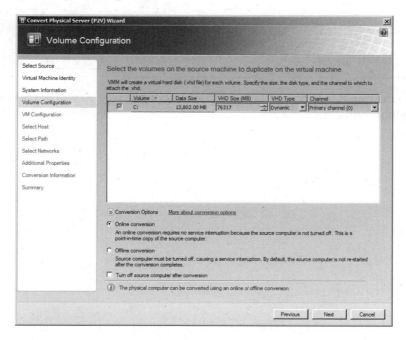

By default, if the operating system supports online conversion, it will be enabled. Choose the conversion type you want to use and whether or not the source system should be turned off after the conversion completes. If you choose to do an offline conversion, an additional option called Offline Conversion Options will appear in the menu.

You will only need to configure this screen if you chose to do an offline conversion.

If you've chosen to do an offline conversion, you will need to provide an IP address for WinPE when it reboots.

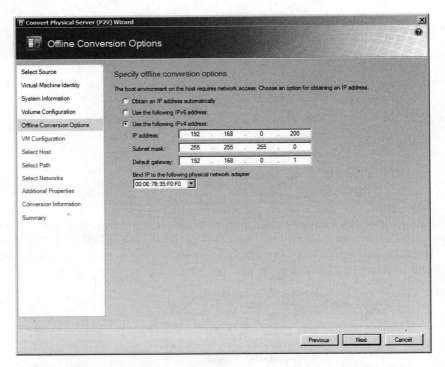

Choose the number of processors and the amount of memory you want in your new virtual machine and click Next.

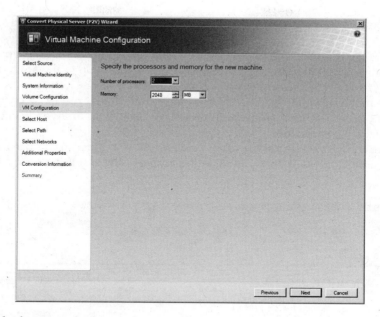

Choose the host to which you want the source computer migrated, and click Next.

Choose the path where the virtual machine files will reside. Remember: If you are going to configure this system to be highly available, it will need to be on a dedicated LUN. Click Next to set up your networks.

When the P2V client scans the system, it will detect the number of NICs available in the system and will create the same number in the virtual machine. Use the drop-down box to set which virtual network each NIC will be associated with, and click Next to move to the next step.

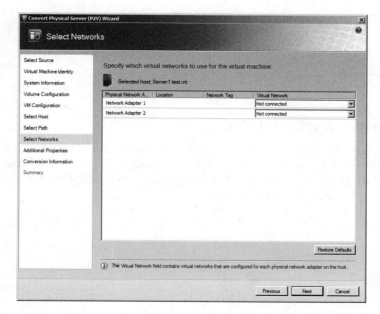

Set the desired automatic start and stop settings you want for this virtual machine. Click Next.

SCVMM 2008 does a quick validation of what you've chosen. If all is good, you will get a "No issues detected" message. If you have any issues, you will want to use the Previous button to go back and remedy any configuration issues. Click Next.

Check to make sure that your configuration settings are correct. Also check the box if you want to connect to the virtual machine after it has been deployed. Click the Create button to start the conversion.

When the conversion starts, the Jobs window will pop up. You can use the Jobs window to watch the process of your conversation and to help troubleshoot should you have any issues.

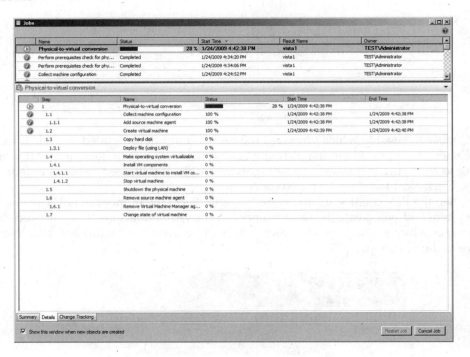

Virtual-to-Virtual Conversion

Virtual-to-virtual (V2V) migration is the act of converting a virtual machine from one virtual platform to another virtual platform. In the case of SCVMM 2008, that conversion is from VMware to Hyper-V or Virtual Server, and is a read-only operation that doesn't delete or affect the original source machine.

Prerequisites

In order to conduct a virtual-to-virtual conversion using SCVMM 2008 as the source you will be converting, the source machine must have a couple of files:

▼   .vmx—The .vmx file is a text file that lists the configuration of the virtual machine such as RAM, disk assignments, and networking information.

▲   A supported VMware virtual hard disk (.vmdk) format file:

- monolithicSparse
- monolithicFlat
- vmfs
- twoGBMaxExtentSparse
- twoGBMaxExtentFlat

The source virtual machine must also be running one of the following operating systems:

▼   Windows 2008 32-bit or 64-bit

- Windows Server 2003 32-bit or 64-bit with SP1 or later
- Windows 2000 Server SP4 or later
- Windows 2000 Advanced Server SP4 or later
- Windows XP 32-bit or 64-bit with SP2 or later

▲   Windows Vista 32-bit or 64-bit with SP1 or later

When you conduct a V2V conversion with the SCVMM 2008 tools, your source computers can be migrated to either Windows Server 2008 with Hyper-V, Windows Server 2008 with Virtual Server R2 SP1 or later, or to Windows Server 2003 with Virtual Server R2 SP1 or later. The VMs that you convert to need to have at least 256MB of RAM for the host plus the memory required for the virtual machine. In addition, they cannot have any port restrictions through a firewall or an IPSEC policy.

Overall, the V2V process is relatively simple. VMM converts the source VMDK hard disk to a VHD hard disk, and configures the source operating system to be compatible with Hyper-V or Virtual Server. There are three different methods that you can use to conduct a V2V conversion depending on where your virtual machine resides:

▼   ESX Host

- VMM Library

▲   From a share (Windows or Network File System [NFS])

Conducting a V2V Conversion

If you are managing your ESX hosts with SCVMM 2008, the following steps are the process that you will follow for conducting a V2V conversion.

Open the SCVMM 2008 console.

Click Convert Virtual Machine from the Virtual Machine Manager tab in the Actions pane on the right of the console to start the Convert Virtual Machine Wizard.

Click Browse to select the virtual machine that you would like to migrate to Hyper-V.

As you can see in our example, we have XP2 on the ESX platform. Click on your conversion candidate and click OK. Then click Next.

Enter a name for the virtual machine. This name is what is displayed in VMM. We recommend that either you give the VM the same name that it was given, or you provide it with a descriptive name so that you know what it is when you're managing your environment. Click Next.

Specify the number and processors that you want for the virtual machine when it migrates. Click Next.

Select your Hyper-V host and click Next.

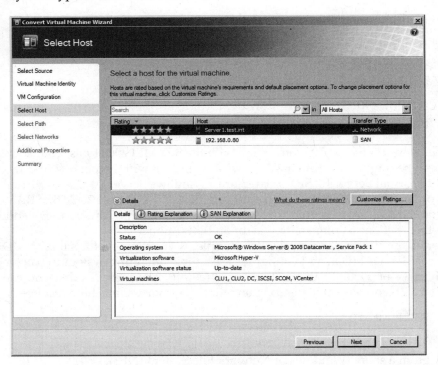

Select the path where you want to deploy the virtual machine and click Next.
Configure the networking for the virtual machine and click Next.
Configure the start and stop information for the virtual machine and click Next.

Verify your settings and click Create to start the migration.

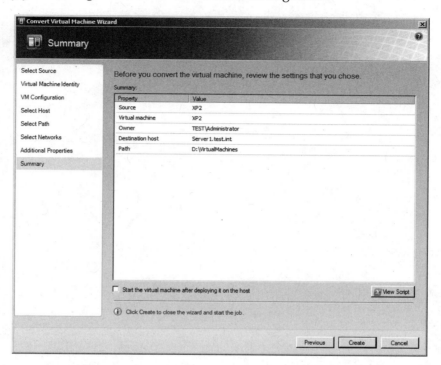

If you're not managing your ESX environment with SCVMM 2008, you can still conduct a V2V conversion. There are two different methods you can use to accomplish the migration:

▼   Manually copy the .vmx and .vmdk files from the ESX host and add them to your library server. Once the library is refreshed, you can use the conversion process described in this section to convert the files to a Microsoft format.

▲   If the .vmk and .vmdk files are accessible from a Universal Naming Convention (UNC) path such as \\Server\Share\Dir, you can use the New-V2V cmdlet in PowerShell to convert the file. You can also use the New-V2V cmdlet in a script to do a standard migration or to batch-migrate several virtual machines.

Virtual machines are fantastically useful tools. Not only do they deliver reliability, but they also make it possible to deploy new systems with a few mouse clicks. And if you decide that a system isn't working out for you, you can just reconfigure a new one and start from scratch with little headache.

CHAPTER 8

Managing Your Virtual Machines

Once the entire infrastructure is in place and you've created some virtual machines, there are a few things you need to know about managing them. Managing your virtual machines isn't much different than managing a physical machine. You need to keep your virtual machines patched, tuned, and running in tiptop shape for your users. In this chapter we'll talk about what you can do to manage your virtual machines.

VIRTUAL MACHINE STATE

A virtual machine can exist in four different states: Powered On, Powered Off, Paused, or Saved. When a virtual machine is powered on, it's almost identical to turning on the power on a physical system. The virtual machine will go through a power-on self-test (POST), similar to hardware, and boot into the OS. When the virtual machine is powered on, you can only make edits to certain components of the virtual machine.

When a virtual machine is powered off, it is in a non-running state just as if you shut down a physical server. All the information that was in RAM is written to the disk or discarded. When the virtual machine is shut down, you can make any edits to the virtual machine configuration, add additional disks, and many other options.

When a virtual machine is in a paused state, the virtual machine is put into a stopped state, except that the information that is in memory is maintained and available to the virtual machine when you resume the virtual machine. When the virtual machine is in a paused state, you will be able to make edits to some, but not all, components of the virtual machine.

When you use the save state function on a virtual machine, the current state of the virtual machine is saved to a file on disk and the virtual machine is moved into a stopped state. Once the virtual machine is in the stopped state, then the CPU and memory resources the virtual machine was using are released to be available for other virtual machines. When you restart the virtual machine from the saved state, the virtual machine will restart to the same place it was when you saved the state.

Starting a Virtual Machine

Starting a virtual machine is a straightforward process regardless of whether you are using the Hyper-V Manager or System Center Virtual Machine Manager.

Starting a Virtual Machine with Hyper-V Manager

Open the Hyper-V Manager.

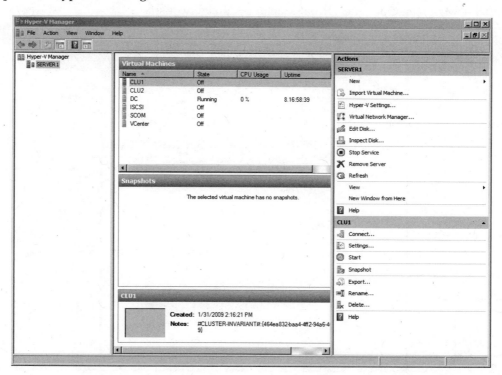

Click on a virtual machine that is in the Off state. From a virtual machine listed in the Actions pane, click Start to start the virtual machine. You can also right-click on the virtual machine in the Virtual Machines pane and choose Start. In Illustration 1 the server CLU1 residing on Server1 has not yet been started. Once selected, you can use the actions in the Actions pane on the right hand side of the Window to start CLU1.

Starting a Virtual Machine with SCVMM 2008

Starting a virtual machine with the SCVMM 2008 console is similar to starting it with the Hyper-V Manager. Open the Virtual Machine Manager console.

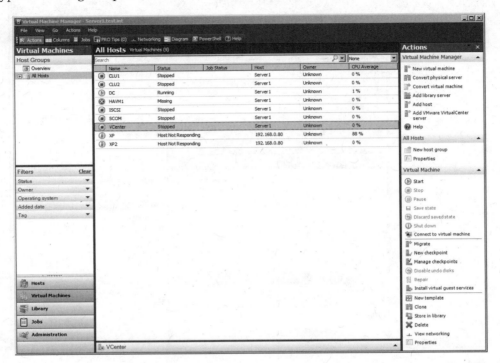

Click on a virtual machine and then from the Virtual Machine tab in the Actions pane, click Start.

You can also right-click on the virtual machine that you want to start and choose Start from the menu.

Stopping a Virtual Machine

There are two different methods to stop a virtual machine: shutting it down and turning it off. When you turn off a virtual machine, it's the same as doing a hard shutdown on a physical server. The shutdown command works with systems that have the Integration Components installed. If you use the shutdown command, the operating system will go through a normal clean shutdown procedure without having to be logged on to the operating system. You can also log into a running virtual machine and use the installed Operating System shutdown command to shut the virtual machine down.

Turning Off a Virtual Machine

Open the Hyper-V Virtual Machine Manager.

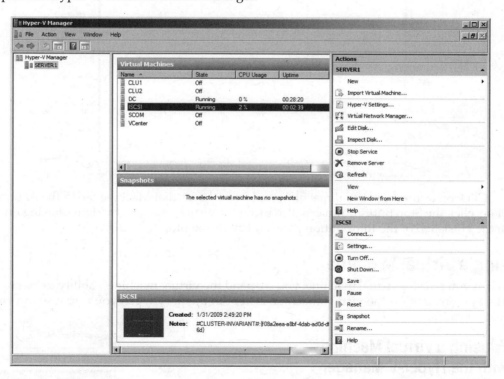

Click on a running virtual machine and then click Turn Off in the virtual machine listed in the Actions pane to turn off the virtual machine.

You can also right-click on the virtual machine in the Virtual Machines pane and choose Turn Off.

Turning Off a Virtual Machine in SCVMM 2008

To turn off a virtual machine in the Virtual Machine Manager, open the Virtual Machine Manager console.

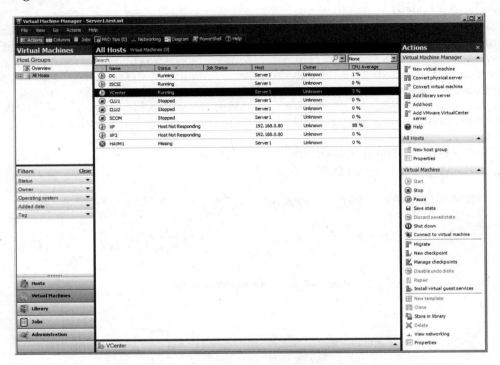

Click on a running virtual machine, and from the Virtual Machine tab in the Actions pane, click the Stop button. You can also turn off a virtual machine by right-clicking on it in the Hosts tab of the Information pane and choosing Stop.

Pausing a Virtual Machine

When you pause a virtual machine, you suspend the virtual machine's ability to execute. The system state for the virtual machine is kept in memory when you unpause the virtual machine.

Pausing a Virtual Machine with the Hyper-V Manager

Open the Hyper-V Manager console and click on the virtual machine that you would like to pause. In the Virtual Machine Name tab in the Actions pane, click Pause. Right-clicking on the virtual machine in the Information pane and choosing Pause can achieve the same result.

Pausing a Virtual Machine with SCVMM 2008

Open the SCVMM 2008 console and click the Virtual Machines tab in the Explorer pane. Click on the virtual machine that you would like to pause. From the Virtual Machine tab in the Actions pane, click Pause.

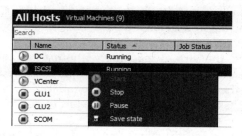

The same result is achieved by right-clicking on the virtual machine in the Information pane and choosing Pause.

Saving Virtual Machine State

When you save state on a virtual machine, you are taking the contents of what's in memory on the virtual machine and saving it to a file on a disk.

Saving Virtual Machine State with Hyper-V Manager

To save the virtual machine state with the Hyper-V Manager, open the Hyper-V Manager console and click on the virtual machine for which you would like to save state. From the Server Name tab in the Actions pane, click Save. You can also right-click on the virtual machine and choose Save from the context menu.

After you have saved state, you can choose to restart the virtual machine with the state you saved, or you can restart the virtual machine without the saved state.

To restart the virtual machine with the saved state, click on the virtual machine and from the Virtual Machine Name tab in the Actions pane, click Start. You can also right-click on the virtual machine and choose Start from the menu.

If you want to restart the virtual machine without the state that you have saved, you will first need to delete the saved state. To delete the saved state, click on the virtual machine and from the Virtual Machine Name tab in the Actions pane, click Discard Saved State. You will be asked if you're sure you want to discard the state; choose Yes to discard the state.

You can also right-click on the virtual machine and choose Discard Saved State from the context menu.

Saving Virtual Machine State with SCVMM 2008

Saving your virtual machine state with SCVMM 2008 is a very similar process to saving state with the Hyper-V Manager. Open the SCVMM 2008 console and click on the virtual machine for which you would like to save state.

From the Virtual Machines tab in the Actions pane, click Save State and click Yes when it prompts asking if you're sure you want to do this. You can also right-click on the virtual machine and choose Save State from the context menu.

After you have saved state, you can choose to restart the virtual machine with the state you saved, or you can restart the virtual machine without the saved state.

To restart the virtual machine with the saved state, click on the virtual machine and from the Virtual Machine tab in the Actions pane, click Start. You can also right-click on the virtual machine and choose Start from the menu.

If you want to restart the virtual machine without the state that you have saved, you will first need to delete that saved state. To delete the saved state, click on the virtual machine, and from the Virtual Machine Name tab in the Actions pane, click Delete Saved State. You will be asked if you're sure you want to delete the state; choose Delete to delete the state.

You can also right-click on the virtual machine and choose Delete State from the menu.

COPYING A VIRTUAL MACHINE

Once you create a virtual machine, a great action you can do with that virtual machine is to copy it and use it on the same host or on a different host, send it to a friend, or send it to a client for review—the options are limitless. There are several methods that you can use to accomplish this task:

▼ Copy the VHD file

■ Export/import a virtual machine

▲ Clone a virtual machine

Copy the VHD File

A method that we have used to send other developers, partners, and customers virtual machines is to simply shut down our virtual machine and send them a copy of our VHD file. When they receive the VHD file, they can then create a new virtual machine on their Hyper-V host and attach the virtual hard disk file to the new virtual machine. You can use this same process to help speed along the creation of virtual machines in your environment. Keep in mind that if you use this process to create a series of virtual machines, you must prepare your guest operating system prior to copying the virtual machine so that you don't get duplicate machines on your network.

Export/Import a Virtual Machine

When you export a virtual machine, a complete copy of that virtual machine is created. This copy includes the virtual machine configuration file, any saved state files, all VHDs associated with the virtual machine, and all snapshots that are associated with the virtual machine. We've used this process to create exact copies of virtual machines that we could then test different scenarios on. One point to note is that when you export and then im-port a virtual machine, you will either need to export that virtual machine again to make another copy, or make a copy of the export prior to importing the virtual machine.

Exporting a Virtual Machine

To export a virtual machine, open the Hyper-V Manager. The virtual machine that you want to export must be shut down. Select the virtual machine that you would like to ex-port and click the Export button under the Virtual Machine name tab in the Actions pane on the right of the console to start the export wizard. You can also start the export wizard by right-clicking on the virtual machine and choosing Export.

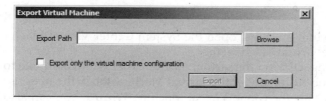

Enter the path that you would like to export the virtual machine to and click Export. You can also choose to export only the virtual machine configuration, which would then not copy the VHD and the snapshot files that would be associated with the virtual machine. If you are exporting the entire virtual machine, it could take a few minutes to complete depending on the size of your VHD files, the number of snapshots, and the speed of your disk and network.

Importing a Virtual Machine

Once you've exported the virtual machine, you can import the virtual machine into an-other host or the same host. Since you can only import a virtual machine once from a given export and you want to import multiple copies of an export, you may want to make a copy of the export. To import a virtual machine, click the Import Virtual Machine button under the Host Name tab in the Actions pane on the right of the console.

Enter the path to the source virtual machine files and click Import. You can choose to reuse the old virtual machine IDs. You may want to do this if you had conducted an export, deleted the virtual machine, and you now want to import the virtual machine exactly the way it was prior to the deletion.

Cloning a Virtual Machine

Cloning a virtual machine is a task that you can use in System Center Virtual Machine Manager. It is very similar to the exporting and importing of a virtual machine with the Hyper-V Manager, except that it's automated and you can clone a virtual machine more than once. You can clone a virtual machine that is in the library or deployed on a host. When you clone a virtual machine, you need to make sure that the virtual machine is in the Off state.

NOTE If you are planning to make multiple clones of a virtual machine that will be on the same network and Active Directory, you will want to consider using the sysprep tool to prepare the system prior to conducting a clone.

To clone a virtual machine, open the System Center Virtual Machine Manager console and click the Virtual Machine tab.

To start cloning, click on the virtual machine that you would like to make a clone of and click the Clone button under the Virtual Machine tab in the Actions pane on the right of the console to start the Clone Virtual Machine Wizard. You can also accomplish this task by right-clicking on the virtual machine and choosing Clone.

If you are cloning the virtual machine to another host, you can leave the name the same if you need to; otherwise we recommend changing the name to avoid any confusion. If you are cloning to the same host, you will need to give the cloned virtual machine a unique name, and it doesn't hurt to give a description of what the clone will be used for. Click Next.

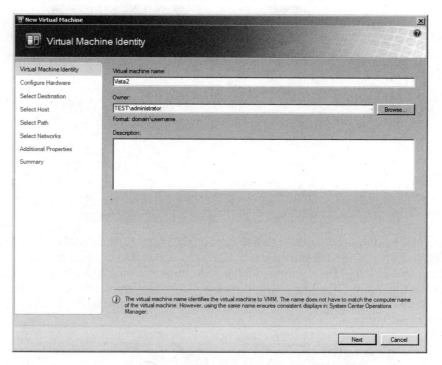

Configure the hardware profile that you want the cloned virtual machine to use and click Next. Choose whether you want to deploy the clone to a host or you would like to store the cloned virtual machine in the library for later use. For this example we are going to deploy our clone to a host. If you choose to save the clone to your library, your next step will be to choose the library and the location to store the virtual machine clone. Click Next to deploy to a host.

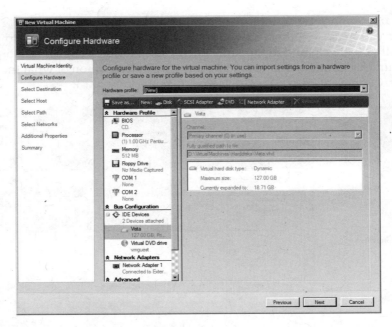

Select the host that you would like to deploy the clone to and choose Next. Enter the path that you are going to deploy the virtual machine clone to. Remember that if you are deploying this clone to be highly available, you must create a LUN on your SAN specifically for the clone prior to making the clone, or if you are running Windows Server 2008 R2 and you want to leverage Live Migration you will want to deploy the clone to a Cluster Shared Volume. Click Next.

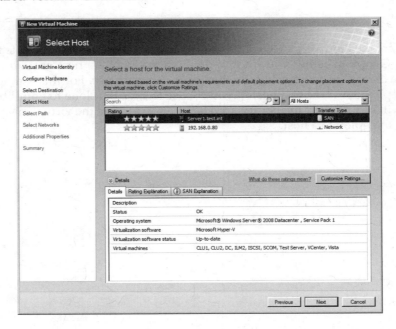

Select the networks that you want this virtual machine to be connected to and click Next. Set any additional properties for the virtual machine and click Next. Verify that your settings are correct and whether or not you would like to start the virtual machine after it is created. If your settings are correct, click the Create button to start the clone of your source virtual machine.

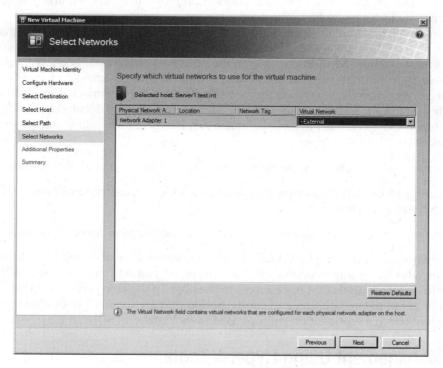

CONNECTING TO A VIRTUAL MACHINE

There are several different methods you can use to connect to your virtual machine. You can set up some form of remote software in your child machine—such as Remote Desktop with Windows or Virtual Network Computing (VNC)—or you can use the remote capabilities of the built-in management tools or use a remote shell. For most of the users in your environments, using RDP or the management tools will be sufficient. For users who require more control of the virtual machines, such as editing state or mounting an ISO image, and you don't want them to log on to the host, you will want to deploy SCVMM 2008, the Self-Service console, or the Hyper-V management tools.

Connecting to a Virtual Machine Using Hyper-V Manager

To connect to a virtual machine using the Hyper-V Manager on a host system, open the Hyper-V Manager console. Click on the virtual machine that you would like to connect to and choose Connect from the Virtual Machine Name tab in the Actions pane. When you click Connect, the Virtual Machine connection tool will be started and will connect to the virtual machine you have chosen.

From the Virtual Machine connection tool you will be able to edit the virtual machine settings, change the state of the virtual machine, and mount media. You can also connect to the virtual machine by right-clicking on the virtual machine and choosing Connect or by double-clicking on the virtual machine you want to connect to.

You can also directly call the vmconnect application to be connected to a virtual machine. If you have the Hyper-V tools installed, vmconnect.exe is located in C:\Program Files\Hyper-V\. To connect to a virtual machine on a local host, follow this process:

Click Start | Run and type:

```
c:\Program Files\Hyper-V\vmconnect.exe localhost virtualmachinename
```

To connect to a virtual machine that is on a remote host, use the following process:
Click Start | Run and type:

```
c:\Program Files\Hyper-V\vmconnect.exe hostservername virtualmachinename
```

If you are using the Hyper-V tools to connect, you will either need to be logged on as a user who has rights to access the host server, or you will need to use the Run As feature to use credentials that have access to the host. In the next section we will discuss in further detail the installation and configuration that are required to be able to use the remote tools from a workstation running Windows Vista with SP1.

Remote Management Using Hyper-V Tools

We're not sure about you, but we don't really like to log on to a host or let other people log on to the hosts unless it's absolutely necessary. If you install the Hyper-V tools on a remote system, this will keep you and other users from having to log on to the server every time you want to make a change to a VM or Hyper-V. The Windows Vista Service Pack 1 Management Tools update now includes the Hyper-V Management Tools and the Virtual Machine Connection tool. For users who need more than just a remote desktop to their virtual machine, this makes life much easier.

Installing and Configuring Hyper-V Tools on Vista

You can download the Vista Service Pack 1 Management Tools for both 32-bit and 64-bit systems from: http://support.microsoft.com/kb/952627. Once you've downloaded and installed the management tools, there are a few steps that you're going to need to complete before you'll be able to connect.

Configuring the Hyper-V tools requires steps on both the host systems as well as the Vista systems that you are trying to connect from. You will need to follow the process described below on each host server that you want to connect to remotely.

Configure the Host The first step of the process is going to be executed on the host servers. Log on to the host system with elevated rights and open a command prompt that has elevated privileges. From the elevated privileges command prompt, run the following command:

```
netsh advfirewall firewall set rule group="Windows Management Instrumentation
(WMI)" new enable=yes
```

If the command runs successfully, the message "Updated 4 rule(s). OK" will be displayed.

You can also open the Windows Firewall with Advanced Security application from the Administrative tools. There should be three WMI inbound rules and one WMI outbound rule.

The next step is to configure the authorization policy for the host server. If the user who is connecting is a part of the administrator group on each machine, you can skip this step.

Click Start | Run and type **azman.msc** to start AZMAN. Right-click on Authorization Manager and click Open Authentication Store.

From the Open Authorization Store window, choose XML File and enter the following path to the Hyper-V store:

system drive\ ProgramData\Microsoft\Windows\Hyper-V\InitialStore.xml

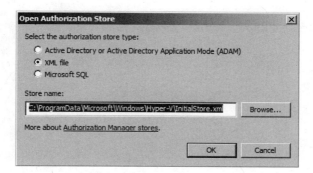

In our case the system drive is C:\.

Click OK. This will open the Hyper-V store. Expand Hyper-V Services, Roles Assignments.

Right-click on Administrators and choose Assign Users and Groups and then From Windows and Active Directory to bring up the Select User, Computer, or Groups window.

Enter the name of the user or group that you want to give rights to and click OK. Then close the authorization manager.

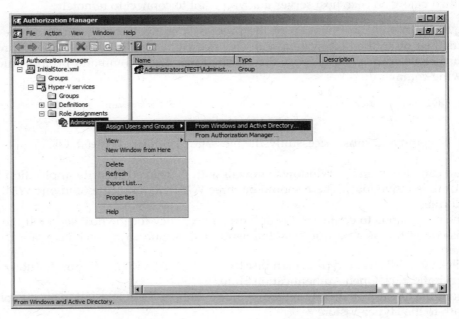

Next you need to add the user or group to the Distributed COM Users group on the host system. To do this, open the Computer Management application from Administrative Tools.

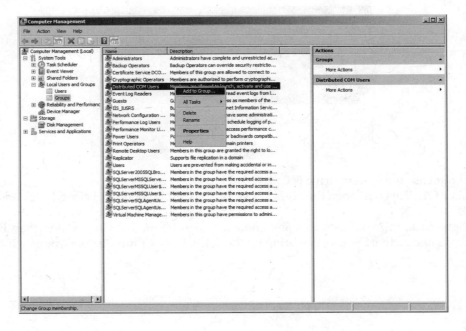

Expand Local Users and Groups, click Groups, right-click on the Distributed Com Users group, and choose Add to Group. Click on Add to bring up the Select Users, Computer, or Groups window.

Add the user or group that you want to have remote access to the host and click OK and then OK again to close the Distributed COM Users Properties window. The remote user or group now needs access to the CIMV2 and virtualization namespace in WMI. To grant access to the user or group, open the Computer Management application from the Administrative Tools.

Expand Services and Applications, right-click WMI Control, and choose Properties. Click the Security Tab, expand the root, click CIMV2, and click the Security button to display the security for the CIMV2 namespace.

Click Add to bring up the Select Users, Computers, and Groups window. Enter the user or group and click OK.

In the Security window, click on the user or group that you just added, and click the Advanced button. Make sure that the user you just added is selected, and click Edit.

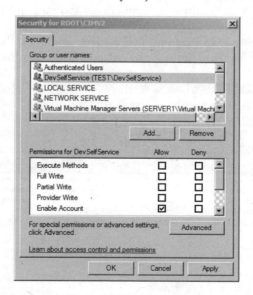

In the Apply To drop-down, choose "This namespace and subnamespaces." In the Allow column, choose Remote Enable. Click the check box by Apply These Permissions to Objects and/or Containers Within This Container Only. Click OK to close the

Permission Entry window, click OK to close the Advanced Security Settings for CIMV2 window, and click OK in the Security for ROOT\CIMV2 window.

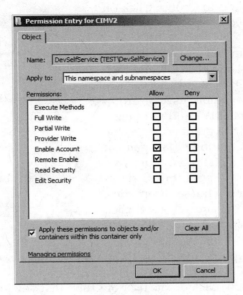

Click on the virtualization namespace and click Security. Click Add to bring up the Select Users, Computers, or Groups window. Enter the name of the user or group, and click OK.

Click on the user or group that you just added, and click the Advanced button to bring up the Advanced Security Setting for Virtualization window.

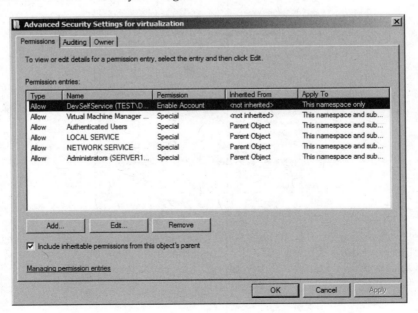

Click on the user or group that you just added and click Edit to bring up the Permission Entry Window.

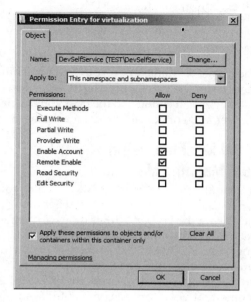

In the Apply To drop-down, choose "This namespace and subnamespaces." In the Allow column choose Remote Enable, and click the check box by Apply These Permissions to Objects and/or Containers Within This Container Only. Click OK to close the Permission Entry window. Click OK to close the Advanced Security Settings for Virtualization window. Click OK on the Security for ROOT\Virtualization window. Click OK to close the WMI Control properties window. You can now close the Computer Management application and reboot the server so that the changes will take effect.

Configure Vista To use the tools in Windows Vista with Service Pack 1 or better, you will need to open a couple of different firewall rules. Log on to the Vista machine where you installed the Hyper-V tools with a user that was just configured on the host and has elevated privileges on the Vista system, and open a command prompt that has elevated privileges. From the elevated privileges command prompt, run the following command:

```
netsh advfirewall firewall set rule group="Windows Management Instrumentation
(WMI)" new enable=yes
```

If the command runs successfully, the message "Updated 4 rule(s). OK" will be displayed.

You can also open the Windows Firewall with Advanced Security application from the Administrative Tools; there should be three WMI inbound rules and one WMI outbound rule.

For the Hyper-V tools to work, the Microsoft Management Console will also need a firewall exception rule. From the elevated command prompt, run the following command to create a firewall exception rule for the MMC:

```
netsh firewall add allowedprogram Program=%windir%\system32\mmc.exe
name="Microsoft Management Console"
```

You can now open the Hyper-V Manager on your Vista machine, and click Connect to Server in the Actions pane. Enter the name of the host server you want to connect to and click OK. The Hyper-V Manager will connect to the host you defined, and you will be able to mange the Hyper-V Server and connect to virtual machines using VMconnect.exe.

Connecting to a Virtual Machine Using System Center Virtual Machine Manager

When you connect to a virtual machine using SCVMM 2008, you connect via VMConnect on port 2179 for Hyper-V, and port 5900 for Virtual Server using the Virtual Machine Viewer application. When using the Hyper-V tools, you can connect to a virtual machine that's not in a started state, but that's not the case with SCVMM 2008. If you want to connect to a virtual machine from SCVMM 2008—whether on Virtual Server, Hyper-V, or VMware—that virtual machine must be in a started state.

To connect to a started virtual machine, open the SCVMM 2008 console and then click on the virtual machine that you want to connect to. From the Virtual Machine tab in the Actions pane, click Connect to Virtual Machine. You can also right-click on the virtual machine and choose Connect to Virtual Machine to connect. In Hyper-V Manager you can double-click the virtual machine to connect, but with SCVMM 2008, when you double-click on a virtual machine, it will bring up the virtual machine properties. To connect to a virtual machine that is hosted on an ESX host, you follow the same procedure to connect. If you are connecting to a virtual machine on ESX for the first time, you will be prompted to install a VMware Active X control for the VMware Viewer.

VIRTUAL MACHINE ADDITIONS

Now that you can build and connect to virtual machines, you will want to install the virtual machine additions to the guest systems that you have. If you are using SCVMM 2008, the virtual machine additions are called the Virtual Guest Services. If you are using Hyper-V, they are called the Integration Services.

Installing Integration Components with Hyper-V Manager

Installing the integration components on a virtual machine using the Hyper-V Manager requires that you are logged on to the server to run the installation. To conduct the installation you can open the Hyper-V Manager. Next, connect to the virtual machine on which you want to install the integration components. Alternately, you can use vmconnect.exe to connect to the virtual machine.

Once you've connected and logged on to the virtual machine where you want to install the integration components, click the Action menu and select Insert Integration Services Setup Disk. This will mount the Integration Services Setup Disk ISO file to the virtual machine.

Once the ISO is mounted, click Install Hyper-V Integration Services. If you are installing on Vista, you may get a UAC message asking if you would like to continue the installation. Accept the UAC message to start the installation of the integration components.

When the installation has completed successfully, click Yes to restart the system or No to restart it at a later time.

Installing Guest Services in SCVMM 2008

Installing the Guest Services on a virtual machine in SCVMM 2008 works in a slightly different fashion than with the Hyper-V Manager. Virtual Guest Services is another name for what is either the Hyper-V integration components or the Virtual Server virtual machine additions. When Virtual Guest Services is being installed, SCVMM 2008 checks to see which virtualization platform the virtual machine resides on and installs the correct virtualization guest service. When you install the guest services, the virtual machine will be brought to a stopped state while VMM installs the guest components.

To install the Virtual Guest Services, open the SCVMM 2008 console and click the Virtual Machines tab in the Virtual Machines pane. In the Results pane, click on the virtual machine where you would like to install the guest services. Click Install Virtual Guest Services from the Virtual Machine tab in the Actions pane. You can also install guest services by right-clicking on the virtual machine in the Results pane and choosing Install Virtual Guest Services from the context menu.

CHECKPOINTS AND SNAPSHOTS

Depending on the console that you are using to manage your virtual machines, a snapshot can be called by a different name. If you are using the Hyper-V console, a snapshot is a called a snapshot. If you are using SCVMM 2008 console, then the snapshot is called a checkpoint. No matter what you call it, at the end of the day a snapshot or checkpoint is a point-in-time image of a virtual machine. You can take a single point-in-time image, or you can take multiple point-in-time images of a virtual machine. Once you've taken a snapshot or checkpoint you can revert to that snapshot. Alternately, you can continue to take snapshots. This functionality comes in extremely handy when you are troubleshooting, patching, installing software, or just trying stuff out to see what happens.

When you take a snapshot of a virtual machine, Hyper-V goes through several steps to actually create the virtual machine. The following steps happen whether the snapshot is taken from the Hyper-V Manager or from SCVMM 2008:

1. The virtual machine is put into a paused state.

2. A differencing disk is created for each virtual hard disk and is linked to the virtual machine.

3. A copy of the virtual machine's configuration file is created.

4. The virtual machine is resumed.

5. When the virtual machine has resumed, the contents of the virtual machine's memory are saved to disk.

While the contents of the virtual machine's memory are being saved to disk, the virtual machine is being monitored for memory activity. If the guest operating system tries to modify something in memory that hasn't been copied yet, those write attempts are queued until the original contents are copied to the disk. When this process is going on, the virtual machine is still available to your end users—they may experience some slowed performance for a very small period of time.

One of the nice features of being able to take a point-in-time view is that you can take multiple snapshots as you go.

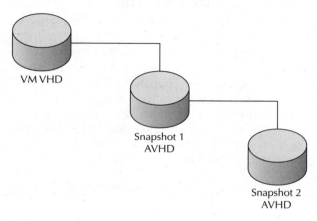

VM VHD

Snapshot 1
AVHD

Snapshot 2
AVHD

Here's an example of how this works: First you create a virtual machine and you install your base Server 2008 image with IIS and ASP.NET. Now you want to install an application, but you're not sure how the installation is going to go and you don't want to have to start over if something doesn't work out. To mitigate this issue, you take a snapshot before you start the installation. This snapshot is created as an AVHD file.

An AVHD file is essentially a differencing disk and is linked to the parent VHD. When changes happen on the virtual machine, the changes occur on the AVHD file and not the parent. So you've taken the snapshot, you've installed the application, and everything worked out. Now the application owner wants to make some changes, but isn't sure about the changes they want to make. You can take another snapshot of the system that has Server 2008, IIS with ASP.NET, and the application installed, so that now the application owner can make their changes. If something doesn't work out, you can revert to either the snapshot where the application is installed, or the base server installation with IIS and ASP.NET.

Once you've created a snapshot of a system, you can take another snapshot; delete a snapshot; revert your system to a previous snapshot; or you can accept your snapshot. Keep in mind that every time you create a snapshot, it uses physical disk space. Also, if you've created a highly available virtual machine, you will want to make sure that your snapshots are on a shared volume. This makes it possible to move the virtual machine between nodes, and the snapshots will move along as well. You don't want to move your virtual machine and have your snapshots back on the other node.

Snapshots

Snapshots are a great way to capture the way your machine is operating right now, and if you need to change back to that moment in time, you simply select the snapshot and you can change your configuration. Let's talk about how to make and use snapshots.

Creating Snapshots with Hyper-V Manager

To create a snapshot using the Hyper-V Manager, open the Hyper-V Manager as a user who has rights to create snapshots.

Click on the virtual machine of which you would like to take the snapshot, and click the Snapshot button under the Virtual Machine Name tab in the Actions pane on the right of the console. When you click the Snapshot button, you will see the state change and text in the Operations column that says "taking snapshot."

When the snapshot is finished, you will see the virtual machine with a date stamp and then below it Now. "Now" is the current state of your running virtual machine. You can take multiple snapshots of the virtual machine and you can choose the point to which you would like to restore the virtual machine.

Managing Snapshots

Managing your snapshots is very important to the health of your virtual machine and your overall mental health as an administrator. As we previously mentioned, when you take a snapshot it uses disk space. Given how easy it is to make snapshots, in the wrong hands this power may be abused. When you create a snapshot, that snapshot is a read-only point in time. When you manage snapshots, you have the option to do a couple of different things. You can:

▼ Apply a snapshot

■ Rename a snapshot

■ Revert the virtual machine to the last snapshot taken

■ Delete a snapshot

▲ Delete a snapshot tree

Applying a Snapshot   When you apply a snapshot to a virtual machine, you are given two choices: Take a snapshot and then apply it, or just apply a snapshot. When you choose to apply a snapshot, that particular point in time becomes "Now." Any snapshots that were taken after that point in time are discarded. You may choose to use this method if you have installed an application and you are testing different configurations of hardware and software to find the ideal configuration.

When you first create a snapshot and then apply that snapshot, you ultimately create a branch in time. The snapshots that may have come after the point in time you applied still exist and are available if you want to apply or revert to a previous snapshot.

This illustration shows where we applied a point in time after we took another snapshot, creating a branch for that virtual machine.

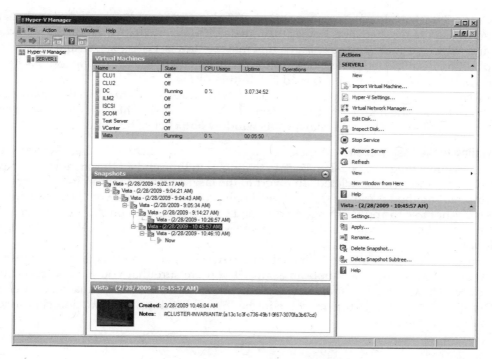

To apply a snapshot from the Hyper-V Manager, click on the virtual machine you would like to work on in the Virtual Machines window.

Now click on the desired snapshot and click the Apply button under the Virtual Machine Name tab in the Actions pane on the right of the console. A window will pop up asking if you would like to take a snapshot and apply, or to just apply the snapshot. You can also right-click on the snapshot that you want to apply in the Snapshots window and choose Apply.

A scenario that we commonly come across is when a series of snapshots have been created and you want to take the virtual machine the way it is and use it as a template. To accomplish this task, you will delete all of the snapshots that you have taken. This makes the AVHD that you are running on the only snapshot. Once you have deleted all of the snapshots, the changes that you are doing on the "Now" snapshot are merged with the parent VHD.

Another scenario that we come across is, "I've taken a series of five snapshots, and I want to create a virtual machine based on snapshot 3." At this time, this scenario is possible. You will just have a few steps to take. To accomplish this task you will need to export the virtual machine, make a copy, and then delete any snapshots that you don't want.

When you export a virtual machine, all of the virtual machine configurations, virtual hard disks, and snapshots are copied to a location. You can then import this copy of the virtual machine and run the tasks that you need to do.

Rename a Snapshot   Renaming your snapshots helps when you have many snapshots to manage. Give your snapshots names that are descriptive of what you took the snapshot of and why you took it. Examples of this may be "pre-service pack install" or "post-application install." Using these descriptions will help if you are setting up test machines and want to revert to a specific period in a testing phase.

To rename a snapshot, click the Rename button under the Virtual Machine Name tab in the Actions pane on the right of the console. You can also right-click on the snapshot that you want to rename in the Snapshots window and choose Rename.

Reverting to the Last Snapshot   When you revert a virtual machine to the last snapshot, the virtual machine will be taken back to that point in time and all the changes that have been made since will be deleted. To revert to the last snapshot, you can follow a couple of different methods. You can follow the above process and choose the last snapshot in the snapshot tree to apply, or you can run the `revert` command on the virtual machine. To run the `revert` command, click on the virtual machine in the Virtual Machine window.

From the Virtual Machine Name tab in the Actions pane on the right of the console, click Revert. A window will pop up asking if you are sure that you want to revert the virtual machine to the last snapshot. Click Revert to revert the virtual machine. You can also right-click on the virtual machine in the Virtual Machine window, and choose Revert from the menu.

Deleting Snapshots   There will come a time when you will want to delete the snapshots that you have amassed. You can delete a single snapshot, or you can delete a tree or section of a snapshot tree. When you delete a snapshot, the memory save file and the configuration files are deleted and removed from the user interface. At this point the AVHD file is still available on the disk. When the virtual machine is shut down, the virtual machine goes through a merging process. During this process, Hyper-V looks at the snapshots that are taken. If any have been deleted, it will find the AVHD file and merge it forward into the snapshot ahead of it. Once you delete a snapshot, you will not be able to return to that point in time.

To delete a snapshot, click on the desired snapshot in the Snapshots window.

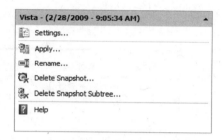

From the Virtual Machine Name tab in the Actions pane on the right on the console, click the Delete Snapshot button. A pop-up will ask if you are sure you want to delete the snapshot. You can also delete a snapshot by right-clicking on it in the Snapshots window and choosing Delete.

If you want to delete a series of snapshots below a certain point, you can use the Delete Snapshot Subtree button. When you use this function, it will delete all the snapshots that are below the period in time that you choose.

Checkpoints

A checkpoint is a part of SCVMM 2008, and the name of what a snapshot is in Hyper-V, but checkpoints have a broader scope and includes VMware. Like a snapshot, a checkpoint saves the state of a virtual machine and its associated virtual hard disks at a point in time. With SCVMM 2008 you can take snapshots of virtual machines that are running on Hyper-V or on VMware ESX.

Creating Checkpoints

To create checkpoints with SCVMM 2008, open the SCVMM 2008 console as a user who has rights to create checkpoints. Click the Virtual Machine tab in the Navigation pane, and then click on the virtual machine you would like to make a checkpoint for.

Under the Virtual Machine tab in the Actions pane, click New Checkpoint (located in the lower right-hand side of the window in the figure above) to bring up the New Checkpoint window.

When you have the window open, enter a name and description for the checkpoint you are creating, and click Create. SCVMM 2008 then instructs Hyper-V or VMware to create a checkpoint for that virtual machine.

Managing Checkpoints

Just as with the Hyper-V Manager, you can manage your checkpoints with SCVMM 2008. When you are managing the checkpoints, the same actions that we described for Hyper-V hold true when you are using SCVMM 2008, but the names are a little different. To manage your checkpoints, click on the virtual machine you want to manage the checkpoints for and click the Manage Checkpoints button under the Virtual Machines tab in the Actions pane on the right of the console to bring up the Virtual Machine Properties window. You can also right-click on the virtual machine and choose Manage Checkpoints.

From the Checkpoints tab in the Virtual Machine Properties window, you are presented with a series of buttons. The New button creates a new checkpoint. The Remove button deletes a checkpoint. The Restore button will apply the checkpoint, and the Properties button allows you to view and edit the name and description for the checkpoint.

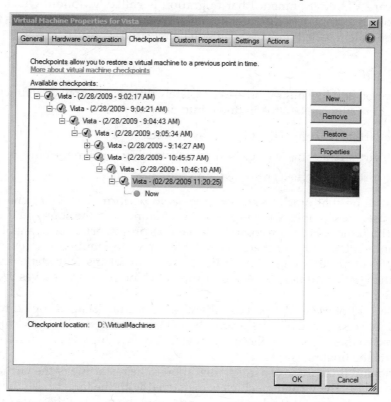

NOTE Be careful with snapshots and certain aspects of your environment. The first major consideration is taking snapshots of domain controllers or any transactional database. Domain controllers are very sensitive to time, and pausing, saving state, and taking snapshots all impact time. Our recommendation is that you don't use any of the state-saving functions of Hyper-V with transactional database-type applications such as domain controllers. The second consideration is also one that is based on time. Machines that are joined to an Active Directory domain will periodically change their machine password for the domain. If you are reverting to a snapshot that has been taken and the machine has changed the password, you will not be able to log on and you will have to reset the machine's account and re-add that machine to AD.

MIGRATIONS

A *migration* is a process that moves a virtual machine from one host server to another host server. With Hyper-V the migration is called a *quick migration*. If you are managing a VMware VI3 environment, that migration is called VMotion. Quick migration and VMotion are completely different animals. When Windows Server R2 is released, a VMotion equivalent called *live migration* will be released.

Quick Migration

Quick migration and live migration are completely different in how they function. Quick migration essentially can be broken down into three steps:

1. The virtual machine is put into a saved state.
2. The virtual machine service is moved to another node in the cluster.
3. The virtual machine is resumed with the saved state.

The first thing that quick migration does is to perform a series of checks. During this first phase, the live migration process will examine both the source and destination hosts to verify if those hosts are compatible (similar processor); have available resources (memory and CPU); and that there is available access to required resources (network, VHD, CD/DVD drives, and so on). If there are no problems with the examination of the hosts, then Quick Motion saves the Virtual Machine state, and moves to the second phase of the process.

In the second phase of the process, the virtual machine state is copied to the target host machine. The storage ownership for the LUNs associated with the virtual machine is transferred to the target host. Once the state and ownership are transferred, quick migration starts the final phase.

The third and final phase of a quick migration is the restarting of the virtual machine. During this phase, the virtual machine is registered with the target host; the network is configured; and the virtual machine is resumed from the point of the state capture prior to migration.

While VMotion and live migration can move a virtual machine between hosts in less than a couple of seconds, quick migrations take a little bit longer. There are two factors that impact the speed at which a quick migration will occur; the amount of memory the VM has and the speed of the connection to your shared storage. Table 8-1 shows some rough average times it takes to conduct a Quick Motion action with different memory configurations and connections speeds to your shared storage.

At the end of the day, you need to make sure that you test your applications and document how those applications react to being migrated. Depending on the application, a few seconds of unavailability won't make an impact. Your end users might not even notice that the virtual machine has moved hosts. Quick migration is a major step in Microsoft's realizing the vision of the Dynamic System Initiative, and leads us into live migration.

Virtual Machine Memory	1GBE ISCSI	2GB FC	4GB FC
512MB	~8 seconds	~4 seconds	~2 seconds
1GB	~16 seconds	~8 seconds	~4 seconds
2GB	~32 seconds	~16 seconds	~8 seconds
4GB	~64 seconds	~32 seconds	~16 seconds
8GB	~2 minutes	~64 seconds	~32 seconds

Table 8-1. Quick Motion Average Times with Varied Connections and Configurations

Like quick migration, live migration has three general steps in the way it moves a virtual machine from one host to another.

The first process that live migration performs is a Pre-Flight Migration. During this first phase, the live migration process examines both the source and destination hosts to verify if those hosts are compatible (similar processor); have available resources (memory and CPU); and there is available access to required resources (network, VHD, CD/DVD drives, and so on). If there are no problems, then the live migration process can proceed to the next phase.

Assuming that all the checks passed, the second phase of the live migration process is to transfer the virtual machine. During this process, the virtual machine state, virtual machine configuration, and device information are transferred to the target host. Only a very small working set of virtual machine processes are left behind on the host system where the virtual machine is migrating from. If there are new writes to the virtual machine memory, those memory writes are intercepted and written to the target host.

The third phase of this process is the final transfer and startup of the virtual machine. The small footprint that was left behind in the second phase of the process is now paused and moved to the target host. Once the remainder of the virtual machine and storage ownership have been moved, the virtual machine is resumed.

While this seems like a lot of steps are happening, this entire process is supposed to occur in less than one second. Given the way that TCP/IP works, you may have a small break in connectivity and TCP/IP can handle that.

VMotion

VMotion is VMware's live migration technology. It allows for the movement of a virtual machine between hosts with a perceived zero downtime, undetectable to users. VMware's VMotion technology fits directly in the idea of a dynamic datacenter, allowing you to move a virtual machine with no perceived downtime to hosts with more power, or move the virtual machine so that you can conduct hardware maintenance. VMotion has been available as an option for your VMware implementations for quite some time now. Similar to Microsoft's live migration, VMotion is a less-than-one-second migration.

Performing a Live Migration

Performing a quick migration is different, depending on whether you use SCVMM 2008 or if you are using the Failover Cluster Administrator. Essentially, a quick migration is failing a cluster resource to another node in the cluster. The process is different, depending on whether you are using SCVMM 2008 or you've built a failover Hyper-V cluster.

Quick Migration Without SCVMM 2008   To migrate the virtual machine you will use the Failover Cluster Manager. Open Cluster Manager, expand your Hyper-V cluster, and click Services and Applications.

You can either right-click on the virtual machine you want to migrate and click Move This Server or Application to Another Node, or you can activate the VM with a single click. This brings up a tab in the Actions pane. From the Actions pane, click Move This Server or Application to Another Node.

Live Migration without SCVMM 2008   To live migrate the virtual machine, you will use the Failover Cluster manager. Open Cluster manager and expand your Hyper-V cluster, and click on Services And Application.

You can either right-click on the virtual machine you want to migrate, and click Live Migrate Virtual Machine To Another Node. Or, you can activate the VM with a single click. This brings up a tab in the Actions pane. From the Actions pane, click on Live Migrate This Server Or Application To Another Node.

Performing a Quick Migration or Live Migration with SCVMM 2008   To perform a quick migration or live migration, open the SCVMM 2008 Console and click the Virtual Machine tab in the Navigation pane. Click on the virtual machine and choose Migrate from the Virtual Machine tab in the Actions pane. You can right-click on the virtual machine and choose Migrate from the context menu to start the Migration Wizard. Remember that if you are running Windows Server 2008 R1, you are performing a quick migration, and there will be a small period of time when the virtual machine you are migrating will be unavailable. If you are running Windows Server 2008 R2 and have configured CSV, your virtual machine will migrate with no interruption to your end users.

From the first page of the wizard, you are asked to choose a host that you want the virtual machine to migrate onto. Each host will have a representative star ranking in front of its name. Choose the appropriate host and click Next.

Select the path to where you want to save the virtual machine file and click Next. Select the virtual network that each physical network adapter should be associated with and click Next.

Verify that your settings are correct. If you are conducting a quick migration, the virtual machine is in a running state when you start the migration and you want it to be running after the migration, check the Start the Virtual Machine after Deploying It on the Host check box and click Move. You can use this same process to conduct VMotion migrations on a supported VMware VI3 configuration.

OFFLINE SERVICING

Microsoft's Offline Virtual Machine Servicing Tool is useful for managing the workflow of updating large numbers of offline virtual machines. The tool works in conjunction with Microsoft System Center Virtual Machine Manager 2008 and with either of these software update management systems:

▼ Windows Server Update Services (WSUS) 3.0 or WSUS 3.0 SP1

▲ System Center Configuration Manager 2007, Configuration Manager 2007 SP1, or Configuration Manager 2007 R2

In order to manage update operations, the servicing tool uses "servicing jobs." For each machine, the servicing job

▼ Deploys it to a host and starts it

■ Triggers the software update process

▲ Shuts down the virtual machine and returns it to the library

---

NOTE   The tool works with Windows Task Scheduler to plan updates.

Using the Offline Virtual Machine Servicing Tool involves a simple workflow:

1. Install the tool to your network.

2. Use the configuration wizard to help connect the tool to VMM and your software management system.

3. For simplicity, you can group virtual machines so that entire groups can be updated at the same time.

4. Establish a schedule for servicing jobs. A servicing job establishes which virtual machines will be updated and what resources will be used for the job.

Getting Ready

Before you install and configure the tool, there are a number of parts of your network that must be prepped and ready. This section examines how you can ensure a smooth installation of Offline Virtual Machine Servicing Tool.

Set Up Your Environment

In order to use the tool, you must have an environment in which Configuration Manager or WSUS is present to perform software updates. The tool uses VMM to manage the virtual machines. Further, updates must be ready for the software update management system to deploy them, and the virtual machines must be configured to accept the updates.

The following section walks you through the steps to prepare your environment for the tool installation and use.

Infrastructure Preparation

There's really only one requirement for your network—that is, to have Active Directory Domain Services running on at least one domain controller with a domain and DNS infrastructure in place. All servers and virtual machines must be joined to the domain.

Microsoft recommends that you have storage area network (SAN) infrastructure. They advise using a Fibre Channel SAN with virtual machines (running 2GB or faster).

Additionally, they recommend an isolated VLAN to manage the virtual machine update process. This is because of security considerations—virtual machines might not be healthy and might attack the network or become susceptible to attack.

Server Preparation

In order to update virtual machines using the Offline Virtual Machine Servicing Tool, different components of the solution have minimum requirements. Table 8-2 lists the components and their minimum and high-capacity requirements for update management servers.

NOTE In Table 8-2 we list "high-capacity" server recommendations. These are recommended in environments in which more than 20 virtual machines are present.

NOTE We talked about the system requirements for the VMM components in Chapter 4.

Also, VMM and its components must be installed and present on your network. Flip back to Chapters 4 and 5 for more discussion on this.

Server Role	Server Type	Minimum Requirements
WSUS	Minimum: Virtual server High capacity: Physical server	CPU: 2GHz dual core or multiple processors Memory: 2GB Network: 1GB Ethernet adapter
Configuration Manager	Minimum: Virtual server or the same physical server as VMM High capacity: Physical server	CPU: 2GHz dual core or multiple processors Network: 1GB Ethernet adapter

Table 8-2.   Management Server Components and Requirements

Virtual Machine Preparation

In order to ensure that the Offline Virtual Machine Tool is able to update your virtual machines, they must be properly prepared. To be used, the virtual machines must meet the following requirements:

▼ Make sure DHCP is enabled.

■ VMM client agents must be installed.

■ If any of your virtual machines are Virtual Server 2005, have the latest version of Virtual Machine Additions installed and registering a heartbeat signal for the virtual machine.

▲ For your Hyper-V virtual machines, ensure that the latest version of Integration Services is installed and registering a heartbeat for the virtual machine.

NOTE   Offline virtual machines that are going to be configured to replace existing servers in case of failure need two network adapters configured: The first will be used by the servicing job. The second will be used by the hot spare virtual machine during its operation as a replacement server.

Preparation for WSUS Updates

If your update plan includes using WSUS, ensure that the following conditions apply:

▼ Each virtual machine has a WSUS client agent installed.

▲ Each virtual machine is part of a Group Policy object that identifies the WSUS server as an update location.

Also, think about grouping your virtual machines together. This makes targeting updates a simpler, more straightforward process.

Preparing for Configuration Manager

If you are going to use Configuration Manager to handle update duties, ensure that the following conditions exist:

▼ Each virtual machine has a Configuration Manager client installed.

■ Each virtual machine is in the Configuration Manager inventory database.

▲ Virtual machines are grouped together in collections in Configuration Manager.

Update Preparation

Virtual machines do not directly connect to an external source (like Microsoft Update) to update. This is where WSUS or Configuration Manager gets involved. And how you use them will vary between WSUS and Configuration Manager.

If you use Configuration Manager:

▼   Make sure that the software update point has downloaded the updates.

■   Make sure the updates have been prepared for deployment.

▲   Manage your deployments for the updates to include a deadline for deployment. To have them updated as soon as possible, set a very short deadline.

If you are using WSUS:

▼   Make sure the WSUS server has synchronized the updates.

■   Approve the updates for the virtual machines.

▲   Set the deployment deadline. To ensure that the update is applied as soon as possible, set the deadline to a date in the past.

Installing the Tool

You're not done yet. Now that you've got all the prerequisites out of the way, you can finally install the tool.

NOTE   Make sure that you install the tool on the VMM server.

NOTE   You must uninstall any previous versions of the Office Virtual Machine Servicing Tool before installing a later version.

To install the tool, follow these steps:

1. Ensure that previous versions of the tool have been uninstalled.
2. Download the setup file (OfflineVMServicing_X86.msi or OfflineVMServicing_X64.msi, depending on your chipset) to a VMM server that has the VMM Administrator Console installed.
3. Open the setup file to begin the installation process.
4. On the Welcome screen, click Next to continue the installation.
5. Accept the license terms by clicking Next
6. On the Features to Install screen, click Next.
7. On the next screen, click Install to install the Offline Virtual Machine Servicing Tool.
8. On the final screen, click Finish to complete the installation.

Configuring the Tool

When you start the tool for the first time, you run through the configuration wizard. This establishes connections between the tool and other applications and services that the tool uses.

To configure the tool, follow these steps:

1. In the Actions pane, click Configure Tool.

2. Enter the name of the VMM server (if asked) and the name of the software update management server. If you are using Configuration Manager to manage updates, also provide the name of the primary site server.

3. Choose the name of the maintenance host group on which the tool will work.

4. Select individual maintenance hosts from the aforementioned group.

5. Specify the time-out limits for servicing jobs. This will depend on how many virtual machines the servicing job can handle at once. If a member of a virtual machine group has not been serviced before the time-out has expired, they will still be updated and not affected by the time-out.

6. Click Finish to complete the wizard.

Installing and configuring virtual machines is just the start of the fun. You'll do it occasionally, but it's when you manage them that you'll really get a lot of experience. This chapter was designed with virtual machine management in mind. It doesn't tell the whole story, but we hope it's enough to point you in the right direction to successfully manage your virtual machines.

CHAPTER 9

Backing Up, Restoring, and Disaster Recovery for Your Virtual Machines

Regardless of whether you are running your servers or workstations on physical hardware or virtual machines, one of the most important things you can do is back up your data. We don't know how many times we've seen customers who had corruption in a system, and they don't have a backup to restore from. To put it quite simply, if you're not backing up your data, you're playing Russian roulette with your company's life. In this chapter we are going to explore different methods and scenarios that you can use to protect the most important asset that your company has: its data.

BACKUP PRIMER

Backing up data is really Computing 101, but it never hurts to go over it again. In fact, it's such a basic task that if you don't know how to do it—or aren't doing it properly—it might be embarrassing to ask about. But in case you need guidance—and for the sake of addressing the issue—let's talk about performing proper backups. Also, Windows Server provides its own tools for performing a proper backup.

Determining Your Needs

In the earlier chapters you spent time determining what kind of recovery point objective (RPO) and recovery time objective (RTO) you needed for your Hyper-V environment and each physical server that you planned to virtualize. Just to give a quick refresher, your recovery point objective—or RPO—is the point in time to which you want to be able to recover. This recovery point can be 1 hour, 12 hours, 24 hours, or more. Depending on the importance of the application, it might even be 30 days from the point of failure. Keep in mind that if you have a 30-day RPO, any data and configurations from the point of failure to the recovered data would be lost. When you are setting recovery point objectives, remember that the shorter the RPO, the more costly the solution can be, both from a resource and dollars perspective.

Your recovery time objective is how fast you want to get to your RPO after a disaster occurs. Determining the RTO for an application your business uses will be heavily dependent on the cost that your organization incurs during the outage period for that application. The other factor that will have a huge impact on your RTO and the backup solution you will need to implement is the amount of data you need to back up and restore.

A little later in the chapter we'll get into the different types of solutions you can use for your backup infrastructure. Bear in mind that everything you do for a backup takes time to complete. If you need to back up and be able to restore several terabytes of data, no matter what solution you choose, it's going to take some time. You'll need to deal with that amount of data, as well as taking into consideration the performance strain that backups can put on your disk performance and your processor performance.

The Data Repository

A backup—in the most basic sense—is a data repository. Data is copied or backed up, and then stored on some form of media. The data repository can exist in three basic models:

▼ Unstructured

■ Full plus delta

▲ Continuous

The *unstructured* data repository model is a grouping of data where there isn't much information about what was backed up. This generally consists of copying data to some form of storage like a CD/DVD, a thumb drive, or an external hard drive.

The *full plus delta* data repository model is closer to what you would consider a traditional backup. A full backup is taken, and then a delta backup is taken. A delta backup can either be from an incremental or differential perspective. In the full plus delta repository model, each file is generally cataloged and tracked to show what was backed up and when.

The final data repository model is the continuous model. The *continuous* model in real time logs all changes that occur on a system. The continuous model tracks at bit and byte levels, the changes that are being made to a file, and allows for a rollback to a point in time to restore that data. A good example of this is shadow copies and previous versions in Windows. With previous versions you can recover a file that was deleted, recover a file that you accidentally overwrote, or compare different versions of a file from different points in time.

No matter which data repository model you implement, you will need to make a decision on how you access and manage that data. Your data repository can exist in three different states: online, near-line, and offline.

Online

An online data repository is the most accessible method of storing your data. You can access your repository to conduct a restore or recovery operation in a matter of seconds and get your end users back to work faster. This kind of access has a high cost of ownership, and the data that you store in your online recovery is still susceptible to being overwritten, deleted, or corrupted. Some examples of an online library include shadow copies of files on a Windows file server, versions in SharePoint, or the local copy of a backup that you save prior to moving to tape and then offsite storage.

Near-Line

Near-line data repository is similar to online data storage, but the time it takes to start a restore or recovery option is generally longer. The reason it takes longer to recover data is that a near-line repository is generally kept in a robotic tape library. Once you've chosen the data that you would like to restore, the backup software instructs the library to retrieve the tape or set of tapes to read the data from.

Offline

An offline data repository is almost identical to a near-line data repository except that a person needs to make the repository media available. This can still work with a robot, but a person will generally have to load a tape that is kept in a tape vault, or that's been received from an offsite location.

We see most organizations making use of all three repository types in their organizations. A common scenario is to make a backup to the online repository, then move the data to the near-line storage, and finally make copies to be stored in an offline and offsite location.

Backup Media

No matter how you back up your data, it will go to some form of media for storage. While there are several different media types you can use—such as CD/DVD and solid state storage—the most common types you will use are magnetic tape, hard disk, or a combination of each.

Magnetic Tape

Magnetic tape, most commonly referred to as just tape, is the most common form of backup media in use today. There are many different types and formats for backup tapes and they vary in size and length of life. The most common formats for tape are DAT, DLT, and LTO.

Hard Disk

For a long time tapes used to be the cheapest form of backup media, but in the past few years the cost of disks has dropped dramatically. You can purchase an affordable disk-based system with redundant SATA or PATA drives relatively inexpensively, and the performance is most often better than that of tape for both backup and for recovery operations.

Most organizations today are running a mix of both tape and hard disk solutions to meet their business needs.

Backup Methods

Backing up data has been around since we started collecting data. The most common problem with backing up of data is whether we actually do it. At a high level there are three different backup types that you need to know about: full backup, incremental backup, and differential backups.

Full Backup

A *full backup* is exactly what it sounds like: backing up everything. This is really the starting point of any backup strategy. Now everything can be definable to a system, a set of data, or a combination of system settings, application settings, and application data.

If you are using a full backup in the classic sense, a really nice outcome of this is your ability to restore your system quickly and get it running extremely fast. In the case of a virtual machine, a full backup can be as simple as backing up the handful of files that make up that virtual machine. Overall, the advantages of full backup are that it is the quickest method of restore, but at the same time the major disadvantage is that this method of backup takes the longest time to create and uses the largest amount of storage media.

Incremental Backup

An *incremental backup* saves only the files that have changed since the most recent backup. This includes whether a file has been backed up using a full, incremental, or differential backup. If you choose to do incremental backups, the first backup that you perform is a full backup. This is because no files have been backed up before your first incremental backup. When you are going to restore incremental backups, you will need all tapes or media in the series of backups to make sure you capture the files that need to be restored. For example, suppose you take a full backup on Sunday, and you do an incremental backup on each weeknight at 10 p.m., and then on Thursday at noon you find out that you need to restore some files.

In order for you to be able to restore these files with incremental backups, you will need access to not only the full backup, but each day's incremental backup media. The advantage of incremental backups is that you're going to use a lot less storage space than you will with full backups. Further, your backups are going to run in the shortest amount of time. The major disadvantage to incremental backups is that you need to have all of your incremental backups available to you when you perform a restore, thus ultimately making your restore take much longer.

Differential Backup

A *differential backup* backs up all files that have changed since a full backup. This is similar to the incremental backup, except the incremental backup backs up files that have changed since the last backup, no matter what type of backup occurred previously. The differential backup stores what has changed since the full backup.

You should be careful when using differential backups. If you go too long between full backups, your differential backup can become as large—if not larger—than your last full backup. The advantages of using a differential backup are that it's faster than a full backup; it doesn't use as much storage as using only full backups; and to conduct restores, it's faster than using incremental backups.

No matter what method or combination of methods you choose, you're going to want to create some form of backup strategy. In this strategy you are going to want to take into consideration a backup schedule, such as conducting full backups on Friday night into Saturday, and using differentials Monday through Thursday. You'll also want to think about backup windows for each application. That means you should consider when the system has scheduled jobs running, and when users are using the system. If you only have one or two hours during which you can make a backup, then you should consider different methods of conducting backups.

Other Backup Styles

Traditionally, backups have been conducted by copying a file from a disk to a backup tape. Because of the amount of data that we have today, this doesn't always work the best, and we've had to adjust based on general physics and the cost of backup tapes. With the cost of disk space becoming cheaper and cheaper, many companies have implemented a virtual tape solution that stores backup files onto a disk, and then that data can be copied onto tape.

While tape is a slower media, it is in no way becoming an outdated medium. We recommend that no matter what solution you have or put in place for backing up your data, you make sure that you have an offsite copy as part of your strategy. In recent years, we've seen too many companies that have had a catastrophic event—such as a fire or flood—and they've lost all of their data, simply because they didn't have an offsite storage strategy.

Tape Rotation

A best practices approach to tape backup is to employ a tape rotation plan. Having only a single copy of your backup data is a bad idea, and is just asking for trouble. What could be worse than your system needing to be restored, and turning to the tape, only to discover that it is faulty? Now, you don't need dozens of backups, but you should have more than one.

Most backup plans employ a combination of incremental backups mixed in with a few full backups. The most common is a differential backup, where all the changes since the last full backup are backed up. This streamlines the backup process because you only need two sets of tapes—the full backup and the last differential backup.

No matter what scheme you follow, you should have access to your tapes at any time. Data storage facilities guarantee this, but most small businesses tend to use sites or safety deposit boxes that don't offer this guarantee. If you need to get the backup tape on an evening or weekend, you probably can't get into the vault until the bank opens.

There are several different types of tape rotation.

Grandfather-Father-Son

The most common tape rotation scheme uses three sets (or generations) of tapes:

▼   **Grandfather**   A full backup conducted monthly

■   **Father**   A full backup conducted weekly

▲   **Son**   A full or partial daily backup

The grandfather and father tapes are typically stored offsite, while the son tapes are used to perform daily backups. This scheme uses daily differential backups followed by a full backup each week. The grandfather tape is stored offsite as long as a permanent backup is needed.

In addition to being the simplest plan, this scheme causes the least wear and tear on the tape drives and media.

Tower of Hanoi

Conversely, the most complex of common backup plans is the Tower of Hanoi plan. It uses the most number of tapes, but it benefits from being the most secure. The system starts with a number of full backup tapes. For example, it could employ five sets of tapes labeled A, B, C, D, and E.

▼   Set A is used for every other backup.

■   Set B is used for every fourth backup.

■   Set C is used for every eighth backup.

■   Set D is used for every sixteenth backup.

▲   Set E is used for every thirty-second backup.

In practice, for the first non-Set A backup, you back up to the Set B media. On the first non-Set A or first non-Set B backup, you use the Set C media, and so forth.

Six-Tape Backup

The six-tape system is ideal for enterprises that have small amounts of data to back up. This version doesn't back up over the weekends and alternates between two tapes on Fridays (thus using six tapes).

NOTE   You can modify this scheme and back up on weekends, thus changing the name to an Eight-Tape Backup.

This scheme uses six backup sets, one for almost every day of the week:

▼   Monday

■   Tuesday

■   Wednesday

■   Thursday

▲   Two on alternate Fridays (Friday1 and Friday2)

The Friday tapes are full backups, and the tape is taken offsite. When the tape is taken offsite, the previous Friday tape is brought back. The Monday through Thursday backups can either be full or incremental backups.

Virtual Tape Library

IBM introduced the idea of a virtual tape library in 1997. The virtual tape library is a collection of hard disks that are presented to standard backup software as tape storage. By backing up to disk, this greatly improves the backup and restore times for an application or a series of applications and servers. With this type of solution you can also take advantage of disk staging.

Disk staging is basically using a disk to hold your data for a period of time prior to moving it to tape to be sent to a secure offsite facility. This method is typically called D2D2T, or disk-to-disk-to-tape. In the event of a failure, the restore first checks to see if the data is available on the disk. If the data cannot be found, it will then request that the required tapes be obtained to finish the restore. This solution is one of the fastest for backing up and restoring your data. Even though disks and tapes have a similar throughput, disks have a much faster seek time and random access than a tape does.

LUN or Storage Replication

Most storage area network vendors have created methods that can replicate a logical unit number (LUN) or an entire storage array to a different LUN or array. You can leverage tools that are built into a single-vendor solution, or you can purchase solutions from companies that can replicate between different vendor solutions and different type of disks. Depending on how you plan to use replication, a common practice is to run the virtual machines on higher-end SAN in your main datacenter, and then replicate data to a lower-cost solution in your recovery datacenter. Even with the cost of disks getting cheaper every day, the availability requirements of your virtual machines and data will ultimately determine whether this solution is worthwhile for your organization.

Backup Solutions

There seem to be a million and one different backup solutions that are available on the market today. Most of the major vendors such as CommVault, Symantec, EMC, and IBM have all added the ability to back up virtual machines, be it from inside the virtual machine or from the host system.

A few years back Microsoft released a feature called Volume Shadow Service (VSS). In a nutshell, VSS is the service that provides the backup infrastructure for Windows Server 2008 and allows for a method to create snapshots of data.

BACKUP SCENARIOS

When you're dealing with virtual machines, there are many different options that you can use to back up your data. You can use a traditional model of installing a backup client on each virtual machine; you can deploy an agent to the host and do snapshot backups; or you can do a combination of both. Determining what is right for you will be governed by cost; what you have for a backup solution; and what kind of data protection you require. Also, keep in mind that when you are conducting a backup, no matter which scenario you choose, the backup will use disk, memory, and processor resources. Keep this in mind when you are designing your solution and picking which backup scenario is best for you.

Backup Host Only

In this scenario, you are only backing up the host and the files that are on the host system. To make this a successful scenario for your environment, you need to use a backup solution that can take advantage of the Hyper-V VSS writers in Windows Server 2008. You can also conduct backups with the Windows Server Backup application and have your existing backup solution back up the file that is produced.

Overall, this scenario works great from a backup point of view, but is a little bit more cumbersome when you need to conduct a restore. In this scenario, when you conduct a restore, you need to restore the entire virtual machine; this may make sense for some of you, but for others you'll probably want to be able to conduct a file-level restore.

Back Up Only the Virtual Machine

In this scenario, you are only running backup jobs on the virtual machine and not on the host. This will give you file-level restore options for each VM that you have backed up. Unfortunately it doesn't provide for an easy method of totally restoring the virtual machine. If you experience an issue that causes you to have to have to fully restore the VM, you will need to either provision a new VM and then run a restore job, or you could use a Windows setup disk and a full backup to recover. You can either do this backup using the native guest operating-system backup tools, or you can use a third-party backup solution and load a client onto the VM.

We've found that a mix of backing up the host and the VM is the most efficient method for backup and recovery.

Backup Host and the Virtual Machine

In this scenario you are running backup jobs in both the host and in the virtual machine. This seems to have become one of the most common backup scenarios that we have seen in the wild. Not only do you have the ability to restore at the file level in the virtual machine, you can also do a full machine restore from the host system. When you configure your backups in this scenario, you need to take into consideration that you could be backing up the virtual machine data twice: once when you do the host backup (you can deselect the virtual machine locations), and once when you do the backup in the virtual machine.

We recommend that you spend some time and think about a backup strategy for your virtual machines. A possible solution when using this method is to take a full backup of the host including virtual machines on a weekly or biweekly basis, while taking a full guest backup once a week. The method also leverages either incremental or differential backups on the days you don't take a full backup.

This method does give you the highest amount of restore flexibility, but the major loss is that your backups will take longer and be much larger in size due to the duplicated data. You will need to weigh the costs of the backup to be able to restore at the file level and also be able to restore the entire virtual machine in the case of a disaster which could be the deletion of the virtual machine or the loss of a datacenter. We'll cover disaster recovery a little later in the chapter.

BACKUPS WITH WINDOWS SERVER

Windows Server comes built-in with many ways you can protect your data. It starts at the desktop, protecting you in case you delete something you didn't want to delete, and moves all the way up to the backup of your entire system. In this section we'll look at the tools that Windows Server brings to the party to help keep your data safe.

Shadow Copies

In the olden days if you deleted a file, it was gone. Poof. Vanished. You couldn't get it back. Then Microsoft added confirmation dialog boxes: "Are you *sure* you want to delete this file?" Even that wasn't enough for people. So then Microsoft added the Recycle Bin. You could delete a file (and still be asked if you want to delete it), but it wasn't completely gone until you "emptied" the Recycle Bin.

Still, this wasn't enough for some users.

The next step in file protection is what's known as Shadow Copies. It's not the title of the latest Tom Clancy book. Rather, it is a way to get back files if you accidentally erase them or save over a file you didn't mean to save over.

For example, let's say you've got an important presentation coming up and you've been artfully crafting your PowerPoint presentation. It's almost perfect. Regrettably, one wrong mouse click later, you've copied over the file with some stupid PowerPoint presentation about mullets that your buddy across town emailed you. It's gone, right?

Not with Shadow Copies.

Once you've altered a file and you want to get it back, you can right-click on the file in question and then select Properties. Click the Previous Versions tab and Windows will start looking for other versions of the file.

You can preview each file in a read-only version to find out which version you want to restore. To restore it, just drag the file to a folder or select it and click Restore to restore it to its original location.

Shadow Files works on individual files as well as entire folders. When you restore a file, all previous versions of the file that are different from the live copy on the disk are shown. When you're examining previous versions of a folder, you can browse the folder's hierarchy as it used to exist.

Windows Server Backup

Windows Server Backup is accessed through a Microsoft Management Console (MMC) snap-in, and command-line tools that provide a solution for day-to-day backup and recovery needs. You can use four wizards to guide you through running backups and recoveries.

Windows Server Backup is used to back up a full server (consisting of all volumes), selected volumes, or the system state. Using this tool, you can recover whole volumes, folders, files, applications, and the system state. If a hard drive dies, you can perform a system recovery, which will restore your system to the new hard disk.

Windows Server Backup can create and manage backups for local computers as well as remote computers. Backups can be scheduled to run automatically, or you can perform one-time backups to complement the scheduled backups.

Windows Server Backup offers these features:

▼   **Speed**   Windows Server Backup uses Volume Shadow Copy Service (VSS) and block-level backup technology to perform backups. After a full backup, you can tell Windows Server Backup to automatically run incremental backups.

■   **Simplification**   Items can be restored by choosing a backup and then selecting the item to restore.

■   **Operating system recovery**   You can recover to the same server or a separate server that has equivalent hardware.

■   **Restore applications**   Using VSS functionality built into applications like SQL Server protects application data.

■   **Offsite removal**   Backups are rotated through multiple disks so that they can be taken offsite for more protection.

■   **Remote administration**   The MMC snap-in allows you to manage other servers by clicking on the Action menu and then clicking Connect to Another Computer.

■   **Disk management**   Once configured for a scheduled backup, Windows Server Backup automatically manages the disk usage. The tool automatically reuses the disk space of older backups when creating new ones. It also displays the backups that are available and the disk usage information.

■   **Command-line support**   The wbadmin command is available if you prefer to use the command line. Backup tasks can also be achieved through command-line scripting.

▲   **Optical support**   Windows Server Backup also supports backing up to an optical media drive, like DVD drives. This is ideal when you want to move backups offsite.

Installing Windows Server Backup

If you've just installed Windows Server and enabled Hyper-V—and you don't have another solution for backups—you can install the Windows Server Backup feature from the Server Manager to conduct backups of your virtual machines from a host perspective.

Open Server Manager and click Features. From the Features menu, click Add Features to start the Add Features Wizard.

Scroll down, select the Windows Server Backup Features, and choose Windows Server Backup. If you would like to be able to schedule and edit backups with Power-Shell, you need to choose PowerShell and the command-line tools as well. Click Next.

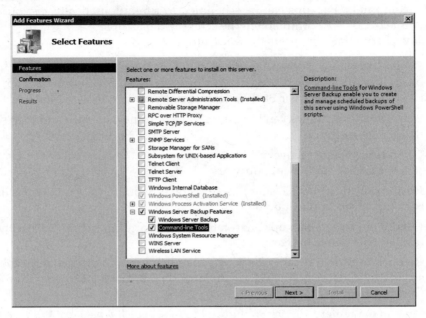

Verify that your settings are correct and click Install to start the installation of the Windows Server Backup Features. Once the installation has completed successfully, click Close to close the Add Features Wizard.

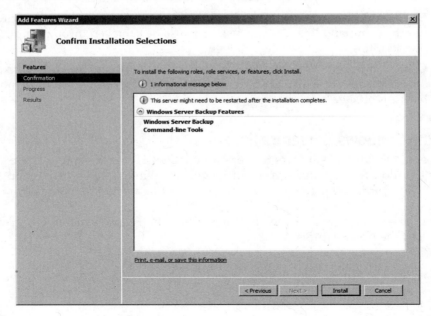

Enabling the Windows Server Backup to Use the Hyper-V VSS Writer

Out of the box, Windows Server backup doesn't support the use of the Hyper-V VSS Writer. Before you make any backup jobs for your virtual machines using Windows Server backup, you first need to manually create a registry key to enable the VSS Writer for Hyper-V. Open the registry editor by clicking Start | Run, and type **regedit**. Or you can use the `reg add` command to add these keys via the command line or as part of a configuration script.

Create the following key:

```
HKEY_LOCAL_MACHINE\Software\Microsoft\Windows NT
\CurrentVersion\WindowsServerBackup\Application Support\{66841CD4-6DED-4F4B-8F17-
FD23F8DDC3DE}
```

Once this registry key is created, you will also need to create a new string value in this location with the following information:

```
Name: Application Identifier
Type: RED_SZ
Value: Hyper-V
```

Creating a Backup with Windows Server Backup

When you create a backup using Windows Server Backup, you can choose to do this as a manual backup or as an automated backup. We're not sure about you, but we like to automate everything we do, so we'll go over setting up an automated backup. Open the Windows Server Backup console by clicking on Start | Administrative Tools | Windows Server Backup.

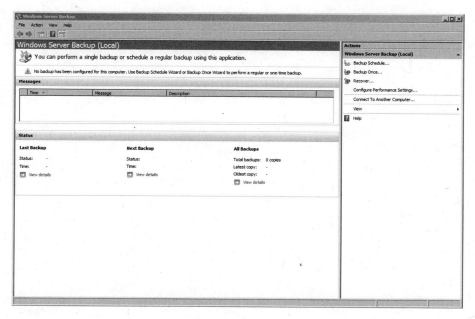

From the Windows Server Backup console, click the Backup Schedule button in the Windows Server Backup tab in the Actions pane on the right of the console to start the Backup Schedule Wizard. Click Next.

Choose either a full backup or a custom backup. For this example we're going to do a custom backup. More than likely you'll run your virtual machines in a cluster configuration, and—like us—you probably have an automated server build process. For us, just rebuilding a host and adding it to a cluster is faster than doing a restore. Anyway, the main difference between Full and Custom is that with custom you choose which volumes you want to back up. Choose Custom and click Next.

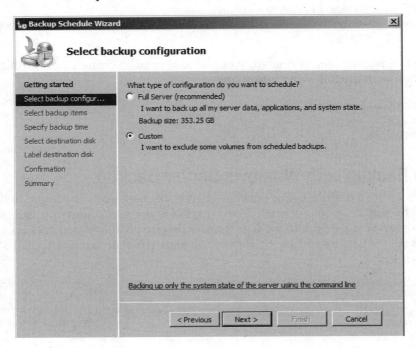

Choose which volumes you want to back up and click Next.

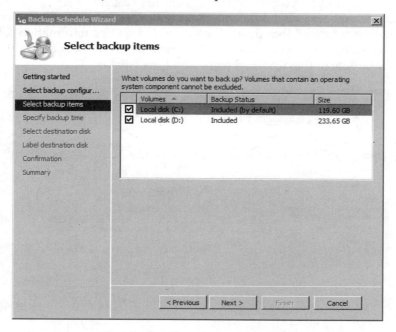

You can either choose a single time to create your backup, or you can choose to do multiple backups run in a given day. Choose the time or times that you would like to have your backup and click Next.

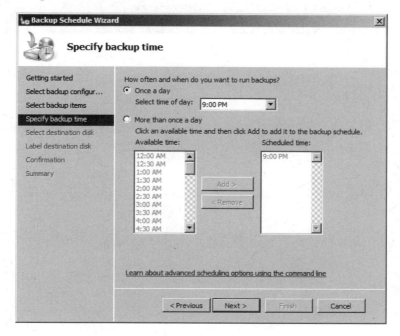

Choose the disk location where you would like to place your backup. If you don't see a disk listed, click the Show All Available Disks button to choose a disk. When you click Next, you will be informed that the disk you selected will be reformatted. Click Yes or choose another disk. When you click Next, you will be given the label for the disk you just added. Take note of the disk label name and click Next.

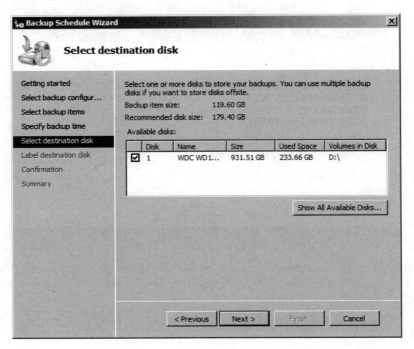

Verify that all information is correct and click Finish for the disk to be formatted and the backup created and scheduled.

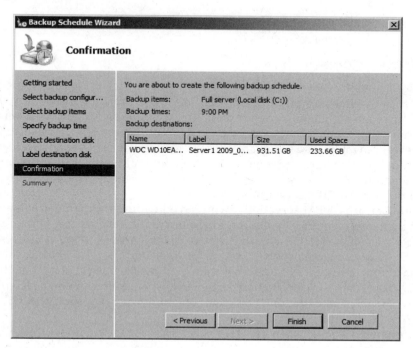

SYSTEM CENTER DATA PROTECTION MANAGER 2007 WITH HYPER-V

We spent a little bit of time on System Center Data Protection Manager (SCDPM) in a previous chapter, but let's go a little deeper and explore how SCDPM can help you with the backing up of your Hyper-V environment. With the release of Service Pack 1, SCDPM now fully supports Windows Server 2008 with Hyper-V and Hyper-V Server.

If you already use SCDPM 2007 SP1 or are planning to use SCDPM 2007 with SP1, a feature that will help you with your disaster recovery is the ability to replicate a backup taken on one SCDPM server, and install it on another SCDPM server in another datacenter. This gives you a pretty good option for working with an SCDPM provider in the cloud, or to provide some disaster recovery capability to your virtual environment.

There are plenty of books and advice available for SCDPM design already, and we don't have all that much room to write about SCDPM. However, we do want to cover a few things about SCPDM design before we show you how to install it. In a nutshell, there are three things you need to take into consideration (besides all the good stuff we wrote above):

▼ What are you backing up?

■ Where are you backing it up from?

▲ Where are you going to put it?

You need to look at the workloads that you want to back up to determine how you want to design your backup strategy for SCDPM. If you're reading this book, we're going to go out on a limb and make an assumption that you'll be backing up virtual machines, but you may also want to back up your SharePoint, Active Directory, and Exchange servers as well, so make sure you plan for them. Remember that you have three different backup scenarios for your virtual machines: host only, VM only, host and VM. You will need to determine your scenario so that you can plan for the type and size of media you will need for your SCDPM server or servers.

The number of SCDPM servers that you have in your environment will also be determined by the number of locations and the number of systems that you have in your environment. Keep in mind that when you are planning your SCDPM servers, a 32-bit platform SCDPM has a data source limit of 150 data sources, while 64-bit systems have a 300-data-source limit. SCDPM also has a limit to the number of snapshots that it can store. SCDPM can store up to 9,000 disk-based snapshots, so when you are creating your protection policies, make sure that you count the number of snapshots that will be taken on a given system.

We recommend that you don't try to do backups over the traditional WAN links that you may have in your environment. If you have dedicated fibre running between your locations, feel free to back up to your heart's content. Backups—even when compressed—can be quite large and they can saturate your network lines. To help alleviate this situation, Microsoft has designed SCDPM so that you can have a SCDPM server in your remote locations, and if needed, you can replicate those backups to another SCDPM server or have some form of tape backup to take those backups off site.

Which leads us to the question of where you are going to put the backup. SCDPM can back up directly to disk or it can back up to tape storage. Once you've figured out the size of your backups and where your SCDPM servers are going to be, you need to determine how you are going to store the data you back up. The benefit with SCDPM is that you can do your first round of backups onto a set of fast disks, then replicate that data set to another SCDPM server that is running on a cheaper disk array, and then to tape or read-only media.

Installation Prerequisites

As with all applications, there are prerequisites that have to be met prior to the installation of SCDPM. To install SCDPM you will need a server that is running one of the operating systems detailed in Table 9-1.

Operating System	Version	Bits: 32-bit, 64-bit, or Both
Windows Server 2008	Standard, Enterprise, Datacenter	Both
Windows Server 2003	Standard, Enterprise, Datacenter, Storage Server with SP2	Both
Windows Server 2003 R2	Standard, Enterprise, Datacenter, Storage Server with SP2	Both

Table 9-1.   SCDPM Server Requirements

SCDPM also comes with the SCDPM Management Shell. The SCDPM Management Shell is a command-line tool that allows you to script SCDPM activities and manage multiple SCDPM servers remotely. You can install the SCDPM Management Shell on the operating systems listed in Table 9-2.

Software Prerequisites

There are prerequisites for both the SCDPM server and the clients that SCDPM will be protecting. From a server standpoint, SCDPM must be a completely dedicated stand-alone server and not installed onto a server that is part of a cluster or is running other

Operating System	Version	Bits: 32-bit, 64-bit, or Both
Windows XP	Service Pack 2or newer	Both
Windows Vista	All	Both
Windows Server 2003	Standard, Enterprise, Datacenter, Storage Server with SP2	Both
Windows Server 2003 R2	Standard, Enterprise, Datacenter, Storage Server with SP2	Both
Windows Server 2008	Standard, Enterprise, Datacenter	Both

Table 9-2.   System Requirements for SCDPM Management Shell

System Center components, Exchange, or Active Directory. The following software needs to be installed prior to installing SCDPM:

▼ Power Shell 1.0

■ Single Instance Storage (for Windows 2008)—If you are running Server 2008, you need to install Single Instance Storage. To do this, open an administrator command prompt and run the following command:

```
start /wait ocsetup.exe /SIS-Limited /quiet /norestart
```

KB 940340 (for Windows Server 2003)—If you are installing SCDPM on Windows Server 2003, the first thing that needs to be done before you start the installation of SCDPM is to install the update described in Knowledg Base article 940349. That update can be found at http://support.microsoft.com/kb/940349 and is an update rollup that covers several different issues with VSS on Server 2003.

■ .Net 2.0

■ Internet Information Server (IIS) 6 or IIS 7

■ SQL Server 2005 SP2 with Reporting Services (or you can install the SCDPM database to an already existing SQL 2005 instance)

▲ SQL Server Workstation Components

Hardware Prerequisites

You can install SCDPM on 32-bit or 64-bit hardware. To take advantage of the additional processing capacity that is available to a 64-bit system, we recommend that you install SCDPM on a 64-bit version of your chosen operating system. We recommend that you run at least the hardware configuration listed in Table 9-3 on your SCDPM server.

Component	Configuration
CPU	Dual quad core at least 2.33GHz
Memory	4GB or more
Disk space	Two to three times the size of the data you are backing up, and this storage should be part of a SAN to provide the throughput that you need.

Table 9-3. Installation Recommendations for 64-bit Systems

Installing System Center Data Protection Manager

To install SCDPM you will need to obtain the installation media and insert it into your server or copy it to a network or local location.

1. From the SCDPM installation media, run setup.exe. When the System Center Data Protection Manager 2007 window comes up, choose Install Data Protection Manager.

2. Read and accept the license terms and click OK to move on with the installation.

3. From the Welcome screen click Next to start the prerequisite check.

4. If your system has passed all the prerequisites, click Next, or remediate any errors that occurred and click the Check Again button to recheck your system.

5. Enter your product registration information and click Next.

6. Choose whether to use a dedicated instance of SQL Server 2005 or to use an existing instance of SQL Server 2005.

7. During setup SCDPM will create two restricted local accounts. The first account is MICROSOFTDPMAcct, which runs the SQL Server instance and the SQL Agent server. The second account is DPMR$BACKUP, which is used to generate reports securely.

8. Choose whether you would like to use Microsoft Update to check for SCDPM updates or not and click Next.

9. Choose whether you would like to participate anonymously in the Customer Experience Improvement Program or not and click Next.

10. Verify that your settings are correct and click Install to start the installation of SCDPM.

The installation process will now install the following components:

▼ SQL Server 2005 Standard

■ SQL Server 2005 tools and Workstation Components

■ SQL Server 2005 SP2

▲ SCDPM

Once SCDPM is finished, you will need to restart your server and then download and install SCDPM Service Pack 1 files. The SCDPM SP1 files can be found at http://technet.microsoft.com/en-us/dpm/dd296757.aspx.

Creating a Virtual Machine Backup with SCDPM 2007 SP1

To create a backup in SCDPM you will first need to open the SCDPM 2007 Administrator Console, which can be found at Start | All Programs | Microsoft System Center Data Protection Manager 2007 | Microsoft System Center Data Protection Manager.

The first thing you will need to do is add a disk to SCDPM. To do this:

1. Click the Management heading, then the Disks tab, and click Add in the Selected Item tab in the Actions pane.

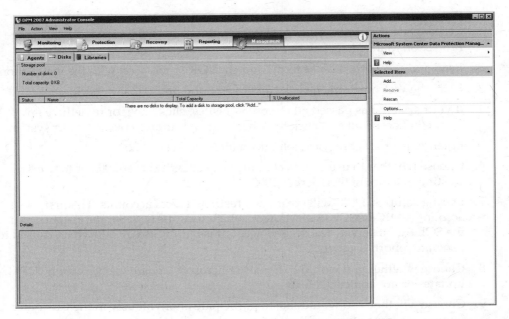

2. Click on the disk that you want to add. Click the Add button to select it to be used with SCDPM, and click OK.

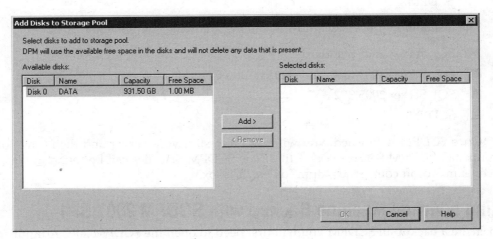

Once you've added your disk to the SCDPM storage pool, you need to install a protection agent on each server that you want to protect.

1. To install the client, click the Management heading and then click the Agents tab.

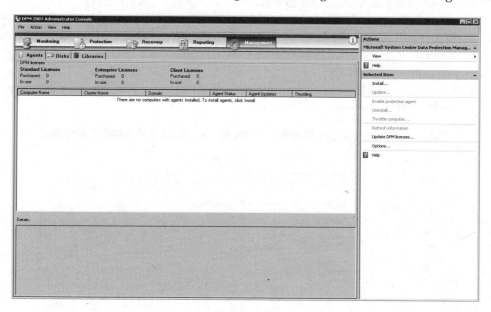

2. Click the Install button under the Selected Item tab in the Actions pane on the right of the console to start the Protection Agent Installation Wizard.

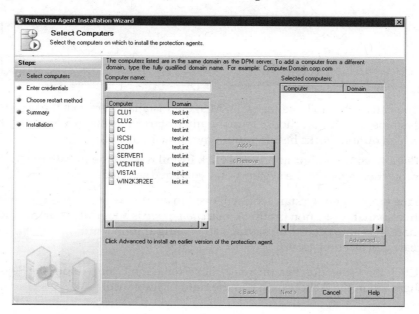

3. Select the computers on which you want to install the protection agent in the left pane and click Add to move them to the Selected Computers pane. Once you've finished selecting computers, click Next.

4. Select how you would like to restart the computers on which you install the protection agent. You can either have the agent install procedure do the restart, or you can restart the systems manually yourself. Click Next.

5. Review your information to verify that it's correct and click Install to deploy the protection agent.

6. Enter credentials for an account that has rights to install the protection agent on the target servers and click Next.

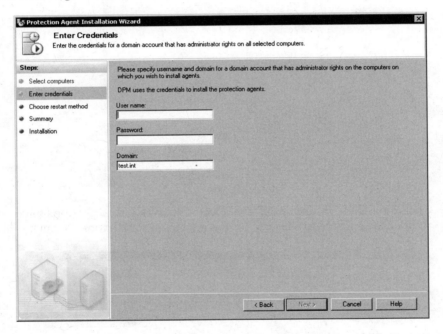

7. You can choose to have the SCDPM agent installation restart the target systems, or you can choose to manually restart the systems yourself. Choose which option works best for your environment and click Next.

8. Review your configurations and click Install to start the installation of the protection agent to the systems that you have selected.

Once the target agents restart, you will need to create a protection group and add the new agent into that protection group. A *protection group* is a logical group of data sources that all share the same protection settings and configuration.

To create a protection group:

1. Click the Protection heading and click Protection Group under the Selected Item tab in the Actions pane on the right of the console.

2. Click Next on the welcome page.

3. Expand the systems that you want to protect and select the data that you want to back up. Click Next.

4. Select the protection method you would like to use for this protection group. This can include short-term protection using disk and/or long-term protection using tape.

5. Specify your short-term goals for your data. This will include the retention time, how often you would like to synchronize the data, and the specific recovery points for files. Once you've set that information, click Next.

6. Verify that your disk allocation information is correct and click Next.

7. Select how you would like to create a replica of the data. You can either do this manually or have SCDPM create the replica for you. Click Next.

8. Review your configuration and click Create Group to create the protection job and start the replication of your chosen data.

There is much more to SCDPM, but we wanted to show you how easy it is to install SCDPM and to create a backup job.

DISASTER RECOVERY

There was a time when an organization had one or two computers; everything was stored in filing cabinets or desk drawers. In this day and age, every organization relies on computers, and there's one on every desk. It is now more important than ever to have a solid disaster recovery plan (DRP) in place. And it isn't just a failed hard drive we have to worry about. Fires, hurricanes, and even acts of terrorism can affect the IT infrastructure of our organizations.

If the network is out for even a few hours, it can have serious consequences for what we do. It might not be important in a candy shop, but if the computer network goes out at the manufacturer making that candy, the consequences can add up. And if the network is unusable at organizations that provide mission-critical services—like power plants, hospitals, or defense agencies—the consequences can be life-threatening.

DRP

A disaster recovery plan (DRP) is a set of measures and procedures that an organization will follow to ensure that essential, mission-critical resources and infrastructures are maintained or backed up by alternatives during various stages of a disaster.

A DRP typically addresses three issues:

▼   **Prevention**   This is the preplanning that takes place to avoid the disaster. For instance, using mirrored servers for mission-critical systems, having hot sites, and training personnel. This will help minimize the overall impact of a disaster on a system. Preplanning is important because it helps you recover in the event of a disaster.

- ■ **Continuity**   This is the process of maintaining core, critical systems or initiating other hot sites during a disaster. Continuity ensures that the organization doesn't buckle in the face of a disaster and can provide essential systems and resources.

- ▲ **Recovery**   These are the steps required to restore all systems and resources to operational status. The time it takes to restore systems can be significantly reduced by subscribing to quick-ship programs, which are third-party service providers that can deliver preconfigured replacement systems.

While the focus of our discussion is about IT infrastructure, a good DRP will be comprehensive and include plans for dealing with all sorts of loss:

- ▼ **IT infrastructure**   Including network, Internet access, and servers
- ■ **Building facilities**   Including power sources, water, and garbage collection
- ■ **Communications**   Including email, telephone, and cellular telephones
- ▲ **Personnel**   What key personnel will do during a crisis

Why is a DRP so important? A DRP protects your organization in a number of ways:

- ▼ Provides a sense of security
- ■ Ensures that certain systems and resources are available and stable during a crisis
- ■ Minimizes system downtime and recovery time
- ■ Minimizes the risk of permanent loss of important assets
- ■ Reduces the risk of confusion during a crisis
- ■ Reduces the need for decision making during a high stress time
- ■ Provides a way to model and simulate various recovery scenarios
- ▲ Ensures the reliability of secondary systems, like hot sites and server mirrors

That candy shop we talked about earlier doesn't really need to prepare for a terrorist attack or worry about what to do if a tornado strikes. But the candy manufacturer might. Nuclear power plants certainly do. It might be cost prohibitive and a little over the top for the candy store, but it's money and time well invested by the nuclear power plant.

Departments within the organization should prioritize the resources in terms of the amount of time required for recovery:

- ▼ Mission-critical systems and resources that must be recovered within minutes of a disaster
- ■ Important systems and resources that must be recovered within a day of the disaster
- ▲ Non-essential systems and resources that can be recovered within a few days or weeks of the disaster

You can't plan for every disaster, but a DRP will help you prepare and give you a good blueprint to follow if there is a crisis.

Sites

In the event of disaster, you may opt to move your organization's IT duties to a different site until you can get the main site back on its feet. There are different types of sites where you can locate backup equipment. Depending on how they are used, they are stocked and called by different names.

Cold Sites

A *cold site* is the least expensive type of backup site for an organization to operate. The site contains no backed-up copies of data or information from the main organization's site. Further, there is no hardware already set up and ready to use. It is because there is no hardware ready and waiting that cold sites are so inexpensive.

While the lack of hardware keeps costs down, it also adds to the amount of time that it will take to get the site up and running.

Hot Sites

A *hot site* is an exact functional duplicate of the original site. This includes full computer systems as well as near-complete backups of user data. To achieve such a match, real-time synchronization between the two sites may be used to mirror the data environment of the original site. This is accomplished through WAN links and backup software.

Following a disaster, the hot site becomes the home for the IT infrastructure and can be switched over to with a minimum of loss to normal operations. Optimally, a hot site will be up and running within a few hours.

Personnel may have to be moved to the hot site, so it may be possible to have the hot site running remotely before personnel arrives.

This is the most expensive solution, because there is so much investment in infrastructure. This type of site is most popular with organizations that run real-time processes, like financial institutions, government agencies, and e-commerce organizations.

Warm Sites

A *warm site* has some hardware and connectivity to the organization, but on a smaller scale than the production site or a hot site. Warm sites have backups on hand, but they likely aren't complete and may be a week old. For example, backup tapes might be sent to the warm site for offsite storage.

The choice of which type of site you'll use is dictated by the organization's cost-versus-benefit strategy.

As we noted, hot sites are more expensive than cold sites, but the hot sites provide a faster turnover in the event of crisis. And if your organization loses a lot of revenue each day because the network is down, it's probably worth it to invest in a hot site.

How Virtualization Helps

As you read this section, the benefits of virtual machines to disaster recovery should be obvious. If a server fails, it is possible to start another virtual machine on another physical device. Many vendors—including Microsoft—report that a new machine can be started so fast that users won't even realize that an outage has occurred.

In the event of a natural catastrophe, one that wipes out your data center, virtual machines make it possible to start functioning at a hot site almost instantly. If your backup plan included backing up to the hot site, you won't lose as much as you would without a fully prepared hot site.

Protecting your data is more important now than ever before. With so many of our organizations relying on their IT infrastructure, it's a necessity that the equipment be safe and that the data on the equipment can be accessed. While there is no dearth of data backup tools, Microsoft does offer some pretty solid mechanisms in Windows Server.

RESTORING

You should look at restoring your virtual machines and your data as *when* it's going to happen versus *if* it's going to happen. You will also want to make sure that you test not only the backups of your virtual machines and data, but also the restores of your data and virtual machines. For this section we're going to go over the recovery of a virtual machine using Windows Server Backup and System Center Data Protection Manager. If you are using another third-party tool to do backup and restores, please contact your vendor for instructions on how to restore virtual machines with their application.

Restoring a Virtual Machine with Windows Server Backup

Restoring your virtual machine with Windows Server Backup is a pretty straightforward process. Keep in mind that when you are using Windows Server Backup to conduct a restore, you will only be able to restore at the volume level. If you want to restore individual virtual machines, you will need to use another tool, such as Data Protection Manager. To conduct a restore for a virtual machine, use the following steps:

1. Start the Windows Server Backup utility from Start | Administrative Tools | Windows Server Backup.

2. From the Action drop-down menu on the toolbar, select Recover.

3. If you are logged on to the host to which you will be restoring the virtual machine, you can choose the This Server radio button. The process is almost the same, but if you are recovering to another server, you will be asked for the location type and the location of the backup data. For this example we're going to restore to the host that we are logged on to.

4. Select the date and time that you want to restore your virtual machine from and click the Next button.

5. Click the Applications Recovery Type and click Next.

6. Select Hyper-V and click Next.

7. Choose where you would like the restore location to be and click Next.

8. Click Restore to start the restore of data.

Now, more than likely you're going to have snapshots that you've taken with your virtual machine. If you have two or more snapshots that you've taken on a virtual machine, those snapshots will not be restored. But there is a little trick that you can use to get around this. To restore a virtual machine with two or more snapshots, follow this process:

1. From the Hyper-V Manager, delete the virtual machine that you need to restore which has two or more snapshots.

2. Start the Windows Server Backup utility from Start | Administrative Tools | Windows Server Backup.

3. From the Action drop-down menu on the toolbar, select Recover.

4. If you are logged on to the host to which you will be restoring the virtual machine, you can choose the This Server radio button. The process is almost the same, but if you are recovering to another server you will be asked the location type and the location of the backup data. For this example we're going to restore to the host that we are logged on to.

5. Select the date and time that you want to restore your virtual machine from and click the Next button.

6. Click the Files and Folders recovery type and click Next.

7. Pick where you have your snapshots stored. If you haven't changed the location, that should be %SystemRoot%\ProgramData\Microsoft\Windows\Hyper-V\Snapshots.

8. Choose the location to which you would like to restore the snapshots.

9. Click the Recover button to start the restore of the snapshot files.

10. After the snapshot files have been restored, follow steps 1 through 9 to restore the virtual machines.

Restoring a Virtual Machine with System Center Data Protection Manager 2007 SP1

When you are protecting Hyper-V hosts with System Center Data Protection Manager (SCDPM), you can recover either the full host, the virtual machine, or if you are protecting the virtual machine, the data inside the virtual machine. We are going to go over the restoring of a virtual machine on a host using SCDPM 2007 Service Pack 1. To recover a virtual machine using SCDPM:

1. Open the SCDPM Administrator console and select Recovery on the navigation bar.

2. Navigate to the host system where the virtual machine resides and select an available recovery point for the virtual machine.

3. Select the virtual machine you want to recover from the Recoverable Item pane.

4. From the Actions pane on the right side of the console, click the Recover link.

5. Review the selection that you have made and click Next.

6. Pick the Recover to Original Instance option and click Next. This will restore the files to the location they were backed up from, overwriting the files that are there.

7. If you've configured SCDPM to use SAN hardware snapshots, you can enable the restore to use SAN-based recovery. Select Enable SAN-Based Recovery if you have that function configured.

8. If you would like to send an email to the end user, or yourself for that matter, when the recovery operation has completed, click Send an Email When the Recovery Completes in the notification area.

9. Make sure that your recovery settings are correct and click Recover to start the recovery process.

Make sure that you test your restores on a regular basis. We've been at many customer locations where they did have a backup but it was never tested, and when we went to conduct a restore, the backups were corrupt and a significant amount of data was lost. We can't stress enough that you consistently test your restores.

CHAPTER 10

Monitoring Your Virtual Solution

One of the most overlooked aspects of any solution is monitoring. It always seems that during a project, monitoring is looked at as an afterthought, instead of looking at it during the planning phases. With a virtual solution, you need to monitor the entire stack from the hardware, network, and disk, to the host/guest operating systems and the applications that are installed on the guests. There are several different methods that you can use to monitor your solution:

▼ Built-in tools with Windows Server 2008

■ Built-in tools with your guest operating systems

■ Using the tools that are a part of your network and SAN infrastructures

▲ Using third-party tools that correlate all of the information and give you a holistic view of your environment

In this chapter we'll talk about different ways to monitor your system, the tools, and the methodologies involved.

MONITORING

When you're monitoring your systems, there are really only two things that you are looking at: performance monitoring and event monitoring. Performance monitoring is examining different system counters to determine how your servers or services are running. Event monitoring is monitoring your system for certain events such as errors that get posted to the event or error logs of a system. The fun part about this is that a performance monitor can be configured so that once it reaches a defined threshold, then the monitoring tool can create an event. Depending on the tools that you use for your event monitoring, you can then make an alert for that particular event.

Performance Monitoring

As we said earlier, performance monitoring is looking at different system counters to determine how your system is running. It seems easy enough, but there are some steps that you need to do beyond just looking at what percentage of your processor time is being used. When you first build your system, you should establish a baseline. A *baseline* is a starting point that you record while your system is running under normal working conditions.

The benefit of having a baseline, or even several baselines, is that you—as the administrator—have a place to start from when figuring out what your system's performance should be. It will also help you track trends over time, and how that server should act at different times. The process of creating the baseline is the same between systems, but will have variations depending on the services running on that system. For example, you will have a standard server baseline that will be made up of a series of performance counters, and then you will have application baselines for applications such as SQL Server, Active Directory, and Hyper-V.

We like to make the two baselines separate, because then you can create your standard server profile and know what the base build trend should look like. Then you can create the application profile to trend how your applications run. This helps when you are trying to troubleshoot bottlenecks in your system.

Some of the common baselines that you will want to add to your system are:

▼   Memory

■   Processor

■   Disk

▲   Network

Memory

Tracking your memory activity will be important from both a host and guest perspective. You need to track the host so that you don't over-allocate your available memory and bog the host down; and at the same time you want to track how your guest is performing so that any installed applications are running at peak performance for your defined service level and performance agreements. There are three main counters that you want to track on both your host and guest systems:

▼   Memory \ Pages/Sec

■   Memory \ Page Reads/Sec

▲   Memory \ Available Bytes

Table 10-1 explains each of these counters and what to consider for each counter.

Counter	Description	Considerations
Memory \ Pages/Sec	The Pages/Sec counter, or pages per second, shows the rate at which pages are read or written to disk to resolve hard page faults. The counter shows you a view of information that is relevant to system-wide delays. A hard page fault occurs when a process references a page in virtual memory that is not in working memory or somewhere in the physical memory, so the process then needs to read from the physical disk to get the information.	When you are looking at this counter, you should start to investigate the system if you are seeing pages/sec in the 500 to 1000 area. If your system is constantly running above 1000 pages per second, you are experiencing a critical issue. Constant basis is the keyword. Even when your system is running at peak performance, this counter will pop into the high range from time to time.

Table 10-1.   Memory Counters to Monitor

Counter	Description	Considerations
Memory \ Page Reads/ Sec	The Page Read/Sec counter, or page reads per second, is used to track the rate at which the disk was read to resolve hard page faults.	When you are looking at this counter and determining if your system is paging more than it should, watch to see if this value is 50 percent greater than the number of logical disk operations on the disk where the page file lives. If you are seeing a high level of paging, you may need to add additional RAM to your system.
Memory \ Available Bytes	The Available Bytes counter is used to track the amount of physical memory that is available for a system or process to use immediately.	When you are looking at this counter, you should be running around 50 percent of the installed RAM on a consistent basis. If your system starts to fall to around 25 percent of the free memory available, you will want to start to monitor your systems. If this counter is running at 10 percent of the free memory available, you are in a warning state and you will want to remediate. If this counter is showing less than 5 percent of free memory available, your system is in a critical state and performance will more than likely be affected.

Table 10-1. Memory Counters to Monitor (*continued*)

No matter how you configure your host or guest systems, there will always be some paging on the system. Use the counters described in Table 10-1 before installing the services that are going to be used to build the system baseline. During this time, make sure you are running your core services such as monitoring agents, backups, and antivirus software to give you a real view of what the system looks like during a normal day.

Processor

Tracking your processor activity in both your host and guest systems helps you determine the number of systems you can have on your virtual host, and it also helps you determine if you've allocated enough processor, or processors, to your guest systems. Trending your processor time may also help you determine when you may need to give a system more processors. One example of such a situation would be if you have virtualized an accounting system that uses small numbers of processor cycles most of the month, but at month end it uses a significant number for month-end reports.

When you are building your processor baseline and determining why you have high CPU usage, there are two scenarios that are common. The first scenario is that you have a runaway process sucking up all of your available CPU resources. The second scenario is that you are having a good, old-fashioned processor bottleneck. That means that the processor is so busy with normally running processes that it can't find time to respond to a request in a reasonable amount of time. As such, you may get some form of timeout errors or your system may lock up. There is just one major performance counter that you can use to track down what your processor is doing:

- Hyper-V Hypervisor Logical Processor(_Total)\% Total Run Time

Table 10-2 explains this counter and what to consider.

When you are creating your baseline profiles and other performance profiles, you need to take into consideration that some applications, such as screen savers, can suck up free processor cycles, so you need to make sure you shut those applications off while you are analyzing your true processor baseline.

Counter	Description	Considerations
Hyper-V Hypervisor Logical Processor(_Total)\% Total Run Time	The Hyper-V Hypervisor Logical Processor(_Total)\% Total Run Time counter is used to show the true percentage of processor time between the host operating system and the guest operating system.	Whenever you talk about the percentage of processor time used, you can get into a deep philosophical discussion tied to what to look for. According to Microsoft, if your system is running at less than 60 percent, your system is healthy. If it's running between 60 to 89 percent, you should be monitoring your system. If it's running at anything between 90 and 100 percent, your system is in a critical state and your performance is degraded. Obviously, if your system is running between 90 and 100 percent utilization on a constant basis, you're having an issue, but that's not the point of contention. The main point of the ongoing debate is where your system should be running to be optimal.

Table 10-2.   Processor Counter to Monitor

Counter	Description	Considerations
		Our opinion is that if you are running a stand-alone system, you should be running around the 70 to 85 percent mark to get your money's worth. If you are running a cluster, you may want to run your workload a little bit lower, in the 50 to 60 percent range. This allows you to have available resources in the event of a failure. With those numbers, we're making an assumption that you are running loads on all nodes. If you are purely running on an active node and one passive node, you may just want to run your utilization on the high side of things.

Table 10-2. Processor Counter to Monitor (*continued*)

When you are experiencing high processor utilization and a larger processor queue, more than likely your processor is overloaded and you will want to consider the purchase of an additional processor, faster processors, or a main board that has a faster bus speed and a larger amount of processor cache.

Disk IO

When you track your disk activity, or disk IO, you will primarily be more concerned with the total amount of IO that the host system uses versus the guest system. That is not to say that the guest isn't important; it's just that the total IO for a host is the host activities plus the guest activities. We covered disk IO previously from a scaling and virtualization candidate perspective, but you also need to continue to monitor IO throughout the life cycle of your environment. When you are looking at disk IO, there are two major counters that you will want to keep track of:

▼ Logical Disk(*)\Avg.Sec/Read

▲ Logical Disk(*)\Avg.Sec/Write

Table 10-3 explains each of these counters and what to consider for each counter.

Use the Logical Disk(*)\Avg.Sec/Read and the Logical Disk(*)\Avg.Sec/Write counters to determine if you are having disk subsystem issues. As we've said in previous

Counter	Description	Considerations
Logical Disk(*)\Avg.Sec/Read	The Logical Disk(*)\Avg .Sec/Read counter is used to measure the amount of time that a read operation takes to respond to the operating system.	When you are looking at either the Logical Disk(*)\ Avg.Sec/Read counter or the Logical Disk(*)\Avg .Sec/Write counter, keep the following readings roughly in mind when you are figuring out your disk performance:
Logical Disk(*)\Avg.Sec/Write	The Logical Disk(*)\Avg .Sec/Write counter is used to measure the amount of time that a write operation takes to respond to the operating system.	One ms to 15 ms is healthy. At 16 ms to 25 ms, you could start to monitor more. At 25 ms and greater, you're having an issue and you need to figure out what's going on with your disk.

Table 10-3.   Disk IO Counters to Monitor

chapters, the disk subsystem is often the cause of many of the problems you will face with your virtualized environment. As such, make sure that you plan your disk layout ahead of time, ensuring that you have plenty of throughput to your disk subsystem. There are a few things that you can do if you are experiencing disk subsystem issues:

▼　Implement a SAN.

■　Use faster disks.

■　Build a RAID array for your virtual machines.

■　Add more disks to your RAID array.

▲　Implement a faster connection method such as 10GB Ethernet or 4GB Fibre.

Network

Network counters are similar to disk counters where you are ultimately monitoring the host system's total network IO. In this case, that IO is made up of mostly guest network traffic. No matter which performance counter you are looking at, you always want to look at both the host and the guest. The reason you want to look at both is that when you have to troubleshoot why your network is slow, you will want to be able to rule out virtual machines that are dormant, and be able to have a view into the virtual machines that may be the cause of the disruption. When you are monitoring the network on the host and the guests, there are four main counters that you need to watch:

▼ Network Interface(*)\ Bytes Total/Sec

▲ Network Interface(*)\Output Queue Length

Table 10-4 explains each of these counters and what to consider for each counter.

Counter	Description	Considerations
Network Interface\ Bytes Total/Sec	The Bytes Total/Sec counter is used to monitor the rate at which the network adapter is processing data bytes. The Bytes Total/ Sec counter also includes protocol information, application data, and file data. This counter is the sum of the Bytes Sent/Sec and the Bytes Received/ Sec. You can calculate the percent of network utilization by multiplying the Bytes/sec by 8 to represent as bits. You then take that total and multiple that by 100 and then divide that number by the NIC's current bandwidth.	When you are figuring out if your system is in a good health state or not, you can use these numbers as a road map to help out. If your interface is running less than 40 percent consumed, your system is healthy. If your interface is running between 41 and 64 percent, you should be monitoring that interface. If your interface is running 65 to 100 percent, you are probably experiencing some negative performance on that interface.
Network Interface(*)\Output Queue Length	The Network Interface(*)\ Output Queue Length measures the number of threads waiting on the NIC.	This is a pretty straightforward counter. If there are no threads in the queue, your system is healthy. If you have one or two threads in the queue, you should be monitoring your interface; and if you have more than two, you've got some form of bottleneck and more than likely you are experiencing some negative performance on that interface.

Table 10-4.   Network Counters to Monitor

Depending on your network infrastructure, you will also want to leverage the tools that your network administrators have to help monitor switch ports and routes, and do inline monitoring of all the traffic coming out of your host systems. You may also want to become familiar with the Microsoft Network Monitor. The Microsoft Network Monitor is a network protocol analyzer that is used to capture a network trace of a problem while it's happening.

Hyper-V Performance Counters

When Microsoft released Hyper-V to the wild, it included 24 different performance counter sets. Amongst the performance counters there is a mix of counters for administrators, developers, and Microsoft support. There is a set of performance counters that you—the reader of this book—will use, so we're only going to cover ones that are the most relevant to you.

Hyper-V Hypervisor

Let's examine the Hyper-V Hypervisor performance counter set. The Hyper-V performance counter set is made up of five performance counters:

▼ Logical Processors
■ Monitored Notifications
■ Partitions
■ Total Pages
▲ Virtual Processors

Table 10-5 explains each of these counters and what to consider for each counter.

Counter	Description
Logical Processors	The Logical Processors counter is used to view the number of cores or hyperthreaded processors that the hypervisor is managing. For example, if you have two quad-core processors running in your server, and you've turned off hyperthreading, you will have eight logical processors. If you have that same configuration, except you've turned on hyperthreading, you will see 16 logical processors.

Table 10-5. Hyper-V Counters Relevant to Users

Counter	Description
Monitored Notifications	The Monitored Notifications counter is used to show the number of interrupts that are being sent via the interrupt-coalescing technique. Hyper-V uses this to help reduce overall virtualization overhead. Basically, when a guest has some data to send out, it will send an interrupt to the root so that the root knows the guest is about to send data over the bus.
Partitions	As we've explained in earlier chapters, each virtual machine that your create in Hyper-V is a partition of the system. The Partitions counter shows you how many partitions are on a system at any given time. If you view this counter when you haven't yet created a virtual machine, you will see that there is one noted partition. This is because the host is the root partition on the system. So when you add your first virtual machine, the count will go up to two and then one more for each new virtual that you create.
Total Pages	When you create a virtual machine, each virtual machine has associated processes the hypervisor uses to manage. This includes such things as tracking virtual processors and guest-to-system address translations that take up memory on the host system. The Total Pages counter will track the total amount of memory that the hypervisor uses to manage the partitions on the system.
Virtual Processors	The Virtual Processors counter shows the total number of virtual processors running on your system. For instance, if you have eight logical processors in the root, you will start with eight virtual processors. Now let's say you add a virtual machine with a single processor. You will now see that you have nine virtual processors. As you add more virtual machines, you will see the number of virtual processors increase.

Table 10-5. Hyper-V Counters Relevant to Users (*continued*)

Hyper-V Hypervisor Logical Processor

The clock is a lie! Okay, that's not always true, but when you're monitoring Hyper-V, knowing which counters are accurate is a story of lies and deceit. That's not exactly true either, but the counters do require careful interpretation. Some of the basic counters that you use to monitor a system do not always reflect what's actually happening on the host. This is because neither the host nor the guest has actual ownership of the PM timer and a handful of other processes. Effectively, this means that the root and the guest time is virtualized.

I'm sure you're either wondering if we've played way too much Half-Life Portal, or you're thinking, "Where is the lie?" The lie actually gets reflected when you are looking at % Processor Time. On a guest system the % processor time may show 100 percent, but on the host at the same time, it may show that the % processor time is in the 60 to 80 percent area. The lie is really just a case of confusion; both counters are showing correctly for the particular instance they are viewing, and this phenomenon has become known as *click skew*.

So what does this have to do with the Hyper-V Hypervisor Logical Processor counter set? The Hyper-V Hypervisor Logical Processor counter set is one of the few counter sets that aren't affected by clock skew. The Hyper-V Hypervisor Logical Processor counter set is made up of 18 different counters:

▼   % C1 Time

■   % C2 Time

■   % C3 Time

■   % Guest Run Time

■   % Hypervisor Run Time

■   % Idle Time

■   % Total Run Time

■   C1 Transitions/Sec

■   C2 Transitions/Sec

■   C3 Transitions/Sec

■   Context Switches/Sec

■   Hardware Interrupts/Sec

■   Inter-Processor Interrupts Sent/Sec

■   Inter-Processor Interrupts/Sec

■   Monitor Transition Cost

■   Scheduler Interrupts/Sec

■   Timer Interrupts/Sec

▲   Total Interrupts/Sec

Table 10-6 explains each of these counters and what to consider for each counter.

Counter	Description
% C1 Time	The C1 process is the power-saving mode for a CPU. The % C1 Time counter is used to track the amount of time that the logical processor is the C1 state. When you are viewing the _Total counter, it is a reflection of how long all of the logical processors are in the C1 state.
% C2 Time	The % C2 Time counter is very similar to the % C1 Time counter except that it tracks the C2 Process, which is a deeper power state than C1.
% C3 Time	The % C3 Time counter is very similar to the % C1 and % C2 Time counter except that it tracks the C3 Process, which is a deeper power state than both the C1 and C2 states.
% Guest Run Time	The % Guest Run Time counter is used to show the percentage of time that a guest is running on a logical processor.
% Hypervisor Run Time	The % Hypervisor Run Time counter is used to track the percentage of time that the hypervisor is running on a logical processor.
% Idle Time	The % Idle Time counter is used to track the percentage of time that the logical processors are waiting for work.
% Total Run Time	The % Total Run Time counter is used to track the percentage of time that is the sum of the % Guest Run Time and the % Hypervisor Run Time counters.
C1 Transitions/Sec	The C1 Transitions/Sec counter is used to show the number of times a logical processor has transitioned into the C1 power state.
C2 Transitions/Sec	The C2 Transitions/Sec counter is very similar to the C1 Transitions/Sec counter except that it tracks the C2 transitions process, which is a deeper power state than C1.
C3 Transitions/Sec	The C3 Transitions/Sec counter is very similar to the C1 Transitions/Sec counter and the C2 Transitions/Sec counter except that it tracks the C3 transition process, which is a deeper power state than both the C1 and C2 states.

Table 10-6.   Hyper-V Logical Processor Counters to Monitor

Counter	Description
Context Switches/Sec	The Context Switches/Sec counter is used to track the number of times in a second that a new virtual processor has been scheduled to a particular logical processor.
Hardware Interrupts/Sec	The Hardware Interrupts/Sec counter is used to track the number of times in a second that a logical processor is processing hardware interrupts.
Inter-Processor Interrupts Sent/Sec	The Inter-Processor Interrupts Sent/Sec counter is used to track the number of times in a second that interrupts are sent between logical processors.
Inter-Processor Interrupts/Sec	The Inter-Processor Interrupts/Sec counter is used to track the number of times in a second that interrupts are received between logical processors.
Monitor Transition Cost	The Monitor Transition Cost counter is used to help determine the relative performance of logical processors.
Scheduler Interrupts/Sec	The Scheduler Interrupts/Sec counter is used to track the number of times in a second that the logical processor is interrupted to handle a scheduler request.
Timer Interrupts/Sec	The Timer Interrupts/Sec counter is used to track the number of times in a second that the logical processor is interrupted to handle a timer request.
Total Interrupts/Sec	The Total Interrupts/Sec counter is used to track the number of times in a second that a logical processor is interrupted to handle any kind of interrupt.

Table 10-6.   Hyper-V Logical Processor Counters to Monitor (*continued*)

Performance and Reliability Monitor

This tool is available in two modes. The mode available from the Performance Information and Tools window gives you a reporting interface that covers system health metrics. You can use the Reliability and Performance Monitor to identify how programs affect your computer performance, both in real time and through collecting log data for later analysis. Like the System Monitor in Windows XP and Vista, the Reliability and Performance Monitor uses performance counters, event trace data, and system configuration information. In Server 2008, you can roll the counters, trace data, and configuration into a Data Collector Set.

NOTE   You have access to the full console and configuration options. To launch this version, type **Perfmon.exe** at the command line.

Data Collector Sets

With Windows Server 2008's Reliability and Performance Monitor comes a new configuration concept known as Data Collector Sets. A *Data Collector Set* enables you to organize multiple data collection points into a single component that can be used to review or log performance. A Data Collector Set can be created and then recorded, grouped with other sets and incorporated into logs, viewed in Performance Monitor, configured to generate alerts, and used by non-Microsoft applications. You can create a Data Collector Set in one of three ways:

▼ **From Performance Monitor**   Create a Data Collector Set using the counters loaded in Performance Monitor by right-clicking anywhere in the Performance Monitor display pane, pointing to New and clicking Data Collector Set to launch the wizard.

■ **From a Template**   This is the simplest way to create a new Data Collector Set. There are several templates from which to choose. Templates are XML files and can be exported and imported. To build a set from a template, open the Reliability and Performance Monitor. Locate the Data Collector Set node in the Navigation pane and double-click it. Right-click the User Defined node and choose New, then click Data Collector Set to start the wizard. After providing a name for your new Data Collector Set, choose Create From a Template and click Next. Complete the wizard.

▲ **Create Manually**   Open the Reliability and Performance Monitor, expand the Data Collector Sets node by double-clicking on it, then right-click the User Defined node, point to New and click Data Collector Set to start the wizard. After providing a name for your new Data Collector Set, choose Create Manually and click Next. Complete the wizard.

You can obtain system diagnostics and generate a report detailing the status of local hardware resources, system response times, and processes on the local system along with system information and configuration data. This report includes suggestions for ways to maximize performance and streamline system operation. Membership in the local Administrators Group is required to run the default Data Collector Set.

Performance Monitor

Performance Monitor is a visualization tool for viewing performance data, both in real time and from data stored in log files. You can render the data in graphs, histograms, or a tabular report. To configure Performance Monitor, add counters by clicking the green plus sign (+) and using the Add Counters screen to select performance objects and counters to monitor. Be sure to check the box next to Show Description to view a very helpful description of the counters as you browse through them.

Reliability Monitor

The Reliability Monitor provides a system stability overview and details events that impact system reliability. You are presented with a Stability Index, which is calculated over the lifetime of the system based on daily measures that are displayed in a graph on the main pane.

The Index is an integer that ranges between 1 and 10, where 10 means that the system was most stable. The daily index is a weighted measure derived from the number of specified failures seen over a rolling historical period. Reliability events in the System Stability Report describe the specific failures.

Event Monitoring

Event monitoring is similar to performance monitoring, but it's based on events, such as errors in the event log, that happen on your systems. When we go out to a client we are often asked about an issue that they are having. One of the first questions that we generally ask is "Have you looked at the event logs?" Unfortunately, the answer is almost always "Well, no." The event logs on your systems are going to be one of your best friends when you're trying to figure out an issue on your host or your guest systems. Almost every application today writes errors to an event log file or to the Windows event logs. If the application doesn't, you need to talk with your vendor to get that fixed, or start looking for another application.

Windows Server 2008 comes with a tool called the Event Viewer. With the release of Windows Server 2008, Microsoft has really beefed up the Event Viewer and added new features like Custom Views and subscriptions. With Event Viewer you can view the Windows Server event logs for Applications, Security, and System events that occur. You can also use Event Viewer to create and save filters so that you can view a certain set of data. You can schedule a task to fire if a certain event occurs. One of the best features of the Windows Server 2008 Event Viewer is that all of the event logs for the Windows Server 2008 Operating System are in the Event Viewer. No longer do you have to dig through file structures to find a log to look at why your BITS client is failing.

Figure 10-1 shows the Windows Server 2008 Event Viewer. As you can see, it's built on the MMC 3.0 platform, with the Navigation pane on the left, the Information pane in the middle, and the Actions pane on the right. The navigation pane has four major sections:

- ▼ Custom Views
- ■ Windows Logs
- ■ Applications
- ▲ Services Logs and Subscriptions

The Custom Views area is used when you want to create a custom view of event data that the Event Viewer has access to. This can be creating a filter to view only Hyper-V errors, or whatever combination of data that you like.

If you've used the Event Viewer in older Microsoft operating systems, then you will be very familiar with the Windows Logs area. The Windows Logs area is where

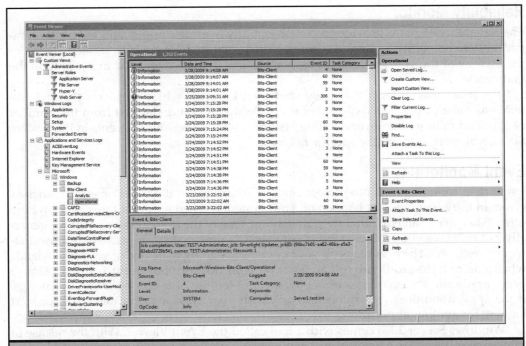

Figure 10-1. The Windows Server 2008 Event Viewer is built on the MMC 3.0 platform.

the standard Application, Security, and System logs are, with the addition of the Forwarded Events and Setup Events logs. The Forwarded Events log is used to store events that are collected from remote computers, where the setup log contains events from application setups.

The Applications and Services logs are a new feature that was added to the 2008 Event Viewer. The Applications and Services logs are broken down into four categories:

- ▼ Admin
- ■ Operational
- ■ Analytic
- ▲ Debug

More than likely, you as the administrator are going to spend more time looking at the Admin and Operational logs, whereas a developer would be more interested in looking at the Analytic and Debug logs.

The Subscriptions area is where you can view events that you've subscribed this computer to receive. Event subscriptions are a great feature if you don't have the ability to implement a system like System Center Operations Manager 2007. You can designate a system to be your Event Viewer system, and configure your other systems to forward events to that system. This means you don't need to spend a significant amount of time going from system to system looking at events. If you are going to have more than a couple of systems, you should invest in getting a system such as Systems Center Operations Manager 2007. It will greatly decrease the amount of time you spend looking at each system's event logs and trying to figure out what's actually going on. Microsoft has spent a significant amount of time building logic and information into Systems Center Operations Manager 2007 to help you with your day.

Opening the Event Viewer   There are three ways to open the viewer. You can open it from the Windows interface, from the Shell Search field, and from the Microsoft Management Console snap-in interface. To open the Event Viewer from the Windows interface, follow these steps.

1. Click the Start button, then click the Control Panel link on the right pane.

2. In the default Control Panel view, click on System and Maintenance (skip this step if you are in the Control Panel classic view).

3. Click on the Administrative Tools icon and then launch the Event Viewer by double-clicking it.

Alternatively, you can type **EventVwr** in the search field from the Start menu and from any Explorer window and press Enter to launch the viewer. For your third choice, you can add the Event Viewer to a custom console using the MMC tool, which you can start by typing MMC into the search field from the Start menu (see the Performance and Reliability section above for adding snap-ins to a custom MMC console).

Navigating Around the New Event Viewer   The Event Viewer in Server 2008 is based on MMC 3.0 and includes the three standard MMC panes.

The first pane on the left holds the computer object that you want to view and the event logs on that computer. You can add computers to the pane by connecting them as follows:

1. Right-click the Event Viewer parent node, located in the top of the left pane.

2. From the context menu that appears, click Connect to Another Computer.

3. In the Select Computer window, provide the resolvable name for the target computer (fully qualified domain name or NetBIOS name depending on your network name resolution service) in the Another Computer field, or click the Browse button to navigate your network and select the target computer from the list of detected computers.

4. Optionally, provide alternate credentials if the account currently in use does not have access to the logs on the target computer. Click the check box for Connect as Another User and then click the Select User button to provide the user credentials.

5. Click the OK button to attempt connection to the target computer. If the attempt is successful, a new computer object will appear in the Connection pane and the logs it carries will be accessible by double-clicking it.

Once you expand the computer node, you will see the major log containers. The containers include the following:

▼ **Custom Views**   You can save your log filters here, in the Custom Views container. The Server 2008 Event Viewer enables you to stitch together output from multiple logs and save the query for ongoing use.

■ **Windows Logs**   The Windows Logs container holds the five system logs that track the system events for later viewing. The logs include the Application, Security, Setup, System, and Forwarded Events logs.

■ **Application log**   The Application log contains events logged by installed applications or programs. The application developers decide which events to log.

■ **Security log**   The Security log contains events such as valid and invalid logon attempts, as well as events related to resource use, such as creating, opening, or deleting files or other objects. You can affect what events are sent to the security log using Group Policy and Local Security Policy.

■ **Setup log**   New for Server 2008, the Setup log contains events related to application setup, including installation activities and configuration updates. Be aware that legacy applications may still send these events to the Application log.

■ **System log**   The System log contains events logged by Windows system components. For example, if a service fails to start, the event is sent to the system log.

■ **ForwardedEvents log**   New for Server 2008, the ForwardedEvents log is used to store events collected from remote computers. To collect events from remote computers, you must create an event subscription.

■ **Applications and Services Logs**   New for Server 2008, logs in the Applications and Services Logs container hold events from a single application or component rather than events that may have system-wide impact. The logs are listed by activity type and vendor. The list of logs varies depending on the services and applications that you have installed. Common logs include

■ **DFS Replication Log**   The Distributed File System (DFS) Replication Service activities are tracked here.

■ **Hardware Log**   Device and peripheral activities are tracked here.

■ **Internet Explorer Log**   Activities tracked by the default Windows web browser.

■ **Key Management Service Log**   Local events created by security association between this computer and remote computers.

▲ **Microsoft\Windows Log Container**   This container is different from the log files listed above. It is itself only a container and holds no events. Under the container, however, are hundreds of logs that are included with Windows and other Microsoft applications you may have installed on your computer.

SYSTEM CENTER OPERATIONS MANAGER 2007

In previous chapters, we've touched a little bit on System Center Operations Manager 2007. We talked about how to configure it for PRO tips and reporting, but there is so much more to SCOM 2007 that you can take advantage of in your environment. SCOM 2007 combines event monitoring and performance monitoring into a single system. SCOM 2007 also has a fantastic correlation engine that takes events that are happening on your system and applies intelligence to help tell you the actual issue with your system. Before we had monitoring systems with correlation engines, we had to deal with a lot of false positive alerts that were generated, or we had to spend a significant amount of time building intelligence into complex event structures.

System Center Operations Manager 2007 also has a feature that will allow you to trend your event and performance data over a period of time. Using SCOM 2007 you can take a historical view of data—let's say 366 days—and with a little analysis, you can start being predictive about what your systems are doing. You can figure out when you need to scale them up or out, and if you can more deeply virtualize your environment.

As we said earlier, Microsoft has spent a significant amount of time building event intelligence into SCOM 2007. They did this by creating management packs. A *management pack (MP)* is a collection of monitors that look at a particular system and look for certain events that occur based on rules and tasks. The events that occur are categorized into different buckets of criticality, and then actions can be assigned to send an email or run some form of action to fix the problem. For Windows Server 2008, there are several different management packs that are broken down into the core operating system and the services that run, such as Active Directory, DNS, DHCP, Clustering, and Hyper-V. The Hyper-V Management Pack provides detailed information about the health of your Hyper-V implementation for both the host and the guest systems. It also looks at components that we talked about earlier in the discussion of Hyper-V performance monitoring, and other components, including clustering of virtual machines.

SCOM has the ability to extract and collect security logs from Windows operating systems and store them for later analysis and reporting. The logs are stored in an Audit Collection database. Audit collection can be used for security analysis, including intrusion detection and unauthorized access attempts.

Audit policies configure which events are recorded to the Windows security log. This log of audit data must then be analyzed and reported on to understand the information. To do this for Windows systems on an enterprise-wide scale, a system is needed to collect, consolidate, analyze, and report on audit data for many distributed systems. Operations Manager 2007 also includes the Audit Collection Services feature, which automates the collection and consolidation of Windows security logs.

Reporting for Audit Collection is built on SQL Reporting Services. Operations Manager 2007 includes a number of default audit reports, including the following:

▼   Account Management
  ■   User account created/deleted, enabled/disabled
  ■   Administrator groups changed

- ■ Group membership changed
- ■ Someone else's password changed
- ■ Computer account created/deleted
- ■ Access Violation
  - ■ Unauthorized access attempts
  - ■ Account locked
- ■ Policy Changes
  - ■ Audit policy changed
  - ■ Object permissions changed
  - ■ Account policy changed
  - ■ Privilege added/removed
- ▲ System Integrity
  - ■ Lost events
  - ■ Audit failure
  - ■ Log cleared

Like all reports in Operations Manager 2007, the default Audit Collection reports can be modified. However, audit reports are modified using SQL Report Builder, not the reporting section of the Operations Manager 2007 console. This separation allows Audit Collection reports to be owned and accessed by individuals who do not have access to regular operational data through the Operations Manager 2007 console.

Not only does SCOM monitor Windows systems, but it also utilizes several MPs for managing non-Microsoft technologies. It uses SNMP messages for the creation of alerts. Syslogs can also be redirected to the management server for analysis and alerting. New to SCOM 2007 is support for the WS-Management standard. WS-Management is a SOAP-based protocol that uses a standard language for systems to interact with management information. WS-Management allows systems to send and receive event and performance information and execute tasks on managed systems.

Monitoring is an important trait of network management, and it is especially so for virtualized networks. Windows Server 2008 comes with the tools you've likely used in one form or another for years, and they can help keep your system optimized as you continue your virtualization efforts.

CHAPTER 11

Hyper-V Security

In days gone by, it always seemed that security was one of the most overlooked concepts and practices when it came to implementing a new service or product into a company. Today things have drastically changed. The shift has a lot to do with the expanding role computers have in our daily lives and with the introduction of government regulations and other audit bodies such as the Payment Card Industry (PCI) and the Health Insurance Portability and Accountability Act (HIPAA). Today, many companies need to know the "who, what, when, where, and how" about what is happening in their technical environments. Depending on the audit compliance regulations, you may even need to have a separate physical network for your customer and a separate physical network for your corporate environment to segregate customer data.

SECURITY BASICS

To truly be able to secure your virtualization solution, you need to understand the process to use to secure your hosts and guests, as well as the stack of technology that makes up your solution and how to secure that. When we talk about the stack of technology we are talking about the following components:

▼ **Network**   How and where your system is connected, as well as how the traffic is getting to that system.

■ **Server**   How your server hardware is configured.

■ **Operating system**   At the very root of it, a hypervisor is an operating system. When we're talking about the operating system, we're talking about the hypervisor, the parent partition operating system, and the guest operating system. We're primarily looking at the services that run on that operating system and what kind of connections that operating system will allow.

■ **Applications**   We've never been to a company that doesn't have some form of application that helps the company run the business or earns that company its revenue. Each application has people who use it either internally or externally, and that application will more than likely hold some form of data. That data could be patient health data, client financial data, internal sales data, or really any type of data. Securing that data is extremely important to your company.

▲ **Process**   Human error is the leading cause of security issues in any company today. No matter what tools you put in to track changes and actions in your solutions, more than likely there is a person in your company who—most of the time unknowingly—can still cause an issue. It could be as simple as an administrative assistant mistakenly attaching an internal quarterly business report instead of a job description for a new position, and then sending the email to a job site.

Even if you have irreproachable users and the best-secured network, servers, and operating system, if you don't have a well-configured application, then you are still open to problems.

Security really is like a chain—the weakest link can compromise your entire chain. The same logic applies to a solution. If you take care of all but one of the key security areas, you still do not have a secure solution. To help you understand your environment, you may want to break down your solutions and think about what each component is. Most applications today have a database, an application server, and a front-end web server. They support web-based clients, or they have "non-browser" clients that connect to the system in a similar manner, skipping the web server front end. In between all of the different components, you will have network switches, access control systems, and firewalls.

We like to view those components as roles. A role is just that—the role your system will play in the solution. By breaking out each role in your environment, you can start to think about what the security concerns are going to be for that role; and define what your standard set of security controls should be. That standard set of security controls is what we call a *security baseline*. You can have different security baselines in your environment and a server may even have more than one baseline applied to it. At a high level you will most likely create baselines for a number of different roles in your environment:

▼   File server

■   Web server

■   Hyper-V host

■   Database server

■   Application server

■   Directory server

■   Network switch

▲   Network router

In each of your baseline configurations you will want to think about things like these:

▼   Auditing user access

■   Turning unneeded services off

■   Turning on a firewall and blocking all unneeded ports, services, and other functions

■   When and how patching should occur

■   Switch port access rights

▲   And many other options

Once you've created standard baseline security profiles for your environment, it becomes easier to manage the security of your environment. You manage to the standard versus the exception, or always having to create something new every time you implement a new solution into your environment. By creating these standards, you create a much more predictable environment, which helps you troubleshoot and figure out what is going wrong in your environment and where.

NETWORK SECURITY 101

Network security involves—as the name suggests—securing the overall network. While security measures exist on individual computers and servers, the network has its own security issues. Access to the network is a primary source of concern. That's because network access is how most hackers and other evildoers get into the network and ultimately do their dirty work. It would be ideal just to cut off network access, a concept that has been the basis for many a dry security joke. But we all know the reality is that an unplugged network would be useless for all of those legitimate users who need to get their work done. We recognize that there is an infinite array of configurations and architectures, so to keep it relatively simple we'll stick to the basics. Let's have a look at three well-known network access technologies that serve to balance the conflicting needs for access and security:

▼ **Firewalls** Conceptually, these are special routers or bridges that intercept, analyze, and apply security controls on the traffic between two or more networks. Commonly this will be between a "trusted" private network and "untrusted" public networks like the Internet or business partner networks.

■ **Virtual private networks (VPNs)** Encryption of private networks operating over a public network (often the Internet) to protect the contents of the network traffic when moving across untrusted networks.

▲ **Access devices** Dedicated devices used to connect remote users to internetworks over the Internet and normal telephone lines. These products include access servers and access routers.

Of the three technologies, only the firewall is solely concerned with enforcing application layer security, and it doesn't provide access so much as permit it. The other two—VPNs and access servers—exist primarily to deliver trusted, cost-effective connectivity at the network layer. Access servers provide remote persons with a way to enter networks. The mission of a VPN is to securely encrypt network traffic as it traverses networks. A combination of access servers and VPN technology serves to allow controlled, secure, network access for an increasingly distributed workforce, and to support customer and business partners who could be coming from the other side of the planet. The solution should ensure that only authorized users are allowed access, while also ensuring data integrity across networks.

FIREWALLS

In the most common deployment scenario, a firewall serves as a traffic control point between a private "trusted" network and one or more public networks. It's a gateway that selectively decides what may enter or leave a given network. To do this, a firewall must be the sole gateway between the network it protects and the outside. If traffic can go around a firewall, the security it provides is worthless. A basic principle is that all inbound and outbound traffic must pass through the firewall.

There is a necessary trade-off between security and network performance. The more traffic that has to pass through a firewall, the slower it may flow. While this may be mitigated by purchasing faster, higher-capacity firewalls, the point is that to deeply inspect traffic for threats, faster, more capable hardware and other resources are required. If security weren't a concern, to boost performance, private networks would use only routers at the perimeter. But we all know security is a major concern, and protecting your network with the very best firewall technology necessary to meet your security requirements is simply a good business practice. The cost of a breach almost always overshadows the expense of having good security in place to prevent it.

Firewall Basics

The firewall is generally thought of as a network traffic filter. Network traffic enters through one network interface and leaves through another. In the case of a routing firewall (as opposed to a Layer 2 firewall), traffic starts being handled at the network layer (OSI Layer 3) of the seven-layer OSI model. Traffic inspection also happens further up the layers of the OSI model in any good, modern firewall. That means the firewall is looking further into the network traffic to see what the applications are actually doing and if there are any attempts to exploit vulnerabilities in those applications.

Firewalls operate by intercepting and inspecting each packet that enters any of their network interfaces. The inspections vary according to the firewall's sophistication and how tight the security policy is. But the goal is always to identify a match between each packet's contents and the security rules the firewall has been configured to enforce. While modern firewalls are very sophisticated, there's nothing topologically fancy about how a firewall intercepts traffic. It does so by accepting all traffic entering its network interfaces over a single path. By having all traffic pass through the firewall's internal data bus and memory, software running on the central processing unit (CPU) is given the opportunity to check each packet against the security rules it has been programmed to enforce.

The actual inspection is performed by reading the packet's header, among other things, for conditions that match rules set up in security tables. Security tables usually include dozens of rules, each designed to explicitly accept or reject specific kinds of traffic by applying a pass/fail test to the packet. If the packet passes, it's forwarded to its destination. If it fails, the packet is dropped.

How Firewalls Work

Security rules are defined for each firewall network interface. Each packet is filtered based on rules applied to the specific network interface card through which it entered the firewall. The act of configuring a firewall, then, is largely a matter of assigning security rules to each firewall interface.

The simplest form of network security technology is the access list. Also called an access control list (ACL), or filter, the access list is a basic component of any firewall's configuration. As the name implies, the access list restricts certain traffic from gaining access to a network. It provides a basic level of network security by filtering packets according to these criteria:

▼ **Source and destination IP address**　The IP address from which the packet originated and is addressed.

■ **Source and destination port number**　The port number from which the packet originated and is addressed.

▲ **Source and destination protocol number**　The protocol number from which the packet originated and is addressed.

There is a whole lot more to firewalls, so much so that we could easily write an entire book on the subject. There are firewalls from companies like Check Point Software, that handle special applications, like Voice over IP (VoIP), and that have the ability to ferret out the stealthiest of shell code hidden in what looks like normal network traffic. The important takeaway here is that firewalls are a very important component of a virtualized system. The selection, configuration, deployment, and management of an appropriate firewall solution should be an early consideration in any virtualization project.

VIRTUAL PRIVATE NETWORKS

What is a virtual private network (VPN)? As so often happens in the computer business, marketing hype can muddle an otherwise clear term. In the case of VPNs, some confusion exists over what's virtual in a VPN—the privacy or the network? Here's the two-part definition of a virtual private network:

▼ VPN topology runs mostly over shared network infrastructure, usually the Internet, and has at least one private LAN segment at each endpoint.

▲ VPN sessions run through an encrypted connection.

To operate through encrypted connections across the Internet, the network segments at each end of a VPN must be under the administrative control of the enterprise (or enterprises) running the virtual network, or each end must be cooperatively configured in the case of a VPN between two organizations. But in practical terms, this means that the endpoint routers must be under a common security and operational regimen. Above all, the endpoint routers or firewalls in a VPN must use a common encryption scheme.

Traditionally, long-distance connectivity to an internetwork relied on a WAN with a leased line. Further, a leased line is simply not an option for an individual who is traveling and cannot be in one place long enough for a leased line to be justified. The following are some reasons why VPNs have been making an impact on the leased-line market for a long time:

▼ **Lower costs**　Leased lines require expensive transport bandwidth and backbone equipment. Additionally, VPNs don't need in-house terminal equipment and access modems.

- ■ **Network agility**   Relatively speaking, VPN links are easy and inexpensive to set up, change, and remove. Because of this, an organization's communications infrastructure won't be traumatized when a VPN is installed, reconfigured, or removed. Further, the availability of the Internet ensures that you can connect your VPN nearly anywhere.

- ▲ **Access**   Because of its availability, subscribers anywhere on the VPN have the same level of access and view of central services (like email, internal and external web sites, security, and so forth).The components making up a VPN are

  - ■ **Tunneling**   Point-to-point connections over a connectionless IP network—in essence, a set of predetermined router hops taken through the Internet to guarantee performance and delivery.

  - ■ **Encryption**   The scrambling of an IP packet's contents to render it unreadable to all but those with a key to unscramble it. (Keys are held by authorized VPN sending and receiving endpoints, concealing the contents of the traffic from anyone in between.)

  - ■ **Encapsulation**   Placing a frame inside an IP packet to bridge dissimilar networks (the IP is unpacked on the other side), effectively allowing tunneling to take place across otherwise incompatible VPN network segments.

  - ■ **Packet authentication**   The ability to ensure the integrity of a VPN packet by confirming that its contents (payload) weren't altered en route.

  - ■ **User authentication**   User authentication, authorization, and accounting (AAA) capabilities enforced through security servers such as TACACS+, RADIUS, or Kerberos.

  - ■ **Access control**   Firewalls, intrusion detection devices, and security auditing procedures used to monitor all traffic crossing VPN security perimeters.

  - ■ **Quality of Service (QoS)**   QoS is a set of internetwork management standards and functions to ensure interoperability of devices and software platforms, and to leverage the platform to guarantee end-to-end network performance and reliability.

This list shows how a VPN is as much about seamlessness as security. Forcing network administrators or users to go through multiple steps to accomplish simple tasks would make using a VPN less attractive. In practical terms, therefore, a VPN must be configured using hardware and software devices with these required characteristics.

Access Devices

Access to your network can be accomplished through a variety of means. Branch offices, small offices, telecommuters, and road warriors may need higher performance and more robust access to the network. As such, access for these connections can be facilitated via access routers, specialized remote access gateways, and firewalls supporting user-based VPN connections.

These solutions provide the functionality for remote workers who need more powerful access to the network. To facilitate these connections, they include beefed-up security and performance features, and provide secure Internet and network access.

Access solutions generally include or support:

▼ Access via cellular, broadband, leased-line, and even other methods of network transport such as satellite

■ Multiservice data/voice integration applications.

■ Secure Sockets Layer (SSL) and IPSec VPN

■ Stateful inspection firewall

■ Intrusion detection and prevention (IDS/IPS)

▲ Many models, scalable and modular, providing design and deployment flexibility

An important feature to consider is support for Quality of Service (QoS) functions. Since they will be asked to channel VoIP, multimedia content, and other applications that would suffer from packet latency right alongside traffic like backup or file transfer, QoS is a necessary mechanism. These capabilities result in smoother, jitter-free conversations and transmissions of voice and multimedia traffic types.

Access Lists

We talked about ACLs earlier in this section, but let's take a closer look at what they do, exactly. *Access lists* are groups of statements based on security policy and are intended to enforce security on network traffic passing though the device. In its simplest form, each statement contains a pattern, or signature, that could be found within an IP packet. As packets enter the device with an access list, the list is checked line-by-line—in the same order it is loaded—for the pattern that matches the incoming packet. A permit-or-deny rule is associated with the pattern and it determines what happens to the packet.

Access lists are entered one line at a time and the list is scanned in that order. Also, once you associate a list with a device, any packet not processed by the list is dropped.

The list can be applied to incoming packets (ingress) or outgoing packets (egress). For egress lists, one would typically filter only on the outgoing interface, rather than on the individual incoming interfaces on the trusted network.

Access lists are broken into two different types:

▼ **Standard access lists** These operate on the network layer of the OSI stack. These are used to block or allow networks from reaching other networks.

▲ **Extended access lists** These function on both Layer 3 and Layer 4 of the OSI model. They allow you to filter by network address, and also the type of traffic that's being sent or retrieved. Extended access lists are more robust and capable, and allow greater control of traffic into and out of your network.

IPSec

IPSec is a set of protocols that supports secure exchange of packets at the IP layer. Because IPSec operates at the network layer (Layer 3), it can provide secure transport capable of supporting any application that uses IP.

IPSec provides three main areas of security when transmitting information across a network:

▼ Authentication of packets between the sending and receiving devices

■ Integrity of data when being transmitted

▲ Privacy of data when being transmitted

IPSec operates in two modes, transport and tunnel:

▼ In transport mode, encapsulated security payload (ESP) and authentication header(AH) reside in the original IP packet between the IP header and the upper-layer extension header information. For instance, Windows 2000 IPSec uses transport mode to provide security between two end systems, for example, a Windows 2000 Professional client and a Windows 2000 Server.

▲ In tunnel mode, IPSec places an original IP packet into a new IP packet and inserts the AH or ESP between the IP header of the new packet and the original IP packet. The new IP packet leads to the tunnel endpoint and the original IP header specifies the packet's destination. You can use tunnel mode between two security gateways, like a tunnel server, router, or firewall.

IPSec tunnel is the most common mode and works like this:

1. A standard IP packet is sent to the IPSec device with the expectation that the packet will be encrypted and routed to the destination system over the network.

2. The first of the two IPSec devices, which in this case would probably be either a firewall or a router, authenticates with the receiving device.

3. The two IPSec devices negotiate the encryption and authentication algorithms to be used.

4. The IPSec sender encrypts the IP packet containing the data, and then places it into another IP packet with an authentication header.

5. The packet is sent across the TCP/IP network.

6. The IPSec receiver reads the IP packet, verifies it, and then unwraps the encrypted payload and decrypts it.

7. The receiver forwards the original packet to its destination.

IDS Network Access Control

An intrusion detection or prevention system (IDS/IPS) is software or hardware that is designed to detect attempts at accessing or modifying a computer system through a network. These attempts can be attacks from the outside, or internal attacks from curious or disgruntled employees, or from someone who has gained unauthorized access to your network.

IDS/IPS systems are used to detect numerous types of malicious behavior that can breach a network's security. This includes network attacks against services, attacks on applications, unauthorized logins, and access to sensitive files.

There can be many components to an IDS/IPS, including the following:

▼ **Sensors** Used to monitor traffic and generate security events

■ **Console** Used to monitor events and alerts and control sensors

▲ **Central engine** Used to record events logged by the sensors in the database; uses a system of rules to generate alerts from security events received

IDS/IPS can be configured in a number of ways, including:

▼ In network-based IDS/IPS, the sensors are located at choke points in the network to be monitored, usually in the demilitarized zone (DMZ), at the network's borders, and in-between user or server LAN segments. The sensor captures network traffic and analyzes it for malicious traffic. They are independent platforms that examine network traffic and monitor multiple hosts. Network-based IDS/IPS can also be configured to passively monitor network traffic by connecting to a switch port configured for port mirroring.

■ Protocol-based IDS/IPS are systems or agents that sit at the front end of a server, monitoring and analyzing communication protocols between a connected device and the server. For instance, for a web server this would normally be an analysis of HTTP or HTTPS protocols.

■ Application protocol-based IDS/IPS systems sit within a group of servers monitoring the communication on certain protocols. For instance, a web server with a database would be monitored for the SL protocol specific to the business logic as it transacts with the database.

■ A host-based IDS/IPS is composed of an agent on a host, identifying intrusions by analyzing system calls, application logs, file-system modifications, and other host activities.

▲ A hybrid IDS/IPS is a combination of two or more approaches. Host agent data is combined with network information to get a comprehensive view of the network.

Network Security Threats

Viruses are malware that inserts malicious code into existing documents or programs, and then propagate to other computers.

▼ **Trojan horses**   This is a type of malware attack that is delivered in an executable file, usually as something innocuous, like an online greeting card or a computer game. This type of code might also be delivered via an infected web site. Once installed on the computer, the Trojan horse is able to execute almost any computer code. An example of a recent Trojan horse delivered via email purported to show the recipient a picture if the user opens an attachment. When the attachment was opened, the Trojan horse code was able to install itself. Once installed, it installed a keylogger on the infected computer. The keylogger recorded every keystroke by the computer's user, and was able to steal financial account information and passwords.

■ **Spam**   The Hormel Corporation—makers of canned Spam—don't like that this name has been used for this type of email. But you can't unscramble an egg, so to speak, so it looks like the term's usage is here to stay. Anyway, it is said that – worldwide – spam makes up 70 to 84 percent of daily emails. That results in billions of dollars in lost productivity and gives IT departments extra work to do to filter out the mess.

■ **Phishing**   This is a method by attackers to try to trick you into giving out sensitive account information. For instance, we may all have seen a fake PayPal email (or one from a variety of major banks) with the subject line "Urgent: Your Account Has Been Breached." Within the message is a link to an unsecure web site that is made to look like PayPal, and where thieves are hoping the recipient will "update" their information by providing credit card numbers or passwords.

■ **Packet sniffers**   These capture data streams over a network, allowing for the capture of sensitive data like usernames, passwords, and credit card numbers. While losing a password or credit card number is problematic enough, IT managers also face the threat of lawsuits for noncompliance of data protection regulations.

■ **Malicious web sites**   Web sites that have been designed with evil in mind can do everything from install Trojan horses to redirecting you to an unrequested site. For instance, a web site could be created to appeal to a user's generous nature. A site offering to help natural disaster victims can ask for your credit card, and when you put it in, then hackers can use it however they see fit.

■ **Password attacks**   These are sundry methods to steal a password, including

■ **Brute force**   A very labor-intensive and unsophisticated method is to try to guess a password by entering different combinations of words and phrases compiled from a dictionary.

- **Packet sniffers** As mentioned earlier, these glean data from a compromised network.

- **IP spoofing** This attack involves the interception of data by pretending to be a trusted server.

- **Trojans** As mentioned above, these install surreptitious software to intercept a password.

- **Hardware loss** The theft of government laptops has caused great concern. Not because the government can't afford to replace one, but because so often there is sensitive data contained on them. Some estimates say that hardware loss is the cause of more than 10 million cases of identity theft each year.

▲ **Zombie computers and botnets** Hackers take over individual computers without the owner's awareness and use them to send out spam. Infected "zombie" computers are organized by spammers into small groups called "botnets." Botnets then transmit the spam that might include phishing attempts, viruses, and worms.

OPERATING SYSTEM SECURITY 101

There are many books available on operating system security that will go into much deeper detail than we will in this book, but we wanted to add a quick review for you and perhaps introduce a new concept that you can then go and find more information about. An operating system is simply an interface between a user and the hardware it's installed on. The operating system hosts applications and makes sure that each of those applications has hardware resources available to them to run. Sound familiar?

As we noted earlier, the hypervisor is an operating system, and all it really does is provide access to hardware resources on a particular server. The parent partition has its responsibilities for providing access to resources, and the guest operating system provides system resources for the applications you want to run. This makes things a little more complex from a perspective of securing the operating system. Knowing that, Microsoft has thrown us a bone on securing the hypervisor part of this equation.

Microsoft has built the Hyper-V hypervisor to be as small as possible, and doesn't allow any third-party software into the hypervisor. By doing this, Microsoft can control the code that's in the hypervisor and can spend more time analyzing the code they wrote to be as secure as possible. Microsoft did this to reduce the attack surface a malicious entity has on a host system. An *attack surface* is the number of things a malicious entity has to access in order to try to compromise a system. The type of things that an entity could try to exploit are device drivers, running services, and code that is running on a system. If a malicious entity gains control of the hypervisor, then it ultimately owns that host.

From a high level, securing your operating system is relatively straightforward. When you create your baseline configuration, you want to determine the following information:

▼ Services that are required to run

■ Core applications and core application configuration that will be installed on the system such as:

    ■ Antivirus

    ■ .NET Framework

    ■ Monitoring clients

    ■ Server management clients and applications

■ Service accounts that needs to be created and what rights they should have on that system

■ Network ports that must be open

■ Network communication protocols to be used

■ Auditing rules for accounts and objects on your computer

▲ Users that need access to the operating system and what rights they will need on that system

Once you document these items, you want to create scripts and/or use tools to automate the installation and configuration of your systems. The reason that you want to automate the installation of your system and configurations is that takes the human factor out of the configuration. Also, your configuration is repeatable and the same on each server. Having this repeatable process will help you troubleshoot, and will give you the ability to know what's happening on your systems.

Generally, when you perform an audit, your auditors will want to see your server build procedures and verify that you follow those procedures. If you are building servers by hand, it can be difficult to verify what you are doing. But if you have automated builds, you can show the auditor your automated build tool and show the build logs of your servers. This can significantly reduce the amount of time you have to spend with the auditor and save your company a considerable amount of money.

If you are using Active Directory as your directory service, leveraging Group Policy is a must for securing your servers. If you're not using Active Directory with your servers today, we highly recommend that you implement it. We also recommend that you implement Active Directory in your corporate networks as well as in the external networks for your servers.

Active Directory contains a feature called Group Policy. Group Policy is used with Active Directory to centralize user and computer settings. Windows 2000 and later Windows versions all have local Group Policy and support Group Policy coming from Active Directory. Figure 11-1 shows the Group Policy console for Windows Server 2008.

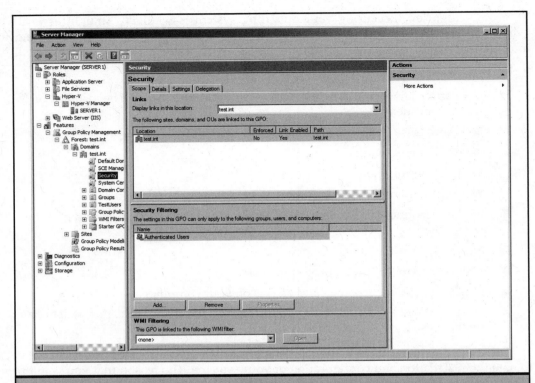

Figure 11-1. The Group Policy console for Windows Server 2008 is a Microsoft Management Console snap-in.

You use the Group Policy console to create, link, and edit Group Policy objects for your forest and domain. An example of this is shown in Figure 11-2.

The Group Policy Management Editor is used to edit a Group Policy and set different values to a policy.

You should consider creating organization units (OU) in your Active Directory to separate your different server roles and create standard group policies for each of the different roles that you implement. For instance, you may choose to create an OU for web servers with multiple organizational units under that for Uber-Secure and Standard security. Each OU would then have a Group Policy attached to it that would have the settings that you want for that particular role. You would then configure your automated build tools to create a corresponding role that would place the machine account in that OU at build time so that the machine would be automatically configured. It's a little bit of work up front, but we like to work really hard up front on solutions so we can have more free time in the future.

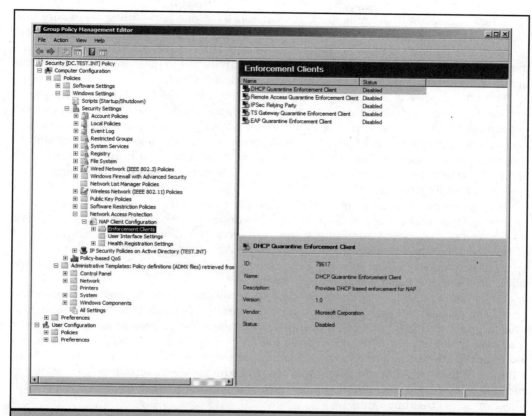

Figure 11-2. The Group Policy console for Windows Server 2008 is used to manage network policy rules for your forest or domain.

APPLICATION SECURITY 101

A server without any applications is a waste of money for an organization. Even when you think about it, a file server is running an application: file sharing. First you secured your network, and then you secured your operating system. Now it's time to secure your applications. At a basic level an application is an interface to some form of data.

Most applications collect, manipulate, and report on data that you have. To allow you to access that data, an application has authentication and authorization components in place so that it knows what to let you do. Just like the server roles you created, user roles can also be created for an application. The user role that you create will define what functions a user can do and what data that user can access in the application.

When you secure the application, you are mostly concerned with making sure that the right people have access to only the data they need to have access to. For instance, you may have a large Enterprise Resource Planning (ERP) application, such as SAP, implemented in your enterprise. You probably wouldn't want to give users in your manufacturing module access to the finance module and vice versa.

You will also want to make sure that when you implement an application in your environment, you are paying close attention to the applications that the new application will use. For instance, if your application uses IIS for web serving, Biztalk for an application server, and SQL Server for a database, you will want to make sure you configure those supporting applications to be secure as well. If you have your front-end web server facing the Internet but you haven't secured the configuration, you may be opening that box up to be compromised.

If your company writes its own applications, you also want to talk with your security organization about having code security reviews done. Many hacking competitions have been won not because an operating system or core application is insecure, but because of how code is implemented in the application. We recommend that you keep up on application patches that are released by your code vendors and implement a defined application lifecycle for each of your applications.

An *application lifecycle* is a process that an application goes through in your enterprise. The process follows the application from concept, planning, design, implementation, support, and upgrades to its eventual tombstone. We've been at many companies that have never implemented application lifecycles with their applications, and this has led to applications that are 20 years old and won't work on modern operating systems. Ultimately these aged applications will cost the companies more money to keep them running than if they had followed a lifecycle and performed updates, replacing the application when the time came.

DEFENSE IN DEPTH

As we said earlier in the chapter, your security is only as strong as the weakest link in a chain. To truly secure your solutions, you need to look at several different methods to secure your environment. Having a secure network doesn't really help if somebody who is authorized on your network has access to data they shouldn't have. "Defense in depth" is a concept of layering different security methods to help protect your environments.

With defense in depth in mind, we recommend that when you look at each of the components that we've listed, you think of them as working together to secure your environment and not just to secure each of the individual components. Ideas of defense in depth with a given solution will require different tools and processes that make up the total solution, for example:

▼ Using application and traditional firewalls between server components

■ Using intrusion detection and prevention systems

■ Using two-factor authentication

- Installing protection tools on servers and workstations
    - Antivirus
    - Firewalls
- Limiting user access
- Auditing user access
- Classifying your data and set rules on how that data can be accessed
- Using Group Policy to centrally secure your servers
- Using automated server builds so that you know how each server is built every time
- ▲ Encrypting the communications between servers and users

There are many other actions you can take on each layer of an application to help you secure it, but the idea is that you are securing your solution at each and every layer and taking a holistic view of your solution.

WINDOWS SERVER 2008 SECURITY FEATURES

As attackers get more wily, they figure out the chinks in an operating system's armor. As such, as new operating systems are introduced, they are hardened. Microsoft has taken some big steps with security in Windows Server 2008.

New and Improved

Windows Server 2008 is touted to be the most secure release of a Windows Server product ever (but then, so were Windows 2000, Windows 2003, and so on). Regardless, the product includes a number of security enhancements, including:

- ▼ Security improvements to the kernel
- Kernel patch protection for 64-bit editions
- Security improvements to the heap manager
    - Security improvements to the registry
    - Code integrity
    - Data Execution Prevention
    - Address Space Layout Randomization
    - Windows Resource Protection
- Security improvements to Windows services
    - Windows service hardening
    - Session 0 isolation

- Named pipe hardening
  - Windows Integrity Mechanism
  - Windows Internet Explorer 7
    - Protected mode
- Extended Validation SSL certificates
  - Internet Explorer Administration Kit 7
  - Extensible logon architecture
  - Cryptography Next Generation
  - Authentication protocol improvements
- Windows implementation of the Kerberos protocol
- TLS/SSL cryptographic enhancements
- ▲ Threats and vulnerabilities mitigation

While existing features have been enhanced, Windows Server 2008 offers a number of new features. Windows Server 2008 includes the following new features for server protection:

- ▼ Server role security configuration
- Server Core installation option
- User Account Control
- Web Server (IIS) role
- ▲ Backup and recovery

New features for network and edge protection in Windows Server 2008 include

- ▼ Windows Firewall with Advanced Security
- ▲ Network Policy and Access Services role
  - Network Policy Server
  - Network Access Protection
  - Routing and remote access
  - Secure configuration assessment and management

New features for secure configuration assessment and management in Windows Server 2008 include

- ▼ Security auditing
- Server security policy management

- Security Configuration Wizard (SCW)
    - More server role configurations and security settings than the version of SCW in Windows Server 2003
    - Scwcmd command-line tool to
        - Apply the policy to one or more servers
        - Roll back policies
        - Analyze and view an SCW policy on multiple servers, including compliance reports that can show any discrepancies in the configuration of a server
        - Transform an SCW policy into a Group Policy object (GPO) for centralized deployments and management by using Active Directory Domain Services (AD DS)
- Authorization Manager
- Group Policy
- ▲ Active Directory Domain Services
    - Fine-grained password policies
    - Auditing
    - Identity and access control

New features for Identity Management in Windows Server 2008 include

- ▼ Smart cards
- 802.1X authenticated wired and wireless access
- Backup and restore of stored user names and passwords
- Credential Security Service Provider and single sign-on for Terminal Services logon
- ▲ Previous logon information

New features for Access Control in Windows Server 2008 include

- ▼ Access control user interface
- TrustedInstaller SID
- Restricted SIDs checks
- File system namespace modifications
- Default permissions changes
- Changes to tokens
- Integrity levels
- Icacls command-line tool
- ▲ OwnerRights SID

New features for information protection in Windows Server 2008 include

▼ BitLocker Drive Encryption

■ Encrypting File System

■ Active Directory Certificate Services

    ■ Cryptography Next Generation

    ■ Online Certificate Status Protocol

    ■ Network Device Enrollment Service

    ■ Web enrollment

    ■ Policy settings

    ■ Restricted enrollment agent

    ■ Enterprise PKI snap-in

■ Active Directory Domain Services

▲ Active Directory Rights Management Services

A Closer Look at Features

Windows Server 2008 continues its promise to deliver products that adhere to its Three D program—secure by design, secure by default, and secure in deployment. Let's take a closer look at some of Windows Server 2008's security highlights.

BitLocker

Windows Server 2008 offers a number of tools to strengthen system security. BitLocker Drive Encryption is an optional way to encrypt OS volumes while protecting the Windows boot process. Encrypting the entire operating system on the hard disk strengthens the OS against software attacks and loss of other data also on the drive.

BitLocker lessens the impact of unauthorized access through two protection procedures: drive encryption and secure startup. User and system files on the volume are encrypted, including individual user data, page, and temporary files. When third-party applications are installed on the encrypted drive, they are also protected by encryption. ·

Drive encryption is designed to work in partnership with a Trusted Platform Module (TPM) chipset, but it will work on any system as long as the BIOS can read from a USB flash drive.

That's all nice and good, but there is some tradeoff for the security. System upgrades require you to decrypt the volume and non-Microsoft software updates will require you to disable BitLocker before starting. Otherwise, the system will enter a recovery mode and require a recovery key or password for access.

NOTE BitLocker setup and management is wizard-based and can be managed through a Windows Management Instrumentation (WMI) interface.

Microsoft claims there are no noticeable performance issues on the server with Bit-Locker enabled, because it only adds a single-digit percentage increase in overhead.

Secure startup—which does require the TPM chipset—protects the boot process and protects data from theft or system tampering when the OS is offline or being installed. It helps make sure that data decryption is performed only if the boot computer does not appear to have been tampered with, and that the encrypted drive is located in the computer. If the system has been tampered with, it will lock down and refuse to boot.

Digital Signatures

Windows Server 2008 also adds to its security arsenal when the server is running. It uses digital signatures to stop hackers and malware from replacing operating system files with malicious code using the same name. All of the operating system's executables and dynamic link libraries (DLLs) have been digitally signed, and the OS checks these signatures before loading the files into memory.

Address Space Layout Randomization

Windows Server 2008 uses a technique called Address Space Layout Randomization to defeat attacks—like buffer overflows—that hone in on known addresses in the system for certain bits of code.

Earlier versions of Windows use tables of hard-coded addresses, which were very easy to exploit. Malware could be written to use those known locations and then moved to the machine through a buffer overflow. The new method randomly arranges portions of key data in a new place each time the system boots, making it look different to malware each time and providing protection against automated attacks.

If a piece of malware targets the wrong location—it uses 256 locations—it will likely crash that process. Windows Server 2008 has a restart limit of 10, so if a process is scheduled for an automatic start, the malware can't blindly make 300 attempts and keep trying until it finds what it's looking for. After the tenth attempt, the server requires a reboot. Then, an administrator should be aware that the system is under attack and take a look at event logs or get a notification from a management utility.

Windows Firewall

Windows Server 2008 offers a host-based Windows Firewall with Advanced Security, which has been improved in recent times and includes the capability to manage outgoing data. Rules can be set based on source and destination IP address, and source and destination ports (TCP and UDP), as well as for numerous ports.

Application rules are based on the path, but you can specify on an individual service by service basis, rather than having to specify the exact path to the service.

In earlier versions of the operating system, firewall behavior and IPsec policy management were handled by different interfaces. This was often confusing for administrators and led to mistakes. Now the firewall is integrated with IPsec as well.

NOTE We consider a server firewall as one part of defense in depth and strongly urge anyone deploying servers to have purpose-built network and application firewalls deployed in addition to those located on a given server.

Service Hardening

Malware developers like to exploit for vulnerable services because they are always on and tend to run under accounts with high privileges. When malware gets to a server, it can use system services to perform nearly any task, like formatting the hard disk, or propagating itself across the network. Earlier versions of Windows had many services turned on and set to run, whether they were being used or not. Microsoft made a change to this in Windows Server 2003, but a lot of unnecessary services were still running by default.

Windows Server 2008 changes that by introducing Windows Service Hardening, which uses low levels of privileges. The number of services installed and running by default has been reduced, providing fewer targets for malware.

Windows Server 2008 expands its user levels to six service accounts, each with a specific scope and capabilities to provide for more granular control. To remove the permissions that services don't require, several services that used to run under the context of the Local System account now run under a less privileged account, like LocalService or NetworkService. Key Windows services are restricted so that they can't behave beyond their normal operating parameters. For instance, the Remote Procedure Call (RPC) service is not allowed to replace system files or change the registry.

NOTE   You can even set the level of privileges or special powers a service can have (like shutdown or audit) so that malware doesn't have access to all the default privileges of the account that the compromised service is running.

Services also have a unique service identifier (SID), so they can't run surreptitiously. In earlier versions of the operating system, a service would run anonymously under the context of a service account, giving extensive privileges on the local computer. As such, you could only apply an Access Control List (ACL) against the service account, not the actual service. This gave administrative control to the anonymous entity. With SIDs, ACLs can be applied to specific services for better control.

Active Directory

Active Directory (AD) is the core component of your security infrastructure. It is where the environment is managed and you establish access. But it is also a risk when it is in a branch office or anywhere you can't prevent tampering.

Windows Server 2008 deals with this problem with a Read-Only Domain Controller (RODC), which is an AD domain controller that contains a read-only version of the AD Directory Services (AD DS) database and is meant to be placed in remote locations or any place else where physical security cannot be guaranteed. Any changes must be made on a writable domain controller and replicated to the RODC. Account passwords are not stored on the RODC, and a Password Replication Policy establishes whether a user's or computer's credentials can be replicated from a writable domain controller.

Local users can also be assigned limited rights to perform maintenance work on the domain controller, like upgrading the driver, but without giving them control over other domain controllers or putting the security of AD DS at risk.

While RODCs are meant to prevent a lot of security risk at places where you cannot guarantee the physical safety of a machine, you still have to keep an eye on what's happening on your writable domain controllers. Previous flavors of Windows Server provided limited security monitoring and logging capabilities. All they did was log the name of an attribute that was changed, but not the new setting. According to its global audit policies, the audit directory service now logs old and new values of an attribute when a change is made to that attribute (for instance, who changed a password).

NAP

Windows Server 2008 uses Network Access Protection (NAP), which is Microsoft's take on the Network Access Control (NAC) issue on Vista clients. NAP lets an organization check a computer's compliance with security policy (is it up to date? what is the patch level? and so on), with the option to quarantine and fix problems. Using software management tools, administrators can automatically update noncompliant computers.

Windows Server 2008 offers a number of tools for NAP, including:

▼ Health policies
■ NAP administration server
■ System health validators
▲ NAP enforcement components (for IPsec communications, 802.1x, VPN, and DHCP)

Logging

If hackers have managed to get through all of the new mechanisms in place, you need to determine which computers in the network have been compromised. This usually required the administrator to go to each system to view its logs, connect remotely to each system, or use a third-party tool to collect data. In Windows Server 2008 and Vista, the Event Viewer has been changed to provide improved event logging and tracing capabilities.

Logs can be collected from multiple remote computers and then stored in a local XML file. You can then use a new cross-log query feature to view, correlate, and analyze specific types of events on your systems. For instance, you could look at all failed logon attempts from multiple machines to see if an attacker is trying to penetrate your network.

HYPER-V—DESIGNED FOR SECURITY

When Microsoft was developing Hyper-V, they created a set of goals about how the Hyper-V hypervisor should be created, from a security standpoint. First and foremost is that there needs to be strong isolation between partitions on the host. If you can't keep the different partitions from talking to each other, or from having the ability to talk to each other through anything other than a network connection, one partition could then take control of another partition.

Each partition has to be able to protect the confidentiality and integrity of the data that is stored on that partition. Essentially what this means is that a partition cannot affect the contents of another partition. This goes from guest to guest, parent to guest, guest to parent, and any of those to the hypervisor. So Microsoft wrote Hyper-V so that each guest is running a unique resource pool on the hypervisor. There are separate worker processes per guest virtual machine and guest-to-parent communications happen over a unique channel.

To meet those goals, Microsoft implemented the following high-level components into Hyper-V:

▼ There is no third-party software code in the hypervisor. Hyper-V only allows Microsoft code to be run in the hypervisor. All third-party software is run on the parent partition if required.

■ The hypervisor runs in a server address space. All of the partitions on a host system run in separate memory spaces so that the chance of memory poisoning and corruptions is limited.

▲ Guests cannot talk to other guests through the hypervisor. Guests can only talk to each other through a network connection. This is done so that you can use a firewall and restrict the communications that occur between guests, as well as to limit the damage should a virtual machine become compromised.

VIRTUALIZATION SOLUTION SECURITY

As we've mentioned before, you need to look at your virtualization implementation as a system and not just focus on one part. We've covered some security basics, and now we're going to go deeper and cover protecting your hosts, protecting the guests, and implementing security in the Hyper-V Manager and System Center Virtual Machine Manager.

Protecting the Host

To put it simply, if your host gets compromised, your VMs will be compromised. With that said, we need to take a look at how we go about protecting your host systems. A large part of protecting your host system is going to be to reducing the attack surface to which a malicious entity would have access.

Reducing the Attack Surface

When you are looking at reducing the attack surface after you install your system, you should absolutely update your system with security patches. At the time of this writing, there are 17 different Hyper-V updates available, and there will likely be one or two additional updates by the time you're reading this. Microsoft has been very gracious to create a comprehensive list of all of the Hyper-V updates. That list can be found at http://technet.microsoft.com/en-us/library/dd430893.aspx.

Part of reducing the attack surface of your host system is also how you configure your hardware for your host system. When you create the host system, you will want to have a dedicated NIC for the parent partition and other NICs for guest traffic. You should consider having the parent partition NIC on a separate, secure management network that has an Access Control List of who can be on that network. You may also want to consider using IPsec to encrypt your traffic, and two-factor authentication to further secure your host system.

The first thing you should consider when reducing the attack surface on your host systems is to implement Hyper-V on servers that are running as Server Core installations. To refresh your memory, Windows Server Core is a stripped-down, minimal installation of Windows Server. Aside from the fact that the operating system footprint is much smaller than that of a full version of Windows, one of the nice things about installing Server Core is that it already has many of the services that you may want to turn off disabled. This smaller footprint allows you to give the parent partition where Core will be installed fewer resources and gives you the opportunity to make more resources available to the guest partitions. Another reason that we like Server Core is that it's all command-line–driven. So any command that you want to run in Core is completely scriptable and the automated build and configuration of the Core installation is very straightforward.

Server Core was built to be a lightweight version of Windows that will only run a specific set of server roles:

▼ Active Directory Domain Services
■ Active Directory Lightweight Domain Services
■ DHCP server
■ DNS server
■ File services
■ Media services
■ Printer services
■ Web services—limited IIS
▲ Hyper-V

Only Run the Hyper-V Role on a Host

Regardless whether you install Hyper-V on a full version of Windows Server 2008 or on a Core version, you should ensure that you only run the Hyper-V role on the parent partition. While it's possible to run other roles and applications in the parent partition, we highly recommend against doing that on the host.

The first reason we recommend not running any other applications or roles in the parent partition is that you will be taking away system resources that can be used by the guest partitions. The second reason is that when you start running more applications in your parent partition, you increase the attack surface that a malicious entity has to work with. The third reason is that with every application you install, there is a greater chance that the application could crash and take down the parent partition and maybe the guest partitions as well. In addition, every application you install is more that you will have to patch on your trusted parent partition.

Limit Access to the Parent Partition

If you are going to run your Hyper-V hosts on a full installation of Windows Server 2008, consider limiting the number of people who will have access to log on to that parent partition and what rights they have to log on with. Microsoft has done a fantastic job of creating tools that can be installed on a Windows desktop and which can be used to manage your services without having to log on to a session on the server itself. If a particular admin only needs to access the server to do backups, you can install the Windows Server backup tools on his desktop and have him access the server using that method.

Not only do you want to limit who can actually log on to the server, but you will also want to limit who has escalated rights on the server. We recommend that if you give administrative rights to a particular guest system administrator, you do not give administrative rights to the parent partition. Just because you give somebody access to a guest doesn't mean that they should have rights that can potentially interact with other systems on that host. A great example of this that we've run into is that some business units have rights to the entire host system. This tends to be a little bit more of a political discussion point, but the question really comes down to whether you want to allow a person outside of your administrator group access to a server that has a mixed workload on it.

What we've typically recommended to our customers who have a business unit is that the business unit build a separate set of hosts, and then give them access to those hosts only. You would still give the other administrative groups the access they require to manage the boxes. You would just have to create a set of process, rules, and guidelines for the business unit administrator to follow.

Networks and Virtual Machine Placement

Remember, the weakest link in a chain defines how strong that chain is, and the least secure guest equals the security level of your host. Currently, there are only theories on how a virtual machine can be compromised, and then through that compromise, the parent partition through the Hyper-V. As of the writing of this book there haven't been any documented cases of that happening, but that just means they haven't been documented. Microsoft continues to test different methods of breaking the isolation between guests and will write patches to keep Hyper-V as secure as possible. This means you need to put a little bit of thought into what networks you plug your host into and what kind of guests reside on those hosts.

Hyper-V is perfectly capable of running multiple networks on a single network card, or running multiple network cards that connect to multiple networks. Most organizations today have several different network types. The network types that an organization may have are:

▼ Public web network

■ DMZ application network

■ DMZ database network

■ Management network

■ Backup network

■ Internal network

▲ External vendor networks

We're pretty sure that there are other networks that organizations have, but this gives you an idea of what we're talking about and gets you thinking about the networks that you have. Each one of those networks could be associated on a host system. But that doesn't always make the best security sense when you are building your solution out. Even though Hyper-V is very secure, and the isolation between networks is rock solid, there really isn't anything that can stop the human condition.

As an example, we wouldn't recommend that when you create a host, you have it plugged into your internal network with your root certificate authority and plugged into your external web network where you host your company's web site. While the host and the guests would more than likely be just fine, it's a fact that someone could accidentally add an external NIC to your root certificate authority and then it would be on a public network.

Protecting Guest Systems

The guest systems are really where all of the magic happens. The guest is the system that will hold the applications your business uses and the data that is becoming more and more valuable to your organization. If you've taken the time to secure everything else in your solution, please make sure that you don't skip securing your guest systems. Follow the steps that we described earlier in the chapter about securing the operating system and your applications.

Roles

When you create security baselines for your operating systems and then create server roles, those concepts should apply to any system, regardless of whether it's physical or virtual. Even if you create templates for your virtual machines to speed up the deployment, you should still be automating the creation of your template so that the server role build is the same, be it physical or virtual. We've seen clients that have a very well-put-together automated build for physical servers, but then build their virtual templates by hand. By doing that, they basically are in the same spot they were before they started doing automated builds.

Updating

Make sure that you patch your virtual machines. A virtual machine is just like a physical server; it needs to be updated from time to time. Don't forget to install the Integration Components to your virtual machine as well. You should look at your virtual machine not much differently than how you look at your physical machines when it comes to updating. If you've defined a patch management strategy, you should follow it with your virtual machines as well as your physical ones.

Just as with a physical box that has been shut down for a while and that might have missed an update cycle, a virtual machine can go through the same situation. When you are updating systems that have been shut down and missed update cycles, you should bring them up in an isolated network where you can install updates or implement some form of network access control or protection that will only allow that operating system to speak to an update server.

NOTE   Keep in mind that if you reboot all of your guests at once, you're going to take a hit on IO to your disk subsystem. The same thing goes for antivirus scans; you're going to want to figure out how you can stagger your AV scans on your virtual machines. If they all fire at the same time, you'll see your disk system all of a sudden start running at very high utilization.

Offline Virtual Machine Servicing Tool   To help with the updating of offline virtual machines, Microsoft has created the Offline Virtual Machine Servicing Tool, which can be found here:

http://www.microsoft.com/downloads/details.aspx?FamilyId=8408ECF5-7AFE-47EC-A697-EB433027DF73&displaylang=en

The Offline Virtual Machine Service tool is a scheduling and workflow tool that updates your offline virtual machines. The Offline Virtual Machine Servicing Tool (OLVMST) is very easy to use. There are three high-level steps to the tool:

1. Install the tool.
2. Configure your virtual machine groups.
3. Create and schedule your update jobs.

The OLVMST is built to be used with Virtual Machine Manager 2007 or Virtual Machine Manager 2008. Since you're reading this book about Hyper-V and you can only manage Hyper-V with Virtual Machine Manager 2008, we're not going to discuss Virtual Machine Manager 2007. When you install the OLVMST, you can install it on one of the following operating systems:

▼   Windows Server 2003 SP 2 or greater 32-bit or 64-bit

■   Windows Server 2003 R2 SP2 or greater 32-bit or 64-bit

▲   Windows Server 2008 32-bit or 64-bit

When you use the OLVMST, you must use one of the following Software Update Management Systems in conjunction with the OLVMST:

▼ Windows Server Update Services (WSUS) 3.0

■ WSUS 3.1 SP1

▲ System Center Configuration Manager 2007, SP1, or R2

Previously we talked about creating a separate network that you can bring your virtual machines up on to do updating. With the OLVMST, we recommend the same configuration by having a separated network where you can install your maintenance hosts. This separate network is where you will deploy offline virtual machines that require updating. You will also multihome your SCVMM, Domain Controllers, DNS, and Software Update Management Server to this network. Figure 11-3 shows an example of using multiple networks.

When you use this example configuration, you will want to make sure that you have a SAN for your disk. This will greatly decrease the amount of time it takes to deploy the virtual machines in need of updating from the library to a maintenance host.

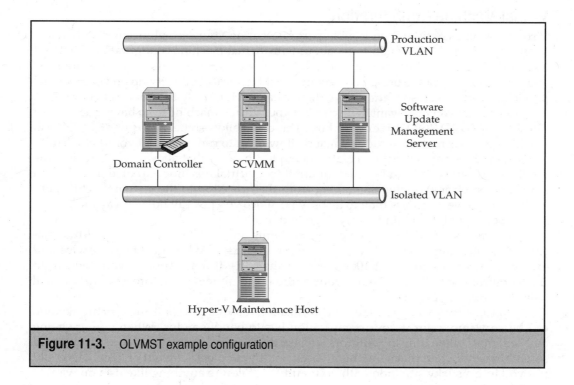

Figure 11-3. OLVMST example configuration

The OLVMST process for updating your virtual machines is pretty straightforward. The OLVMST has five steps that it goes through:

1. The servicing job to update your virtual machines is triggered.

2. The virtual machines that are targeted for updates are deployed to a maintenance host you define from the VMM Library.

3. The process to update the virtual machines is started.

4. The appropriate updates are identified and gathered from the Software Update Management System and the virtual machine is updated.

5. The virtual machine is returned to the VMM Library for storage.

Spend some time with the Offline Virtual Machine Service Tool solution accelerator to make sure that it will be right for your environment. We think that the OLVMST is a must-have even if you are using a software update management tool that isn't supported by the OLVMST. The time that you save in managing your offline virtual machines will be worth the effort of implementing WSUS or System Center Configuration Manager for your updating environment.

Virtual Machine Configuration

Virtual machine configuration is a big part of securing your virtual machines. There are several things that you should think about with virtual machine configuration. First and foremost is that your virtual machine is on the correct network. As in our previous example, you don't want to bring your internal root certificate authority up on your external public network. You also want to give the virtual machine only the devices that it needs. This means that you may want to disconnect your virtual machine from having access to a physical CD/DVD ROM drive on the host. This could allow someone to put a CD/DVD in the drive that has malicious code on it and allow them to run it without your knowledge.

You might want to consider creating a request process that allows you to review the media before you create an ISO and mount it to a virtual machine. Granted, this doesn't stop someone from copying something from their desktop to the virtual machine, but it's better to have a process than to just say no. Once you just say no, it always seems the asking person will try to find a way to get it done.

You may also want to impose processor limits on virtual machines. If a virtual machine becomes compromised with a virus, that virus may be attacking a service and causing that service to run at 100 percent of the CPU. If that happens, you don't want that compromised VM to take out your entire host; implementing processor limits will help that from happening.

Also consider setting up time synchronization for your guests. Time synchronization can be very important if your organization has to handle audits. When you are being audited, most of the time the auditors will ask that you show them evidence that you did something and when that something occurred. If your clocks are out of sync, this could put you into a sticky situation with your auditor. If you're anything like us, you want to get the audits done and over with so you can get back to playing some video games.

Virtual Machine Placement

We talked about host placement of virtual machines, but you will also want to think about what kind of disk you want to place your virtual machines on. If your company is large, more than likely you're going to have your virtual machines on a SAN. If your company is smaller, you may have your virtual machines on local disks. If you're a traveling consultant, more than likely all of your virtual machines are on an external USB hard drive. No matter what your situation is, you will want to protect your virtual machine files and your snapshot files. If you lose those files to a malicious entity, they will have the information that is kept in those files. Windows Server 2008 comes with the ability to perform full disk encryption with the BitLocker feature. While encryption isn't the answer for everything, it certainly does help you out if someone gets a disk that has your information on it.

You will also want to lock down who has access to the file folders where your virtual machine files and your snapshots are located. The fewer people who have access, the better.

Limiting Access Through Hyper-V Manager and SCVMM

Earlier in this chapter we talked about using user roles to help secure your environment. A *role* is a definition of what a particular user can do in an application. A particular role in an IT organization may be a backup operator. A backup operator doesn't need full administrator access to a server, but the backup operator needs to be escalated beyond what a standard user needs.

By using the Microsoft Authorization Manager (AZMAN) software, you can create user roles for Hyper-V Manager and for System Center Virtual Machine Manager (SCVMM). In Chapter 8 we showed you how to use AZMAN, but we wanted to make sure to really push this concept home with you, our reader. Using AZMAN and creating a role is really delegating administration of your environment. For administrators who are managing only a couple of hosts, this might not make sense to implement, but for large enterprises and for companies who have a situation like the one we described with the business unit, you may want to review Chapter 8.

Security is no small issue, and while we tried to talk about as many facets as we could regarding Windows Server 2008, we couldn't possibly cover everything. Also, security is such a moving target that there will always be something new to learn about tomorrow. That said, we hope this chapter helped explain some of the issues germane to your system's security.

CHAPTER 12

Virtual Desktop Infrastructure

With the economy in its current state, companies are trying to squeeze every penny that they can from their current investments. We've seen companies stretch desktop refresh intervals from 3 years to 4 to 5 years on average, and at a couple of companies that we've visited, they are trying to stretch their investments out to 20 years on some machines. Twenty years is an extreme case of trying to stretch out a refresh cycle, but moving to 5 or even 7 years is a pretty common reality.

You're probably wondering how the heck these companies are doing this. Well, to start, Windows XP has been a rock solid operating system for most companies. It ran all of the applications the company had with little to no remediation and it's been very easy to deploy. Between that and all of the negative press that Vista got, it seems that companies are waiting for Windows 7.

Even though Windows XP has been a rock solid operating system—and runs very well on older hardware—some companies are dreading the idea of having to refresh their desktop fleet. It's complicated and resource intensive, which means it's an expensive proposition. So in many ways, it makes sense to consider an implementation of virtual desktop infrastructure where the processing happens on a server versus the desktop. We've all heard this before—with Terminal Services and Citrix you could run a desktop someplace else and reuse your hardware, but the configuration and management are just too much. This time around things have changed. We think it might be a good time to talk about it, since you've just implemented server virtualization.

WHAT IS A VIRTUAL DESKTOP INFRASTRUCTURE?

It's actually pretty tough to define what a virtual desktop infrastructure, or VDI, is these days. But if you look at it in the simplest form, it is using virtualization to provide your end users with desktops. Many of you reading this book have already installed a guest partition with Windows Vista for testing, or are running Virtual PC and have a desktop operating system running in a virtual machine, so the concept is not completely new. But the VDI that we're talking about is a little bit more complex than just running VPC, VMware workstation, ACE, or MED-V. We're talking more about hosting desktop operating systems on your Hyper-V hosts. VDI is still very similar to Citrix or Terminal Services in that you are performing the processing in the datacenter, versus on a desktop system. The main difference between VDI and Citrix or Terminal Services is that with VDI you are creating a dedicated virtual machine for the end user to work in, versus having a shared environment.

Once you've created the virtual desktop, you can connect to it using some form of remote control software, like Remote Desktop Protocol (RDP), which is built into Windows, VNC, or really any remote control software. This works okay for a couple of virtual desktops, but when you start getting a large number of virtual desktops, you may want to consider adding a connection broker in front of your virtual desktops. Originally, the connection broker was basically used to help determine which virtual desktop an end user should be connecting to or is assigned to. Today you can consider it to be much more than that. You can really consider the connection broker as almost an infrastructure access gateway for an end user. You can leverage that connection broker to give access to your virtual desktops, and also to your blade PC, servers, and even applications.

Just a few years ago there weren't all that many connection brokers on the market. Primarily we used a Citrix presentation server as front-end RDP sessions to the virtual desktops. Today the connection brokers are much more sophisticated, with features like temporary and permanent assignments, virtual machine power management, graphics acceleration, and multimonitors. This allows your virtual desktop users to use media-rich applications, and many others.

WHY VDI AND WHAT AM I GOING TO USE IT FOR?

You're probably saying to yourself, "We've got our desktop and laptop fleet deeply managed. Why and what would we use VDI for?" To be completely up front with you, VDI isn't a silver bullet that will completely change your lives by fixing all your problems. The major benefits of VDI for an organization are:

▼ Security

■ Centralization

■ Speed of deployment

■ Reliability

▲ Cost reduction

Security and Centralization

When we talk about security for your desktops, it's really about the fact that your data is not stored in a location where it can easily get up and walk away or just disappear. What we mean by that is we've found that a significant number of users store their data to their desktops or laptops, but don't back up that data. This may sound a little paranoid, but there are people who will get a job as a night cleaning staff person so that they can steal desktops, laptops, and data from your companies. Sometimes it can even be coworkers, and it can happen during the day. We know this from firsthand experience, since one of our laptops was stolen right off one of our desks during the middle of the day and we lost quite a bit of data that wasn't backed up. Let us tell you—it's really changed the way we handle our laptop and desktop systems and we make sure that we get our data up on servers.

VDI doesn't necessarily work for people who are running around with their laptops on planes, trains, and automobiles, but think of it for your accounting or human resources departments. Your accountants and HR reps more than likely don't have too much work that they bring home with them. They probably have a desktop, and if they do have a laptop, perhaps it doesn't leave the office all that often. Let's face it; all of us store data locally when we should make sure that it's up on the network, so having HR or company accounting data on one of those systems is quite probable, and losing one of those systems would be painful. With VDI your desktops are stored in your datacenter, so it makes it a lot harder for those systems and data to take a hike.

VDI also works nicely when you have a large number of remote sites where you don't want to install servers. You can deploy a thin client device, and they connect to the central servers using a thin protocol such as RDP or Independent Computing Architecture (ICA). Then all the data is stored centrally in your datacenters. From an administrative perspective, you don't have to worry about having servers in a remote site and having to deal with remote backups and administration.

Speed of Deployment and Reliability

When you have a new user start or need a desktop, it's nice to have them up and running as soon as possible. We've seen some companies where it can take two to three weeks for a desktop to be provisioned to the requestor. If you're anything like us, performing desktop administration isn't really high on our list of fun stuff. Let's face it; desktop admin isn't as interesting as performing virtualization. With VDI you can get a new desktop provisioned in just a matter of minutes using templates. Another facet of speed of deployment is when a user may go between locations or moves in a building. If you've deployed thin client devices, when a user is moved to a new cube or location, they can simply go to that location, sit down at a terminal, log on, and they're right where they were when they left their desk. You don't have to worry about moving a computer, monitor, or data that may be on a file server.

It always seems that with deployment comes the idea of reliability. When you first get new desktops, you generally image them and let them burn in for a couple of hours or days before you take them to your end user. It never seems to fail that even though you burn them in, you'll get hardware failures in a percent of your desktops. Any device that has moving parts is—sooner or later—going to have a failure. Once that failure occurs, you not only have to fix the issue, but you may have a larger issue on your hands if the user wasn't keeping his or her data on a file server, or performing regular backups. With VDI, and if you've architected your virtual solution correctly, you don't have to worry as much about failures, since your virtual desktops would be on redundant servers and stored on redundant disks in your datacenter.

Cost Reduction

Reducing costs is always on a company's mind. It doesn't matter if it's the best or worst of times; companies always want to do more with less. Most of the companies that we regularly work with are on about a three-year hardware refresh cycle with desktops. Desktops keep getting cheaper, and the bang for your buck continues to keep going up. But those aren't the only costs that are associated with a desktop environment. When we look at desktop cost we look at the following factors:

▼ Purchase price and maintenance

■ Monitor and peripheral expense

■ The amount of power to run the desktop and peripherals

■ Operating system and application costs

▲ Labor to build, deploy, move, and maintain

As we were saying, the purchase price of a desktop, laptop, and all the accessories has gone down quite a bit, but they're still more expensive than a thin client device, and it's still more expensive if you always have to buy a third of your desktops every year. You can generally get a thin client device for about half the cost of purchasing a desktop or laptop, and the thin client device is going to use significantly less power and have much less maintenance time than a traditional desktop or laptop. If you look at the solution from a hardware-only perspective, it tends to be about even from a cost perspective. When you look at it from the bigger view of power and labor, VDI tends to win the cost argument every time.

VIRTUAL DESKTOP INFRASTRUCTURE COMPONENTS

We've touched on some of the VDI components a little bit, and now we're going to go deeper into each component. VDI in its basic form is really made up of three components:

▼ Host

■ Connection broker

▲ Endpoint

The following diagram represents, at a high level, what a VDI architecture may look like. The architecture is made up of three major components:

1. The host systems
2. The connection broker
3. The endpoints

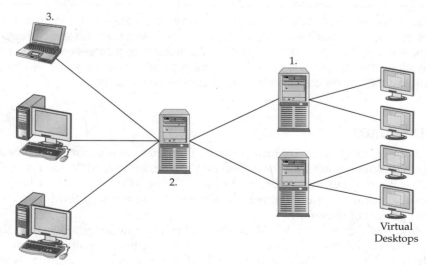

Virtual
Desktops

A user at an endpoint has a logon to that endpoint with some form of username and password, smart card, or two-factor authentication. The endpoint is then directed to the connection broker and the connection broker will look at the credentials and allow the endpoint to access the virtual machine on a host system. One of the most powerful features of the connection broker is that it will load-balance the endpoint connections between host systems, making sure that if the end user is disconnected from their virtual machine, they get the correct virtual machine when they reconnect.

Host

As with most every technology that's out on the market, there are multiple solutions and products. VDI is a solution that is composed of multiple different products. But since this is a book about Hyper-V, we're going to go out on a limb and make the assumption that you're going to use Hyper-V as your host. We feel that we've pretty much covered the host in the first 11 chapters of the book, so we're going to give you some tips for hosts when you are setting up your VDI solution.

You may want to consider having a separate host cluster for your virtual desktops. You can absolutely use the same hosts and clusters that you store your servers on, but with desktops you can get a higher number of virtual systems per host if you keep all your desktops together. You can also use a cheaper disk for your desktops than you might for your server workloads. For example, you may be virtualizing servers that have some pretty big IO requirements. Overall, desktop operating systems tend to access a disk more frequently than a server operating system does, but require much less IO on a consistent basis. Instead of putting your desktops on your SAN that is costing you 10 to 20 dollars a gigabyte, you can have your desktops on an iSCSI disk that will cost you around 2 to 5 US dollars a gigabyte.

NOTE   While we're on the topic of disks and IO, you'll want to make sure that you try to offset when you're doing antivirus scans and backups on your systems. Antivirus scans and backups are very IO-intensive, and if you are running 30 to 40 virtual desktops on a host—and all of your antivirus scans start at the same time—it can lead to a serious performance hit on your SAN—maybe even leading to a crash. We've been there before and it's not exactly a fun time.

Connection Broker

As we said above, the connection broker can be thought of as a traffic cop. A connection request for a desktop comes into the connection broker, and based on the configuration and security, it's pointed to the correct desktop. Today Microsoft doesn't have a very good connection broker option that will work for VDI, and relies on third-party partners for that component of the solution.

With Windows Server 2008 R2, Microsoft will release the Remote Desktop Connection Broker, which will provide access to both remote applications, and desktops. It will also really help Microsoft create a solid VDI story. As VDI becomes more frequently adopted in enterprise environments, we feel that the connection broker will be one of the first areas to get huge functionality increases as Microsoft continues to develop its VDI platform.

Until the release of Windows Server 2008 R2, you're going to want to rely on third-party partner connection brokers. There are several different companies that have created VDI connection brokers. The most popular of the VDI solutions today are Citrix XenDesktop, Quest vWorkspace, and Sun VDI Software.

Citrix

Citrix is widely thought of as a Terminal Services add-on product, but let's remember that Citrix actually created the components that are Terminal Services, and licensed them to Microsoft. Citrix has come a long way since the early days of Terminal Services. They've created several different products to help with Terminal Services security, as well as continuing to refine their ICA protocol for thin communications. In 2007 Citrix made the jump from presentation virtualization to server and desktop virtualization with the purchase of XenSource. XenSource is the company that created the Xen virtualization software, which is very similar to what Hyper-V and VMware are. Today Citrix has become one of the innovators of virtualization products by releasing Citrix XenDesktop as well as Citrix Essentials for Hyper-V.

Citrix XenDesktop is much more than just a simple connection broker. With Citrix XenDesktop you can have:

▼ Single-image desktop management

■ Real-time desktop assembly

■ High-definition user experience

■ High level of security

■ Monitoring

▲ Integration with Hyper-V and System Center Virtual Machine Manager and other systems

Single Image Desktop Management   The idea of a single image has been almost the Holy Grail of sorts in the IT community. We've gotten close, and we all have a friend who knows somebody who's done it, but it just never seems to be real. A large part of multiple images has been dealing with the hardware abstraction layer (HAL) that is a part of Windows XP and prior operating systems. With the release of Windows Vista, Microsoft has helped us by making Vista—and soon Windows 7—HAL independent. Virtualization, in general, also helps with this since you can set what your standard virtual machine should be configured as. What this means is that we can truly have a single image. With XenDesktop, Citrix has built upon that and helps you reduce patch and upgrade maintenance time. You can significantly cut down the amount of disk that's needed for your virtual desktop environment.

Real-Time Desktop Assembly   In previous chapters we talked about dynamic systems and about roles in your organization. Citrix created the real-time desktop assembly feature with those concepts in mind. When you provision a virtual desktop, that desktop is assembled with the user's settings and applications already incorporated, regardless from where the desktop is accessed. This allows your users to roam between locations and still have the same user experience.

High-Definition User Experience   For any technology to be adopted by the end-user community, it really comes down to the user experience. If a user can't do the things they need to do, they're going to complain and the technology will never truly be adopted. But if you can give the user an experience that may not be much different than what they are used to, then the new technology will be adopted quite rapidly. It really comes down to the fact that even though people want change, when it happens they tend to reject it if the change seems too disruptive.

When you think about it, virtualization was disruptive to how we go about doing our day-to-day jobs as IT staff. Instead of building physical servers that take us weeks and weeks, we've gone to spinning up virtual machines in a matter of minutes. But for the general population of a company, they really don't know what virtualization is until it affects them on a day-to-day basis. Both Microsoft and Citrix are working diligently to ease virtualization to the end users. A major step in the right direction is the HDX technology that Citrix has in XenDesktop. HDX delivers a high-definition user experience that is media rich. *Media rich* means that the end users are able to use multiple monitors, watch videos, and even use graphic-intense applications on pretty much any network.

High Level of Security   Any VDI solution will get the benefits of having your company data in a centralized location. Citrix brings a little bit more than that to the table for VDI. With the Citrix components you will get encrypted delivery and you can implement an SSL VPN device that you can use to leverage multifactor authentication for your users, which will give you a nice check mark with your audit compliance group.

Monitoring   Citrix XenDesktop has built-in monitoring that will proactively identify performance issues. Once a performance issue is found, XenDesktop can then reallocate resources to make sure that your desktops are always running and at peak performance.

Integration with Hyper-V, SCVMM, and Other Systems   Because of Citrix's long history of thin computing and partnership with Microsoft, Citrix XenDesktop works with pretty much every major thin-client vendor that's around right out of the box. There isn't all that much that you need to do to get it configured and working with Hyper-V, System Center Virtual Machine Manager, and any thin client devices that you may already have. This integration story helps you get your solution up and running faster, which means you get to start saving money sooner rather than later.

Versions   Citrix XenDesktop comes in five different editions for you to choose from:

▼   Platinum—This is the Cadillac version of the software, which gives you

- Desktop lifecycle management
- VDI connection broker
- Provisioning

- ■ Virtual application delivery (XenApp)
- ■ Complete performance monitoring and Quality of Service
- ■ Remote Virtual Desktop Support
- ■ Enterprise
  - ■ Desktop lifecycle management
  - ■ VDI connection broker
  - ■ Provisioning
  - ■ Virtual Application Delivery (XenApp)
- ■ Advanced
  - ■ Desktop lifecycle management
  - ■ VDI connection broker
  - ■ Provisioning
- ■ Standard
  - ■ Desktop lifecycle management
  - ■ Entry-level desktop virtualization
- ▲ Express
  - ■ Desktop lifecycle management
  - ■ Ten-user limited trial

We recommend that—as with any solution you put into place—you do your home-work and perform a cost/benefit analysis. You should document your requirements and then map each feature in each version and determine if it's a need-to-have, a nice-to-have, or a not-needed feature. We recommend that you clearly define your requirements. And remember, you needed to walk before you learned to run. You may find that the standard or advanced versions of the product are more than you need for your solution. Plus, you don't want to purchase a more expensive version and then not use the features. That might put you in some hot water with your higher-ups.

Quest vWorkspace

Quest vWorkspace, formerly Virtual Access Suite, is the desktop management solution spanning multiple hypervisors and desktop deployment models. vWorkspace offers the following features:

▼ **Desktop automation management** Automates virtual desktop management, from power management to task scheduling, including application deployment and operating system operations

■ **Desktop lifecycle management** Automates the provisioning and mass production of desktops and servers from a single golden image including Active Directory integration

■ **Desktop integrity management**   Automates the reversal of the desktop state to its original condition upon reboot

■ **Delegated administration management**   For large-scale deployments, enables the logical presentation of desktop infrastructure assets in geographic zones, and allows fine-grained delegated administrative responsibility to be shared among staff members

▲ **Desktop reclamation management**   Automates the deletion of desktops and their removal from Active Directory upon expiration

Experience Optimized Protocol   Quest says its Experience Optimized Protocol (EOP) makes vWorkspace more like working on an actual PC. vWorkspace capabilities include:

▼ **Multimedia acceleration**   Multimedia content is redirected to both Windows and Linux end-points for local playback.

■ **Graphics acceleration**   From web content to Flash animations to graphics embedded in applications, performance over the LAN or WAN is enhanced by as much as 800 percent.

■ **Latency reduction**   Quest EOP delivers local text echoing, ensuring immediate keystroke feedback.

▲ **Bidirectional audio**   Quest EOP enables applications such as dictation, collaboration, and VoIP.

User Experience   Focus on the user experience was important to Quest for the adoption of vWorkspace. Whether it's integrated universal printing capabilities, the USB PDA support, application publishing, or the enhanced multimonitor support, vWorkspace further extends these essential last-mile features to include:

▼ **Virtual profile management**   Fifth-generation hybrid profile management capability is now available for VDI deployments.

■ **Virtual USB management**   Any USB device is supported through the remote session on Windows and Linux endpoints, including support for isochronous devices such as webcams and headsets.

■ **Integrated support for Expand networks**   vWorkspace offers the capability to automatically enable the compression and acceleration features of Expand appliances, enabling customers with limited bandwidth at branch offices to support larger numbers of centralized user sessions without having to acquire more bandwidth.

▲ **Integrated support for HP Remote Graphics Software (RGS)**   vWorkspace offers the capability to support and broker HP RGS connections, enabling HP customers who have standardized on HP RGS to leverage that investment.

Sun VDI Software

Sun Microsystems offers its Sun Virtual Desktop Infrastructure (VDI) Software 3. The third version of the product offers VDI storage economics, built-in virtualization capabilities, and support for a wide variety of virtual desktop operating systems. The open architecture of Sun VDI Software 3 gives users access to a broader choice of client devices and virtualization hosts—increasing flexibility, management efficiency, and data security.

Sun VDI Software 3 represents a solution that leverages core open-source technologies including Sun's Open Storage, OpenSolaris, VirtualBox, and MySQL. With Sun VDI Software 3, customers can deploy a number of virtual desktop operating systems, including Windows XP, Windows Vista, Windows 2000, OpenSolaris, and Ubuntu, and access these operating systems from a variety of client devices—such as traditional PCs or Macs, Sun Ray thin clients, or thin clients from other vendors. In addition, to host virtual desktop environments, IT architects can opt to use the improved integration with VMware Infrastructure, leverage Sun built-in virtualization, or use a mixture of the two.

"The open architecture of our Sun VDI Software 3 creates a new dimension of choice and integration with Sun's high-performing Open Storage systems," said Jim McHugh, Vice President of Datacenter Marketing, Sun Microsystems. "Customers can now increase the utilization of existing IT assets; gain greater flexibility in client, desktop operating systems, and host virtualization; increase scalability and simplify management; and mitigate the number one issue facing all VDI deployments—the cost of storage. In today's volatile economy, these advantages and capabilities can bring significant benefits to virtualization customers."

Sun touts VDI Software 3's management capabilities, which they say result in lower equipment costs, less energy consumption, reduced system cooling requirements, simplified system administration, and reduced e-waste. Since desktops are centrally hosted, only the display is sent to the client device; critical data never leaves the corporate network and can be managed and backed up by IT. Moreover, built-in Sun Ray technology support takes advantage of the excellent performance and inherent security features of Sun Ray thin clients, which contain no resident operating system or applications—making them virtually immune to client-side viruses.

Additional Sun VDI Software 3 features include:

▼   **Integration with Solaris ZFS and Open Storage**   Enables data integrity for business continuity and exceptional data throughput in an economical storage footprint with simplified management design. When coupled with a Sun Storage 7000 Unified Storage System or other Open Storage architecture, Sun VDI Software 3 can reduce storage consumption and costs.

■   **Expanded VMware support**   Enables customers to rapidly and efficiently scale larger deployments of Sun VDI Software paired with VMware Infrastructure.

■   **Active Directory support**   Permits customers to easily assign virtual desktops to users in Active Directory.

■ **Built-in support for Remote Desktop Protocol (RDP) clients**   Allows customers to connect directly to a Sun VDI Software 3 server from nearly any RDP-enabled device, without installing any software on the client.

▲ **Simplified installation**   Provides a single installer for the core components to reduce complexity.

Endpoints

For VDI you don't have to buy special endpoints. You can leverage the investment that you've already made in your desktops and laptops, extending the duration that you can keep that hardware out in the field. Now, if you are going to go the route of keeping your desktops and laptops, you're not going to get the power savings that you can with a thin device, but just moving to a virtual desktop solution will still help you from a manageability perspective and with cost avoidance (not having to buy new desktops or laptops).

If you do decide that it makes a good business decision to purchase endpoints, there are several different products on the market today that you can buy. The two products that stand out amongst the others today are Wyse and Sun Microsystems.

Wyse

Wyse has been around the Terminal Services game for quite a while. They were really one of the first companies to create a thin computing device that could connect to Citrix or to Microsoft Terminal Services. Wyse brings small economical devices that can connect to different systems using different protocols. You have two different types of terminals that you can choose from:

▼ Thin client

▲ No client

The thin client has a very small operating system on the device that can be configured to connect to a specific location, or you can run very small applications on some of the models. With the Wyse devices you can get them installed with the Wyse Thin OS, Windows CE, Wyse Linux, or Windows XP Embedded. Wyse also makes a device that is specifically designed to connect to Citrix XenDesktop and is built to provide a media-rich end-user experience.

Sun Microsystems

Sun has been pushing thin client computing with its Sun Ray line of thin devices for quite a long time. Sun has truly embraced virtualization, not just from a server and VDI software perspective, but also by running their solution at all of their campuses. If you ever get the chance to visit a Sun campus you will see Sun Ray devices at most of the virtual office spaces they have. Each Sun employee is issued a smart ID badge that is inserted into the Sun Ray device and logs him or her on to a virtual desktop session. When the badge is removed from the device and the user walks over to another of the Sun Ray devices, the virtual session is picked up exactly where it was left off.

Sun offers three different Sun Ray devices:

▼   Sun Ray 2

■   Sun Ray 2 FS

▲   Sun Ray 270

The Sun Ray 2 and the Sun Ray 2 FS are very similar to a Wyse device. You connect a network cable, keyboard, monitor, and mouse and you're ready to go. What we really like about the Sun Ray 270 is that it's a thin device that is integrated with a monitor, so the only thing you need to add is the network, keyboard, mouse, and power. With Sun's newest line of servers and the release of this generation of thin devices, Sun has really raised the bar from a power consumption and conservation perspective.

THE DYNAMIC DESKTOP

The dynamic desktop really transcends the physical and virtual machine worlds. It's the idea that you can automatically create the correct environment for your users quickly, and on the fly. When you use a more traditional VDI solution, you are installing the desktop operating system, and then you're installing applications either by hand or in a more managed fashion with a deployment tool, such as System Center Configuration Manager. The major problem with the installation of applications is the potential compatibility issues that can arise. To help combat application compatibility issues, you ultimately want to isolate applications from each other. Wouldn't it be great if you could quickly provision the desktop to your users, and then have the most recent version of the applications automatically installed based on the user's role in your organization?

In a traditional desktop installation, that's pretty much not going to happen unless you look into using a couple of different options. To help isolate your applications, you can either install them into a Terminal Services or Citrix environment; or publish the application to the desktop; or you can leverage application virtualization. The way application virtualization works is that a client is installed on a desktop that will run only the needed components of the application in an isolated runtime on the operating system.

Microsoft App-V

For organizations that use Terminal Services, server growth gets to be an expensive problem. To avoid conflicts, applications have to be put through a lot of testing to find out which applications will clash and must be separated and run on different Terminal Server devices. This is both time-consuming and expensive. And running multiple separate terminal servers for unique applications results in servers being underutilized, since each one is configured differently and serving a limited set of applications. Often, this accounts for just 25 percent of capacity.

To mitigate this problem, Microsoft offers its Microsoft App-V for Terminal Services. App-V offers the following features: Servers can be easily consolidated to end server siloing and to increase the ROI on your datacenter. App-V's application virtualization allows applications to run next to each other, even if they conventionally clash.

It also allows you to run multiple versions of the same application and applications that previously could not run on Terminal Services. This reduces the number of physical servers you need and improves utilization on the hardware you do use. Ultimately, the number of servers you need is much lower, operating costs are less, and the datacenter ROI is increased.

Some benefits of App-V include:

▼ **Application conflicts and testing are eliminated**   With App-V, you no longer need to permanently install applications on servers and shield the operating system and applications from changes created when the application runs. Also, you no longer need to perform long and complicated regression testing.

■ **Speed up application deployment**   If you use App-V, applications only need to be packaged once for desktop or Terminal Services platforms. This eliminates the need to "double package" the application when it will be used in both environments.

■ **Moderate deployment risk**   In the past, installing a new application on a terminal server was a gamble. First you had to make sure all your users were logged off; then you had to change the mode of the terminal server, and finally perform reboots. Software updates and uninstalls were even more complicated. App-V allows applications to be deployed and updated to users without having to reboot or log off users.

▲ **Easy profile management**   App-V keeps application settings and data stored in a single network location. This makes users' application settings available, no matter what terminal server is used, and without the need for roaming profiles. This feature also makes mandatory profiles an option for Terminal Services. That means that the OS settings can remain locked within the mandatory profile while per-application settings can be modified by the user.

Windows Server 2008 Terminal Services RemoteApp

Terminal Services is one of the most widely used features in previous versions of Windows Server. Terminal Services makes it possible to run an application remotely in one location but have it be controlled and managed in another. Microsoft has evolved this concept considerably in Windows Server 2008 R2, and they decided to rename Terminal Services to Remote Desktop Services (RDS) to better reflect these new features and capabilities.

To expand the Remote Desktop Services feature set, Microsoft has been investing in the virtual desktop infrastructure, also known as VDI, in collaboration with their partners, which include Citrix, Unisys, HP, Quest, Ericom, and several others. VDI is a centralized desktop delivery architecture, which allows customers to centralize the storage, execution, and management of a Windows desktop in the datacenter. It enables Windows Vista Enterprise and other desktop environments to run and be managed in virtual machines on a centralized server.

Increasingly businesses aim to enable their employees and contractors to work from home or from an offshore, outsourced facility. These new work environments provide better flexibility, cost control, and lower environmental footprint, but they increase demand for security and compliance so that corporate data is not at risk. VDI addresses all these challenges with the following features:

▼ **Improved user experience**   The version of VDI and remote desktop services in Windows Server 2008 improves the end-user experience through new Remote Desktop Protocol capabilities. These new capabilities, enabled with Windows Server 2008 R2 in combination with Windows 7, help make the user experience for remote users almost identical to that for local users.

■ **Improved RemoteApp & Desktop Connections**   New RemoteApp & Desktop Connection (RAD) feeds provide a set of resources, such as RemoteApp programs and Remote Desktops. These feeds are presented to Windows 7 users via the new RemoteApp & Desktop Connection control panel, and resources are integrated into both the Start menu and the system tray.

▲ **New Remote Desktop Protocol capabilities**   These new capabilities, enabled with Windows Server 2008, improve the experience of remote users, making it more similar to the experience enjoyed by users accessing local computing resources. These improvements include:

■ **Multimedia redirection**   Provides high-quality multimedia by redirecting multimedia files and streams so that audio and video content is sent in its original format from the server to the client and rendered using the client's local media playback capabilities.

■ **True multiple monitor support**   Enables support for up to 10 monitors in almost any size, resolution, or layout with RemoteApp & Remote Desktops; applications will behave just as they do when running locally in multimonitor configurations.

■ **Audio input and recording**   VDI supports any microphone connected to a user's local machine and enables audio recording support for RemoteApp and Remote Desktop. This is useful for VoIP scenarios and also enables speech recognition.

■ **AeroGlass support**   VDI provides users with the ability to use the AeroGlass UI for client desktops; ensuring that remote desktop sessions look and feel like local desktop sessions.

■ **DirectX redirection**   DirectX 9, 10, and 11 applications will render on the server and will be remoted using bitmaps (requiring Direct3D-compatible hardware). If the application supports the new DirectX 10.1 API with remoting extensions, the DirectX (2D and 3D) graphics are redirected to the local client to harness the power of the GPU on the user's local device, removing the need for a GPU on the server.

- **Improved audio/video synchronization**   RDP improvements in Windows Server 2008 R2 are designed to provide closer synchronization of audio and video in most scenarios.

- **Language bar redirection**   Users can easily and seamlessly control the language setting (for example, right to left) for RemoteApp programs using the local language bar.

- **Task Scheduler**   This adds the ability in Task Scheduler to ensure that scheduled applications never appear to users connecting with RemoteApp. This reduces user confusion.

While RAD improves the end-user experience, it also reduces the desktop and application management effort by providing a dedicated management interface that lets IT managers assign remote resources to users quickly and dynamically. Windows Server 2008 includes the following RAD management capabilities to help reduce administrative effort:

- ▼ **RemoteApp & Desktop Connections control panel applet**   Users can connect to RemoteApp programs and Remote Desktops using the RemoteApp & Desktop Connections control panel applet.

- ■ **Single administrative infrastructure**   Both RemoteApp & Desktop Connections, and RemoteApp & Desktop Web Access are managed from a single management console. This ensures that connections can still be used from Windows XP and Vista by using a web page.

- ■ **Single sign-on experience within a workspace**   Ensures that only a single logon is required to access all applications and resources with a RAD connection.

- ▲ **RemoteApp & Desktop Web access**   This capability provides full integration with RemoteApp & Desktop Connections to ensure that a consistent list of applications is available to the user at all times, no matter which desktop OS is used. The default web page provides a fresh and inviting look and feel, and includes a new web-based login with integrated single sign-on.

Administrators faced with larger RAD deployment scenarios will also find additional management features in Windows Server 2008's Remote Desktop Services. These are aimed at improving the management experience for all existing scenarios previously addressed by Terminal Services, as well as the exciting new scenarios available via RAD. These improved management features include:

- ▼ **PowerShell provider**   Easily manage multiple servers and repetitive tasks; almost all Remote Desktop Services administrative tasks can now be scripted; view and edit configuration settings for the Remote Desktop Gateway, Remote Desktop Server, and more.

- ■ **Profile improvements**   The user profile cache quota removes the need to delete profiles at logoff, speeding up user logon. Group policy caching can now be performed across an RDS farm to speed up group policy processing during logon.

■ **Microsoft Installer (MSI) compatibility**   Microsoft has fixed multiple MSI-related issues with Windows Server 2008's Terminal Services to ensure that MSI install packages can be installed normally and that per-user install settings are correctly propagated. The updates also remove the need to put the server in "install mode," meaning that users no longer need to be logged off during RAD management operations.

▲ **Remote Desktop Gateway**   RDG provides access to RAD resources from the Internet without the need for opening additional ports or the use of a VPN. Partners and independent software vendors (ISVs) also get tools with the new service to more easily enable third-party software manufacturers to built RAD-optimized products. These tools include:

   ■ **RemoteApp& Desktop Web access customization**   It is now possible to extend the look and feel of web access by both customers and partners, using support for cascading style sheets. Developers can also create custom web sites that utilize the RAD connection XML feed and transform these with XSLT.

   ■ **RemoteApp & Desktop connection**   Though RAD connections are currently only used for Remote Desktop Services, it is possible to extend both the server-side infrastructure and Windows 7 client shell to add support for any type of application or service—even ones that don't use RDP or remoting protocols. This provides a single UI and point of discoverability for any service.

   ■ **Session broker extensibility**   The session broker offers broad extensibility to enable customers and ISVs to take advantage of the built-in RDP redirection features, while providing significant additional unique value through the various types of plug-ins; for example:

      ■ **Policy (policy plug-in)**   Determines the proper farm or VM for a connection

      ■ **Load Balancing (filter plug-in)**   Chooses the proper endpoint based on load

      ■ **Orchestration (filter plug-in)**   Prepares a VM to accept RDP connections

Citrix XenApp

Citrix Systems, Inc. offers its Citrix XenApp 5, which provides for delivering Windows applications as an on-demand service. These new features for its latest release are designed to make the most of XenApp implementations by offering capacity planning, server provisioning, and application management tools, all the while providing users with a seamless experience anytime, from anywhere, with any device.

"Citrix understands the challenges that our customers face today with shrinking budgets and the pressures of 'doing more with less,' and we are committed to helping businesses meet these challenges using proven technology that impacts the bottom line," said

Mick Hollison, vice president of XenApp product marketing at Citrix Systems. "As a core component of the Citrix Delivery Center product family, XenApp is now even more valuable in helping organizations manage and deliver applications using fewer resources by adding hundreds of dollars in value on top of what they already get with XenApp for no additional cost."

Citrix XenServer is available as a core feature of all editions of Citrix XenApp, extending the value of its enterprise-class server virtualization to the more than 1 million servers currently running XenApp in datacenters. Using XenServer with XenApp allows organizations to virtualize XenApp server workloads, effectively converting a single physical server with idle capacity into multiple, virtual servers running at full capacity. Customers benefit from server consolidation with virtually no overhead and increased agility through flexible, enterprise-class virtual infrastructure.

Included in the enhancements to XenApp 5 is the ability to manage a single, standardized XenApp server image in a central location, and dynamically provision it to hundreds of XenApp servers across a large, distributed datacenter environment in minutes. Organizations can now save money on storage and ongoing management, while streamlining application management to respond faster to business needs.

New user-profile management capabilities in XenApp 5 allow organizations to maintain and consolidate a user's profile, eliminating common profile reconciliation problems such as write/overwrite issues when accessing user settings on different devices. Additionally, XenApp 5 users have a faster logon experience with personal preferences that are always present.

Local application virtualization, previously only available in the Enterprise and Platinum editions of XenApp, is available in every edition of XenApp 5. This capability allows customers to stream centrally managed applications to an end user's PC or laptop and run them locally in a virtualized environment, even when the user is disconnected from the network. As a result, XenApp customers no longer need to purchase separate licenses to enable offline access for mobile laptop users.

The management toolset included with XenApp Enterprise and Platinum Editions creates realistic simulations that help IT benchmark XenApp hosting servers. This capability eliminates the need for third-party benchmarking software, and ensures that organizations are using server capacity in the most efficient way.

VDI Architecture with Dynamic Applications

So what does this all mean? It means that not only are you saving money with your desktops, but you're also saving money by reducing the amount of time your administrators spend with desktops and the amount of time that an end user may be down because of application compatibility issues or if you need to rebuild the desktop. You can use application virtualization in conjunction with desktop virtualization and folder redirection to make the desktop completely dynamic.

Leveraging the idea of creating roles for business functions that your users will do and tying applications to those roles allows you to create roles within tools like System Center Configuration Manager. Let's say that a manager in the accounting department has just hired a new accountant who will start in a couple of days. Since you've moved your entire accounting department to a virtual desktop environment, you can leverage templates to get the virtual machine up and working very quickly.

But that's only the start. Sure, you may have the Office suite in your base image, but what about the other applications that new accountant will need on the first day? Since you've defined a role for accountant, and you know that role needs five additional applications, you could install them by hand, but that will take you a whole day because two of the applications don't tend to work well together, and you have other responsibilities to manage. By leveraging App-V to create and virtualize the application, and System Center Configuration Manager (SCCM) to deploy those virtual applications to your desktops (virtual or physical), you can get back to working on the other projects that you have.

You can create a dynamic collection in SCCM that is for the accountant role, and then advertise the virtual applications to members of that collection. What happens is that when you create that virtual machine, it is dynamically added to the SCCM collection, and the applications are automatically installed to the desktop.

APPENDIX A

Third-Party Virtualization Tools for Hyper-V

OVERVIEW

Throughout the book we've talked about many third-party tools that can help you with your Hyper-V deployment. We've put together an appendix listing the tools we wrote about and a couple that we didn't get a chance to write about.

Hardware Providers

When you're building a virtual environment, you're going to want to purchase hardware that will allow you to accomplish your goals. Many of the companies below sell total solutions for virtualization, while some of the vendors provide just disk subsystems. Disk subsystems are one of the most important components to your virtual solution. Many of the storage vendors that are in the market today take virtualization into account when they work with you to design your storage solution.

Vendor	Description	Link
NetApp	NetApp is a storage vendor that has storage solutions for both desktop and server virtualization as well as for several other technologies.	www.NetApp.com
EMC	EMC is a storage vendor with hundreds of solutions from backup to SAN storage.	www.emc.com
HP	HP has been in the computing business for a very long time and has pioneered many different technologies. HP has disk, server, and workstation solutions for nearly anything you can think of for your enterprise.	www.HP.com
Dell	Dell started out building desktop systems and shipping direct to the customer. Over the years Dell has become one of the largest hardware manufactures for the enterprise.	www.dell.com
IBM	In a list of hardware vendors, you can't forget IBM. IBM is one of the originators of enterprise computing and continues to blaze new trails.	www.IBM.com
Hitachi	Hitachi makes a wide range of solutions from consumer goods to enterprise solutions. Hitachi is one of the leading disk innovators for your storage needs.	www.hitachi.com

Vendor	Description	Link
Sun	That's right, Sun. In the last couple of years Sun has released an x64 line of servers that have proven to be amazing servers for virtualization. With the sale of Sun to Oracle, we're not sure what's going to happen with the servers.	www.sun.com
Cisco	Cisco is probably the most popular networking gear on the planet. They create switches for both your Ethernet and fibre networks. Cisco has many network virtualization options to help you with building your environment.	www.cisco.com

iSCSI Target Software

If you don't have a SAN today and you want to build up your test lab solution, there are several products that you can buy to make a Windows server an iSCSI target and effectively a storage provider for your host and guest systems. When you are looking for iSCSI software and you are going to build a Hyper-V cluster, make sure that your iSCSI software will support Windows 2008 Clustering, in particular SCSI3 – Persistence.

Vendor	Description	Link
Microsoft	Microsoft released a storage server version of Windows Server 2003 and Windows Server 2008 that includes an iSCSI target configuration.	http://www.microsoft.com/windowsserversystem/wss2003/default.mspx
Rocket Division	Rocket Division created the StarWind product to provide an iSCSI target for Windows Server. The product comes in multiple versions. Check out their web site to see which is right for you.	www.rocketdivision.com
iSCSI Cake	iSCSI Cake is created by Youngzsoft. There are three different versions you can choose from that are very affordable. Check out their web site to find the right version for you.	www.iscsicake.com

Physical to Virtual Software

We don't think virtualization would have become as widely adopted if it weren't for Physical to Virtual (P2V) conversion software. P2V software will convert your physical machines to virtual machines in a matter of a couple of hours. This is much easier than having to rebuild and reinstall each of the physical machines as virtual machines. Some of the software listed will even allow you to keep your physical and virtual machines in sync as you're doing your conversion over a period of a couple of days.

Vendor	Description	Web site
PlateSpin	PlateSpin is one of the pioneers of P2V technology now owned by Novell. They have always supported the concept of the dynamic datacenter and have striven to build their products to support that idea. PlateSpin also offers a very powerful tool to collect system data and to help you make informed decisions on whether a system is a virtualization candidate or not.	http://platespin.com/ products/migrate/
Microsoft	As part of the System Center Virtual Machine Manager 2008 tool, there are built-in functions for conducting P2V conversions.	http://www.microsoft.com/ systemcenter/ virtualmachinemanager/ en/us/default.aspx
Vizioncore	Vizioncore vConverter can be used with VMware, Microsoft, or Virtual Iron platforms. The vConverter tool can be used to do P2V conversions with zero downtime to your end users.	http://www.vizioncore.com/ products/vConverter/
Doubletake	Doubletake has been in the disk replication business for a very long time and have now added a solution for conducting P2V and other X2X conversions.	http://www.doubletake .com/english/products/ double-take-move/Pages/ default.aspx
Acronis	True Image Echo with Universal Restore is a conversion tool that can be used to do P2V or V2P conversions.	http://www.acronis.com/ enterprise/products/ATICW/ universal-restore.html

Management Software

When you are going to manage your virtual environment, you need to take into consideration the big picture of your environment. It's not just the host and the guest you need to monitor and manage; you also have backups, performance of the network and disk, and the performance of your physical systems. The reason you need to keep an eye on your physical boxes to is to trend performance over a period of time and determine whether they may be virtualization candidates to help you to continue to save money and the environment.

Vendor	Description	Website
Microsoft	The Microsoft System Center suites of products are all built to help you easily and effectively manage your environments. With the combination of Operations Manager and Virtual Machine Manager, you can monitor and manage your virtual environment. Add in Data Protection Manager and Configuration Manager and you have an end-to-end solution to managing deployment, performance, historical trending, and data protection.	http://www.microsoft.com/systemcenter/en/us/default.aspx
Citrix	Citrix not only has presentation and VDI software, but they also have created management software that can be used with Hyper-V. Citrix Essentials is a management product that helps with automating lab management, dynamic provisioning, and taking full advantage of the disk systems that you already have in place.	http://www.citrix.com/English/ps2/products/feature.asp?contentID=1687093
Vizioncore	Vizioncore released the vControl software to be a cross-platform management tool. They've done a great job with the tool; its main features are Self-Service Provisioning, Multi-VM Control, task automation, task-based HA, and virtual infrastructure discovery to help you identify hosts that are in your environment.	http://www.vizioncore.com/products/vControl/
PlateSpin	Since PlateSpin has been purchased by Novell they have continued to innovate their virtualization products. PlateSpin released PlateSpin Orchestrate, which does multivendor support.	http://platespin.com/products/orchestrate/

Virtual Desktop Infrastructure Software

There are two major components to your Virtual Desktop (VDI) solution, the connection broker and the provision for the desktops.

Vendor	Description	Website
Citrix	It almost seems that when VDI was created, Citrix was born to be the first out-of-the-gate connection broker. In the early days of VDI, Citrix Presentation Server was used to serve RDP connections via ICA for virtual desktops. Today Citrix has taken XenDesktop to a whole new level in the virtual desktop world.	http://www.citrix.com/English/ps2/products/product.asp?contentID=163057
LeoStream	LeoStream has been focusing on the connection broker component of VDI since the very early days of hosting desktops.	http://www.leostream.com/products/connection_broker.php
Quest	The Quest vWorkspace solution combines a connection broker as well as very powerful desktop management features. The vWorkspace software helps with:	http://vworkspace.com/solutions/vworkspace/enterprise.aspx

- Desktop automation
- Desktop lifecycle management
- Desktop integrity management
- Delegated administration
- Desktop reclamation management

As you can see, there are many different products for you to choose from today, and there will be five times this number in just a short time. Our advice to you as you're building your environment out is to make sure that you thoroughly vet out your requirements and make sure that the tools you already own can't meet those requirements. The idea of virtualization has always been to do more with less and save money in the process, so try to keep that idea in mind when you're reviewing third-party products.

APPENDIX B

Windows Server 2008 Hyper-V Command-Line Reference

B ack in the days of DOS, there was only one way to get your computer to do what you wanted—you had to type in long, nonsensical commands. Users hated it, and once graphical user interfaces (GUIs) came around, we were finally free of the command line. But something interesting happened—it turns out that some of us actually like the command line. And, if you are using Windows Serve 2008 Core, you'll have to use the command line.

The command line still exists in Windows Server 2008 Hyper-V, and it has its own unique commands. To use the command line, you use the PowerShell Graphical Interface. You can read more about it and download it here:

http://www.microsoft.com/technet/scriptcenter/topics/msh/download2.mspx.

POWERSHELL COMMANDS

In order to run the PowerShell commands, you also need to download the Hyper-V Management Library for them to appear. It can be downloaded from http://pshyperv .codeplex.com.

The following are some of the commands that are unique to Hyper-V:
Finding a VM

- ▼ Get-VM
- ■ Choose-VM
- ▲ Get-VMHost

Connecting to a VM

- ■ New-VMConnectSession

Discovering and manipulating machine states

- ▼ Get-VMState
- ■ Set-VMState
- ■ Convert-VmState
- ■ Ping-VM
- ■ Test-VMHeartBeat
- ■ Shutdown-VM
- ■ Start-VM
- ■ Stop-VM
- ■ Suspend-VM
- ■ Get-VMKVP

- Add-KVP
- Remove-KVP
- ▲ Get-VMJPEG

Backing up, importing, exporting, and taking snapshots of VMs

- ▼ Export-VM
- Import-VM
- Get-VMSnapshot
- Choose-VMSnapshot
- Apply-VMSnapshot
- New-VMSnapshot
- Remove-VMSnapshot
- Rename-VMSnapShot
- Update-VMSnapshot
- Get-VMSnapshotTree
- ▲ Get-VmBackupScript

Adding and removing VMs, configuring motherboard settings.

- ▼ New-VM
- Remove-VM
- Set-VM
- Get-VMCPUCount
- Set-VMCPUCount
- Get-VMMemory
- Set-VMMemory
- ▲ Set-VMSerialPort

Manipulating disk controllers, drives, and disk images

- ▼ Get-VMDiskController
- Add-VMSCSIController
- Remove-VMSCSIController
- Get-VMDriveByController
- Add-VMDRIVE
- Remove-VMdrive
- Get-VMDiskByDrive

- Add-VMDISK
- Set-VMDisk
- Get-VMDisk
- Get-VMFloppyDisk
- Add-VMFloppyDisk
- ▲ Add-VMNewHardDisk

Manipulating network interface cards

- ▼ Get-VMNic
- List-VMNic
- Choose-VMNIC
- Add-VMNIC
- Remove-VMNIC
- Set-VMNICAddress
- Set-VMNICConnection
- Get-VMNicport
- Get-VMnicSwitch
- Choose-VMSwitch
- New-VMSwitchPort
- Get-VMByMACaddress
- Choose-VMExternalEthernet
- New-VMExternalSwitch
- New-VMInternalSwitch
- ▲ New-VmPrivateSwitch

Working with VHD files

- ▼ Get-VHDDefaultPath
- Get-VHDInfo
- New-VHD
- Compact-VHD
- Test-VHD
- Convert-VHD
- Merge-VHD
- Mount-VHD
- ▲ Unmount-VHD

WMI COMMANDS

There are dozens of WMI commands for Windows Server 2008 Hyper-V. The following list breaks down the commands by their respective classes and provides Microsoft's description of what they do.

BIOS Classes

▼ **Msvm_BIOSElement**   Represents the low-level software that is loaded into RAM to configure and start the system.

▲ **Msvm_SystemBIOS**   Used to associate a virtual system with its BIOS.

Input Classes

▼ **Msvm_Keyboard**   Represents a keyboard device.

■ **Msvm_Ps2Mouse**   Represents a PS2 mouse device.

▲ **Msvm_SyntheticMouse**   Represents a synthetic mouse device.

Integration Components Classes

▼ **Msvm_HeartbeatComponent**   Represents the state of the heartbeat component, which is responsible for monitoring the state of a virtual machine by reporting a heartbeat at regular intervals.

■ **Msvm_HeartbeatComponentSettingData**   Represents the configured state of the heartbeat component.

■ **Msvm_KvpExchangeComponent**   Represents the state of the key/value pair exchange component, which provides a mechanism to exchange data between the virtual machine and the operating system running on the parent partition.

■ **Msvm_KvpExchangeComponentSettingData**   Represents the configured state of the key/value pair exchange component.

■ **Msvm_KvpExchangeDataItem**   Represents a key/value pair.

■ **Msvm_ShutdownComponent**   Represents the state of the shutdown component, which provides a mechanism to shut down the operating system of the virtual machine from the management interfaces on the host system.

■ **Msvm_ShutdownComponentSettingData**   Represents the configured state of the shutdown component.

■ **Msvm_TimeSyncComponent**   Represents the state of the time synchronization component, which is responsible for synchronizing the system time of a virtual machine with the system time of the operating system running in the parent partition.

- ■ `Msvm_TimeSyncComponentSettingData`   Represents the configured state of the time synchronization component.
- ■ `Msvm_VssComponent`   Represents the state of the Volume Shadow Copy Service (VSS) component, which implements the VSS Requester in the guest operating system.
- ▲ `Msvm_VssComponentSettingData`   Represents the configured state of the Volume Shadow Copy Service (VSS) component.

Memory Classes

- ▼ `Msvm_Memory`   Represents the memory currently allocated to a virtual system.
- ▲ `Msvm_MemorySettingData`   Represents the configured state of the memory for a virtual system.

Networking Classes

- ▼ `Msvm_ActiveConnection`   Connects a switch port to the LAN endpoint to which the port is connected. The existence of this object means that the switch port and the LAN endpoint are actively connected and the Ethernet port associated with the LAN endpoint can communicate with the network through the switch port.
- ■ `Msvm_BindsTo`   This association establishes a service access point as a requester of protocol services from a protocol endpoint.
- ■ `Msvm_DeviceSAPImplementation`   An association between a service access point (SAP) and how it is implemented.
- ■ `Msvm_DynamicForwardingEntry`   Represents an entry in the forwarding (filtering) database associated with the transparent bridging service.
- ■ `Msvm_EmulatedEthernetPort`   Represents an emulated Ethernet adapter. This adapter is used when a virtual machine is not capable of running the synthetic Ethernet port.
- ■ `Msvm_EmulatedEthernetPortSettingData`   Represents the configured state of an emulated Ethernet adapter.
- ■ `Msvm_ExternalEthernetPort`   This class represents an external Ethernet port (network adapter).
- ■ `Msvm_GlobalEthernetPortSAPImplementation`   This association connects a LAN endpoint to a global Ethernet port (either an external or internal Ethernet port).
- ■ `Msvm_HostedAccessPoint`   This association connects a virtual switch service to a switch port inside the Microsoft Hyper-V platform.

- **Msvm_HostedSwitchService** This association connects a virtual switch service to a transparent bridging service.

- **Msvm_InternalEthernetPort** This class represents an internal Ethernet port (network adapter).

- **Msvm_NetworkElementSettingData** Logically connects the virtual system with the various LAN endpoints scoped by the virtual system.

- **Msvm_NetworkJob** Represents a network operation job created by the Network VSP WMI management service.

- **Msvm_SwitchLANEndpoint** A LAN endpoint connected to an external or internal Ethernet port.

- **Msvm_SwitchPort** Represents a port on the switch.

- **Msvm_SwitchPortDynamicForwarding** Connects a switch port to a dynamic forward entry (learned MAC address). This is useful in finding all of the learned MAC addresses for a specified port.

- **Msvm_SyntheticEthernetPort** Represents a synthetic Ethernet adapter.

- **Msvm_SyntheticEthernetPortSettingData** Represents the configured state of a synthetic Ethernet adapter.

- **Msvm_TransparentBridgingDynamicForwarding** Connects a transparent bridging service to a dynamic forward entry (learned MAC address).

- **Msvm_TransparentBridgingService** Serves as a placeholder for the service inside the switch that learns MAC addresses.

- **Msvm_VirtualSwitch** Represents a virtual switch.

- **Msvm_VirtualSwitchManagementService** Controls the definition, modification, and destruction of global networking resources such as virtual switches, switch ports, and internal Ethernet ports.

- **Msvm_VLANEndpoint** This class represents the VLAN endpoint of a switch port.

- **Msvm_VLANEndpointSettingData** This class represents the settings for a VLAN endpoint of a switch port.

- ▲ **Msvm_VmLANEndpoint** A LAN endpoint connected to a virtual machine.

Processor Classes

- ▼ **Msvm_Processor** Represents the virtual processor in a virtual computer system.

- **Msvm_ProcessorPool** Aggregates the processor resources that may be allocated to a virtual system.

- ▲ **Msvm_ProcessorSettingData** Represents the virtual processor settings for a virtual system.

Profile Registration Classes

▼ **Msvm_ResourcePoolComponent**   Represents a resource pool component of the Microsoft Windows Hyper-V platform.

■ **Msvm_ResourcePoolRegistration**   Registers a component that provides global resource pool-related objects.

■ **Msvm_ResourceTypeDefinition**   Defines a mapping of a resource type to its implementation classes.

■ **Msvm_VirtualizationComponent**   Represents a component of the Microsoft Windows Hyper-V platform.

■ **Msvm_VirtualizationComponentRegistration**   Abstract association class that represents the registration of a component in the Microsoft Hyper-V platform.

■ **Msvm_VirtualSystemResourceComponent**   Represents a virtual device component of the Microsoft Windows Hyper-V platform.

▲ **Msvm_VirtualSystemResourceRegistration**   Registers a component that provides virtual system-specific resource-related objects.

Resource Management Classes

▼ **Msvm_AllocationCapabilities**   Defines the means by which a client can discover the valid range of default settings for a virtual resource.

■ **Msvm_ElementAllocatedFromPool**   Associates an instance of an allocated resource with the resource pool from which it was allocated.

■ **Msvm_ElementCapabilities**   Represents the association between managed elements and their capabilities.

■ **Msvm_ResourceAllocationFromPool**   Associates an instance of a resource allocation with the resource pool from which it is allocated.

■ **Msvm_ResourceAllocationSettingData**   Represents the current and recorded allocation states of a virtual resource.

■ **Msvm_ResourcePool**   Describes a type of virtual resource available for use in virtual systems.

▲ **Msvm_SettingsDefineCapabilities**   Provides a link between the CIM_AllocationCapabilities instance and the minimum, maximum, incremental, and default settings for a resource.

Serial Devices Classes

▼ **Msvm_SerialController**   Represents the capabilities and management of the serial controller.

- ■ **Msvm_SerialPort**   Represents a serial port associated with the serial controller.
- ▲ **Msvm_SerialPortOnSerialController**   Associates a serial port with a serial controller.

Storage Classes

- ▼ **Msvm_AffectedStorageJobElement**   Represents the association between a Job and the ManagedElement(s) that may be affected by its execution.
- ■ **Msvm_ControlledBy**   Associates a storage device with the storage controller that owns the device. This association is used with both IDE and floppy controllers.
- ■ **Msvm_DiskDrive**   Represents a hard drive inside a virtual machine.
- ■ **Msvm_DisketteController**   Represents the floppy controller in the virtual machine.
- ■ **Msvm_DisketteDrive**   Represents a floppy drive inside the virtual machine.
- ■ **Msvm_DVDDrive**   Represents a DVD drive inside a virtual machine.
- ■ **Msvm_IDEController**   Represents an IDE controller.
- ■ **Msvm_ImageManagementService**   Manages the virtual media (.vhd, .is, or .vfd files) for a virtual machine.
- ■ **Msvm_LogicalDisk**   Represents storage drive media and is used to populate the storage drives. The media types supported include virtual hard disk files, virtual floppy files, ISO files, and physical device media.
- ■ **Msvm_MediaPresent**   Associates a storage drive with the media inserted into the drive. This association is used for all storage drive objects.
- ■ **Msvm_MountedStorageImage**   This class provides detailed information about a manually mounted storage image.
- ■ **Msvm_ProtocolControllerForUnit**   This association indicates that a subclass of LogicalDevice (for example, a storage volume) is connected through a specific ProtocolController.
- ■ **Msvm_SCSIProtocolController**   Represents a synthetic SCSI controller.
- ■ **Msvm_StorageJob**   This class represents an image operation job created by the Microsoft Hyper-V Image Management Service.
- ▲ **Msvm_VirtualHardDiskInfo**   Provides detailed information about an existing virtual hard disk image.

Video Classes

- ▼ **Msvm_S3DisplayController**   Represents the state of the emulated S3 controller that is present in each virtual machine configuration.
- ■ **Msvm_SyntheticDisplayController**   Represents the state of the synthetic display controller that is present in each virtual machine configuration.

- **Msvm_SystemTerminalConnection**   Associates a virtual computer system with a terminal connection.

- **Msvm_TerminalConnection**   Indicates the state of an active remote session interacting with a virtual computer system.

- **Msvm_TerminalService**   Manages all remote terminal connections to a particular host. The service uses a configurable port to initiate all terminal connections.

- **Msvm_VideoHead**   Describes the primary drawing surface on a display controller.

- ▲ **Msvm_VideoHeadOnController**   Associates a video head with the video controller that includes it.

Virtual System Classes

- ▼ **Msvm_ComputerSystem**   Represents a hosting computer system or virtual computer system.

- **Msvm_ConcreteComponent**   A generic association used to establish "part of" relationships between ManagedElements.

- **Msvm_LastAppliedSettingData**   An association between a virtual system and the setting data of the snapshot that was most recently applied to the virtual system.

- **Msvm_ParentChildSettingData**   An association between an instance of CIM_VirtualSystemSettingData and the CIM_VirtualSystemSettingData instance that represents the most recent snapshot upon which this object is based.

- **Msvm_PreviousSettingData**   An association between a virtual system and the setting data of the snapshot that is the parent to the virtual system.

- **Msvm_SummaryInformation**   Used in the GetSummaryInformation method in the Msvm_VirtualSystemManagementService class to quickly retrieve common information related to a virtual system or snapshot.

- **Msvm_SystemDevice**   LogicalDevices can be aggregated by a system. This relationship is made explicit by the Msvm_SystemDevice association.

- **Msvm_VirtualSystemGlobalSettingData**   Represents the global settings for a virtual system. These settings do not change if a new snapshot is applied to the virtual system.

- **Msvm_VirtualSystemSettingData**   Represents the virtualization-specific settings for a virtual system.

- ▲ **Msvm_VirtualSystemSettingDataComponent**   A generic association used to establish "part of" relationships between one instance of Msvm_VirtualSystemSettingData and one or more instances of Msvm_ResourceAllocationSettingData.

Virtual System Management Classes

▼ **Msvm_AffectedJobElement** Represents an association between a Job and the ManagedElement(s) that may be affected by its execution.

■ **Msvm_ConcreteJob** A concrete version of Job. This class represents a generic and instantiable unit of work, such as a batch or a print job.

■ **Msvm_ElementSettingData** Associates a managed element with its configuration data. Some of the more notable applications of this association are its use in linking a virtual computer system and the logical devices that have been assigned to that system with their snapshot configuration information.

■ **Msvm_Error** A specialized class that contains information about the severity, cause, recommended actions, and other data related to the failure of a CIM operation.

■ **Msvm_HostedDependency** Associates a virtual computer system instance with the computer system object representing the physical, hosting system.

■ **Msvm_HostedService** Associates a service with its hosting computer system.

■ **Msvm_ServiceAffectsElement** Associates a virtual computer system instance with the management service that controls its state.

■ **Msvm_SettingsDefineState** Associates a virtual system and its devices with an instance of Msvm_ComputerSystem.

■ **Msvm_SystemExportSettingData** Associates a virtual system and its export setting data.

■ **Msvm_VirtualSystemExportSettingData** Represents export settings of a virtual system.

■ **Msvm_VirtualSystemImportSettingData** Represents import settings of a virtual system.

■ **Msvm_VirtualSystemManagementService** Represents the virtualization service present on a single host system.

▲ **Msvm_VirtualSystemManagementServiceSettingData** Represents the settings for the virtualization service present on a single host system.

COMMAND-LINE EXAMPLE—SNAPSHOTS

Let's use an example to show how command-line scripting works. To explore the subject, let's look particularly at snapshots—how you take one, how you apply it, and how you manage it.

Hyper-V uses a feature called snapshots. These are different from SAN or VSS snapshots. Hyper-V snapshots allow you to save the current state of a VM while it's still running.

You can change the VM back to this state later, if need be. This is an excellent feature if you are testing new configurations or applications, and things don't go right. If that happens, you just revert to an old snapshot and try again.

Taking the Snapshot

To take the snapshot of your VM, open PowerShell and enter the following code:

```
$VMManagementService = Get-WmiObject -Namespace root\virtualization -Class
Msvm_VirtualSystemManagementService
$SourceVm = Get-WmiObject -Namespace root\virtualization -Query "Select * From
Msvm_ComputerSystem Where ElementName='VmToSnapshot'"
$result = $VMManagementService.CreateVirtualSystemSnapshot($SourceVm)
#ProcessWMIJob($result)
```

Applying a Snapshot

If you decide you need to revert back to an earlier snapshot, enter this code:

```
$VMManagementService = Get-WmiObject -Namespace root\virtualization -Class
Msvm_VirtualSystemManagementService
$SourceVm = Get-WmiObject -Namespace root\virtualization -Query "Select * From
Msvm_ComputerSystem Where ElementName='VmToSnapshot'"
$Snapshot = Get-WmiObject -Namespace root\virtualization -Query "Associators Of
{$SourceVm} Where AssocClass=Msvm_ElementSettingData
ResultClass=Msvm_VirtualSystemSettingData"
$result = $VMManagementService.ApplyVirtualSystemSnapshot($SourceVm, $Snapshot)
#ProcessWMIJob($result)
```

Deleting a Snapshot

If you're done with a given snapshot, it's straightforward enough to delete it. Using this code will delete the snapshot:

```
$VMManagementService = Get-WmiObject -Namespace root\virtualization -Class Msvm_
VirtualSystemManagementService
$SourceVm = Get-WmiObject -Namespace root\virtualization -Query "Select * From
Msvm_ComputerSystem Where ElementName='VmToSnapshot'"
$Snapshot = Get-WmiObject -Namespace root\virtualization -Query "Associators Of
{$SourceVm} Where AssocClass=Msvm_ElementSettingData
ResultClass=Msvm_VirtualSystemSettingData"
$result = $VMManagementService.RemoveVirtualSystemSnapshot($Snapshot)
#ProcessWMIJob($result)
```

INDEX

F

G

W

X

 Y

 Z